Intelligent Innovations in Multimedia Data Engineering and Management

Siddhartha Bhattacharyya
RCC Institute of Information Technology, India

A volume in the Advances in Data Mining and
Database Management (ADMDM) Book Series

Published in the United States of America by
IGI Global
Engineering Science Reference (an imprint of IGI Global)
701 E. Chocolate Avenue
Hershey PA, USA 17033
Tel: 717-533-8845
Fax: 717-533-8661
E-mail: cust@igi-global.com
Web site: http://www.igi-global.com

Library of Congress Cataloging-in-Publication Data

Names: Bhattacharyya, Siddhartha, 1975- editor.
Title: Intelligent innovations in multimedia data engineering and management
 / Siddhartha Bhattacharyya, editor.
Description: Hershey, PA : Engineering Science Reference, an imprint of IGI
 Global, [2019] | Includes bibliographical references and index.
Identifiers: LCCN 2018016418| ISBN 9781522571070 (hardcover) | ISBN
 9781522571087 (ebook)
Subjects: LCSH: Image processing--Digital techniques. | Multimedia systems. |
 Imaging systems.
Classification: LCC TA1637 .I494 2019 | DDC 006.6--dc23 LC record available at https://lccn.loc.gov/2018016418

This book is published in the IGI Global book series Advances in Data Mining and Database Management (ADMDM) (ISSN: 2327-1981; eISSN: 2327-199X)

Advances in Data Mining and Database Management (ADMDM) Book Series

David Taniar
Monash University, Australia

ISSN:2327-1981
EISSN:2327-199X

MISSION

With the large amounts of information available to organizations in today's digital world, there is a need for continual research surrounding emerging methods and tools for collecting, analyzing, and storing data.

The **Advances in Data Mining & Database Management (ADMDM)** series aims to bring together research in information retrieval, data analysis, data warehousing, and related areas in order to become an ideal resource for those working and studying in these fields. IT professionals, software engineers, academicians and upper-level students will find titles within the ADMDM book series particularly useful for staying up-to-date on emerging research, theories, and applications in the fields of data mining and database management.

COVERAGE

- Customer Analytics
- Enterprise Systems
- Data Warehousing
- Data quality
- Database Testing
- Database Security
- Educational Data Mining
- Factor Analysis
- Data Mining
- Heterogeneous and Distributed Databases

IGI Global is currently accepting manuscripts for publication within this series. To submit a proposal for a volume in this series, please contact our Acquisition Editors at Acquisitions@igi-global.com or visit: http://www.igi-global.com/publish/.

Titles in this Series

For a list of additional titles in this series, please visit: www.igi-global.com/book-series

Predictive Analysis on Large Data for Actionable Knowledge Emerging Research and Opportunities
Muhammad Usman (Shaheed Zulfikar Ali Bhutto Institute of Science and Technology, Pakistan) and M. Usman (Pakistan Scientific and Technological Information Center (PASTIC), Pakistan)
Information Science Reference • copyright 2018 • 177pp • H/C (ISBN: 9781522550297) • US $135.00 (our price)

Handbook of Research on Big Data Storage and Visualization Techniques
Richard S. Segall (Arkansas State University, USA) and Jeffrey S. Cook (Independent Researcher, USA)
Engineering Science Reference • copyright 2018 • 917pp • H/C (ISBN: 9781522531425) • US $565.00 (our price)

Bridging Relational and NoSQL Databases
Drazena Gaspar (University of Mostar, Bosnia and Herzegovina) and Ivica Coric (Hera Software Company, Bosnia and Herzegovina)
Information Science Reference • copyright 2018 • 338pp • H/C (ISBN: 9781522533856) • US $185.00 (our price)

Advancements in Applied Metaheuristic Computing
Nilanjan Dey (Techno India College of Technology, India)
Engineering Science Reference • copyright 2018 • 335pp • H/C (ISBN: 9781522541516) • US $225.00 (our price)

Applications of Finite Markov Chains and Fuzzy Logic in Learning Contexts Emerging Research and Opportunities
Michael Voskoglou (Graduate Technological Educational Institute of Western Greece, Greece)
Engineering Science Reference • copyright 2018 • 193pp • H/C (ISBN: 9781522533283) • US $175.00 (our price)

Exploring the Convergence of Big Data and the Internet of Things
A.V. Krishna Prasad (K.L. University, India)
Engineering Science Reference • copyright 2018 • 332pp • H/C (ISBN: 9781522529477) • US $245.00 (our price)

Deep Learning Innovations and Their Convergence With Big Data
S. Karthik (SNS College of Technology, Anna University, India) Anand Paul (Kyungpook National University, South Korea) and N. Karthikeyan (Mizan-Tepi University, Ethiopia)
Information Science Reference • copyright 2018 • 265pp • H/C (ISBN: 9781522530152) • US $205.00 (our price)

Modern Technologies for Big Data Classification and Clustering
Hari Seetha (Vellore Institute of Technology-Andhra Pradesh, India) M. Narasimha Murty (Indian Institute of Science, India) and B. K. Tripathy (VIT University, India)
Information Science Reference • copyright 2018 • 360pp • H/C (ISBN: 9781522528050) • US $215.00 (our price)

701 East Chocolate Avenue, Hershey, PA 17033, USA
Tel: 717-533-8845 x100 • Fax: 717-533-8661
E-Mail: cust@igi-global.com • www.igi-global.com

Prof. (Dr.) Siddhartha Bhattacharyya would like to dedicate this book to his father, Late Ajit Kumar Bhattacharyya, his mother, Late Hashi Bhattacharyya, his beloved wife, Rashni, and his dearest classmates Kakali, Satadal, Lakshminarayan, Ranabir, Rajarshi, and Partha.

List of Reviewers

Abhijit Das, *RCC Institute of Information Technology, India*
Rik Das, *Xavier Institute of Social Service, India*
Sourav De, *Cooch Behar Government Engineering College, India*
Sandip Dey, *OmDayal Group of Institutions, India*
Shibakali Gupta, *University Institute of Technology, India*
Debanjan Konar, *Sikkim Manipal Institute of Technology, India*
Dipankar Majumdar, *RCC Institute of Information Technology, India*
Anirban Mukherjee, *RCC Institute of Information Technology, India*
Soumen Mukherjee, *RCC Institute of Information Technology, India*
Pankaj Pal, *RCC Institute of Information Technology, India*
Indrajit Pan, *RCC Institute of Information Technology, India*

Table of Contents

Detailed Table of Contents

Ranit Karmakar, Tata Consultancy Services, India
Abhishek Basu, RCC Institute of Information Technology, India

Electronic health records (EHR) contain patients' medical as well as personal details. With the increased use of digital media, these data are stored and transferred through the electronic media all over the world. This makes it vulnerable to unauthorized people. Digital image watermarking can be a useful process of protecting these data from attacker but causes severe and unrecoverable damage to cover media. In the case of highly sensitive images like medical images, this might creates a problem during further diagnosis. In this chapter, a reversible data hiding algorithm is proposed which also is capable of holding a large chunk of data without affecting the cover media. The main cover image is first reconstructed and hidden behind a bigger media and then the extra pixels are used to hide encrypted forms of EHR data along with an authentication signature. As EHR data and the digital signature is passed through various encryption stages while encoding, it is made more secure. The algorithm is developed on the spatial domain adding some cautious measures which made it fragile as well.

Kanimozhi Suguna S., SASTRA University, India
Dhanya V. S., SASTRA University, India

This chapter throws light on major multimedia data security techniques. It has become so essential in today's society which uses multimedia data in almost all walks of life. There are a lot of multimedia data transactions carried out every day. Thus, to ensure data security the techniques, steganography and watermarking are frequently used. In steganography and watermarking techniques, the data to be hidden is encrypted and fed into a transparent layer like documents, images, and it is decrypted at the receiving end by the recipient. Generally, steganographic communications are one-to-one while watermarking is one-to-many. Besides these techniques, certain other techniques are also used in the application for providing security to multimedia data. From this chapter, a detailed content about steganography and watermarking can be obtained.

Abhishek Basu, RCC Institute of Information Technology, India
Soumadeb Dutta, RCC Institute of Information Technology, India

The recent developments of enormous computer networks have invoked insecurities related to copyright theft of digital media. To be precise, the virtual sharing of medical images over networks with a novel desire of improved medical diagnosis has led to the tampering of sensitive patient identity information. In this chapter, the authors have exemplified the need of watermarking with fragile medical image watermarking using saliency and phase congruency. Initially, the saliency and phase congruency methodologies are applied on the original medical image to highlight the object features. Based on the feature map, a mask is generated which segregates the area of interest from the portions containing visual medical information. An encrypted text, containing identity of the patient, is embedded into the area of interest of the image. The results of imperceptibility and fragility criteria are satisfactory towards the implementation of a fragile watermark as the extracted watermark is found to be corrupted upon unfaithful image processing modifications.

Barnali Gupta Banik, St. Thomas' College of Engineering and Technology, India

In this digital era, with the advent of technology like 4G network and VOIP, video calling is the most cost effective and cutting-edge communication technique. Simultaneously, video sharing through social networking sites is very popular, as it can reach a wider public domain in seconds. This enormous use of video motivates the fact that as digital medium video can be effectively utilized for secret sharing. Using video steganography, any kind of secret data like text, image, audio, even a short video can be hidden inside another video object, which can be securely transmitted to the recipient over the internet. In this chapter, an effort has been made to relate various techniques of video steganography under a single header to identify future scope of research. Also, all possible quality metrics for videos and for measuring robustness have been studied, and different steganalysis attacks on video have been analyzed. The broad mission of this chapter is to be a quick reference to future researchers of video steganography.

Mehul S. Raval, Ahmedabad University, India

The chapter presents an application of reversible data hiding for the authentication of image travelling over a hostile and insecure communication channel. The reversible data resides in the image and tracks any changes done to it on a communication channel. The extraction of data and any modification to its structure reveals changes in the image. This allows the use of data hiding for forensic purpose. The reversible data hiding provides an additional advantage along with active forensics. The image regains original form after removal of the embedded data. However, reversible data hiding is an interplay between the image quality and watermarking capacity. The chapter presents the generic framework for data hiding and discusses its special case reversible data hiding. It presents capacity-behavior analysis of the difference expansion scheme. It performs in-depth analysis on the type of predictor and its impact on the capacity of the reversible data hiding scheme. Finally, the chapter presents a case study to showcase the use of reversible data hiding for image authentication.

Chapter 6

Roland Schmitz, Stuttgart Media University, Germany

Shujun Li, University of Kent, UK

Christos Grecos, Central Washington University, USA

Xinpeng Zhang, Shanghai University, China

Histogram-based watermarking schemes are invariant to pixel permutations and can thus be combined with permutation-based ciphers to form a commutative watermarking-encryption scheme. In this chapter, the authors demonstrate the feasibility of this approach for audio data and still image data. Typical histogram-based watermarking schemes based on comparison of histogram bins are prone to desynchronization attacks, where the whole histogram is shifted by a certain amount. These kind of attacks can be avoided by synchronizing the embedding and detection processes, using the mean of the histogram as a calibration point. The resulting watermarking scheme is resistant to three common types of shifts of the histogram, while the advantages of previous histogram-based schemes, especially commutativity of watermarking and permutation-based encryption, are preserved. The authors also report on the results of testing robustness of the still image watermark against JPEG and JPEG2000 compression and on the possibility of using histogram-based watermarks for authenticating the content of an image.

Chapter 7

Amit Khan, RCC Institute of Information Technology, India

Dipankar Majumdar, RCC Institute of Information Technology, India

In the last few decades huge amounts and diversified work has been witnessed in the domain of de-noising of binary images through the evolution of the classical techniques. These principally include analytical techniques and approaches. Although the scheme was working well, the principal drawback of these classical and analytical techniques are that the information regarding the noise characteristics is essential beforehand. In addition to that, time complexity of analytical works amounts to beyond practical applicability. Consequently, most of the recent works are based on heuristic-based techniques conceding to approximate solutions rather than the best ones. In this chapter, the authors propose a solution using an iterative neural network that applies iterative spatial filtering technology with critically varied size of the computation window. With critical variation of the window size, the authors are able to show noted acceleration in the filtering approach (i.e., obtaining better quality filtration with lesser number of iterations).

Chapter 8

Jayati Ghosh Dastidar, St. Xavier's College, India

Debangshu Chakraborty, St. Xavier's College, India

Soumen Mukherjee, RCC Institute of Information Technology, India

Arup Kumar Bhattacharjee, RCC Institute of Information Technology, India

Identification and recognition of a human subject by monitoring a video/image by using various biometric features such as fingerprints, retina/iris scans, palm prints have been of interest to researches. In this chapter, an attempt has been made to recognize a human subject uniquely by monitoring his/her gait. This has been done by analyzing sampled frames of a video sequence to first detect the presence of a human form and then extract the silhouette of the subject in question. The extracted silhouette is then used to find the skeleton from it. The skeleton contains a set of points that retains the connectivity of the form and maintains the geometric properties of the silhouette. From the skeleton, a novel method has been proposed involving the neighborhood of interest pixels to identify the end points representing the heel, toe, etc. These points finally lead to the calculation of gait attributes. The extracted attributes represented in the form of a pattern vector are matched using cosine distance with features stored in the database resulting in identification/rejection.

Chapter 9

    Dilip Kumar Choubey, National Institute of Technology Patna, India
    Sanchita Paul, Birla Institute of Technology Mesra, India
    Kanchan Bala, Birla Institute of Technology Mesra, India
    Manish Kumar, Birla Institute of Technology Mesra, India
    Uday Pratap Singh, Madhav Institute of Technology and Science, India

This chapter presents a best classification of diabetes. The proposed approach work consists in two stages. In the first stage the Pima Indian diabetes dataset is obtained from the UCI repository of machine learning databases. In the second stage, the authors have performed the classification technique by using fuzzy decision tree on Pima Indian diabetes dataset. Then they applied PSO_SVM as a feature selection technique followed by the classification technique by using fuzzy decision tree on Pima Indian diabetes dataset. In this chapter, the optimization of SVM using PSO reduces the number of attributes, and hence, applying fuzzy decision tree improves the accuracy of detecting diabetes. The hybrid combinatorial method of feature selection and classification needs to be done so that the system applied is used for the classification of diabetes.

Chapter 10

    Soumen Mukherjee, RCC Institute of Information Technology, India
    Arunabha Adhikari, West Bengal State University, India
    Madhusudan Roy, Saha Institute of Nuclear Physics, India

Nature-inspired metaheuristic algorithms find near optimum solutions in a fast and efficient manner when used in a complex problem like finding optimum number of neurons in hidden layers of a multi-layer perceptron (MLP). In this chapter, a classification work is discussed of malignant melanoma, which is a type of lethal skin cancer. The classification accuracy is more than 91% with visually imperceptible features using MLP. The results found are comparably better than the related work found in the literature. Finally, the performance of two metaheuristic algorithms (i.e., particle swarm optimization [PSO] and simulated annealing [SA]) are compared and analyzed with different parameters to show their searching nature in the two-dimensional search space of hidden layer neurons.

Preface

With the ever-increasing volume of data, proper management of data is a challenging proposition to the scientists and researchers and multimedia data is no exception in this regard. Multimedia data exhibits in different fashions, be it continuous or discrete. Continuous multimedia data includes audio, video and animation where there is an element of synchronization associated with the data with respect to time. On the other hand, discrete multimedia data refers to text and images/graphics where the information content is static with time.

Given the vast storage space required for multimedia data, scientists and researchers are investing a lot of efforts to discover new space efficient methods for storage and archival of these data. Newer higher dimensional data structures have been involved for this purpose. In addition, a huge amount of bandwidth is required for faithful transmission of these voluminous data. So, efforts are also being invested for evolving proper transmission mechanisms for multimedia data. As a consequence, advanced encryption techniques are also envisaged for maintaining the data secrecy.

Apart from these issues, multimedia data also exhibits varied types of uncertainty and imprecision. Traditional computing techniques cannot handle these uncertainties. Hence, scientists have resorted to intelligent tools and techniques to handle the uncertainties. These intelligent techniques include several soft computing techniques in the form of neural networks, fuzzy sets and evolutionary techniques.

This volume will benefit the readers from various spheres of engineering community. These include budding researchers and practitioners. In addition, the volume would also benefit the teaching community since the academicians will find new avenues for knowledge dissemination.

This volume comprises ten well-versed self-contained chapters dealing with the recent innovations in multimedia data engineering and management.

Chapter 1 discusses the implementation of a reversible watermarking technique for medical images. Electronic Health Record (EHR) contains patient's medical as well as personal details. With the increased use of digital media, these data are stored and transferred through the electronic media all over the world. This makes it vulnerable to unauthorized people. Digital image watermarking can be a useful process of protecting these data from attacker but causes severe and unrecoverable damage to cover media. In case of high sensitive images like medical images this might create a problem during further diagnosis. In this chapter, a reversible data hiding algorithm is proposed which also is capable of holding a large chunk of data without affecting the cover media. The main cover image is first reconstructed and hidden behind a bigger media and then the extra pixels are used to hide encrypted forms of EHR data along with an authentication signature. As EHR data and the digital signature is passed through various encryption stages while encoding, it made it more secure. The algorithm is developed on the spatial domain adding some cautious measures which makes it fragile as well.

Chapter 2 throws light on major multimedia data security techniques. It has become so essential in today's society which uses multimedia data in almost all walks of life. There are a lot of multimedia data transactions carried out every day. Thus to ensure data security the techniques namely Steganography and Watermarking are frequently used. In Steganography and Watermarking techniques, the data to be hidden is encrypted and fed into transparent layer like documents, images and it is decrypted at the receiving end by the recipient. Generally, steganographic communications are one-to-one while watermarking is one-to-many. Besides these techniques, certain other techniques are also used in the application for providing security to multimedia data. From this chapter discussion, a detailed content about steganography and watermarking can be obtained.

The recent developments of enormous computer networks have invoked insecurities related to copyright theft of digital media. To be precise, the virtual sharing of medical images over networks with a novel desire of improved medical diagnosis has led to the tampering of sensitive patient identity information. In Chapter 3, the authors have exemplified the need of watermarking with fragile medical image watermarking using saliency and phase congruency. Initially, the saliency and phase congruency methodologies are applied on the original medical image to highlight the object features. Based on the feature map, a mask is generated which segregates the area of interest from the portions containing visual medical information. An encrypted text, containing identity of the patient, is embedded into the area of interest of the image. The results of imperceptibility and fragility criteria are satisfactory towards the implementation of a fragile watermark as the extracted watermark is found to be corrupted upon unfaithful image processing modifications.

In this digital era, with the advent of technology like 4G network and VOIP, video calling begins to be the most cost effective and cutting-edge communication technique. Simultaneously, video sharing through social networking sites becomes very popular, as it can reach a wider public domain in seconds. This enormous use of video motivates the fact that as digital medium, video can be effectively utilized for secret sharing. Using video steganography, any kind of secret data like text, image, audio, even a short video, can be hidden inside another video object, which can be securely transmitted to the recipient over the internet. In Chapter 4, an effort has been made to relate various techniques of video steganography under a single header to identify future scope of research. Also, all possible quality metrics for videos have been studied and for measuring robustness, different steganalysis attacks on video have been analyzed. The broad mission of this chapter is to be a quick reference to future researcher of video steganography.

Chapter 5 presents an application of reversible data hiding for the authentication of image travelling over a hostile and insecure communication channel. The reversible data resides in the image and tracks any changes done to it on a communication channel. The extraction of data and any modification to its structure reveals changes in the image. This allows the use of data hiding for forensic purpose. The reversible data hiding provides an additional advantage along with active forensics. The image regains original form after removal of the embedded data. However, reversible data hiding is an interplay between the image quality and watermarking capacity. The chapter presents the generic framework for data hiding and discusses its special case reversible data hiding. It presents capacity-behavior analysis of the Difference Expansion scheme. It performs in-depth analysis on the type of predictor and its impact on the capacity of the reversible data hiding scheme. Finally, the chapter presents a case study to showcase the use of reversible data hiding for image authentication.

Histogram-based watermarking schemes are invariant to pixel permutations and can thus be combined with permutation-based ciphers to form a Commutative Watermarking-Encryption scheme. In Chapter 6, the authors demonstrate the feasibility of this approach for audio data and still image data.

Typical histogram-based watermarking schemes based on comparison of histogram bins are prone to de-synchronization attacks, where the whole histogram is shifted by a certain amount. This kind of attacks can be avoided by synchronizing the embedding and detection processes, using the mean of the histogram as a calibration point. The resulting watermarking scheme is resistant to three common types of shifts of the histogram, while the advantages of previous histogram-based schemes, especially commutativity of watermarking and permutation-based encryption, are preserved. The authors also report on the results of testing robustness of the still image watermark against JPEG and JPEG2000 compression and on the possibility of using histogram-based watermarks for authenticating the content of an image.

Since the last few decades huge amounts and diversified form of work has been witnessed in the domain of de-noising of binary images through the evolution of the classical techniques. These principally include analytical techniques and approaches. Although the scheme was working well but the principal drawback of these classical and analytical techniques are that the information regarding the noise characteristics is essential beforehand. In addition to that time complexity of analytical works amounts to beyond practical applicability. Consequently most of the recent works are based on heuristic based techniques conceding to approximate solutions rather than the best ones. In Chapter 7, the authors propose a solution using an iterative neural network that applies iterative spatial filtering technology with critically varied size of the computation window. With critical variation of the window-size, the authors are able to show noted acceleration in the filtering approach i.e. obtaining better quality filtration with lesser number of iterations.

Identification and recognition of a human subject by monitoring a video/image by using various biometric features such as finger prints, retina/iris scans, palm prints has been of interest to researches since long. In Chapter 8, an attempt has been made to recognise a human subject uniquely by monitoring his/her gait. This has been done by analysing sampled frames of a video sequence to first detect the presence of a human form and then extract the silhouette of the subject in question. The extracted silhouette is then used to find the skeleton from it. The skeleton contains a set of points that retains the connectivity of the form and maintains the geometric properties of the silhouette. From the skeleton, a novel method has been proposed involving the neighbourhood of interest pixels to identify the end points representing the heel, toe, etc. These points finally lead to the calculation of gait-attributes. The extracted attributes represented in the form of a pattern vector are matched using Cosine Distance with features stored in the database resulting in identification/rejection.

The main motto of Chapter 9 is to present a best classification of diabetes. The proposed approach work consists in 2 stages: (1) In the first stage The Pima Indian Diabetes Dataset obtained from the UCI repository of machine learning databases. (2) In the second stage (a) Have performed the classification technique by using Fuzzy Decision Tree on Pima Indian Diabetes Dataset. (b) Apply PSO_SVM as a Feature Selection Technique followed by the classification technique by using Fuzzy Decision Tree on Pima Indian Diabetes Dataset. In this chapter, the optimization of SVM using PSO reduces the number of attributes and hence after applying Fuzzy Decision Tree improves the accuracy of detecting Diabetes. The hybrid combinatorial method of feature selection and classification needs to be done so that the system applied is used for the classification of diabetes.

Nature-inspired metaheuristic algorithms finds near optimum solution in a fast and efficient manner when used in a complex problem like finding optimum number of neuron in hidden layers of a Multi-Layer Perceptron (MLP). In Chapter 10, a classification work is discussed of malignant Melanoma, which is a type of lethal skin cancer. The classification accuracy is more than 91% with visually imperceptible features using MLP. The results found are comparably better than the related work found in the literature.

Finally the performance of two metaheuristic algorithms, i.e. Particle Swarm Optimization (PSO) and Simulated Annealing (SA) are compared and analyzed with different parameters to show their searching nature in the two dimensional search space of hidden layer neurons.

The primary objective of the proposed book is to address the challenges encountered in multimedia data management by devising both classical and intelligent techniques. The secondary objective is to highlight the essence of multimedia data management and engineering involved. The outcome of the present endeavor would benefit the readers with insights into the multimedia technology assisted by different novel algorithms to manage the multimedia data content. Hence, the readers would be motivated to embark on research in this direction and evolve more novel algorithms beneficial for the mankind.

Siddhartha Bhattacharyya
RCC Institute of Information Technology, India
May 2018

Chapter 1
Implementation of a Reversible Watermarking Technique for Medical Images

Ranit Karmakar
Tata Consultancy Services, India

Abhishek Basu
RCC Institute of Information Technology, India

ABSTRACT

Electronic health records (EHR) contain patients' medical as well as personal details. With the increased use of digital media, these data are stored and transferred through the electronic media all over the world. This makes it vulnerable to unauthorized people. Digital image watermarking can be a useful process of protecting these data from attacker but causes severe and unrecoverable damage to cover media. In the case of highly sensitive images like medical images, this might creates a problem during further diagnosis. In this chapter, a reversible data hiding algorithm is proposed which also is capable of holding a large chunk of data without affecting the cover media. The main cover image is first reconstructed and hidden behind a bigger media and then the extra pixels are used to hide encrypted forms of EHR data along with an authentication signature. As EHR data and the digital signature is passed through various encryption stages while encoding, it is made more secure. The algorithm is developed on the spatial domain adding some cautious measures which made it fragile as well.

INTRODUCTION

The history of imaging dates back in 1826 when a Frenchman Joseph Nicéphore Niépce was able to produce the first picture in the human history, a view through his window. Using the lithographic technique and 8 hours exposure to light, it was possible to capture the first image. Later that century a lot of work has been done for the improvement but it wasn't until late twentieth century when digital imaging was developed. This gave a cheaper and easier solution to the old film-based methods used in photography. In the 1960s, the digital image processing has become a large area of interest in different research facilities

DOI: 10.4018/978-1-5225-7107-0.ch001

around the globe, especially for the applications in satellite imagery, wire-photo standards conversion, medical imaging, videophone, character recognition, and photograph enhancement. However, the cost of processing was fairly high because of low-quality computer equipment available in that era. The scenario soon started changing with the advancement in computer science and in the 2000s, digital images and signal processing have become the most common form of image processing for different applications.

The internet boom of the late 90s and early 2000 allowed this digital media to float all around the globe in real-time. With improvements in technology and digital devices, the amount of digital data started increasing exponentially. A recent paper by IDC, Data Age 2025, predicts that by the year 2025, our world will have 163 ZB (Zetta Byte) of data, almost 10 times than what we have today. But most alarmingly, it suggests that 90% of this data will require some form of security and only about half of this will have it. So, security has become a big concern. For the purpose of securing digital images from different attacks and data theft, a new technique was introduced, named Digital Watermarking. The term digital watermarking was first coined by Andrew Tirkel and Charles Osborne in December 1992 and soon after in 1993 was demonstrated in their paper Electronic Water Mark. Although, watermarking content for IP protection is in use from 13th century, its application in digital media is relatively recent.

- **Digital Watermarking Life-Cycle:** The watermarking of a digital signal is distributed in three steps, Embedding, Attacking and Detecting. In the embedding stage, the watermark signal is embedded under the cover signal or host signal. After transmitting this signal, it may gone through some attacks such as compression, cropping, addition of noise etc. This is known as the attack stage. In the last stage, the watermark signal is tried to be recovered. If the recovered signal is unaltered, it proves that the host signal is not affected anyway. The digital watermarking can be classified in the following ways:
  - ◦ **Robustness:** A watermarking algorithm can be called as robust if it can withheld different attacks and transformations. Whereas a fragile watermarking algorithm is easily destroyed with slight modification on the mail signal.
  - ◦ **Perceptibility:** Perceptibility deals with the understanding of the signal. If the signal is perceptually indistinguishable even after applying the watermark, it is called perceptible.
  - ◦ **Capacity:** Differentiated in two different methods zero-bit and multiple-bit, as the name suggests, capacity determines the size of watermark signal that can be hidden under the host or cover signal.

One of the most widely used application of digital signal processing is on medical images. Medical images contain very sensitive data and can be easily manipulated. Without proper protection, these images are highly vulnerable. The information infrastructure system of modern health care is formed by HIS (Hospital Information System), and its special cases of RIS (Radiology Information System), PACS (Picture Archiving and Communication System). These digitization and recent developments in information and communication technology provide in fact new ways to store, access and distribute medical data. It introduces new practices for the profession, as well as the patient themselves by accessing to their own medical files. Over many advantages these techniques are vulnerable in protecting the Electronic Health Records (EHR), and highly personal documents shared in the open network. The systematized collection of patient and population electronically-stored health information in a digital format is known as Electronic Health Record (EHR), or Electronic Medical Record (EMR). Because of being digital, these information can be shared across different health care settings through network-connected, enterprise-wide information systems or other information networks and exchanges easily. Generally these EHR data includes personal information of the patient's such as demographics, medical history, medication and allergies, immunization status, laboratory test results, radiology images, vital signs, personal statistics like age and weight, and billing information of the patent. A recent study, Medical Identity Theft in Healthcare, shows alarming facts about it as well. So protecting this data from unauthorized access is essential.

If we look closely, we can find that there are two problems that need to be addressed. One, the vulnerability of highly sensitive medical images which can be easily twitched a little to probably misguide the treatment, and two, classified information of the patients that can be stolen. As a solution we can incorporate old watermarking technique to conquer the problems. According to domain based classification, watermarking can be of two types; Spatial Domain and Frequency Domain. Based on human perception it can have Visible and Invisible watermarking where invisible watermarking can again be classified as Robust and Fragile. For the medical images and EHR data to be protected, we require a technique that would both be fragile and robust. This may sound a little contradictory, but we would require a technique that would be fragile enough to destroy the patient's personal information if it faces even a little distortion. On the other hand, it needs to be robust enough to protect the main image after some kind of attack. In the paper "Watermarking Medical Images with Patient Information", A. Deepthi and U.C. Niranjan showed how LSB replacement technique in the spatial domain can be a useful method to find a feasible solution. But the problem with this method was, it made permanent distortion on the cover image. For highly sensitive medical images, this can cause problems. Later in many different research papers scientists have tried to come up with different solutions such as finding the ROI, but the cover image always faced some unrecoverable distortion as the image pixels were modified to hide data. As most cases of data hiding, the cover media experiences some distortion due to hidden data and the exact cover image can never be recovered back to its original form even after extracting out the hidden information from it. In applications like medical diagnosis and law enforcement, it is essential to revert back the hidden media from the original cover media for some legal considerations. On the other hand in applications like remote sensing and high-energy particle physical experimental investigation, the original cover media should be recovered as those contain high-precision data. These type of hiding techniques are famously referred as reversible, invertible, lossless, or distortion-free data hiding techniques. So in reversible data hiding technique the cover media can exactly be recovered even after hiding some important information behind it. But generally lossless data hiding techniques have limitations over the amount of data hidden.

So in this paper we have proposed a data hiding technique specially designed for the highly sensitive images like medical images and to the hide the vulnerable EHR data from attack. First the main image is interpolated to a larger image. The larger image contained image pixels from main image as well as some extra pixels on which the classified data can be hidden. The interpolated image looks almost similar to the main image and can hardly be identified as different by any human being. This made the technique even secure. The text based EHR data is first encrypted with a private key which is only known to the encryption and decryption blocks. Every text bit is then again encoded using UTF-8 standard and divided into 4-bit long blocks. Each 4-bit block replaces the last 4-bits of the extra pixels of the interpolated image. Near the ROI region, the extra pixels are used to hide one doctor's signature. Any try to twitch any pixel near the ROI area will cause a change in the signature image as well. From extracted image we can then find out what type of changes made, if any, and also can predict a form of reverted image.

The algorithm is tested with 40 medical images but it can have a wider scope of implementation. From the results, the algorithm is found to be highly effective and capable of detecting even small attacks.

During testing we found that the every time the EHR data is destroyed after any attack and the doctor's signature shows significant proof of that. But even after that, the main cover image can be restored to a certain level and can be used for further evaluation. As the algorithm combines images and data together, it also saves storage space as two different files don't need to be stored separately.

LITERARY SURVEY

According to the data published in http://www.internetlivestats.com/internet-users/, around 40% of the world's population has internet connection now which is about 3.5 billion and still counting. About 20 years back in 1995 it was less than 1%. But in 2005 it reached its first billion, in 2010 the second billion and in 2014 the third billion. This data clearly shows the rapid spread of internet and its high penetration rates even in underdeveloped parts of the world. With the digital revolution and the rapid development in internetwork technology, the health care systems also evolved from its old manual based type to the electronic-based and fully automated type. It led to a new area of technology named telemedicine. In their paper Technology Meets Healthcare: Distance Learning and Telehealth (2001), White LAE, Krousel-Wood MA, Mather F., defined telemedicine as the use of electronic information and communication technologies to provide healthcare to patients who are separated by distance. On a wide geographical scale, this technology is possessing an important role in providing medical sector with the capability of connecting all participants in the healthcare process as well as this information is used for medical related research. However, the paper Learning through telemedicine networks (2003) talks when the data is digitally archived and transferred through any medium of communication, there is one important aspect and that is the security and protection of the EHR. In another paper, Medical Identity Theft (2012), W. Walters, and A. Betz, shows another example of the critical information security crimes is medical identity theft (MIDT).

M. Terry in the paper Medical identity theft and telemedicine security talks about the same. MIDT gets attention from a large number of hackers because this contains the personal and financial information of the patient. Another problem added to it is the alteration of the medical data. If the data is open to the hacker he may change the information of medication, patient's current status and other sensitive details which causes misleading in the further medical diagnostics, and consequently, jeopardizing the patient's life. A report shows that in 2006 approximately 18,000 cases of MIDT reported to Federal Trade Commission (FTC). In 2012, a study conducted at Ponemon Institute shows about 1.5 million victims of MIDT only in America with an estimated total cost of $28.6 billion or approximately $20,000 per victim. This has led an increased awareness over the MIDT protection. In 2014, HHS Budget Makes Smart Investments, Protects the Health and Safety America's Families budget report allocates $80 million for work to spread the adoption and use of health information technology by US govt. is a big proof of this. Digital watermarking can play an important role in protecting this data while transmitting it safely as well as it can play important role in authentication over many other available methods.

L. Xuanwen et al in his paper A lossless data embedding scheme for medical images in application of e-diagnosis, in 2003 showed a lossless data embedding scheme is proposed for medical images where each binary bit- plane is compressed with roughly and later data is embedded to save space. The digital information is integrated prior to embedding process on the medical images. While recovering the data, the first the compressed image is extracted and then decompressed. In the mentioned process, when the data is embedded in the higher bit-plane level, the distortion to the medical image becomes outsized. The data embedding in special domain results less robustness which is another limitation.

In Tamper detection and recovery for medical images using near-lossless information hiding technique (2008), J H K Wu et al. proposed two methods. The first method is based on modulo 256, where initially the medical image was divided into several chunks and each chunk is embedded with the watermarks, which are the combination of an authentication message which is the hash value of the chunk, and the recovery information of other chunk. But as these chunks are too small and extremely compressed, in second method discrete cosine transform (DCT) was introduced with the idea of ROI. From the non-tampered chunks exactly the same image can be obtained but where the chunks are tampered, we can only get an approximately same image. As here only authentication and recovery data are embedded, this method shows a limitation on the watermark hiding capacity. The scheme is non-reversible as well because of the prEHRocessing involved.

In Data hiding scheme for medical images a search based technique was introduced by R. Rodriguez-Colin, C. Feregrino-Urabe, B. G. Trinidiad, where the search started from the center of the image and depending upon the bit to be embedded, the luminance is either increased or decreased. When the embedding bit is 1, the luminance is was changed by adding the grayscale mean value of the block with luminance of block and when it is 0, the luminance is was changed by subtracting the grayscale. The similar search method was implemented while decoding the bits. As some bits are lost in the extraction process, the extracted data is unreadable. Another limitation of this process is, ROI is not implemented which is a big concern in telemedicine.

F. Rahimi and R. Hossein in A dual adaptive watermarking scheme in contourlet domain for DICOM images suggested a blind watermarking technique with an intention of enhancing robustness, confidentiality and authentication. In the ROI the EHR information is hidden which gave them ability to enhance authentication and confidentiality. And a coded digital signature of the physician is hidden in the RONI for the purpose of origin detection. This technique has a high hiding capacity with confidentiality and authentication. However, due to the fact that watermark bit were not scattered in the embedded region, the hidden watermark is not safe and it receive very low protection against various attack which lead to the non-robustness of the technique.

Using the characteristics of ultrasound medical images a 4-rectangle organized as a pyramid was used to locate region ROI in Reversible medical image watermarking for tamper detection and recovery. The rest of the region is assumed to be RONI. Some ROI block holds the watermark bits while the RONI holds the actual LSB values of the ROI for restoration. For this purpose a mapping sequence was used. This technique is fragile and even a small attack on the RONI can destroy the whole image from recovery, however the main limitation is it only can be applied on the ultrasound medical images.

In a paper by A. Deepthi, U.C. Niranjan in Watermarking Medical Images with Patient Information, two data files are used to implement a digital watermarking process into the greyscale level of a medical image using the LSB replacement scheme. The two data files used while watermarking are one test document and an ECG graph. Though this is a realistic model of embedding watermark in medical images, it has limitations because of the permanent distortion on the image. This distortion causes some permanent loss of data. Because of this loss the recovered image can never be used further in telemedicine for diagnosing patient.

In a recent paper on reversible data hiding technique for medical images, A New Reversible and high capacity data hiding technique for E-healthcare applications, authors have introduced interpolation method and then embedded EHR data using LSB replacement technique. Using parity checksum method, the authors have set last two digits of the image pixel to zero. As the main image pixels are still in use and changed some distortions occur on the main image which might be crucial for high sensitive medical images. Also, the EHR data is stored as jpeg pixels which make them less fragile. Even after the attack, in some cases the patient's information is clearly understandable which is not expected.

In the paper A fair benchmark for image watermarking systems, Martin K., and Fabien P. have presented an evaluation procedure of image watermarking systems. On robust digital watermarking systems, a number of papers have been presented, but the criteria has never been discussed clearly. In this paper they tried to address this problem by suggesting a useful benchmark. In another the paper A Benchmark for Medical Image Watermarking, authors, Navas K. A, Sasikumar M and Sreevidya S, have proposed a benchmark for for the evaluation of watermarking techniques used for embedding EHR data on medical images. With a number of medical images available in different modalities and different sizes, the paper tries to talk about the Bounds of capacity, imperceptibility and robustness. Perceptual model based data embedding in medical images, by S. Dandapat, Opas Chutatape and S. M. Krishnan, proposes a perceptual model based technique for embedding patient information in a medical image. The suggested that the distortions in the diagnostic information-content arised due to data embedding can be controlled using a Perceptual Quality Measure (PQM).

In many a different papers different embedding techniques for medical images have been discussed. In A lossless data embedding scheme for medical images in application of e-diagnosis, authors discuss about the data embedding technique but the scheme was still unable to produce a distortionless system. The paper A survey on watermarking application scenarios and related attacks focuses on different applications of digital image watermarking.

SYSTEM IMPLEMENTATION

Watermarking is a very useful technique in hiding EHR data behind a medical image. Among the various methods of watermarking, the hiding of encrypted ERP data using the LSB replacement is very useful. But LSB replacement always causes some irrecoverable damage on the cover media and as medical images are very sensitive this can hamper the quality of image causing loss of data permanently. To avoid this problem we have applied a method which increases the data hiding capacity as well as this method is totally lossless. So even after embedding EHR data behind the cover image the exact main image can be extracted for further use.

As the Fig. 1 suggests, the main image is first interpolated into a bigger image where the main image pixels are distributed through the image. Then on the extra pixels the data is hidden by using LSB replacement technique. We could have used all the pixels for data hiding but that could have resulted in permanent destruction of the main image. The steps are as follow.

1. Pre-Processing

Step 1: First the cover image, say I, of size M x N is taken. If the image is an RGB image, it is converted to a grayscale image of same size. Let the grayscale image be I_{gr}.

Figure 1. Encoding Block

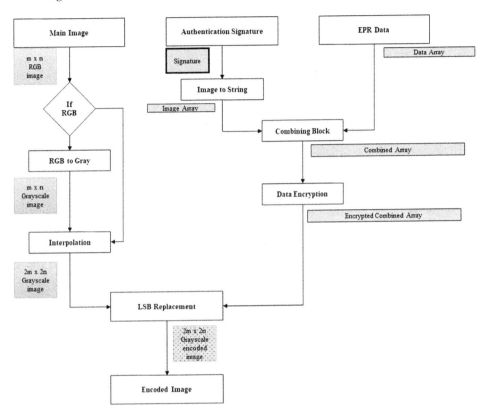

$$I = \begin{bmatrix} i_r(m,n) \\ i_g(m,n) \\ i_b(m,n) \end{bmatrix} \mid 0 \le m \le M, 0 \le n \le N, i_r(m,n) \in [0,255],$$

$$i_g(m,n) \in [0,255], i_b(m,n) \in [0,255]$$

$$I_{gr} = i_{gr}(m,n) \mid 0 \le m \le M, 0 \le n \le N, i_{gr}(m,n) \in [0,255]$$

Step 2: Then the grayscale cover image is interpolated into a bigger image of dimension 2M x 2N. Let the image be I_n.

$$I_n = i_n(m,n) \mid 0 \le m \le 2M, 0 \le n \le 2N, i_n(m,n) \in [0,255]$$

The interpolation steps are as followed.

2. Interpolation

Step 3: First a blank image of dimension 2M x 2N is taken.

$$I_n = i_n\left(m,n\right) \mid 0 \le m \le 2M, 0 \le n \le 2N, i_n\left(m,n\right) = 0$$

Step 4: From the main image I_{gr}, image pixels are replaced in the new interpolated image I_n.

$$I_n\left(2i-1, 2j-1\right) = i_{gr}\left(i,j\right), where\ i \in 1:m, j \in 1:n$$

Step 5: Now the values of the neighborhood pixels are used to fill the entire image in the given fashion,

$$I_n\left(i,j\right) = \begin{bmatrix} I_n\left(m-1,n-1\right) + I_n\left(m-1,n+1\right) + \\ I_n\left(m+1,n-1\right) + I_n\left(m+1,n+1\right) \end{bmatrix} / 4\ ;\ for\ i = 2, 4, 6, \ldots, 2m\text{-}2\ and\ j = 2, 4, 6, \ldots, 2n\text{-}2$$

$$I_n\left(i,j\right) = \left\{ I_n\left(m-1,n-1\right) + I_n\left(m+1,n-1\right) \right\} / 2; for\ i = 2, 4, 6, \ldots, 2m\text{-}2\ and\ j = 2n$$

$$I_n\left(i,j\right) = \left\{ I_n\left(m-1,n-1\right) + I_n\left(m-1,n+1\right) \right\} / 2; for\ i = 2m\ and\ j = 2, 4, 6, \ldots, 2n\text{-}2$$

$$I_n\left(i,j\right) = \left\{ I_n\left(m-1,n-1\right) \right\}; for\ i = 2m\ and\ j = 2n$$

$$I_n\left(i,j\right) = \left\{ I_n\left(m,n-1\right) + I_n\left(m+1,n\right) \right\} / 2; for\ i = 1\ and\ j = 2n$$

$$I_n\left(i,j\right) = \left\{ I_n\left(m,n-1\right) + I_n\left(m+1,n\right) + I_n\left(m,n+1\right) \right\} / 3; for\ i = 1, 3, 5, \ldots, 2m\text{-}1\ and\ j = 2, 4, 6, \ldots, 2n\text{-}2$$

$$I_n\left(i,j\right) = \left\{ I_n\left(m-1,n\right) + I_n\left(m+1,n\right) + I_n\left(m,n+1\right) \right\} / 3; for\ i = 2, 4, 6, \ldots, 2m\text{-}2\ and\ j = 1$$

$$I_n\left(i,j\right) = \begin{bmatrix} I_n\left(m,n-1\right) + I_n\left(m+1,n\right) + \\ I_n\left(m,n+1\right) + I_n\left(m-1,n\right) \end{bmatrix} / 4\ ;\ for\ i = 2, 4, 6, \ldots, 2m\text{-}2\ and\ j = 1, 3, 5, \ldots, 2n\text{-}1$$

$$I_n\left(i,j\right) = \left\{ I_n\left(m,n-1\right) + I_n\left(m-1,n\right) \right\} / 2; for\ i = 2m\ and\ j = 1$$

$$I_n\left(i,j\right) = \left\{ I_n\left(m,n-1\right) + I_n\left(m,n+1\right) + I_n\left(m-1,n\right) \right\} / 3; for\ i = 2m\ and\ j = 1, 3, 5, \ldots, 2n\text{-}1$$

3. Data Encryption

Step 6: The EHR data and the doctor's authentication signature is then taken as input. The EHR data is first encrypted using a private key that is only known to the encryption and decryption blocks. Every alphabet of the EHR data is then converted using UTF-8 conversion to get its binary values. The signature taken is in grayscale, so its each pixel also has an 8-bit value. Between the EHR data, the signature's pixel values are concatenated using some private encryption key. After this process EHR data and the signature rEHResents as a single unit of data. This data is again encrypted using some encryption algorithm before it is passed for the LSB replacement behind the interpolated image. Let the signature be represented as I_L.

$$I_L = i_l(m,n) \mid 0 \le x \le X, 0 \le y \le Y, i_l(x,y) \in [0, 255]$$

4. LSB Replacement

Step 7: The main image is only available on the $I_n(2i-1, 2j-1)$ pixels where i ∈ 1:m and j ∈ 1:n. In all the other pixels this encrypted data is hidden in last 4-bits of the image pixels. As every single data unit has an 8-bit value, we needed two pixels to hide one single data unit. The last 4-bits of the first extra pixel is replaced by first 4-bits of the data unit and the last 4 bits of the second pixel is replaced by the last 4 bits of the data unit. After this LSB replacement we get the final image. Let it be I_{en}.

$$I_{en} = i_{en}(m,n) \mid 0 \le m \le 2M, 0 \le n \le 2N, i_{en}(m,n) \in [0, 255]$$

During the reconstruction, there are total three things are recovered. Those are-

1. Main medical image,
2. Doctor's authentication signature,
3. EHR data. For this purpose below mentioned steps are followed. The decoding process of the system is shown in Figure 2.

5. Medical Image Reconstruction

Step 8: Let the reconstructed medical image is represented as Ire. Then,

$$I_{re} = i_{re}(m,n) \mid 0 \le m \le 2M, 0 \le n \le 2N, i_{re}(m,n) \in [0, 255]$$

$$I_{re} = I_{en}(2i-1, 2j-1); where\ i = 1:m\ and\ j = 1:n$$

Step 9: In LSB extraction block the last 4-bits from the abandoned pixels are extracted and stored in a single array. While encoding, this signature is first concatenated as an 8-bit data with the EHR data array and then encrypted using some private encryption key. So before decoding first the whole data array is decrypted to its real form.

Figure 2. Decoding Block

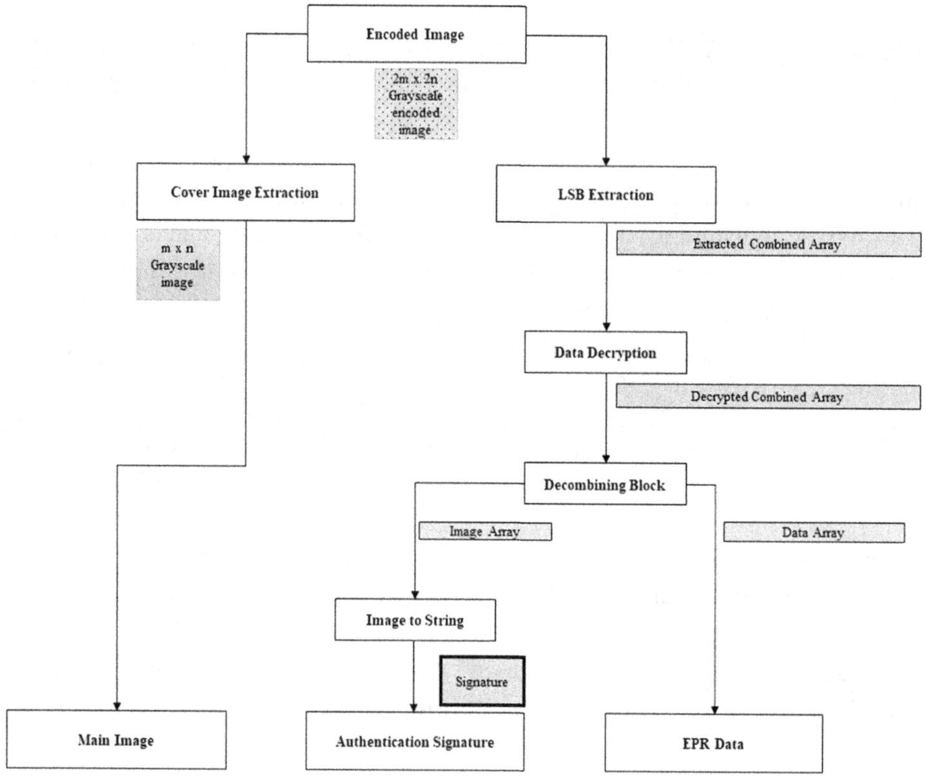

6. Doctor's Authentication Signature

Step 10: Using the known concatenation key, the pixels are first identified and then extracted to construct the signature image. Without the knowledge of this key, reconstruction of the signature is impossible. Let the reconstructed doctor's authentication signature is represented as I_{Lre}. Then,

$$I_{Lre} = i_{Lre}\left(x,y\right) \mid 0 \leq x \leq X, 0 \leq y \leq Y, i_{Lre}\left(x,y\right) \in \left[0,255\right]$$

7. EHR Data Extraction

Step 11: After the reconstruction of the signature those data are removed from the array which makes it a pure EHR data. This data is then collected and stored for further use.

Figure 3. Data Embedding and Watermarking

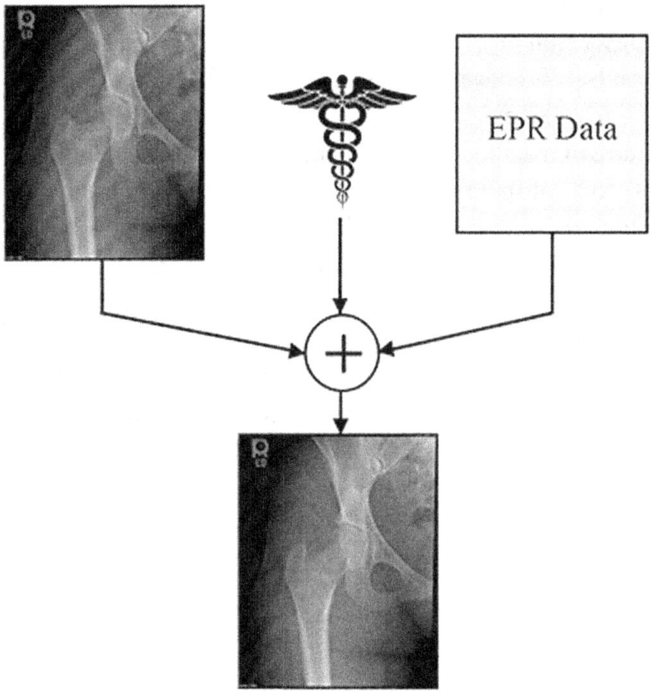

RESULT AND DISCUSSION

Our main motto was to find an efficient algorithm to hide a large chunk of EHR information behind the cover image without effecting it. For this purpose, as mentioned above, we first interpolated the image into a larger image and hide cover image pixel behind them. It gave us extra space for the EHR data to be hidden without even effecting a single bit of the cover image. We took a set a 40 different types of radiological medical images and implemented our algorithm. As the result shows it is fragile in nature which protects the information from attack.

Figure 4 shows the intermediate stages of the image interpolation. The shown image had a dimension of 960x1200 pixels. After the interpolation is performed, the image dimension doubled, increasing it

Figure 4. Intermediate steps of image interpolation

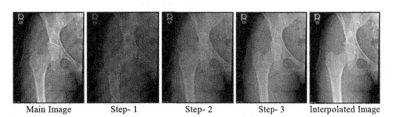

Main Image   Step- 1   Step- 2   Step- 3   Interpolated Image

to 1920x2400 pixels. By performing this, we got three times more pixels to hide information behind it without affection the main image.

In Table 1 (A-C) the test result of an image is shown where the main image taken was in dimension 960x1200. After interpolation it is converted into an image of size 1920x2400. Because of this interpolation extra 3,456,000 pixels where created where EHR data and the authenticating logo can be hidden. For authentication any signature of a doctor or the hospital or the medical center can be taken into account. This signature can be the logo of the medical center, any particular symbol or any specific biometric data. In our test-case we took the doctor's logo of dimension 132x117. Fig. 4 shows the encoding stages. Even after hiding the logo there were total 3,417,120 number of pixel left where 1,708,560 number of characters total can be hidden. With a normal margin on an A4 page total 6217 characters can be accommodated approximately with a size 10 font in Times New Roman font style. Which means with a cover image of size 960x1200 approximately a report with 275 pages can be hidden. The hiding capacity increases with the increase of size of the main image. Though the payload capacity of this algorithm is 3, the average PSNR stand at 34.31 with a 13.26% bit error rate. The details is given in Fig. 6.

Fragility is a big concern for medical information. It is better for the information to be destroyed completely than to be obtained by some unknown attacker. As the algorithm is implemented on the spatial domain it was already less tolerant to any external attack. The fragility is further increased by

Figure 5. Images used for test with their dimension

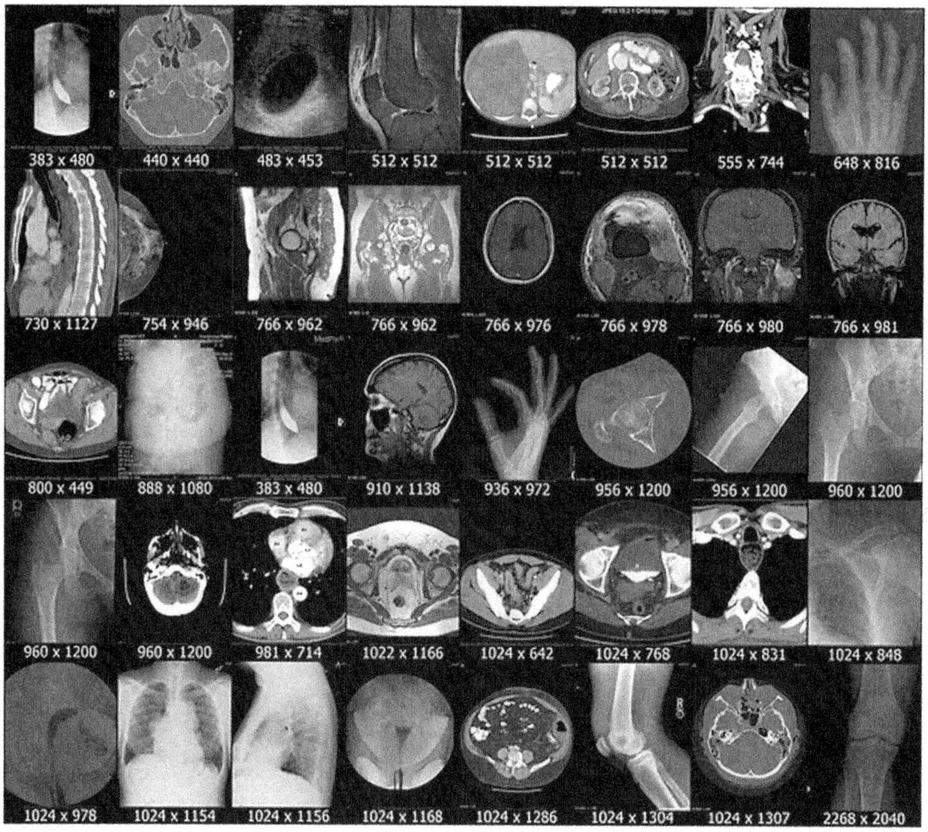

Table 1. Result against attacks

Attack	Attacked Image	Extracted Image	Testing Data	
No Attack			PSNR	Inf
			SC	1
			MI	1
			BERR	0
			JCS	1
			SSIM	1
			WPSNR	Inf
Adjust Filter			PSNR	15.93294
			SC	0.434355
			MI	0.147926
			BERR	0.409812
			JCS	0.865855
			SSIM	0.899609
			WPSNR	14.89779
Average Blur Filter			PSNR	36.03213
			SC	0.990457
			MI	0.249055
			BERR	0.231469
			JCS	0.981948
			SSIM	0.866512
			WPSNR	24.62162
Disk Blur Filter			PSNR	32.01688
			SC	0.999251
			MI	0.261129
			BERR	0.236152
			JCS	0.981948
			SSIM	0.836326
			WPSNR	24.62162
Entropy Filter			PSNR	10.54234
			SC	0.001801
			MI	0.762806
			BERR	0.399054
			JCS	0.981948
			SSIM	0.257359
			WPSNR	24.62162
Erode Filter			PSNR	30.43538
			SC	0.924124
			MI	0.223587
			BERR	0.172721
			JCS	0.987395
			SSIM	0.927024
			WPSNR	27.49026
Gaussian Filter			PSNR	44.71956
			SC	0.997238
			MI	0.181837
			BERR	0.155709
			JCS	0.98195
			SSIM	0.96558
			WPSNR	24.62231
Gaussian Noise Filter			PSNR	20.70157
			SC	0.914377
			MI	0.942072
			BERR	0.380137
			JCS	0.866622
			SSIM	0.130572
			WPSNR	18.21772
GSlid Filter			PSNR	36.21941
			SC	0.99309
			MI	0.23291
			BERR	0.176108
			JCS	0.982747
			SSIM	0.864833
			WPSNR	24.86775

Table 2. Result against attacks

Attack	Attacked Image	Extracted Image	Testing Data	
Guided Filter			PSNR	39.12411
			SC	0.994291
			MI	0.224282
			BERR	0.21663
			JCS	0.981948
			SSIM	0.899957
			WPSNR	24.62162
Laplacian Blur Filter			PSNR	10.56314
			SC	0.017128
			MI	0.983727
			BERR	0.434199
			JCS	0.611522
			SSIM	0.119174
			WPSNR	11.34216
Log Blur Filter			PSNR	10.65159
			SC	0.036499
			MI	0.96109
			BERR	0.437888
			JCS	0.612738
			SSIM	0.107432
			WPSNR	11.2901
Motion Blur Filter			PSNR	32.63777
			SC	0.999297
			MI	0.259161
			BERR	0.232341
			JCS	0.981948
			SSIM	0.848915
			WPSNR	24.62162
Median Blur Filter			PSNR	36.1909
			SC	0.993291
			MI	0.234442
			BERR	0.17642
			JCS	0.98277
			SSIM	0.863933
			WPSNR	24.88879
Order Filter			PSNR	25.69851
			SC	0.824716
			MI	0.318193
			BERR	0.314695
			JCS	0.981948
			SSIM	0.744835
			WPSNR	24.62162
Poisson Noise Filter			PSNR	30.1453
			SC	0.989745
			MI	0.383754
			BERR	0.295682
			JCS	0.948162
			SSIM	0.638632
			WPSNR	22.62786
Prewitt Filter			PSNR	10.53923
			SC	0.013297
			MI	0.0711
			BERR	0.388469
			JCS	0.463216
			SSIM	0.194419
			WPSNR	11.09414
Sobel Filter			PSNR	10.56765
			SC	0.018634
			MI	0.07882
			BERR	0.388564
			JCS	0.464954
			SSIM	0.194935
			WPSNR	11.02777

Table 3. Result against attacks

Attack	Attacked Image	Extracted Image	Testing Data	
Scaling			PSNR	37.37021
			SC	0.992764
			MI	0.236941
			BERR	0.214577
			JCS	0.981987
			SSIM	0.891605
			WPSNR	24.6469
Speckle Noise			PSNR	23.23075
			SC	0.953547
			MI	0.423346
			BERR	0.3304
			JCS	1
			SSIM	0.44848
			WPSNR	Inf
Salt-Pepper Noise Filter			PSNR	21.55007
			SC	0.921233
			MI	0.148829
			BERR	0.010015
			JCS	0.989888
			SSIM	0.523359
			WPSNR	34.91221
Standard Filter			PSNR	10.61324
			SC	0.004054
			MI	0.483577
			BERR	0.395069
			JCS	0.981906
			SSIM	0.231262
			WPSNR	24.61988
Wiener Filter			PSNR	25.23489
			SC	0.951851
			MI	0.524682
			BERR	0.35738
			JCS	0.981948
			SSIM	0.373462
			WPSNR	24.62162

Table 4. Result of EPR and watermark against attack

Attack	Sample Data	Extracted Image	Testing Data	
No Attack	This is a 43 year i. Saccadic eye mov ;aze to the right, ;ide. Bidirectional :orsion swing test lead hanging, left appropriate direct tin. ANALYSIS OF P		PSNR	Inf
			SC	1
			MI	1
			BERR	0
			JCS	1
			SSIM	1
			WPSNR	Inf
Adjust Filter	|z$¦v$vy@.$\|$|@|1$ |y|.$\|¦v¦\|$v|y|.$v XYYZbWy$Z$$v$*)$@\| $$|$\|.$v«|$$\|$.$vz zy\|vz¦y/yv$«v$@v ILdXF^bVWF_$WLdbWZ z.$¦y$v¦\|$w\|\|$\|z$$ $y|v|$$||y@1$Z¦$|z		PSNR	5.311014
			SC	0.365763
			MI	0.944419
			BERR	0.431163
			JCS	0.877981
			SSIM	0.078664
			WPSNR	17.85829
Average Blur Filter	◻)◻+(◻+*◻◻◻+)◻*◻◻;;;ⵕ ◻◻*◻+:*+◻◻◻◻◻◻◻)◻◻: ◻◻+*(◻:)◻◻))◻*◻◻)◻+*◻ *,*+◻◻ ◻(◻◻◻◻++*+<◻++◻*◻+,*¦ *)◻◻)◻ ◻*(+◻)◻´◻+ ◻◻*◻)(◻◻)◻)*◻◻(◻ ¬ª◻.		PSNR	4.871865
			SC	0.331791
			MI	0.775617
			BERR	0.47707
			JCS	0.878901
			SSIM	0.048648
			WPSNR	16.15405

implementing an encryption algorithm to the EHR data and the authenticating signature. As the result in Table II (A-D) shows, it is intolerant to any external attack. After any attack performed the output EHR data is nothing but a garbage. We took a patient's report as our test case data, but the result we got after any attack was some random special characters. The sample is shown in Table 4-7. The whole algorithm

Table 5. Result of EPR and watermark against attack

Attack	Sample Data	Extracted Image	Testing Data	
Disk Blur Filter			PSNR	4.144873
			SC	0.326375
			MI	0.530686
			BERR	0.534941
			JCS	0.862519
			SSIM	0.010745
			WPSNR	15.4858
Entropy Filter			PSNR	2.325885
			SC	0.038016
			MI	0.180211
			BERR	0.62636
			JCS	0.719907
			SSIM	0.022446
			WPSNR	14.01108
Erode Filter			PSNR	3.362764
			SC	0.222408
			MI	0.558244
			BERR	0.554123
			JCS	0.756751
			SSIM	0.053693
			WPSNR	14.21912
Gaussian Filter			PSNR	12.19521
			SC	0.616529
			MI	0.736436
			BERR	0.359104
			JCS	0.898458
			SSIM	0.332082
			WPSNR	17.67683
Gaussian Noise Filter			PSNR	4.437733
			SC	0.360862
			MI	0.595233
			BERR	0.527778
			JCS	0.841157
			SSIM	0.018555
			WPSNR	16.1354
GSlid Filter			PSNR	3.96664
			SC	0.318259
			MI	0.53579
			BERR	0.534083
			JCS	0.824409
			SSIM	0.018645
			WPSNR	14.45511
Guided Filter			PSNR	4.309671
			SC	0.316843
			MI	0.607664
			BERR	0.524419
			JCS	0.875909
			SSIM	0.021366
			WPSNR	16.05964
Laplacian Blur Filter			PSNR	0.911608
			SC	0.053854
			MI	0.865058
			BERR	0.859889
			JCS	0.101188
			SSIM	0.080714
			WPSNR	6.805706
Log Blur Filter			PSNR	0.895973
			SC	0.060916
			MI	0.857452
			BERR	0.860342
			JCS	0.102493
			SSIM	0.087327
			WPSNR	6.819588

Table 6. Result of EPR and watermark against attack

Attack	Sample Data	Extracted Image	Testing Data	
Disk Blur Filter	:::::::::::::::::: %º):::::::;_³ŏ :::::))**:::*:::*: :::::::::*::::::: íîZ::::::;pÔc=Å õä)))))))))))))*** ::::::))*::::::*: :::::<ŏ		PSNR	4.144873
			SC	0.326375
			MI	0.530686
			BERR	0.534941
			JCS	0.862519
			SSIM	0.010745
			WPSNR	15.4858
Entropy Filter	)))))))))))))))))))): :))))))))))))))))))) '))))))))))))))))))) :))))))))))))))))))))))))))))))))))))))):))))))))))))))))))) :))))))))))))))))))))))))))))))))))))))))Ⅲ		PSNR	2.325885
			SC	0.038016
			MI	0.180211
			BERR	0.62636
			JCS	0.719907
			SSIM	0.022446
			WPSNR	14.01108
Erode Filter	Ⅲ]IY)Ⅲ8ⅢⅢ&ⅢH'ⅢGⅢⅢⅢ \ⅢVⅢ)ⅢⅢ9ⅠF⅃H' ⅢⅢN(9ⅢⅢⅢ)Ⅲ&ⅢⅢⅢI6ⅢFⅢ)Ⅲ hⅡVⅢ6ⅢⅡ-ⅢⅢⅢⅢ9Ⅲ8ⅠHⅠ ⅢⅢⅢHⅢⅢⅢⅢⅢ&Ⅱ<ⅠYⅢⅢ ⅠVⅢ6ⅢH6ⅢⅡL ⅢⅢ9H6ⅠHⅠ ⅢⅢⅢWⅢⅢⅢⅢⅢVwⅢⅢⅢⅢVⅢ /Ⅲ6ⅢH6ⅢⅡL ⅢⅢ9ⅠK⅃H⅃Ⅲ		PSNR	3.362764
			SC	0.222408
			MI	0.558244
			BERR	0.554123
			JCS	0.756751
			SSIM	0.053693
			WPSNR	14.21912
Gaussian Filter	QMA??IOXQQ-?IQI_QP. HQAOQXJ`YPI@QZAO?LⅠ PI>MHXMX,LQGQK>QAP M,@A;;>@H*B\RPQ`^] QOQZPNPJ]OPZNJ`N[^` RRLMN`QAI[N_QXJ^QP(Q``]QAOPO]POYNIQ?KⅠ ⱢNwQMIPNPRPLHQXAOY.Ⅰ		PSNR	12.19521
			SC	0.616529
			MI	0.736436
			BERR	0.359104
			JCS	0.898458
			SSIM	0.332082
			WPSNR	17.67683
Gaussian Noise Filter	m¦Ø æ Ć Áŋ Ⅲ F&å¦ Ǫv ⅣR Ǫv v ěZv(Ⅲ ¶6à ⌐ Ⅱ& ⅢⅢ ! oⅢ Ⅱn6 @ÉⅡ Ø FⅡ Ⱦæ F_å 2 1 »p/o -F vf Øf ⅢVØ-VǬæ ⅠⅠØ Ⅱ ¢Ⅱ c Ɇ & :aⱢ Ⅱ Ɫv21 ⱢⅠ ¶ 2Ⅱ		PSNR	4.437733
			SC	0.360862
			MI	0.595233
			BERR	0.527778
			JCS	0.841157
			SSIM	0.018555
			WPSNR	16.1354
GSlid Filter	)ⅢⅢ ⅢⅢⅢ ⅢⅢⅢ ⅢⅢⅢ 9(ⅢⅢⅢⅢ(Ⅱ ⅢⅢⅢ ⅢⅢ Ⅱ(ⅡⱢ)) (Ⅱ)ⅢⅢ(ⅢⅢⅢⅢⅢⅢⅢⅢ :>89 n¾\é^M?ß>ⱢⅠ19*J ⅢⅢⅢⱢ :x1m())ⅠⅡ ZⅡ)9		PSNR	3.96664
			SC	0.318259
			MI	0.53579
			BERR	0.534083
			JCS	0.824409
			SSIM	0.018645
			WPSNR	14.45511
Guided Filter	:::::::::::9);::::; ;KKKJKK:K::::;;:: ;::::::;:::::;:: :::;::;::::;KK;:: ;::;KKKKKK;;KK::: ;;;::<K::;;;;;:: :***;:);;::::::::::; :;KL		PSNR	4.309671
			SC	0.316843
			MI	0.607664
			BERR	0.524419
			JCS	0.875909
			SSIM	0.021366
			WPSNR	16.05964

Laplacian Blur Filter	ⱢXà Vⱦ & ⱢX
	   Ⱡ &
	                      Ⱡ
	   & Ⱡ &
	; Ⱡ & 6
	   & ⱢⱢ FⱢ
	   Ⱡ Ⱡ &
	         Ⱡ Ⱡ Ⱡ
			PSNR	0.911608

			SC	0.053854
			MI	0.865058
			BERR	0.859889
			JCS	0.101188
			SSIM	0.080714
			WPSNR	6.805706
Log Blur Filter	6 ⱡ 6 & Ⱡ ⱢF V Ⱡ 6 Ⱡ6 F F V Ⱡ Ⱡ F V V Ⱡ ⱢF Ⱡ F Ⱡ 6 6 F V Ⱡ V		PSNR	0.895973
			SC	0.060916
			MI	0.857452
			BERR	0.860342
			JCS	0.102493
			SSIM	0.087327
			WPSNR	6.819588

is designed in a way so that the image and the data are passed through various encryption techniques along with private key hiding locations. So with even one unknown parameter, there will be no data available. It shows the security of the algorithm. After even a minor attack the signature and EHR data gets affected such a manner that it can be noticed. If the attacker wants to change any information that

Table 7. Result of EPR and watermark against attack

Attack	Sample Data	Extracted Image	Testing Data	
Standard Filter	▯+,,**-+,+++--▯,*,, ,,,,++,,,,,,+)+),7- j+*-,*+*--+,"▯++,,; +,**9*,,+*-+,+,,,,' <+,*▯,+,++*,+▯',+;, +<,*+-,,*,,*+,,-,)' ,-)▯,*-,++*,+,,*,*, -+-++▯,+-▯+-,*,-,-,)+		PSNR	3.02158
			SC	0.073582
			MI	0.489356
			BERR	0.598169
			JCS	0.874049
			SSIM	0.065961
			WPSNR	17.65505
Wiener Filter	ð]+m1¾m▯H%_I▯+▯j]£▯ö Ŝ{£▯åàÈM% ▯#|>V▯ #Ñ` •]9h 9%▯▯ 6^Â¨¾T"▯ôÀ¢ ?W:*Ïz#8Z´óÕØ▯c▯)Tæ :8I̊Q Z▯▯X▯ V̊0⁹7Ñ▯ ▯ ^A'$ d^jm,4-~á§åÈ¿ U ẑÕQ Ô×ôÒ▯à°ó§µˇYBv9ı		PSNR	4.93287
			SC	0.429224
			MI	0.626097
			BERR	0.500251
			JCS	0.866874
			SSIM	0.005669
			WPSNR	15.49666

Table 8. Comparison with different defined techniques

Sl. No.	Technique	PSNR (dB)	Payload (bits)
1.	A New Reversible And High Capacity Data Hiding Technique For E-Healthcare Applications	46.51	196,608
2.	A high capacity reversible watermarking approach for authenticating images: Exploiting down-sampling, histogram processing, and block selection	52.71	700
3.	A blind and fragile watermarking scheme for tamper detection of medical images preserving ROI	57.95	35,000
Proposed Technique			
4.	On the Implementation of a Reversible Watermarking Technique for Hiding in Medical Images	Inf†	13,824,000

†Discussion: While comparing the watermarked image with the interpolated image we found PSNR as 34.31 but the main image pixels in the interpolated image remained untouched. Hence the PSNR for main image and watermarked image will be infinite.

Figure 6a. Imperceptibility of main images with data hiding capacity: PSNR vs. WPSNR

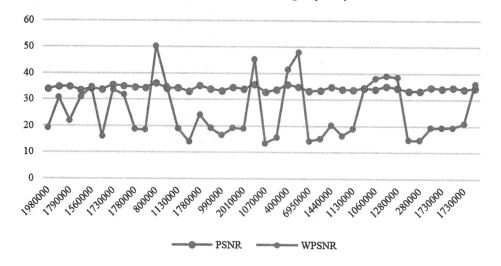

Figure 6b. Imperceptibility of main images with data hiding capacity: JCS vs. MI

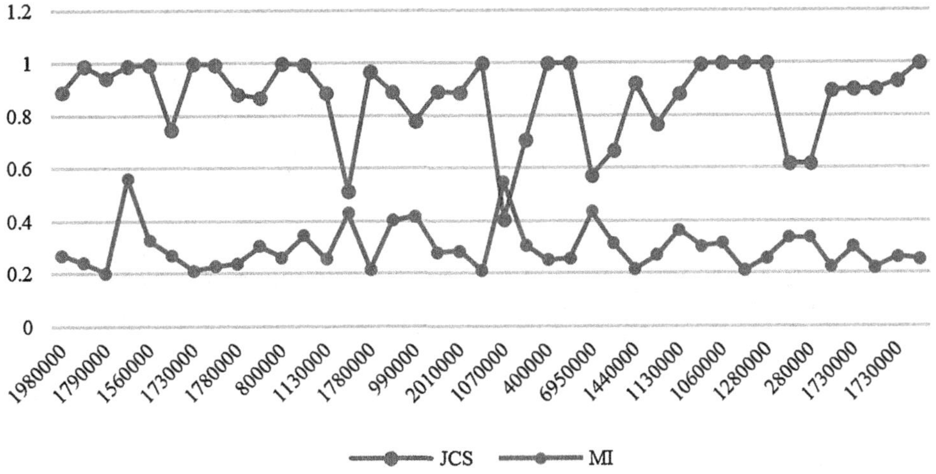

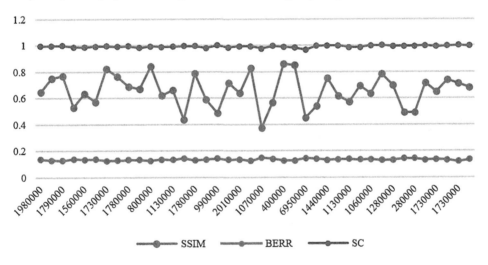

Figure 6c. Imperceptibility of main images with data hiding capacity: SSIM vs. BERR vs. SC

is also not possible without the knowledge of signature's location. The test data result is shown graphically in Figures 6-8. Though the hidden data is destroyed, the main cover image can be reconstructed to some extent if needed, shown in Table I (A-C).

The result of recovered EHR and watermark against different types of attacks are presented in Table 2 (A to D). To test the efficiency of this proposed scheme, results has been compared with some existing scheme in terms of imperceptibility and hiding capacity and presented in Table 3 The results of Imperceptibility and hiding capacity are respectable and fragility of the proposed scheme has been established. Moreover efficiency the method against other state-of-the-art schemes certifies the supremacy of the projected scheme.

Figure 7a. Fragility of cover image: PSNR vs. WPSNR

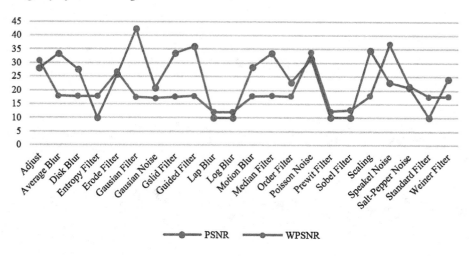

Figure 7b. Fragility of cover image: JCS vs. MI

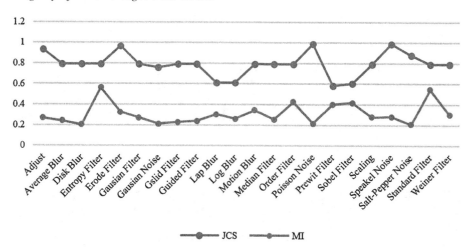

Figure 7c. Fragility of cover image: SSIM vs. BER vs. SC

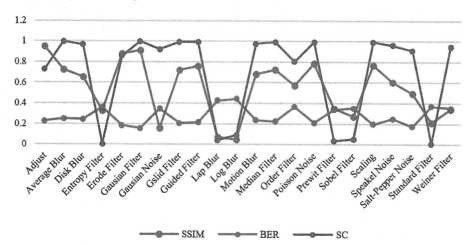

Figure 8a. Fragility of signature

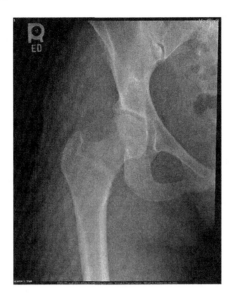

Figure 8b. Fragility of signature: PSNR vs. WPSNR

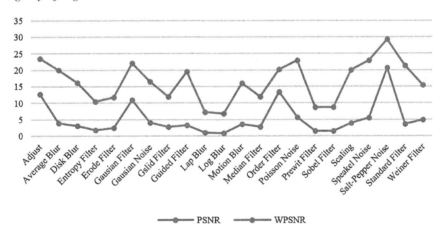

Figure 8c. Fragility of signature: JCS vs. MI

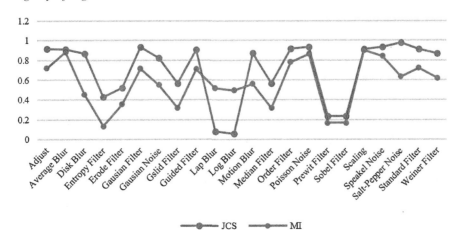

Figure 8d. Fragility of signature: SSIM vs. BER vs. SC

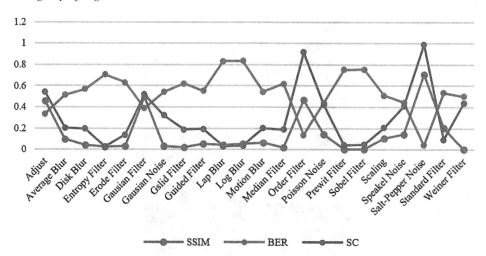

CONCLUSION

In this paper a fragile watermarking technique for highly sensitive medical images has been proposed. The proposed algorithm is useful for its highly fragile nature along with high capacity of hiding EHR (Electronic Patient Record) data. However the technique is also robust when the image authentication is considered. It has been rigorously tested with 40 standard medical images to determine its fragility of data and robustness of the authentication watermark. As the result shows it was able to hide large amount of patient's data inside the image without harming even a single pixel of the main image. In the algorithm with the EHR data, an authentication image has been inscribed as well. The image and data were fragile enough to be destroyed with even a small attack. For the test we have used medical images but the algorithm can be used and implemented on any type of highly sensitive images.

Though the suggested algorithm is highly secured with a high data hiding capacity and fragility, the limitation of it comes in case of size. Because of interpolation the image size is increased which can be a concern but as it is designed keeping cloud storage in mind, this limit can be afforded for the better security. In future research we would work on this algorithm to minimize the image size keeping the high security intact.

REFERENCES

Latham, A. (1999). *Steganography*. Retrieved from http://linux01.gwdg.de/ alatham/stego.html

Leon-Garcia, A. (1994). *Probability and random processes for electrical engineering*. Addison-Wesley.

Aamodt, A., & Plaza, E. (1994). Case-based reasoning: Foundational issues, methodological variations, and system approaches. *AI Communications*, *7*(1), 39–59.

Acharya, R., Bhat, P. S., Kumar, S., & Min, L. C. (2003). Transmission and storage of medical images with patient information. *Computers in Biology and Medicine*, *33*(4), 303–310. doi:10.1016/S0010-4825(02)00083-5 PMID:12791403

Acharya, R., Niranjan, U. C., Iyengar, S. S., Kannathal, N., & Min, L. C. (2004). Simultaneous storage of patient information with medical images in the frequency domain. *Computer Methods and Programs in Biomedicine*, *76*(1), 13–19. doi:10.1016/j.cmpb.2004.02.009 PMID:15313538

Acharya, U. R., Acharya, D., Bhat, P. S., & Niranjan, U. C. (2001). Compact storage of medical images with patient information. *IEEE Transactions on Information Technology in Biomedicine*, *5*(4), 320–323. doi:10.1109/4233.966107 PMID:11759838

Alattar, A. M. (2004). Reversible watermark using the difference expansion of a generalized integer transform. *IEEE Transactions on Image Processing*, *13*(8), 1147–1156. doi:10.1109/TIP.2004.828418 PMID:15326856

Al-Qershi, O. M., & Khoo, B. E. (2011). Authentication and data hiding using a hybrid ROI-based watermarking scheme for DICOM images. *Journal of Digital Imaging*, *24*(1), 114–125. doi:10.100710278-009-9253-1 PMID:19937363

Anand, D., & Niranjan, U. C. (1998, October). Watermarking medical images with patient information. In *Engineering in Medicine and Biology Society, 1998. Proceedings of the 20th Annual International Conference of the IEEE* (Vol. 2, pp. 703-706). IEEE.

Annadurai, S. (2007). *Fundamentals of digital image processing*. Pearson Education India.

Antani, S., Kasturi, R., & Jain, R. (2002). A survey on the use of pattern recognition methods for abstraction, indexing and retrieval of images and video. *Pattern Recognition*, *35*(4), 945–965. doi:10.1016/S0031-3203(01)00086-3

Artz, D. (2001). Digital steganography: Hiding data within data. *IEEE Internet Computing*, *5*(3), 75–80. doi:10.1109/4236.935180

Avcibas, I., Bayram, S., Memon, N., Ramkumar, M., & Sankur, B. (2004, October). A classifier design for detecting image manipulations. In *Image Processing, 2004. ICIP'04. 2004 International Conference on* (Vol. 4, pp. 2645-2648). IEEE.

Badran, E. F., Sharkas, M. A., & Attallah, O. A. (2009, March). Multiple watermark embedding scheme in wavelet-spatial domains based on ROI of medical images. In *Radio Science Conference, 2009. NRSC 2009. National* (pp. 1-8). IEEE.

Bao, F., Deng, R. H., Ooi, B. C., & Yang, Y. (2005). Tailored reversible watermarking schemes for authentication of electronic clinical atlas. *IEEE Transactions on Information Technology in Biomedicine*, *9*(4), 554–563. doi:10.1109/TITB.2005.855556 PMID:16379372

Barni, M., & Bartolini, F. (2004). Data hiding for fighting piracy. *IEEE Signal Processing Magazine*, *21*(2), 28–39. doi:10.1109/MSP.2004.1276109

Barni, M., Bartolini, F., & Piva, A. (2002). Multichannel watermarking of color images. *IEEE Transactions on Circuits and Systems for Video Technology*, *12*(3), 142–156. doi:10.1109/76.993436

Barre, S. (n.d.). *DICOM Medical image samples*. Retrieved from http://barre.nom.fr/medical/samples/

Barreto, P. S., Kim, H. Y., & Rijmen, V. (2002). Toward secure public-key blockwise fragile authentication watermarking. *IEE Proceedings. Vision Image and Signal Processing*, *149*(2), 57–62. doi:10.1049/ip-vis:20020168

Basu, A., Chatterjee, A., Datta, S., Sarkar, S., & Karmakar, R. (2016, October). FPGA implementation of Saliency based secured watermarking framework. In *Intelligent Control Power and Instrumentation (ICICPI), International Conference on* (pp. 273-277). IEEE. 10.1109/ICICPI.2016.7859716

Basu, A., Karmakar, R., Chatterjee, A., Datta, S., Sarkar, S., & Mondal, A. (2017, March). Implementation of salient region based secured digital image watermarking. In *Computer, Communication and Electrical Technology: Proceedings of the International Conference on Advancement of Computer Communication and Electrical Technology (ACCET 2016)* (p. 9). CRC Press. 10.1201/9781315400624-4

Bayram, S., Avcibas, I., Sankur, B., & Memon, N. (2005, September). Image manipulation detection with binary similarity measures. In *Signal Processing Conference, 2005 13th European* (pp. 1-4). IEEE.

Beer, G. (1992). Topological completeness of function spaces arising in the Hausdorff approximation of functions. *Canadian Mathematical Bulletin*, *35*(4), 439–448. doi:10.4153/CMB-1992-058-1

Boncelet, C. G. (2006). The NTMAC for authentication of noisy messages. *IEEE Transactions on Information Forensics and Security*, *1*(1), 35–42. doi:10.1109/TIFS.2005.863506

Boucherkha, S., & Benmohamed, M. (2004). A Lossless Watermarking Based Authentication System For Medical Images. In *International Conference on Computational Intelligence* (pp. 240-243). Academic Press.

Bounkong, S., Toch, B., Saad, D., & Lowe, D. (2003). ICA for watermarking digital images. *Journal of Machine Learning Research*, *4*(Dec), 1471–1498.

BW, T.A., & Permana, F.P. (2012, July). Medical image watermarking with tamper detection and recovery using reversible watermarking with LSB modification and run length encoding (RLE) compression. In *Communication, Networks and Satellite (ComNetSat), 2012 IEEE International Conference on* (pp. 167-171). IEEE.

Cao, F., Huang, H. K., & Zhou, X. Q. (2003). Medical image security in a HIPAA mandated PACS environment. *Computerized Medical Imaging and Graphics*, *27*(2-3), 185–196. doi:10.1016/S0895-6111(02)00073-3 PMID:12620309

Cao, P., Hashiba, M., Akazawa, K., Yamakawa, T., & Matsuto, T. (2003). An integrated medical image database and retrieval system using a web application server. *International Journal of Medical Informatics*, *71*(1), 51–55. doi:10.1016/S1386-5056(03)00088-1 PMID:12909158

Cauvin, J. M., Le Guillou, C., Solaiman, B., Robaszkiewicz, M., Le Beux, P., & Roux, C. (2003). Computer-assisted diagnosis system in digestive endoscopy. *IEEE Transactions on Information Technology in Biomedicine*, *7*(4), 256–262. doi:10.1109/TITB.2003.823293 PMID:15000352

Celik, M. U., Sharma, G., Tekalp, A. M., & Saber, E. (2002). Reversible data hiding. In *Image Processing. 2002. Proceedings. 2002 International Conference on* (Vol. 2, pp. II-II). IEEE. 10.1109/ICIP.2002.1039911

Chamlawi, R., Usman, I., & Khan, A. (2009, December). Dual watermarking method for secure image authentication and recovery. In *Multitopic Conference, 2009. INMIC 2009. IEEE 13th International* (pp. 1-4). IEEE. 10.1109/INMIC.2009.5383118

Chao, H. M., Hsu, C. M., & Miaou, S. G. (2002). A data-hiding technique with authentication, integration, and confidentiality for electronic patient records. *IEEE Transactions on Information Technology in Biomedicine*, 6(1), 46–53. doi:10.1109/4233.992161 PMID:11936596

Chen, J., Shan, S., He, C., Zhao, G., Pietikainen, M., Chen, X., & Gao, W. (2010). WLD: A robust local image descriptor. *IEEE Transactions on Pattern Analysis and Machine Intelligence*, 32(9), 1705–1720. doi:10.1109/TPAMI.2009.155 PMID:20634562

Chen, K., & Ramabadran, T. V. (1994). Near-lossless compression of medical images through entropy-coded DPCM. *IEEE Transactions on Medical Imaging*, 13(3), 538–548. doi:10.1109/42.310885 PMID:18218529

Cheng, S., Wu, Q., & Castleman, K. R. (2005, September). Non-ubiquitous digital watermarking for record indexing and integrity protection of medical images. In *Image Processing, 2005. ICIP 2005. IEEE International Conference on* (Vol. 2). IEEE. 10.1109/ICIP.2005.1530242

Chiang, K. H., Chang-Chien, K. C., Chang, R. F., & Yen, H. Y. (2008). Tamper detection and restoring system for medical images using wavelet-based reversible data embedding. *Journal of Digital Imaging*, 21(1), 77–90. doi:10.100710278-007-9012-0 PMID:17333416

Coatrieux, G., Huang, H., Shu, H., Luo, L., & Roux, C. (2013). A watermarking-based medical image integrity control system and an image moment signature for tampering characterization. *IEEE Journal of Biomedical and Health Informatics*, 17(6), 1057–1067. doi:10.1109/JBHI.2013.2263533 PMID:24240724

Coatrieux, G., Le Guillou, C., Cauvin, J. M., & Roux, C. (2009). Reversible watermarking for knowledge digest embedding and reliability control in medical images. *IEEE Transactions on Information Technology in Biomedicine*, 13(2), 158–165. doi:10.1109/TITB.2008.2007199 PMID:19272858

Coatrieux, G., Lecornu, L., Sankur, B., & Roux, C. (2006, August). A review of image watermarking applications in healthcare. In *Engineering in Medicine and Biology Society, 2006. EMBS'06. 28th Annual International Conference of the IEEE* (pp. 4691-4694). IEEE. 10.1109/IEMBS.2006.259305

Coatrieux, G., Maitre, H., & Sankur, B. (2001, August). Strict integrity control of biomedical images. In *Security and watermarking of multimedia contents III* (Vol. 4314, pp. 229–241). International Society for Optics and Photonics. doi:10.1117/12.435403

Coatrieux, G., Maitre, H., Sankur, B., Rolland, Y., & Collorec, R. (2000). Relevance of watermarking in medical imaging. In *Information Technology Applications in Biomedicine, 2000. Proceedings. 2000 IEEE EMBS International Conference on* (pp. 250-255). IEEE. 10.1109/ITAB.2000.892396

Coatrieux, G., Montagner, J., Huang, H., & Roux, C. (2007, August). Mixed reversible and RONI watermarking for medical image reliability protection. In *Engineering in Medicine and Biology Society, 2007. EMBS 2007. 29th Annual International Conference of the IEEE* (pp. 5653-5656). IEEE. 10.1109/IEMBS.2007.4353629

Coatrieux, G., Puentes, J., Lecornu, L., Le Rest, C. C., & Roux, C. (2006, April). Compliant secured specialized electronic patient record platform. In *Distributed Diagnosis and Home Healthcare, 2006. D2H2. 1st Transdisciplinary Conference on* (pp. 156-159). IEEE. 10.1109/DDHH.2006.1624820

Coatrieux, G., Puentes, J., Roux, C., Lamard, M., & Daccache, W. (2006, January). A low distorsion and reversible watermark: application to angiographic images of the retina. In *Engineering in Medicine and Biology Society, 2005. IEEE-EMBS 2005. 27th Annual International Conference of the* (pp. 2224-2227). IEEE.

Coltuc, D., & Chassery, J. M. (2007). Very fast watermarking by reversible contrast mapping. *IEEE Signal Processing Letters*, *14*(4), 255–258. doi:10.1109/LSP.2006.884895

Cox, I. J., Kilian, J., Leighton, F. T., & Shamoon, T. (1997). Secure spread spectrum watermarking for multimedia. *IEEE Transactions on Image Processing*, *6*(12), 1673–1687. doi:10.1109/83.650120 PMID:18285237

Crespi, M., Delvaux, M., Schaprio, M., Venables, C., & Zwiebel, F. (1996). Working Party Report by the Committee for Minimal Standards of Terminology and Documentation in Digestive Endoscopy of the European Society of Gastrointestinal Endoscopy. Minimal standard terminology for a computerized endoscopic database. Ad hoc Task Force of the Committee. *The American Journal of Gastroenterology*, *91*(2), 191. PMID:8607482

Criminisi, A., Pérez, P., & Toyama, K. (2004). Region filling and object removal by exemplar-based image inpainting. *IEEE Transactions on Image Processing*, *13*(9), 1200–1212. doi:10.1109/TIP.2004.833105 PMID:15449582

Dandapat, S., Chutatape, O., & Krishnan, S. M. (2004, October). Perceptual model based data embedding in medical images. In *Image Processing, 2004. ICIP'04. 2004 International Conference on* (Vol. 4, pp. 2315-2318). IEEE. 10.1109/ICIP.2004.1421563

De Vleeschouwer, C., Delaigle, J. F., & Macq, B. (2003). Circular interpretation of bijective transformations in lossless watermarking for media asset management. *IEEE Transactions on Multimedia*, *5*(1), 97–105. doi:10.1109/TMM.2003.809729

Delp, E. J. (2005). Multimedia security: The 22nd century approach. *Multimedia Systems*, *11*(2), 95–97. doi:10.100700530-005-0193-4

Deng, L., & Poole, M. S. (2003, January). Learning through telemedicine networks. In *System Sciences, 2003. Proceedings of the 36th Annual Hawaii International Conference on* (pp. 8-pp). IEEE.

Dong, C., Chen, Y. W., Li, J., & Bai, Y. (2012, May). Zero watermarking for medical images based on DFT and LFSR. In *Computer Science and Automation Engineering (CSAE), 2012 IEEE International Conference on* (Vol. 1, pp. 22-26). IEEE. 10.1109/CSAE.2012.6272540

Ekici, O., Coskun, B., Naci, U., & Sankur, B. (2001, November). Comparative assessment of semifragile watermarking techniques. In *Multimedia Systems and Applications IV* (Vol. 4518, pp. 177–189). International Society for Optics and Photonics. doi:10.1117/12.448202

Farid, H., & Lyu, S. (2003, June). Higher-order wavelet statistics and their application to digital forensics. In *Computer Vision and Pattern Recognition Workshop, 2003. CVPRW'03. Conference on* (Vol. 8, pp. 94-94). IEEE. 10.1109/CVPRW.2003.10093

Farid, H. (2009). Image forgery detection. *IEEE Signal Processing Magazine, 26*(2), 16–25. doi:10.1109/MSP.2008.931079

Fridrich, J., Goljan, M., & Du, R. (2001, April). Invertible authentication watermark for JPEG images. In *Information Technology: Coding and Computing, 2001. Proceedings. International Conference on* (pp. 223-227). IEEE. 10.1109/ITCC.2001.918795

Fridrich, J., Goljan, M., & Du, R. (2001, August). Invertible authentication. In *Security and Watermarking of Multimedia contents III* (Vol. 4314, pp. 197–209). International Society for Optics and Photonics. doi:10.1117/12.435400

Fu, D., Shi, Y. Q., & Su, W. (2006, November). Detection of image splicing based on hilbert-huang transform and moments of characteristic functions with wavelet decomposition. In *International workshop on digital watermarking* (pp. 177-187). Springer. 10.1007/11922841_15

Garimella, A., Satyanarayana, M. V. V., Kumar, R. S., Murugesh, P. S., & Niranjan, U. C. (2003, January). VLSI implementation of online digital watermarking technique with difference encoding for 8-bit gray scale images. In *VLSI Design, 2003. Proceedings. 16th International Conference on* (pp. 283-288). IEEE.

Ghosh, S., Kundu, B., Datta, D., Maity, S. P., & Rahaman, H. (2014, February). Design and implementation of fast FPGA based architecture for reversible watermarking. In *Electrical Information and Communication Technology (EICT), 2013 International Conference on* (pp. 1-6). IEEE. 10.1109/EICT.2014.6777819

Giakoumaki, A., Pavlopoulos, S., & Koutouris, D. (2003, September). A medical image watermarking scheme based on wavelet transform. In *Engineering in medicine and biology society, 2003. Proceedings of the 25th annual international conference of the IEEE* (Vol. 1, pp. 856-859). IEEE. 10.1109/IEMBS.2003.1279900

Giakoumaki, A., Pavlopoulos, S., & Koutsouris, D. (2006). Multiple image watermarking applied to health information management. *IEEE Transactions on Information Technology in Biomedicine, 10*(4), 722–732. doi:10.1109/TITB.2006.875655 PMID:17044406

Guo, X., & Zhuang, T. G. (2009). Lossless watermarking for verifying the integrity of medical images with tamper localization. *Journal of Digital Imaging, 22*(6), 620–628. doi:10.100710278-008-9120-5 PMID:18473141

He, H. J., Zhang, J. S., & Tai, H. M. (2009, June). Self-recovery fragile watermarking using block-neighborhood tampering characterization. In *International Workshop on Information Hiding* (pp. 132-145). Springer. 10.1007/978-3-642-04431-1_10

Hilbert, M., & López, P. (2011). The world's technological capacity to store, communicate, and compute information. *Science, 332*(6025), 60-65.

Honsinger, C. (2002). Digital watermarking. *Journal of Electronic Imaging, 11*(3), 414. doi:10.1117/1.1494075

Hrsa.gov. (2014). *HHS Budget Makes Smart Investments, Protects the Health and Safety America's Families.* Available at: http://www.hrsa.gov/about/news/pressreleases/2010/100201a.html http://www.internetlivestats.com/internet-users/ https://pulse.embs.org/january-2017/electronic-health-records-data-delivers-better-patient-outcomes/

Hu, M. K. (1962). Visual pattern recognition by moment invariants. *I.R.E. Transactions on Information Theory, 8*(2), 179–187. doi:10.1109/TIT.1962.1057692

Huang, H., Coatrieux, G., Shu, H., Luo, L., & Roux, C. (2012). Blind integrity verification of medical images. *IEEE Transactions on Information Technology in Biomedicine, 16*(6), 1122–1126. doi:10.1109/TITB.2012.2207435 PMID:22801523

Huang, H., Coatrieux, G., Shu, H. Z., Luo, L. M., & Roux, C. (2010, July). Medical image tamper approximation based on an image moment signature. In *e-Health Networking Applications and Services (Healthcom), 2010 12th IEEE International Conference on* (pp. 254-259). IEEE. 10.1109/HEALTH.2010.5556561

Huang, J., & Shi, Y. Q. (1998). Adaptive Image Watermarking Scheme Based on Visual masking. *Electronics Letters, 34*(8), 748–750. doi:10.1049/el:19980545

Huang, Y., Lin, S., Stan, Z., Lu, H., & Shum, V. (2004). Face Alignment under Variable Illumination. *IEEE International Conference on Automatic Face and Gesture Recognition.*

Huang, Y., Lin, S., Stan, Z., Lu, H., & Shum, V. (2004). Noise removal and impainting model for iris image. *International Conference on Image Processing.*

Hussain, N., Wageeh, B., & Colin, B. (2013). A Review of Medical Image Watermarking Requirements for Teleradiology. *Journal of Digital Imaging, 26*(2), 326–343. doi:10.100710278-012-9527-x PMID:22975883

Hwai-Tsu, H., & Ling-Yuan, H. (2016). A mixed modulation scheme for blind image watermarking. *International Journal of Electronics and Communications, 70*(2), 172–178. doi:10.1016/j.aeue.2015.11.003

Imran, U., Asifullah, K., Rafiullah, C., & Abdul, M. (2008). *Towards a Better Robustness-Imperceptibility Tradeoff in Digital Watermarking.* Innovations and Advanced Techniques in Systems, Computing Sciences and Software Engineering.

İsmail, A. (2001). *Image Quality Statistics And Their Use In Steganalysis and Compression* (PhD Thesis). Institute for Graduate Studies in Science and Engineering, Uludağ University.

Ismail, A., Bulent, S., & Khalid, S. (2002). Statistical Evaluation of Image Quality Measures. *Journal of Electronic Imaging, 11*(2), 206–223. doi:10.1117/1.1455011

Itti, L., & Koch, C. (2000). A saliency-based search mechanism for overt and covert shifts of visual attention. *Vision Research, 40*(10-12), 1489–1506. doi:10.1016/S0042-6989(99)00163-7 PMID:10788654

Itti, L., & Koch, C. (2001). Computational Modeling of Visual Attention. Nature Reviews. *Neuroscience, 2*(3), 194–203. doi:10.1038/35058500 PMID:11256080

Jalal, F., Jalil, F., & Peter, W. (1999). *Digital Certificates: Applied Internet Security* (Vol. 1). Addison-Wesley.

Janeczko Paul, B. (2006). *Top Secret: A Handbook of Codes, Ciphers and Secret Writing.* Candlewick Press.

Jaseena & John. (2011). Text Watermarking using Combined Image and Text for Authentication and Protection. *International Journal of Computer Applications, 20*(4).

Jianquan, X., Qing, X., Dazu, H., & Duosi, X. (2010). Research on imperceptibility index of image Information Hiding. *Second International Conference on Networks Security Wireless Communications and Trusted Computing (NSWCTC).* 10.1109/NSWCTC.2010.148

Jiansheng, Q., Dong, W., Li, L. C. D., & Xuesong, W. (2014). Image quality assessment based on multi-scale representation of structure. *Digital Signal Processing, 33,* 125–133. doi:10.1016/j.dsp.2014.06.009

Jianzhong, L., & Xiaojing, C. (2009). An adaptive secure watermarking scheme using double random-phase encoding technique. *2nd International Congress on Image and Signal Processing, CISP '09.*

Johnson, N. F., Duric, Z., & Jajodia, S. (2001). *Information Hiding: Steganography and Watermarking-Attacks and Countermeasures: Steganography and Watermarking: Attacks and Countermeasures* (Vol. 1). Springer Science & Business Media. doi:10.1007/978-1-4615-4375-6

Karthigaikumar, P., & Baskaranc Anumol, K. (2011). FPGA Implementation of High Speed Low Area DWT Based Invisible Image Watermarking Algorithm. *International Conference on Communication Technology and System Design.*

Kaushal, S., Upamanyu, M., Manjunath, B. S., & Shiv, C. (2005). Modeling the Print-Scan Process for Resilient Data Hiding, Security, Steganography, and Watermarking of Multimedia Contents. *SPIE, 5681,* 418–429.

Kautilya. (1992). *The Arthashastra* (L. N. Rangarajan, Trans.). Penguin Books India.

Keskinarkaus, A., Pramila, A., & Seppänen, T. (2012). Image watermarking with feature point based synchronization robust to print–scan attack. *Journal of Visual Communication and Image Representation, 23*(3), 507–515. doi:10.1016/j.jvcir.2012.01.010

Kester, Q. A., Nana, L., Pascu, A. C., Gire, S., Eghan, J. M., & Quaynor, N. N. (2015, June). A Security Technique for Authentication and Security of Medical Images in Health Information Systems. In *Computational Science and Its Applications (ICCSA), 2015 15th International Conference on* (pp. 8-13). IEEE. 10.1109/ICCSA.2015.8

Khan, A., & Malik, S. A. (2014). A high capacity reversible watermarking approach for authenticating images: Exploiting down-sampling, histogram processing, and block selection. *Information Sciences, 256,* 162–183. doi:10.1016/j.ins.2013.07.035

Kharittha, T., Pipat, S., & Thumrongrat, A. (2015). Digital Image Watermarking based on Regularized Filter. *14th IAPR International Conference on Machine Vision Applications.*

Ki-Hyeok, B., & Sung-Hwan, J. (2001). A study on the robustness of watermark according to frequency band. *IEEE International Symposium on Industrial Electronics.* 10.1109/ISIE.2001.932024

Kim, B. S., Kwon, K. K., Kwon, S. G., Park, K. N., Song, K. I., & Lee, K. I. (2002, July). A robust wavelet-based digital watermarking using statistical characteristic of image and human visual system. In *Proc. of ITC-CSCC* (*Vol. 2*, pp. 1019-1022). Academic Press.

Kim, C. Y. (1998). Compression of color medical images in gastrointestinal endoscopy: A review. *Studies in Health Technology and Informatics, 52*, 1046–1050. PMID:10384620

Kobayashi, L. O., & Furuie, S. S. (2009). Proposal for DICOM multiframe medical image integrity and authenticity. *Journal of Digital Imaging, 22*(1), 71–83. doi:10.100710278-008-9103-6 PMID:18266035

Kong, X., & Feng, R. (2001). Watermarking medical signals for telemedicine. *IEEE Transactions on Information Technology in Biomedicine, 5*(3), 195–201. doi:10.1109/4233.945290 PMID:11550841

Kundur, D., & Hatzinakos, D. (1998, May). Digital watermarking using multiresolution wavelet decomposition. In *Acoustics, Speech and Signal Processing, 1998. Proceedings of the 1998 IEEE International Conference on* (*Vol. 5*, pp. 2969-2972). IEEE.

Kundur, D., & Hatzinakos, D. (1998). Improved robust watermarking through attack characterization. *Optics Express, 3*(12), 485–490. doi:10.1364/OE.3.000485 PMID:19384399

Kundur, D., & Hatzinakos, D. (1999). Digital watermarking for telltale tamper proofing and authentication. *Proceedings of the IEEE, 87*(7), 1167–1180. doi:10.1109/5.771070

Kutter, M., & Petitcolas, F. A. (1999, April). Fair benchmark for image watermarking systems. In *Security and Watermarking of Multimedia Contents* (Vol. 3657, pp. 226–240). International Society for Optics and Photonics. doi:10.1117/12.344672

Le Guillou, C., Cauvin, J. M., Solaiman, B., Robaszkiewicz, M., & Roux, C. (2000, November). Information processing in upper digestive endoscopy. In *Information Technology Applications in Biomedicine, 2000. Proceedings. 2000 IEEE EMBS International Conference on* (pp. 183-188). IEEE. 10.1109/ITAB.2000.892383

Lee, H. K., Kim, H. J., Kwon, K. R., & Lee, J. K. (2005, June). Digital watermarking of medical image using ROI information. In *Enterprise networking and Computing in Healthcare Industry, 2005. HEALTHCOM 2005. Proceedings of 7th International Workshop on* (pp. 404-407). IEEE.

Lehmann, T. M., Güld, M. O., Thies, C., Fischer, B., Spitzer, K., Keysers, D., ... Wein, B. B. (2004). Content-based image retrieval in medical applications. *Methods of Information in Medicine, 43*(4), 354–361. doi:10.1055-0038-1633877 PMID:15472746

Li, C., & Liu, L. (2008, May). An image authentication scheme with localization and recovery. In *Image and Signal Processing, 2008. CISP'08. Congress on* (Vol. 5, pp. 669-673). IEEE. doi:10.1109/CISP.2008.374

Li, C. T., & Yang, F. M. (2003). One-dimensional neighborhood forming strategy for fragile watermarking. *Journal of Electronic Imaging*, *12*(2), 284–292. doi:10.1117/1.1557156

Li, M., Poovendran, R., & Narayanan, S. (2005). Protecting patient privacy against unauthorized release of medical images in a group communication environment. *Computerized Medical Imaging and Graphics*, *29*(5), 367–383. doi:10.1016/j.compmedimag.2005.02.003 PMID:15893452

Liew, S. C., & Zain, J. M. (2010, July). Reversible medical image watermarking for tamper detection and recovery. In *Computer Science and Information Technology (ICCSIT), 2010 3rd IEEE International Conference on* (Vol. 5, pp. 417-420). IEEE.

Lim, Y., Xu, C., & Feng, D. D. (2001, May). Web based image authentication using invisible fragile watermark. In *Proceedings of the Pan-Sydney area workshop on Visual information processing-Volume 11* (pp. 31-34). Australian Computer Society, Inc.

Lin, C. Y., & Chang, S. F. (2000, May). Semifragile watermarking for authenticating JPEG visual content. In *Security and Watermarking of Multimedia Contents II* (Vol. 3971, pp. 140–152). International Society for Optics and Photonics. doi:10.1117/12.384968

Lin, E. T., Podilchuk, C. I., & Delp, E. J. (2000, May). Detection of image alterations using semifragile watermarks. In *Security and Watermarking of Multimedia Contents II* (Vol. 3971, pp. 152–164). International Society for Optics and Photonics. doi:10.1117/12.384969

Lu, C. S., & Liao, H. Y. (2001). Multipurpose watermarking for image authentication and protection. *IEEE Transactions on Image Processing*, *10*(10), 1579–1592. doi:10.1109/83.951542 PMID:18255500

Luo, X., & Cheng, Q. (2003, October). Health information integrating and size reducing. 2003 IEEE nuclear science symposium,'medical imaging conference, and workshop of room-temperature semiconductor detectors'. In *Nuclear Science Symposium Conference Record, 2003 IEEE* (*Vol. 4*, pp. 3014-3018). IEEE.

Luo, X., Cheng, Q., & Tan, J. (2003, September). A lossless data embedding scheme for medical images in application of e-diagnosis. In *Engineering in Medicine and Biology Society, 2003. Proceedings of the 25th Annual International Conference of the IEEE* (*Vol. 1*, pp. 852-855). IEEE.

Macq, B., & Dewey, F. (1999, October). Trusted headers for medical images. In DFG VIII-D II Watermarking Workshop (Vol. 10). Erlangen.

Madsen, M. T., Berbaum, K. S., Ellingson, A. N., Thompson, B. H., Mullan, B. F., & Caldwell, R. T. (2006). A new software tool for removing, storing, and adding abnormalities to medical images for perception research studies. *Academic Radiology*, *13*(3), 305–312. doi:10.1016/j.acra.2005.11.041 PMID:16488842

Maeder, A. J., & Eckert, M. P. (1999, July). Medical image compression: Quality and performance issues. In *New Approaches in Medical Image Analysis* (Vol. 3747, pp. 93–102). International Society for Optics and Photonics. doi:10.1117/12.351629

Me, L., & Arce, G. R. (2001). A class of authentication digital watermarks for secure multimedia communication. *IEEE Transactions on Image Processing*, *10*(11), 1754–1764. doi:10.1109/83.967402 PMID:18255516

Medical Identity Theft in Healthcare. (2010). Retrieved 09, July, 2013. https://www.securetechalliance.org/publications-medical-identity-theft-in-healthcare/

Medical Image Database. https://medpix.nlm.nih.gov/home

Meerwald, P., & Uhl, A. (2001, August). Survey of wavelet-domain watermarking algorithms. In *Security and Watermarking of Multimedia Contents III* (Vol. 4314, pp. 505–517). International Society for Optics and Photonics. doi:10.1117/12.435434

Miaou, S. G., Hsu, C. M., Tsai, Y. S., & Chao, H. M. (2000). A secure data hiding technique with heterogeneous data-combining capability for electronic patient records. In *Engineering in Medicine and Biology Society, 2000. Proceedings of the 22nd Annual International Conference of the IEEE* (Vol. 1, pp. 280-283). IEEE.

Mohanty, S. P., Ranganathan, N., & Namballa, R. K. (2003, August). VLSI implementation of invisible digital watermarking algorithms towards the development of a secure JPEG encoder. In *Signal Processing Systems, 2003. SIPS 2003. IEEE Workshop on* (pp. 183-188). IEEE. 10.1109/SIPS.2003.1235666

Mohanty, S. P., Ranganathan, N., & Namballa, R. K. (2005). A VLSI architecture for visible watermarking in a secure still digital camera (S/sup 2/DC) design (Corrected). *IEEE Transactions on Very Large Scale Integration (VLSI) Systems*, *13*(8), 1002–1012.

Mostafa, S. A., El-Sheimy, N., Tolba, A. S., Abdelkader, F. M., & Elhindy, H. M. (2010). Wavelet packets-based blind watermarking for medical image management. *The Open Biomedical Engineering Journal*, *4*(1), 93–98. doi:10.2174/1874120701004010093 PMID:20700520

Moulin, P., & Ivanovic, A. (2003). The zero-rate spread-spectrum watermarking game. *IEEE Transactions on Signal Processing*, *51*(4), 1098–1117. doi:10.1109/TSP.2003.809370

Mukundan, R., & Ramakrishnan, K. R. (1998). *Moment functions in image analysis-theory and applications*. World Scientific. doi:10.1142/3838

Mwangi, E. (2007, December). A geometric attack resistant image watermarking scheme based on invariant centroids. In *Signal Processing and Information Technology, 2007 IEEE International Symposium on* (pp. 190-193). IEEE. 10.1109/ISSPIT.2007.4458073

Nambakhsh, M. S., Ahmadian, A., Ghavami, M., Dilmaghani, R. S., & Karimi-Fard, S. (2006, August). A novel blind watermarking of ECG signals on medical images using EZW algorithm. In *Engineering in Medicine and Biology Society, 2006. EMBS'06. 28th Annual International Conference of the IEEE* (pp. 3274-3277). IEEE. 10.1109/IEMBS.2006.259603

Navas, K. A., & Sasikumar, M. (2007, March). Survey of medical image watermarking algorithms. In *Proc. Internation Conf. Sciences of Electronics, Technologies of Information and Telecommunications* (pp. 25-29). Academic Press.

Navas, K. A., Sasikumar, M., & Sreevidya, S. (2007, June). A benchmark for medical image watermarking. In *Systems, Signals and Image Processing, 2007 and 6th EURASIP Conference focused on Speech and Image Processing, Multimedia Communications and Services. 14th International Workshop on* (pp. 237-240). IEEE. 10.1109/IWSSIP.2007.4381197

Nayak, J., Bhat, P. S., Acharya, R., & Niranjan, U. C. (2004). Simultaneous storage of medical images in the spatial and frequency domain: A comparative study. *Biomedical Engineering Online*, *3*(1), 17. doi:10.1186/1475-925X-3-17 PMID:15180899

Nayak, J., Bhat, P. S., Kumar, M. S., & Acharya, U. R. (2004, December). Reliable and robust transmission and storage of medical images with patient information. In *Signal Processing and Communications, 2004. SPCOM'04. 2004 International Conference on* (pp. 91-95). IEEE. 10.1109/SPCOM.2004.1458363

Nayak, J., Bhat, P. S., Kumar, M. S., & Acharya, U. R. (2004, December). Reliable transmission and storage of medical images with patient information using error control codes. In *India Annual Conference, 2004. Proceedings of the IEEE INDICON 2004. First* (pp. 147-150). IEEE. 10.1109/INDICO.2004.1497726

Ni, Z., Shi, Y. Q., Ansari, N., & Su, W. (2006). Reversible data hiding. *IEEE Transactions on Circuits and Systems for Video Technology*, *16*(3), 354–362. doi:10.1109/TCSVT.2006.869964

Nikolaidis, A., Tsekeridou, S., Tefas, A., & Solachidis, V. (2001). A survey on watermarking application scenarios and related attacks. In *Image Processing, 2001. Proceedings. 2001 International Conference on* (Vol. 3, pp. 991-994). IEEE. 10.1109/ICIP.2001.958292

Oh, G. T., Lee, Y. B., & Yeom, S. J. (2004, June). Security mechanism for medical image information on PACS using invisible watermark. In *International Conference on High Performance Computing for Computational Science* (pp. 315-324). Springer.

Osada, M., & Tsukui, H. (2002, August). Development of ultrasound/endoscopy pacs (picture archiving and communication system) and investigation of compression method for cine images. In *Electronic Imaging and Multimedia Technology III* (Vol. 4925, pp. 99–103). International Society for Optics and Photonics. doi:10.1117/12.481574

Parah, S. A., Ahad, F., Sheikh, J. A., Loan, N. A., & Bhat, G. M. (2017). A New Reversible and high capacity data hiding technique for E-healthcare applications. *Multimedia Tools and Applications*, *76*(3), 3943–3975. doi:10.100711042-016-4196-2

Parameswaran, L., & Anbumani, K. (2008). Content-based watermarking for image authentication using independent component analysis. *Informatica, 32*(3).

Pereira, S., Voloshynovskiy, S., Madueno, M., Marchand-Maillet, S., & Pun, T. (2001, April). Second generation benchmarking and application oriented evaluation. In *International Workshop on Information Hiding* (pp. 340-353). Springer. 10.1007/3-540-45496-9_25

Piva, A., Barni, M., Bartolini, F., & De Rosa, A. (2005). Data hiding technologies for digital radiography. *IEE Proceedings. Vision Image and Signal Processing*, *152*(5), 604–610. doi:10.1049/ip-vis:20041240

Planitz, B., & Maeder, A. (2005, February). Medical image watermarking: a study on image degradation. In *Proc. Australian Pattern Recognition Society Workshop on Digital Image Computing*. WDIC.

Podilchuk, C. I., & Delp, E. J. (2001). Digital watermarking: Algorithms and applications. *IEEE Signal Processing Magazine*, *18*(4), 33–46. doi:10.1109/79.939835

Prokop, R. J., & Reeves, A. P. (1992). A survey of moment-based techniques for unoccluded object representation and recognition. *CVGIP. Graphical Models and Image Processing*, *54*(5), 438–460. doi:10.1016/1049-9652(92)90027-U

Puech, W., & Rodrigues, J. M. (2004, September). A new crypto-watermarking method for medical images safe transfer. In *Signal Processing Conference, 2004 12th European* (pp. 1481-1484). IEEE.

Qi, X., & Qi, J. (2007). A robust content-based digital image watermarking scheme. *Signal Processing*, *87*(6), 1264-1280.

Quellec, G., Russell, S. R., & Abramoff, M. D. (2011). Optimal filter framework for automated, instantaneous detection of lesions in retinal images. *IEEE Transactions on Medical Imaging*, *30*(2), 523–533. doi:10.1109/TMI.2010.2089383 PMID:21292586

Queluz, M. P. (2001). Authentication of digital images and video: Generic models and a new contribution. *Signal Processing Image Communication*, *16*(5), 461–475. doi:10.1016/S0923-5965(00)00010-2

Radharani, S., & Valarmathi, M. L. (2010). A study on watermarking schemes for image authentication. *International Journal of Computers and Applications*, *2*(4), 24–32. doi:10.5120/658-925

Rahimi, F., & Rabbani, H. (2011). A dual adaptive watermarking scheme in contourlet domain for DICOM images. *Biomedical Engineering Online*, *10*(1), 53. doi:10.1186/1475-925X-10-53 PMID:21682862

Rey, C., & Dugelay, J. L. (2002). A survey of watermarking algorithms for image authentication. *EURASIP Journal on Applied Signal Processing*, (1): 613–621.

Ritenour, E. R., & Maidment, A. D. (1999). Lossy compression should not be used in certain imaging applications such as chest radiography. *Medical Physics*, *26*(9), 1773–1775. doi:10.1118/1.598783 PMID:10505862

Rodriguez-Colin, R., Claudia, F. U., & Trinidad-Blas, G. D. J. (2007, February). Data hiding scheme for medical images. In *Electronics, Communications and Computers, 2007. CONIELECOMP'07. 17th International Conference on* (pp. 32-32). IEEE. 10.1109/CONIELECOMP.2007.14

Schneier, B. (1997). *Applied Cryptography* (2nd ed.). Paris: International Thomson Publishing.

Schneier, B. (1996). *Applied cryptography: protocols, algorithms, and source code in C*. Wiley.

Schou, C. D., Frost, J., & Maconachy, W. V. (2004). Information assurance in biomedical informatics systems. *IEEE Engineering in Medicine and Biology Magazine*, *23*(1), 110–118. doi:10.1109/MEMB.2004.1297181 PMID:15154266

Sebald, D. J., & Bucklew, J. A. (2000). Support vector machine techniques for nonlinear equalization. *IEEE Transactions on Signal Processing*, *48*(11), 3217–3226. doi:10.1109/78.875477

Seitz, J. (2005). *Digital watermarking for digital media*. IGI Global. doi:10.4018/978-1-59140-518-4

Shih, F. Y., & Wu, Y. T. (2005). Robust watermarking and compression for medical images based on genetic algorithms. *Information Sciences*, *175*(3), 200–216. doi:10.1016/j.ins.2005.01.013

Singh, A., & Dutta, M. K. (2014, November). A blind & fragile watermarking scheme for tamper detection of medical images preserving ROI. In *Medical Imaging, m-Health and Emerging Communication Systems (MedCom), 2014 International Conference on* (pp. 230-234). IEEE. 10.1109/MedCom.2014.7006009

Solachidis, V., Tefas, A., Nikolaidis, N., Tsekeridou, S., Nikolaidis, A., & Pitas, I. (2001). A benchmarking protocol for watermarking methods. In *Image Processing, 2001. Proceedings. 2001 International Conference on* (Vol. 3, pp. 1023-1026). IEEE. 10.1109/ICIP.2001.958300

Srinivasan, Y., Nutter, B., Mitra, S., Phillips, B., & Ferris, D. (2004, June). Secure transmission of medical records using high capacity steganography. In *Computer-Based Medical Systems, 2004. CBMS 2004. Proceedings. 17th IEEE Symposium on* (pp. 122-127). IEEE. 10.1109/CBMS.2004.1311702

Tagliasacchi, M., Valenzise, G., & Tubaro, S. (2009). Hash-based identification of sparse image tampering. *IEEE Transactions on Image Processing*, *18*(11), 2491–2504. doi:10.1109/TIP.2009.2028251 PMID:19635704

Terry, M. (2009). Medical identity theft and telemedicine security. *Telemedicine Journal and e-Health*, *15*(10), 928–933. doi:10.1089/tmj.2009.9932 PMID:19908998

Tian, J. (2002, April). Wavelet-based reversible watermarking for authentication. In *Security and Watermarking of Multimedia Contents IV* (Vol. 4675, pp. 679–691). International Society for Optics and Photonics. doi:10.1117/12.465329

Unser, M., & Aldroubi, A. (1996). A review of wavelets in biomedical applications. *Proceedings of the IEEE*, *84*(4), 626–638. doi:10.1109/5.488704

Van Leest, A. R. N. O., van der Veen, M., & Bruekers, F. (2003, September). Reversible image watermarking. In *Image Processing, 2003. ICIP 2003. Proceedings. 2003 International Conference on* (Vol. 2, pp. II-731). IEEE. 10.1109/ICIP.2003.1246784

Voloshynovskiy, S., Pereira, S., Iquise, V., & Pun, T. (2001). Attack modelling: Towards a second generation watermarking benchmark. *Signal Processing*, *81*(6), 1177–1214. doi:10.1016/S0165-1684(01)00039-1

Wakatani, A. (2002, January). Digital watermarking for ROI medical images by using compressed signature image. In *System Sciences, 2002. HICSS. Proceedings of the 35th Annual Hawaii International Conference on* (pp. 2043-2048). IEEE. 10.1109/HICSS.2002.994129

Walia, E., & Suneja, A. (2013). Fragile and blind watermarking technique based on Weber's law for medical image authentication. *IET Computer Vision*, *7*(1), 9–19. doi:10.1049/iet-cvi.2012.0109

Walia, E., & Suneja, A. (2014). A robust watermark authentication technique based on Weber's descriptor. *Signal, Image and Video Processing*, *8*(5), 859–872. doi:10.100711760-012-0312-6

Walters, W., & Betz, A. (2012). Medical identity theft. *Journal of Consumer Education*, 75.

Watson, A. B. (1993, September). DCT quantization matrices visually optimized for individual images. In *Human vision, visual processing, and digital display IV* (Vol. 1913, pp. 202–217). International Society for Optics and Photonics. doi:10.1117/12.152694

White, L. A. E., Krousel-Wood, M. A., & Mather, F. (2001). Technology meets healthcare: Distance learning and telehealth. *The Ochsner Journal*, *3*(1), 22–29. PMID:21765713

Woo, C.S., Du, J., & Pham, B.L. (2005). *Multiple watermark method for privacy control and tamper detection in medical images*. Academic Press.

Wu, J. H., Chang, R. F., Chen, C. J., Wang, C. L., Kuo, T. H., Moon, W. K., & Chen, D. R. (2008). Tamper detection and recovery for medical images using near-lossless information hiding technique. *Journal of Digital Imaging*, *21*(1), 59–76. doi:10.100710278-007-9011-1 PMID:17393256

Wu, M., & Liu, B. (1998, October). Watermarking for image authentication. In *Image Processing, 1998. ICIP 98. Proceedings. 1998 International Conference on* (Vol. 2, pp. 437-441). IEEE.

Wu, X., Liang, X., Liu, H., Huang, J., & Qiu, G. (2006). Reversible semi-fragile image authentication using zernike moments and integer wavelet transform. In *Digital Rights Management. Technologies, Issues, Challenges and Systems* (pp. 135–145). Berlin: Springer. doi:10.1007/11787952_11

Xin, Y., Liao, S., & Pawlak, M. (2007). Circularly orthogonal moments for geometrically robust image watermarking. *Pattern Recognition*, *40*(12), 3740–3752. doi:10.1016/j.patcog.2007.05.004

Xu, B., Wang, J., Liu, X., & Zhang, Z. (2007, August). Passive steganalysis using image quality metrics and multi-class support vector machine. In *Natural Computation, 2007. ICNC 2007. Third International Conference on* (Vol. 3, pp. 215-220). IEEE. 10.1109/ICNC.2007.544

Yadav, N., Pahal, N., Kalra, P., Lall, B., & Chaudhury, S. (2011, February). A Novel Approach for Securing Forensic Documents Using Rectangular Region-of-Interest (RROI). In *Emerging Applications of Information Technology (EAIT), 2011 Second International Conference on* (pp. 198-201). IEEE.

Yang, H., & Kot, A. C. (2006). Binary image authentication with tampering localization by embedding cryptographic signature and block identifier. *IEEE Signal Processing Letters*, *13*(12), 741–744. doi:10.1109/LSP.2006.879829

Yang, M., Trifas, M., Chen, L., Song, L., Aires, D. B., & Elston, J. (2010). Secure patient information and privacy in medical imaging. *Journal of Systemics, Cybernetics and Informatics*, *8*(3), 63–66.

Yeung, M. M., & Mintzer, F. (1997, October). An invisible watermarking technique for image verification. In *Image Processing, 1997. Proceedings., International Conference on* (Vol. 2, pp. 680-683). IEEE. 10.1109/ICIP.1997.638587

Zain, J., & Clarke, M. (2005). Security in telemedicine: issues in watermarking medical images. Sciences of Electronic, Technologies of Information and Telecommunications, Tunisia.

Zain, J. M., & Fauzi, A. R. (2006, August). Medical image watermarking with tamper detection and recovery. In *Engineering in Medicine and Biology Society, 2006. EMBS'06. 28th Annual International Conference of the IEEE* (pp. 3270-3273). IEEE. 10.1109/IEMBS.2006.260767

Zhao, X., Ho, A. T., Treharne, H., Pankajakshan, V., Culnane, C., & Jiang, W. (2007, November). A novel semi-fragile image watermarking, authentication and self-restoration technique using the slant transform. In *Intelligent Information Hiding and Multimedia Signal Processing, 2007. IIHMSP 2007. Third International Conference on* (Vol. 1, pp. 283-286). IEEE. 10.1109/IIH-MSP.2007.50

Zhou, X. Q., Huang, H. K., & Lou, S. L. (2001). Authenticity and integrity of digital mammography images. *IEEE Transactions on Medical Imaging, 20*(8), 784–791. doi:10.1109/42.938246 PMID:11513029

Anand, D., & Niranjan, U. C. (1998). Watermarking medical images with patient information. *Proceedings of the 20th Annual International Conference of the IEEE Engineering in Medicine and Biology Society, 20,* 703-706. doi: 10.1109/IEMBS.1998.745518

Chapter 2
Multimedia Data Security With Recent Trends and Technologies:
A Survey

Kanimozhi Suguna S.
SASTRA University, India

Dhanya V. S.
SASTRA University, India

ABSTRACT

This chapter throws light on major multimedia data security techniques. It has become so essential in today's society which uses multimedia data in almost all walks of life. There are a lot of multimedia data transactions carried out every day. Thus, to ensure data security the techniques, steganography and watermarking are frequently used. In steganography and watermarking techniques, the data to be hidden is encrypted and fed into a transparent layer like documents, images, and it is decrypted at the receiving end by the recipient. Generally, steganographic communications are one-to-one while watermarking is one-to-many. Besides these techniques, certain other techniques are also used in the application for providing security to multimedia data. From this chapter, a detailed content about steganography and watermarking can be obtained.

INTRODUCTION TO MULTIMEDIA DATA SECURITY

The recent growth in Multimedia communication has been enormous. Multimedia data comprises of various media types namely image, video, audio etc. These data have vast source of information of different file types or different file formats. Managing different types of multimedia data is called as MultiMedia Database Management System (MM-DBMS). Using this MM-DBMS, storing, delivering, modifying and many other operations can be performed. The contents of the MM-DBMS include media data, format of the data, keyword of the data, and also feature of the data. Media data is the main and

DOI: 10.4018/978-1-5225-7107-0.ch002

actual data that represent an object. Various information about the format of the data like resolution, sampling rate, encoding scheme etc., can be obtained. This information is obtained after making certain process with the multimedia data. The phases on multimedia include acquisition, processing and encoding phase. Next to media data format, media keyword is the point to be considered. Keywords of media will give information about the created data. This information includes date, time, and also place of observation of the data. Last content of the MM-DBMS is the feature of the data. The feature content of the multimedia speaks about the colors in the media with their distribution, what kind of texture is used in it, and also the types of shapes present in the data.

Multimedia data is used in almost every walk of life like social networking, science, research etc. along with their contents. As the volume or size of the MM-DBMS is increasing rapidly, the developers still face many challenges to meet the requirements of the end users. Some of the major challenges to be focused by the developers are modelling, design, storage, performance, queries & retrieval, security, etc. Multimedia databases can be applied to wide range of areas. Some of them to be noted are Documents & record management, knowledge dissemination, education & training, real-time control & monitoring, and so on.

After having a short description about the multimedia, MM-DBMS, the concept can be forwarded towards multimedia communications. Communication is needed to transfer data or information from person to person. The data to be communicated can be of any file format like text, images, audio, and video. These file formats can be classified based on the media types. Four major classifications of media types are Audio, Video, Graphics, and Text. Audio media type is used for music, VoIP, and Podcasts and some of the file formats that are included in this type are MP3, Waveform Audio File Format (WAV), and Audio Interchange File Format (AIFF). Video is used for video streaming, also for films and video conferencing. MPEG, Audio Video Interleave (AVI), and MP4 are certain file formats supported in this type. All types of images, icon, infographics, charts and visual representations are grouped under Graphics. File formats supported under this classification are JPEG, PNG, TIFF, GIF and many more. Among the four major classifications of media types, only Text will be in human readable form like HyperText Markup Language (HTML), TeXT (TXT), Rich Text Format (RTF). Each and every file format of graphics has their own sub-classification.

Almost every stream of society has become a major user of multimedia communication. Today a lot of data transformations are carried out. Each and every person is posting images and text messages in social networking cites for example Facebook, Twitter and also sharing information through Whatsapp, Messenger etc., So it is necessary to ensure data security from the intruders. In that case, it is particularly important for the protection and enforcement of intellectual possessions. In these scenarios, the greatest challenge for the developers is to increase the security; also the application should be user friendly. If the application is more user friendly, there is a huge possibility of attacks. If the application has implementation of complex security, then the application lowers in friendliness to the users. The balancing of both the criteria is biggest research challenge. This chapter throws light on multimedia data security. Though there are lot many algorithms or techniques proposed in day to day technology, most of the multimedia data security concentrates on steganography and watermarking techniques. In existing technologies, much research is going to provide better security for any type of application domain. Researchers are striving hard to give solution to the challenges they face in data security, in specific multimedia security. As advancement towards security, the researchers are working on hybrid techniques, to check whether the combination provides improved security. The detailed description about different types of multimedia data security is presented in this chapter.

This chapter has the following subsections. Introduction to the multimedia security is followed by literature review and the next to it is different methods of implementing multimedia security is discussed. In this section, security techniques such as steganography and watermarking are discussed in detail with their types. These sections are followed by algorithms that can implement these techniques. The chapter is concluded with conclusion.

LITERATURE REVIEW

In the paper (Peerzada et al, 2014) the author focuses on the methods to provide security to the storage and access methods of the multimedia contents over the content delivery at the cloud edge servers is discussed. In this paper the encryption mechanism such as Blowfish and Data Encryption Standard (DES) is used and control mechanism like Challenge-Handshake Authentication Protocol (CHAP) is also discussed. The Rivest-Shamir-Adleman (RSA) algorithm is also specified. In this paper, the author also provided the list of data security issues that can occur in cloud. The issues presented are Privacy & Confidentiality, Data integrity, Data Location & Relocation, Data Availability, and Storage, Backup & Recovery.

Wireless Multimedia Sensor Network (WMSN), a new generation of the network is elaborated in (Mathur et al, 2016). In this paper, the authors have focused on symmetric cryptography and the most popular algorithms of this approach are DES, the Triple DES, the Advanced Encryption Standard (AES) and the Blowfish. In this paper, the authors have proposed the Shift – AES that consumes less energy when compared to AES algorithm.

Security and privacy issues for MM-DBMS are elaborated in (Thuraisingham, 2007). MM-DBMS is the Database Management System (DBMS) that will manage multimedia data. For explaining the concepts of MM-DBMS, the researchers may be in need of differentiated architectures and data models to manage database functions such as query processing, transaction management, metadata management, storage management, and security & integrity management. This paper also concentrates on data mining.

The authors of (Kundur et al, 2008) have discussed the security and privacy issues in relation to designing a Distributed Multimedia Sensor Networks (DMSN). The major features of Wireless Sensor Networks are (Kundur et al, 2008) distributed, data-centric, collaborative, redundant, autonomous, application – specific, hierarchical, and resource constrained. Multimodal sensors are the sensors that collect diversed types of information. Certain protocols that implements DMSN are explained in this paper. A short description of data security issues in cloud storage is presented in (Rao et al, 2017) and also the multimedia data transfer using multi-layered security mechanisms is given. The concept is also discussed in (Lakshmi et al, 2017). In this paper, the encryption standards are classified and tabulated. Towards the end of this paper, the authors have projected the necessities to improve security for medical data. The authors have also performed performance analysis based on capacity ratio and Peek-Signal Noise Ratio (PSNR).

In paper (Susanto et al, 2010), the authors have discussed about Information Security Management System (ISMS) which is proposed in ISO 17799. The basis of ISMS is continuous activity cycle that is proposed and explained in Plan-Do-Check-Act (PDCA) model. This PDCA model has four processes, they are Plan process establishes ISM, Do process will implement and operate ISM, Check process does the role of monitoring and reviewing the ISM, and Act process is to maintain and improve ISM. In this paper, the authors have discussed about four phases of the E-Security Business Architecture. In this architecture, constant feedback is received in all the phases. Four phases of the architecture are Assess, Plan, Deliver, and Operate phases. Next to this architecture is the ISM architecture which is a mixture of five aspects such as security infrastructure, security policies, security culture, monitoring compliance, and security program. Information Security Architecture Blueprint by another author also presented in it. In the proposed Multimedia Information Security Architecture (MISA), along with the aspects of ISM architecture extra more points are considered. The extra aspects are multimedia information sharing, enterprise security, and security awareness. In enterprise security, certain key standards should be followed to deploy and manage security in applications. The major key standards are Enterprise Antivirus, Enterprise Patch Management, Enterprise Security Agent, Internet Content Filtering & Access Control, and Enterprise Administrator Monitoring.

The key challenges in the design of multimedia-based scalable techniques for threat management and information security framework is explained in (Joshi et al, 2008; James, 2006). In this paper the author has come with a solution for large-scale distributed multi-domain multimedia application environments. In this paper, the author has presented a conceptual design of a single domain and multi domain multimedia application environments. Paper (Kalaivani et al, 2011; Kalaivani et al, 2012) discusses the classification of standard encryption methods such as Data Encryption Standard (DES), the Advanced Encryption Standard (AES), the Rivest-Shamir-Adelman (RSA) algorithm, the Triple DES (3DES), and the International Data Encryption Algorithm (IDEA) and Scalable encryption algorithm (SEA). In this paper, the authors have tried to improve the security and quality of the medical data. The techniques to enhance the security of medical data are abbreviated in this paper. The lists of techniques explained in it are (1) content-based watermarking technique, (2) digital watermarking of medical image, (3) lossless watermarking method based on Haar wavelet transform, (4) watermarking techniques for medical images, (5) approaches to medical image integrity and authenticity, (6) a lossless data embedding scheme for medical images, (6) multiple digital watermarking applied to medical imaging, (7) medical image watermarking with tamper detection and recovery, (8) integration of medical data, (9) data hiding scheme for medical images, (10) reversible watermarking of medical image, and (11) medical image security in a PACS environment.

The applications and architecture of Participatory Sensing technique is given in (Lakshmi et al, 2017). In recent days, most of the individuals use highly configured mobile phones to collect data using cloud services for analyzing it. The applications and the model of this technique help in monitoring the health and wellness of the individual. When the self-monitoring application is installed in mobile phone, the private information of the individual should not be accessed by the intruders. The system architecture of their proposed system has five major elements and they are design rationale, coding, transferring, reconstructing, and analysis. In certain papers like (Ouelati et al, 2018), the authors have implemented the watermarking technique to various recent applications. Similarly some authors used steganography techniques for implementing security for the multimedia data. To improve security, some authors are working on proposing hybrid of watermarking and steganography with optimization algorithms and soft computing techniques. Hence in this chapter detailed descriptions about the basic watermarking and steganography techniques are presented.

METHODS FOR IMPLEMENTING MULTIMEDIA SECURITY

Steganography

The word "Steganography" (stegos-cover, grafia-writing) found its origin in Greek. It means "covered writing". It is named so, as it conceals the very existence of the secret message (Kahn et al, 1996). This method found its use as the need for hiding the data grew. In this method the secret message is encrypted and is hidden on different storage cover media like images, audio, video etc., using prescribed algorithms. This file is transferred to the recipient where the content is decrypted and the message is received. With this process we can bring down the chances of the secret message being hacked.

Steganography mainly deals with the concealment of data by embedding the encrypted data in the digital signal and making the users completely oblivious to the changes carried out in the object taken. In this process, the Object which is used as a carrier to embed the information is called the cover object. The one which holds the embedded information is called the stego object. Thus a steganography when given a cover object converts it into a stegos object (Umamaheswari et al, 2010).

Requirements that steganography techniques must satisfy the following two conditions.

1. The integrity of the hidden information after it has been embedded inside the stegos object must be correct.
2. The stegos object must remain unchanged or almost unchanged to the naked eye (Shiguo et al, 2009).

Categories of Steganography

Steganography has three major categories, they are listed below:

1. Pure Steganography
2. Secret Key Steganography
3. Public Key Steganography

In Pure Steganography, both the sender and receiver have no prior exchange of information and they rely on secret through obscurity. Figure 1 from (Shiguo et al, 2009) explains the concept of pure steganography.

In Secret Key steganography, the sender uses a publicly known algorithm but relies on a secret key, shared between the two parties which are indispensable for both embedding and extracting. Anyone who is not aware of the key cannot access the secret. Figure 2 from (Shiguo et al, 2009) depicts the process of secret key steganography.

Figure 1. Pure steganography

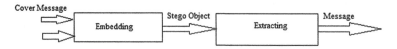

Figure 2. Secret key steganography

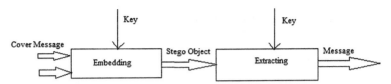

In Public Key Steganography, two keys are maintained. One is publicly known and the other is restricted only to the receiver. Here, using the public key the information is embedded and even the sender cannot extract the information from the stego object (Mustafa et al, 2011). The process of public key steganography is represented in Figure 3 (Shiguo et al, 2009).

Types of Steganography

The major types of steganography are described in (Umamaheswari et al, 2010).

Fragile Steganography

This involves embedding information and the files are destroyed when modified. These are used in situations where the files are not to be tampered.

Robust Steganography

This focuses on embedding information into a file that cannot be destroyed. These techniques are comparatively difficult to implement.

Classification of Steganography

Steganography is classified is explained in Figure 4 and are explained in detail in (Kaur et al, 2014).

1. **Linguistic Steganography:** In this method, the information is hidden such that it is not evidently seen. The major classification of Linguistic Steganography includes Semagrams and Open codes.
   a. **Semagram:** This method uses symbols to hide the secret message. This is further classified into visual semagram and text semagram.

Figure 3. Public key steganography

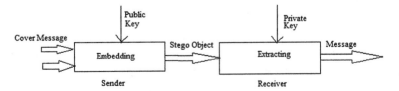

Figure 4. Classification of steganography

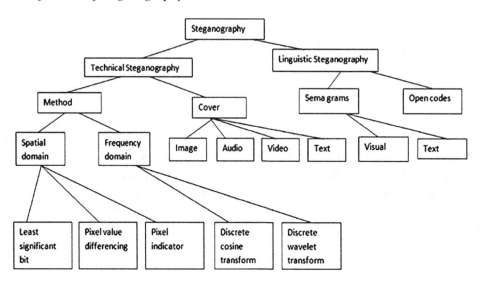

i.   **Visual Semagram:** This uses the day to day physical objects to hide the message. For example, the positioning of objects on a particular website.

ii. **Text Semagram:** This uses text to hide but changes their appearance by modifying the font size, style or by displaying them with spaces in between such that the change is not apparently visible.

b. **Open Code:** Here the code is embedded in legitimate paraphrases of the cover text but it is made not so obvious to the intruder. It is done in two ways. By using the jargon (technical terms) or by using cipher which uses ciphers to hide the message.

2. **Technical Steganography:** This method uses specified tools or other specifically designed scientific methods to hide the secret facts. This is done using invisible inks, microdots etc. Technical Steganography has two major classifications such as Method and Cover.

a. **Cover Image:** This contains the secret. E.g. image, video, audio, text. The cover image is divided into blocks and the message bits are hidden in them.

i.   **Image Steganography:** This is the most frequently used method in the recent years due to the availability of a wide range of electronic image information. This process involves hiding in the pixels which is decoded at the receiving end.

ii. **Audio Steganography:** Here the secret is hidden in the frequencies which are inaudible to humans. Audio steganography can be problematic and can be useful for transmitting covert information in an innocuous cover audio signal. There are many types of Audio Steganography. They are Echo Hiding, Phase Coding, Parity Coding, Spread Spectrum and Tone insertion.

iii. **Video Steganography:** In this method the information is hidden in a video. This method is better because the probability of finding the data by the intruder is lesser.

iv. **Text Steganography:** As the name suggests, the cover is the text in which the message is hidden by changing the words using context-free grammer.

b. **Methods:** These Methods are explained in the later part.

Factors Affecting Steganographic Methods

1. **Robustness:** It is the ability to remain intact, even if the stego image is modified by linear or non-linear filtering, sharpening or blurring, addition of random noise, lossy compression etc.
2. **Imperceptibility:** It refers to the invisibility of steganographic algorithm. The strength of this method lies in its ability to remain oblivious.
3. **Payload Capacity:** It is the amount of information that the cover object can hold obscure from the intruder.
4. **PSNR (Peak Signal to Noise Ratio):** It is defined as the ratio between the maximum possible power of a signal and the power of corrupting noise that affects the fidelity of its representation. This ratio measures the quality between the original and a compressed image. The higher value of PSNR represents the better quality of the compressed image.
5. **SNR (Signal to Noise Ratio):** It is the ratio between the signal power and the noise power. It compares the level of a desired signal to the level of background noise (Li et al, 2017).

Steganalysis Tools

Various tools are available for Steganalysis.

Digital Invisible Tool Kit

It is a java based steganography tool capable of hiding information in a 24 bit color image. This tool also performs statistical analysis.

Steganography Analyzer Signature Scanning (StegAlyzerSS)

This tool efficiently scans the existence of hexadecimal byte patterns in a Stego File.

Steganography Analyzer Artefact Scanner (StegAlyzerAS)

StegAlyzerAS scans a file system as a whole or a single file system on a Stego File for the existence of the embedded information in the Stego File (Poornima et al, 2013). After the process, the cover (vessel) image and the stego image will appear as shown in the Figure 5 (James et al, 2008).

Figure 5. Example for steganography

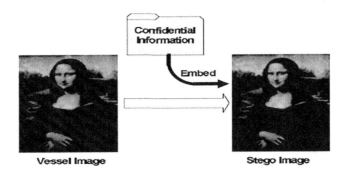

Methods of Implementing Steganalysis

Steganalysis is a process of extracting the hidden information from a stego object by decrypting the embedded message. For different applications, Steganalysis is done in different methods as follows:

1. **Stegos Only:** Extracts only stego image
2. **Known Carrier:** Extracts both the carrier/cover image and stego image
3. **Known Payload:** Known the hidden secret message in the embedded file
4. **Chosen Stegos:** Extracts only the required information, by using tools
5. **Chosen Payload:** It is a most powerful and efficient tool among other different attacks (Poornima et al, 2013).

WATERMARKING

Like Steganography, Watermarking is also used in hiding information into the host data. They differ in the aspect that watermarking covets the data about the actual content of the digital signal, whereas in steganography the embedded data is in no way related with the digital signal (Vasudev et al, 2016). Both follows content-based immunity concept. Watermarking is primarily used to verify the integrity and to reveal the owner's identity.

Watermarking technique is known to have existed in Italy in later 13th century (Mustafa et al, 2011). At first it was made by altering the thickness of the paper and thus creating shadow like image. Thus a watermark is an image which is viewed in various shades in light. This later gave rise to the idea of digital watermarking. In this society of multimedia it has become so simple to copy and create duplicate files without any loss in the quality. Thus the need for watermarking is realized and is almost used in every digital data transformation. Watermarking is a procedure in which the information about the digital file is embedded to reveal the owner's identity and to prevent copyright issues.

CLASSIFICATION OF WATERMARKING TECHNIQUES

Classification Based on Characteristics

1. **Robust Watermarking:** This type is used to sign copyright information of the data and it is named so because it resists the changes like image processing, Lossy compressing etc.
2. **Fragile Watermarking:** As the name suggests these watermarks are very sensitive to changes and are used to detect if the file has been tampered.

Classification Based on Visibility

1. **Visible Watermarking:** The watermark is visible and the change made in the original data is so evident. This type is mainly used in revealing the owner's identity.
2. **Invisible Watermarking:** The changes carried out are oblivious to users as the watermark is invisible. The receiver needs an authorized key to extract the message (Sharddha et al, 2012).

Goals of Watermarking

- Does not impair the image. The main concern is not to affect the cover image too much, if not it is not an effective watermarking.
- Cannot be removed.
- Holds only a less amount of data. As it contains only the essential data, it does not support watermarking a large amount of data (Cole, 2003).

An example for a watermarked image is given in the Figure 6.

ALGORITHMS

Algorithms are generally classified into two major types (1) Spatial domain and (2) Frequency domain. The detailed descriptions about these domains are given in the following subsections.

Spatial Domain

In spatial domain, the modifications have to be carried out only in the selected pixels of the original image. There are different algorithms in this domain. Some of them are LSB method, patchwork technique etc. In this method, no. of pairs of image points (a, b) are chosen as two patches (say A, B). This algorithm works by slightly brightening the points in patch A and darkening those points in patch B. Patchwork method resists many types of attacks. But it can hold only a very little amount of information (Cole et al, 2003).

LSB Method

One of the very common methods used in image steganography is the replacing the Least Significant Bit (LSB) method. The embedding process consists of sequential substitution of LSB of the pixel of the image with the bit message. The redundant bits of the pixel are considered to be the Least Significant Bit, which are replaced at the time of embedding. Generally, 24-bit BMP (Bit Map) file format is preferred for LSB technique, because of its efficiency, good quality and high resolution. The changes made in the cover image are oblivious to the intruder.

Figure 6. Example for watermarking

800X600 pixel BMPs are used to store nearly 1,440,000 bits or 180,000 bytes of data.BMP file formats are used by Windows which is native image format in Microsoft Windows Operating System. It can support image with 16 and 32 bit per pixel (Poornima et al, 2013).

Algorithm for embedding the secret message:

1. Read the cover image from the source.
2. Divide the image into [R x C] smaller blocks. Where R & C are the first & second bytes of the key respectively.
3. Each smaller block is a combination of number of pixels.
4. Further, in this step the LSBs of the pattern bits are replaced depending on the secret message bits. The pattern bits are considered in sequence form its MSB.
5. If the pattern bit is 0, then the first LSB of the pixel is changed [i.e. if data bit is 1 and pixel bit is 0, then pixel bit is made to1 or else it is retained as it is.]

If the pattern bit is 1, then the next LSB should be searched and that is changed accordingly.

6. This single bit message is distributed throughout the block, so that there is enough information at the time of decryption.
7. Same steps are carried out to hide other bits among other blocks. In case of large amount of data, secret bits are stored in more than one frame.
8. To decrypt, operations contrary to the above are carried out and the message is obtained by the receiver (Shiguo et al, 2009).

The same procedure is used in case of watermarking but, there we embed the secret bits of the water image. The following are the advantages and disadvantages of LSB method.

Advantages of LSB method are given in the following points.

*   Changes made in the cover image are obscure.
*   Implementation is very simple when compared with the other techniques.
*   Highly perceptual transparency

Disadvantages of LSB method are given in the following points.

*   The stego image is very sensitive to any kind of filtering.
*   Scaling, rotating and other modifications can destroy the secret message (Gupta et al, 2013).

Frequency Domain

In this method, the cover image is transformed to the frequency domain using the transformation techniques and the secret message (in case of steganography) or information of the water image (in case of watermarking) is embedded by adding them to the values of transform coefficients (Cole, 2003). For extraction, the inverse transform should be used. The frequently used transforms are DCT, DWT and DFT. These methods are widely used today.

Discrete Cosine Transform

1. Generation and embedding of watermark
   a. Calculate the DCT transform of the cover image.
   b. Select N random numbers according to normal distribution N (0, 1). Generally, the larger N is, the Better watermark effect has X=x1, x2... xN.
   c. Do linear transformation for the coefficients vi of DCT transform vi = vi (1+xi αi) where, αi is control variable .
   d. Compute inverse transform coefficients of DCT, and embed the watermark information into digital images.
2. Extraction and detection of watermark
   a. Calculate the DCT transform coefficient X of image after adding watermark.
   b. Calculate the DCT transform coefficient X0 of the Original image.
   c. Compare X and X0.
   d. Define S as the inner product of two vectors to detect the watermark information (Shraddha et al, 2012).

APPLICATIONS OF STEGANOGRAPHY AND WATERMARKING

Applications of Steganography

1. **Modern Printers:** Steganography is implemented in some modern printers like HP printers. In these printers small yellow dots are printed in all pages where information like time stamp, serial number etc. (Poornima et al, 2013) are hidden.
2. **Smart IDs:** In IDs, some information about the person is maintained confidential by hiding them in their image by steganography (Poornima et al, 2013).

Applications of Watermarking

1. **Fingerprinting:** It is used in preventing the duplication of the original content and its distribution. This is very much efficient because fingerprints cannot be forged.
2. **Broadcast Monitoring:** This system, using the watermark in the media files like audio, video etc., recognizes the place and time of broadcast. This is also used in sound tracking (Shraddha et al, 2012)>
3. **Access Control:** As per this application, any media file with a unique watermark permits only the authorized users to carryout changes in the file (Vasudev et al, 2016).
4. **Annotation of Photographs:** Sometimes we see that some information like date, logo, copyright sign or even the highlights of some aspects of the photo are provided in the image and this is called photo annotation. This is done by watermarking.
5. **Medical Application:** This is used in many hospitals and other medical institutions, where the documents and files contain watermark to provide confidentiality and authentication without disturbing the images and other information in the cover image (Shashikala et al, 2009).

CONCLUSION

The need for data hiding is highly indispensable in this environment where frequently carry out data transformations. Certain recent algorithms and challenges in the multimedia data security is discussed. Though there are many updated algorithms available, the traditional data hiding mechanisms have their own specialty. Thus when compared to other data hiding methods, the two major approaches such as watermarking and steganography approaches solves the problem in a very efficient and easy ways.

REFERENCES

Channalli & Jadhav. (2009). Steganography An Art of Hiding Data. *International Journal on Computer Science and Engineering, 1*(3), 137-141.

Cole. (2003). *Hiding in plain sight: Steganography and the Art of covert communication*. Academic Press.

Gupta & Brar. (2013). An Enhanced Security Technique for Storage of Multimedia Content over Cloud Server. *International Journal of Engineering Research and Applications, 3*(4), 2273-2277.

Gupta, B. B. (2017). *Advances in Security and Privacy of Multimedia Big Data in Mobile and Cloud Computing*. Springer.

Katariya. (2012). Digital Watermarking: Review. *International Journal of Engineering and Innovative Technology, 1* (2).

James, B. D. (2008). *A Multimedia – Based Threat Management and Information Security Framework*. IGI Global.

James, B. D., & Joshi, A. (2006). *Multimedia – Based Threat Management and Information Security Framework*. IGI Global.

Kahn, D. (1996). The history of steganography. In R. Anderson (Ed.), Lecture Notes in Computer Science: Vol. 1174. *Information Hiding. IH 1996*. Berlin: Springer.

Kalaivani, K., & Sivakumar, B. R. (2012). Survey on Multimedia Data Security. *International Journal of Modeling and Optimization, 2*(1).

Kalaivani, K., & Sivakumar, R. (2011). Survey on Multimedia Data Security. *International Conference on Signal, Image Processing and Applications With workshop of ICEEA 2011*.

Kaur, N., & Behal, S. (2014). A Survey on various types of Steganography and Analysis of Hiding Techniques. *International Journal of Engineering Trends and Technology, 11*(8), 388–392. doi:10.14445/22315381/IJETT-V11P276

Kundur & Okorafor. (2008). Security and Privacy for Distributed Multimedia Sensor Networks. *Proceedings of the IEEE, 96*(1).

Lakshmi, K., & Hemalatha, J., & Basha, F. (2017). K-Anonymous Privacy Preserving Technique for Participatory Sensing With Multimedia Data Over Cloud Computing. *International Journal of Computer Engineering In Research Trends, 4*(2), 48-52.

Li, D., Yang, C., Li, C., Jiang, Q., Chen, X., Ma, J., & Ren, J. (2017). A Client – based Secure Deduplication of Multimedia Data. *IEEE ICC 2017 Communication and Information Systems Security Symposium.*

Li, Y. (2017). *Crowdsensing Multimedia Data: Security and Privacy Issues.* IEEE.

Lian, Kanellopoulos, & Ruffo. (2009). Recent Advances in Multimedia Information System Security. *Informatica, 33,* 3-24.

Mathur, A., Modh, D., Kulkarni, P., & Roy, S. (2016). Multimedia Big Data Security. *Survey (London, England).*

Msolli, A., Helali, A., Ameur, H., & Maaref, H. (2017). Secure Encryption for Wireless Multimedia Sensors Network. *International Journal of Advanced Computer Science and Applications, 8*(6). doi:10.14569/IJACSA.2017.080643

Mustafa, A.E., ElGamal, A.M.F., ElAlmi, M.E., & Ahmed, B.D. (2011). A Proposed Algorithm For Steganography In Digital Image Based on Least Significant Bit. *Research Journal Specific Education,* (21).

Ouelati, S., & Solaiman, B. (2018). Watermarking medical images with patient identificationto verify authenticity. *International Journal of Medical Engineering and Informatics, 10*(1).

Peerzada & Chawla. (2014). An Analytical Review of the Multimedia Data and Encryption Mechanism at Cloud Server. *International Journal of Innovative Research in Computer and Communication Engineering, 2*(2).

Poornima, R., & Ishwarya, R.J. (2013). An Overview of Digital Image Steganography. *International Journal of Computer Science & Engineering Survey, 4*(1).

Rao & Hasan. (2017). Secure Multimedia Data Storage in Cloud Computing. *International Journal of Engineering Sciences & Research Technology, 6*(5).

Reena, Shah, & Bhavna. (2014). Multimedia Security Techniques. International Journal of Innovative Research In Electrical, Electronics, Instrumentation And *Control Engineering, 2*(5).

Supriya & Shetty. (2017). A Survey on Multimedia Content Protection. International Research *Journal of Engineering Technology, 4*(5).

Susanto & Muhaya. (2010). Multimedia Information Security Architecture Framework. In 5th *International Conference on Future Information Technology.* IEEE.

Thuraisingham. (2007). Security and Privacy for multimedia database management systems. *Springer Science, 33,* 13-29.

Umamaheswari, M., Sivasubramanian, S., & Pandiarajan, S. (2010). Analysis of Different Steganographic Algorithms for Secured Data Hiding. *International Journal of Computer Science and Network Security, 10*(8).

Vasudev. (2016). A Review on Digital Image Watermarking and its Technique. *India Journal of Image and Graphics, 4*(2).

Chapter 3

On the Implementation of a Fragile Medical Image Watermarking Technique Using Saliency and Phase Congruency

Abhishek Basu
RCC Institute of Information Technology, India

Soumadeb Dutta
RCC Institute of Information Technology, India

ABSTRACT

The recent developments of enormous computer networks have invoked insecurities related to copyright theft of digital media. To be precise, the virtual sharing of medical images over networks with a novel desire of improved medical diagnosis has led to the tampering of sensitive patient identity information. In this chapter, the authors have exemplified the need of watermarking with fragile medical image watermarking using saliency and phase congruency. Initially, the saliency and phase congruency methodologies are applied on the original medical image to highlight the object features. Based on the feature map, a mask is generated which segregates the area of interest from the portions containing visual medical information. An encrypted text, containing identity of the patient, is embedded into the area of interest of the image. The results of imperceptibility and fragility criteria are satisfactory towards the implementation of a fragile watermark as the extracted watermark is found to be corrupted upon unfaithful image processing modifications.

INTRODUCTION

In the past decade or so, science and technology have developed in leaps and bounds. Over time, technology has evolved into different generation, as reported by P. Letaba, M. W. Pretorius and L. Pretorius (2015). These developments can be attributed to several reasons, well explained by Basalla, George (1988). As years have passed by, the world population has grown at a significant rate. With this, human

DOI: 10.4018/978-1-5225-7107-0.ch003

mind has evolved and so has the curiosity of humans. Competition amongst the existing technologies was tremendous. To survive in the present technical era, there has been a need to improve existing technology and thereby develop modern unmatched technical specimens. The different nations hereby reap a sustained economic benefit. Also, the fact that modern techniques and technology leads to the betterment of society and global community emergence, is mostly undeniable.

The Digital Revolution, during the period of late 1950s to late 1970s, sparked off the shift from analogue technological methodologies to digital electronics. Digital Information, which is basically a discontinuous or discrete form of information, continues to remain at the forefront of all cutting edge technologies, as proposed by Negroponte, Nicholas (1995). There's a general sense of agreement to the fact that digital information sustains to dominate analogue information which is information in the form of a continuous function, as given by B. J. Bamgbade, B. A. Akintola, D. O. Agbenu, C. O. Ayeni, O. O. Fagbami and H. O. Abubakar (2015). None is screened to the statement that digital information has the capability to carry more information at a faster rate as compared to analogue information. Also, processing ease of the former form of information is far more superior compared to the latter. Since digital information is mostly obtained by sampling the analogue information that is analogue-to-digital conversion, well described by M. Verhelst and A. Bahai (2015) and E. J. Candes and M. B. Wakin (2008), the resulting discrete data or numbers can be easily encrypted through various ways. Thus, digital information is more secured and because of these reasons it should continue to be the primary medium of data storage and transmission for most of the state of the art technologies in the future, also stated by Lori McCay-Peet, Elaine G. Toms and Gary Marchionini (2017). Software, web pages and websites, data and databases, digital images, digital video, digital audio, are some of the notable examples of digital media. As suggested by the idiom 'Two sides of the same coin', digital information poses different threats which may lead to severe financial losses. These threats usually come up in two ways: either the confidentiality or integrity of data is at stake or the availability of information is hampered because of malicious activities. This manuscript focusses on the concerns raised by digital information's potential threat of copyright protection, described by M. J. Baeth and M. Aktas (2015) and B. Vukelić and K. Škaron (2013). There has been a persisting problem of copyright violation of digital information which happens through distribution and duplication of such media without the owner's consent. Since the issue of copyright infringement arose, architects of digital content have been trying to portray a secure and fully established solution to the aforementioned problem. The projected solution has to be fully equipped to handle the different security threats to information systems. But before contemplating on the solution, one has to be very clear with the problem statement at hand that is the different security threats need to be fully understood and kept in mind, in reference with Mouna Jouini, Latifa Ben Arfa Rabai and Anis Ben Aissa (2014).

As quoted by H.L. Mencken, "For every complex problem there is an answer that is clear, simple and wrong", the concept of information hiding came into existence as a countermeasure to copyright protection threats. Information hiding is a secure way of communication wherein the owner of digital media encapsulates certain information within the original content. This distinguishable imperceptible information ensures copyright protection, as explained by F. A. P. Petitcolas, R. J. Anderson and M. G. Kuhn (1999). Information hiding is achieved through the techniques of steganography, cryptography and digital watermarking.

The following section explains the terms steganography and cryptography with respect to information hiding.

Johannes Trithemius (1499) is credited for bringing the word 'Steganography' into existence. Steganography revolves around the concept of hiding any digital media, which maybe image, audio or video, into the original content. This ideology was well enlightened by M. M. Amin, M. Salleh, S. Ibrahim, M. R. Katmin and M. Z. I. Shamsuddin (2003) and W. Bender, D. Gruhl, N. Morimoto and A. Lu (1996). On the contrary, cryptography is the art of designing heavy computational algorithms which are encoded along with the original message when a secure communication channel is set up between a sender and a receiver in the presence of adversaries. This was earlier synonymous to encryption. The different directions of cryptography are well noted by W. Diffie and M. Hellman (1976). There's an obvious advantage of steganography over cryptography that being the former drives almost negligible attention of the intruder as compared to the latter. Since cryptography manages encoding visible codes onto the original document, therefore these encoded codes raise a general sense of curiosity amongst any observer of the document. Hence, this might possibly lead to the tampering of the encoded data as well as the original document. But steganography focusses on hiding data which is invisible to any viewer. Thus, it ensures concealing the imperceptible mark along with the original data, thereby making it difficult for anyone to know that something has actually been hidden in the document. The advantages of steganography over cryptography mentioned here are well in accordance to L. Kothari, R. Thakkar and S. Khara (2017). So, understanding and classifying the different steganography techniques is of immense relevance. According to C.P.Sumathi, T.Santanam and G.Umamaheswari (2013), pure steganography, secret key steganography and public key steganography are the different steganography categories. Steganography techniques are categorised as substitution, transform domain, spread spectrum, statistical, distortion and cover generation. Different steganography techniques find their applications in various domains like military and defence organisations, medical image based associations, digital content spread over the internet. All these are in reference with N. Provos and P. Honeyman (2003). Spread spectrum image steganography by L. M. Marvel, C. G. Boncelet and C. T. Retter (1999), DCT and DWT are designed for higher security as mentioned by N. M. Surse and P. Vinayakray-Jani (2017), A. Girdhar and V. Kumar (2018) remarks about the three dimensional image steganography, least significant bit steganography by G. Prashanti, B. V. Jyothirmai and K. S. Chandana (2017), G. Hamed, M. Marey, S. A. El-Sayed and M. F. Tolba (2016) establishes different DNA based steganography techniques, text steganography can be referred to S. Sharma, A. Gupta, M. C. Trivedi and V. K. Yadav (2016), hiding video in a video file by R. Patel and M. Patel (2014), steganography technique in spatial domain proposed by D. Singla and M. Juneja (2014), CES technique by J. Gaba and M. Kumar (2013), speeded up robust feature technique for steganography by N. Hamid, A. Yahya, R. B. Ahmad and O. Al-Qershi (2012) are listed as some of the widespread steganography techniques.

In the following segment, the authors have mentioned about the use of digital watermarking.

Digital intellectual property is widely accessible in different corners of the world. This is the positive impact that the global networks have had on the entire society and the nations. Different forms of digital media have started interacting with each other. They have begun to establish a coherent system involving each other. Before the dawn of multimedia, this was something totally unimaginable. Digitization of content has led to the industries distributing data to consumers via electronic means. Thus there has been a major shift from analogue to digital form.

Digital watermarking is an efficient copyright protection tool, wherein the owner embeds data, like any sequence of characters or code, into any digital media. This embedded data serves as an identification of the actual owner of the digital media such as audio, video or image, as proposed by R. G. van Schyndel, A. Z. Tirkel and C. F. Osborne (1994). Digital watermarking can be perceptible or imperceptible to human eye or ear, but both need to ensure that the digital media is not stolen or redistributed without the owner's approval. This is in accordance to E. Izquierdo, Hyoung Joong Kim and B. Macq (2003). It can be achieved in two ways: either through robust digital watermarking, whereby the watermark remains intact even amidst external attacks and also maintains the quality of the original digital media, or through fragile digital watermarking, wherein the watermark gets damaged under any external attack. Fragile watermarking is a very sensitive technique and the watermark is destroyed under any modification of the watermarked signal. There can also be a third way which includes implementing both the above mentioned ways. Realising and understanding the different aspects of digital watermarking, as mentioned by F. Mintzer, G. W. Braudaway and M. M. Yeung (1997), is crucial. Digital watermarking has its application in copyright protection, video authentication, broadcast monitoring, source tracking, content management on social networks, and software crippling on screen casting and video editing software programs, in reference to C. I. Podilchuk and E. J. Delp (2001). This unique domain of copyright marking is used in innumerable digital fields spread over associated networks, as published by J. H. Saturwar and D. N. Chaudhari (2017).

The inherent advantages of digital watermarking contributing towards high security of information through its robustness or fragility feature and its capability to protect data even after being decoded are well proposed by Desai, H. V. (2012) and F. Hartung and M. Kutter (1999). Thus, the authors have intended to propose this manuscript revolving around the domain of digital watermarking as their main field of research.

Before digital watermarking, the terminology of paper watermark was hugely relevant. This method was adopted based on the fact that a watermark, which included any image or design, was visible as different shades of lightness or darkness when reflected light was made to fall on the paper, well-illustrated by Biermann, Christopher J. (1996). In 1826, John Marshall developed the dandy roll. This was a water-coated metal stamp which was used as a watermark on paper. In 1848, cylinder mould watermark came into use. It was the modification of the dandy roll process. The dandy roll process used the wire covering, but the latter used areas of relief on the roll's surface to create the watermark. A.Z.Tirkel, G.A. Rankin, R.M. Van Schyndel, W.J.Ho, N.R.A.Mee and C.F.Osborne (1993) are recognised for the advent of the term 'digital watermark'. Since then, it has emerged as one of the encouraging field of study for researchers and industry associates. The classification of digital watermarking is well explained by Saraju P. Mohanty (1999) and Gaurav Chawla, Ravi Saini, Rajkumar Yadav and Kamaldeep (2012). According to the working domain, they are classified as spatial domain and frequency domain. The visibility of the former domain of watermark depends on the application of a specific colour band whereas for the latter a specific frequency has to be applied. The classification based on human perception has already been mentioned above. Based on the type of document, there are four types of watermarks, namely text, image, audio and video. Image based digital watermarking is mostly the prominent one as compared to the other three types of watermark.

Since its birth various techniques of digital watermarking have emerged. The authors have tried to highlight some of the notable mechanisms in this domain and related work. This should enable any reader to comprehend the comparative study between the technique proposed herewith by the authors and the methodologies published by other researchers. The document published by V. M. Potdar, S. Han and E. Chang (2005) focusses on the various digital watermarking and steganography schemes. These techniques are well elaborated with their advantages and limitations. Added to this, the techniques have been properly classified in the different existing domains of watermarking, as noted in an earlier section. The spatial and frequency domain of digital watermarking, with their pros and cons have been mentioned by S. Tyagi, H. V. Singh, R. Agarwal and S. K. Gangwar (2016). Chiou-Ting Hsu and Ja-Ling Wu (1999) illustrates on embedding digital watermarks, which are essentially visually recognizable patterns, into the images by adjusting the middle frequency parts of the images. The method has the potential to withstand image processing modifications and Joint Photographic Experts Group (JPEG) lossy compression. Discrete cosine transform is another way to implement digital watermarking, as published by J. R. Hernandez, M. Amado and F. Perez-Gonzalez (2000). This method has the advantage of enabling two different tests, namely watermark decoding and watermark detection. The decoding part is used to decode the watermark whereas detection ensures the presence of a watermark with a certain key in the image. The two tests are ensured by the algorithm of generalized Gaussian distributions to statistically model the DCT coefficients. It has a greater performance towards Gaussian noise attacks. Ching-Yung Lin and Shih-Fu Chang (2001) proposed a method of image authentication, which centred on the invariance of the associations among discrete cosine transform coefficients at the same location in distinct portions of the image, to protect against undesirable manipulations but allow JPEG lossy compression. D. Kundur and D. Hatzinakos (1999) have addressed the technique of fragile digital watermarking to ensure the tamper proofing of still images. Tamper detection is conceivable at certain spatial and frequency regions. Hence, this process embedded a watermark in the discrete wavelet domain of the image by quantizing the equivalent coefficients. Reversible image watermarking scheme using an interpolation technique, as suggested by L. Luo, Z. Chen, M. Chen, X. Zeng and Z. Xiong (2010), could embed a hefty amount of hidden data into images with imperceptible alteration. This methodology can restore the original image without any changes after the hidden data is extracted. The techniques based on least significant bit prediction and Sweldens' lifting scheme and development of Tian's technique of difference expansion, could allow one to implant significant amounts of data into digital media such that the original content could be reconstructed from the watermarked image, as published by L. Kamstra and H. J. A. M. Heijmans (2005). The digital watermarking technique, as proposed by I. J. Cox, J. Kilian, T. Leighton and T. Shamoon (1996), inserted a watermark into the spectral elements of the data using methodologies analogous to spread spectrum communication, concealing a narrow band signal, the data, in a wideband channel. This had the potential to ensure protection against perceptual degradation of the signal that is the original digital content. A hybrid watermarking method revolving around discrete wavelet transform (DWT) and singular value decomposition (SVD) was released by C. C. Lai and C. C. Tsai (2010). The above two theories were combined together in the sense that watermark was embedded on the elements of singular values of the cover image's DWT sub-bands. A digital watermark, generated by filtering a PN-sequence with a filter that approximates the frequency masking characteristics of the human auditory system, could be embedded on digital audio signals, as entitled by L. Boney, A. H. Tewfik and K. N. Hamdy (1996). M. M. Yeung and F. Mintzer (1997) raised the ideology on invisible watermarking images for ensuring image verification applications, wherein it can be realized whether the content of the image has been altered or not by any mischievous individual. The document referenced by M. Ahmad, A. Shahid, M. Y. Qadri, K. Hussain and N. N. Qadri (2017) stresses on a robust fingerprinting method on the basis of distinct pattern creation and row association schemes, able to counter malicious attacks. The fingerprinting scheme uses a secret key and buyer's unique identity. Using this data along with the application of Fibonacci series, the rows were selected for fingerprinting. To ensure a higher security towards protection of ownership rights, RSA encryption was also used. Considering the fact that little importance has been given to the constrained signal to noise ratio (SNR) with respect to the embedded parameter optimization, the manuscript by Z. Su, G. Zhang, F. Yue, L. Chang, J. Jiang and X. Yao (2018) established the empirical association between the scaling parameter, robustness, and imperceptibility and then a SNR- constrained optimization model is brought forward. Ultimately, using the binary search algorithm and heuristic search scheme, the watermark is embedded in the audio watermarking domain. To highly secure digital image, a combination of least significant bit mechanism and discrete cosine transform algorithm was implemented to develop the watermark, as stated by E. Mathur and M. Mathuria (2017). The capability of the technique, advocated by C. N. Sujatha and P. Satyanarayana (2016), against 12 different intentional and unintentional attacks using the transform domain techniques to embed logo into colour host images, is another similar watermarking scheme. The robustness of the digital watermarking technique was established on the basis of the combination of entropy of block image and least significant bit substitution against various types of image processing attacks, by S. Kumar and A. Dutta (2016). The method proposed by G. W. R. Sandaruwan and L. Ranathunga (2017) used Sobel operator and LoG filter for improving the edge detection and upgrading the robust invariant feature identification. This is simply based on transformation of low level features of digital image and through this the data is recovered dynamically. Fourier transform for time and frequency domain analysis on wav file format for different audio files and then using the cyclic data preservation and similarity computation between two audio files help in audio data based forgery detection, as published by D. Namdev and A. Bansal (2015). Due to the growth of data transmission rates, audio watermarking emerged as one of the promising fields. The watermarking system can be designed as a discrete wavelet transform (DWT) approach which is later divided into smaller sections, along with the usage of Fibonacci numbers to embed the watermark, as documented by U. R. Nair and G. K. Birajdar (2016). Its robustness is measured with the help of SNR values along with error rate. The method of using spread spectrum communication techniques and matrix transformations to design the watermark to be embedded in grey scale digital images was remarked by J. J. K. O. Ruanaidh, W. J. Dowling and F. M. Boland (1996). It could convey the watermark information and used optimal detectors for watermark identification. In the paper designed by A. Piva, M. Barni, F. Bartolini and V. Cappellini (1997), robust digital watermarking technique of embedding codes or pseudo random sequence of real numbers in a selected set of DCT coefficients of images in the frequency domain, was discussed. Instead of depending on the comparison of the watermarked image and the original image, the extraction process doesn't resort to the original image. The technique of embedding a watermark through the implementation of discrete cosine transform in the middle band of an original image and the computation of the watermark image using a differential pulse code modulation method, proved to an effective way to digital watermarking with the added advantage of decreasing noise, as stated by Weili Tang and Y. Aoki (1997). Due to the property of multi-resolution of images, in the time- frequency domain data is changed in closed vicinity of a specific vector. This principle was the basis of laying a watermarking technique without the need of the actual image for detection, as published by G. Berbecel, T. Cooklev and A. N. Venetsanopoulos (1997). To lay down the base for the future applications of digital watermarking to emerge, the document by M. M. Yeung, F. C. Mintzer, G. W. Braudaway and A. R. Rao (1997) classified the different digital watermarking techniques based on their appearance and application domain and also highlighted the research in the Image Library Applications group of the IBM Thomas J. Watson Research Centre on digital watermarking of high quality images. A robust watermarking technique of encoding the information in the histogram domain, a unique method of adaptive watermarking algorithm centring on the transform based domain for the creation of digital fingerprint of the image, was initiated by K. K. Wong, C. H. Tse, K. S. Ng, T. H. Lee and L. M. Cheng (1997), which was robust against hacking, degradation and attack. The process of engaging multi-resolution fusion techniques and incorporating a model of the human visual system (HVS) resulted in the generation of a highly robust watermarking scheme, as can be found from the work released by D. Kundur and D. Hatzinakos (1997). G. C. M. Silvestre and W. J. Dowling (1997) demonstrated a watermarking technique using cryptography, error control coding and spread spectrum techniques which was robust against the image processing distortions. The technique, applicable to all levels of design process namely the algorithm, system and behavioural synthesis and physical design levels of the DSP design examples, emphasised on the selection of constraints keeping in mind the minimal hardware overhead while embedding the unique, difficult to detect signature, as explained by I. Hong and M. Potkonjak (1998). When the watermarked image is subjected to 75% wavelet compression and 85% JPEG lossy compression, the quantity of hidden data is quite significant and the quality of the watermarked image is superior due to the variation of the number of quantization levels for the signature and a scale factor for data embedding, as shown by J. J. Chae, D. Mukherjee and B. S. Manjunath (1998). The manuscript, by Tae-Yun Chung, Min-Suk Hong, Young-Nam Oh, Dong-Ho Shin and Sang-Hui Park (1998), proposed a robust watermarking method for the MPEG- 2 video coding system though modulation of the strength and area of embedding with respect to the global and local characteristics of the video sequences. This technique enabled the direct extraction of watermark from the watermarked MPEG – 2compressed video stream without the usage of the original video sequences. By modifying the geometric features of the image, a watermark can be designed by a predefined dense pixel pattern, such as a collection of lines and to make the modifications imperceptible, the prominent portions of an image are warped into the vicinity of the line pattern, as published by M. J. J. J. B. Maes and C. W. A. M. van Overveld (1998). The watermarking methodology using the luminance component, through the spread spectrum techniques, both in space and frequency, helped in the generation of watermarks which could be recovered with zero probability of error, as can be reflected from the effort by J. Vidal and E. Sayrol (1998). The transparent and robust watermarking procedure by C. I. Podilchuk and Wenjun Zeng (1998) is used to determine the image dependent upper bounds on watermark insertion, using two guidelines specifically that of discrete cosine transform and multi- resolution wavelet framework, thereby providing maximum strength transparent watermark. The non - invertible watermarking scheme for MPEG video discuss in detail about the construction requirement and usage of such different types of non - invertible watermarking methods, as proposed by L. Qiao and K. Nahrstedt (1998). A watermark can be developed by leveraging the unique characteristics of field – programmable gate arrays (FPGAs) that is by mapping it into an FPGA and thereby applying the watermark to the physical layout of a digital circuit, as shown by J. Lach, W. H. Mangione-Smith and M. Potkonjak (1998). Based on the context of intellectual property protection (IPP), the watermarking techniques for graph colouring (GC) problem was established by Gang Qu and K. Potkonjak (1998). It was proven that high credibility was determined by at most a single colour overhead for the prescribed watermarking technique. The digital signature, designed on the basis of the quasi m – array property and thereby implementing the bit plane alteration of the least significant bit, made the extraction process simple along with the potential to withheld JPEG processing, as discovered by C. H. Yeh and C. J. Kuo (1999).

The authors' over here have focussed on a specific domain of digital watermarking, that being medical image watermarking. In this manuscript, the need to have a secure fragile medical image watermarking technique which is imperceptible to human senses, has been given primary emphasis. For the purpose of better diagnosis, the methodology of medical imaging, which centres on the creation of visual representations of the interior organs and tissues of a human body, arose. X-ray, CT, molecular imaging, MRI, ultrasound are some of the widespread fields of medical imaging. Due to the emerging modern technologies widespread access across different computer networks, medical images concerning a patient, are uploaded on cloud for doctors from across the world to speculate and analyse the condition of the patient better. To elucidate better, one of the aspects of cloud computing is that it serves as a virtual storage machine and hence the same storage space can be used multiple instances of multiple applications. The various aspects and impacts of cloud computation has been well illustrated by Mouna Jouini and Latifa Ben Arfa Rabai (2016). The different risks associated with it, along with their viable solutions has been suggested. The computer paradigms of service oriented computing and grid computing and their association with cloud computing has been realised and it is predicted to have a huge impact on information communication technology (ICT), as discussed by T. Dillon, C. Wu and E. Chang (2010). More importantly, it mentions about the distinct challenges associated with cloud computing adoption methodologies. On one side, this flourishes the prospect of better medical treatment for the patient as the condition of the patient can be diagnosed through tested medical images by any prominent doctor present in any corner of the world, but on the other side it raises apprehensions over patient identity theft and health data management issues. These sensitive data can be manhandles for one's undesirable self-centred requirements. This appeals for some strategic efficient ways to curb the problem. Hence, the need of a Fragile Medical Image Watermarking method arises which eliminates all embedded hidden confidential data from a medical image when attacked by illegitimate operators.

This section provides an insight into the other related works on medical image watermarking. The technique suggested by M. E. Brummer, R. M. Mersereau, R. L. Eisner and R. R. J. Lewine (1993) deals with the automatic detection of brain contours, dealing with a histogram based thresholding, from single – echo 3 - D MRI data. After the thresholding, morphological procedure with the knowledge of anatomy is implemented. Finally, coherent 2 – D brain masks on 23 coronal brain data sets, are propagated through the third dimension. For copyright protection of MRI images, a text image having patient details serves as the watermark which is embedded using the discrete wavelet transform and singular value decomposition algorithms. This method generates a robust watermark, as published by A. M. S. D. Mashalkar and S. S. Shirgan (2017). The methodology of L. Venkateswarlu, N. V. Rao and B. E. Reddy (2017) uses arnold transform (AT), discrete wavelet transform (DWT) and discrete cosine transform (DCT) to generate a semi – fragile (RDWTSF) watermark for medical images. After the host image is subjected to AT, this technique superimposes DCT on DWT. Through this complete method a robust medical image watermark is generated. The combination of discrete wavelet transform, fast Walsh – Hadamard transform (FWHT) and singular value decomposition generates two watermark into a single medical image, as illustrated by I. Assini, A. Badri, K. Safi, A. Sahel and A. Baghdad (2017). To be specific, the generation of the robust watermark comprises of the following steps: dividing the original image until the third level of DWT and then transforming the high frequency sub bands by FWHT and SVD. According to A. Singh, J. Nigam, R. Thakur, R. Gupta and A. Kumar (2016), the patient details can be embedded into the singular values of wavelet domain with negligible distortion to the original content. The watermark has a good result of imperceptibility, improved security and it doesn't get corrupted on external attack or modification. The security model based on Arnold transform considering the spatial domain correlation, as suggested by L. Venkateswarlu, B. E. Reddy and N. V. Rao (2016), inserts a watermark using discrete wavelet transform. The watermarked image parameters are computed for MRI and US – Scan images. Using the algorithms of discrete wavelet transform (DWT), singular value decomposition (SVD) and advanced encryption standard (AES), the image after being divided into four sub parts in the second level of the DWT and applying SVD to the higher bands, the watermark was implanted by modifying the singular values, as proven by S. Ajili, M. A. Hajjaji and A. Mtibaa (2015). For further security, encryption was also resorted to in this technique. Instead of searching all threshold values in HPS method or choosing threshold values unsystematically, the reversible watermark is selected after choosing a number of thresholds whose frequencies satisfy the vital capacity to gain the best imperceptibility, for usage in medical and military images, as shown by T. H. Nguyen and D. M. Duong (2015). To generate robust watermarks, E. Rayachoti and S. R. Edara (2014) segmented the medical image into three regions: region of interest (ROI), region of non interest (RONI) and border, wherein the hash value of ROI, data for identifying the ROI region and patient's information were embedded in the border pixels, recovery data of ROI was implanted into RONI using integer wavelet transform (IWT). N. H. Divecha and N. N. Jani (2015) proposed a reversible watermarking technique, wherein they partitioned the image into different blocks and it was observed that that there was higher correlation in the neighbouring pixels. This laid the foundation to the creation of the data embedding space based on the difference between fixed point pixel and its neighbour pixels in vertical, horizontal and diagonal direction for a particular block. Using this method, extraction could be done in an inverse manner and the original image along with the watermark could be obtained. Another way of watermarking medical image is to create an AES encrypted reversible watermark using the three different constituents: MD5 hash value of the original medical image, lossless compressed R – S vector of the different segregated groups of the image and patient ID, as entitled by Sarani N and Amudha K (2015). A robust watermark was generated by first encrypting the watermark image, then the discrete wavelet transform coefficients were altered to embed the watermark. After the generation of the watermark, the original medical image was divided into four bands in the frequency domain and singular value decomposition was applied to each band to implant the watermark through the modification of the singular values, as stated by Y. Pathak and S. Dehariya (2015). G. Suganya and K. Amudha (2014), came up with a technique to test 8 – bit ultrasound images and 16 – bit Positron Emission Tomography (PET) images, using two encryption algorithm: RC4, AES are stream cipher, block cipher respectively. Thus the combination of the watermarking algorithm, quality index modulation (QIM), with an encryption algorithm helped in securing medical images. The method of segregating the original medical image into region of interest (ROI) and region of non interest (RONI) was used for inserting the authentication information, which is compressed using run length encoding (RLE) technique, and the recovery information into the RONI. This method of least significant bit (LSB) based fragile watermarking method for tamper detection and recovery of medical images was published by R. Eswaraiah and E. S. Reddy (2014).

Over here, the authors' have come up with a critical method of implementing saliency map and phase congruency map to employ the fragile medical image watermarking technique. As the name suggests, a saliency map of an image is used to highlight the salient features of the image which in general is more noticeable to humans. It segments an image based on the quality of each pixel. Quality of a pixel is computed on the basis of its colour, intensity, orientation or texture. Thus, the pixels in the saliency map are similar to each other built on these computed properties. The saliency computation techniques have immensely improved over time and presently they have a capability to produce real time or almost real time good quality saliency images. Hence, saliency detection has its applications rooted to the fields of adaptive image display, object recognition, image retrieval, image segmentation, content-based retargeting and advertising design. Object recognition is the main application which the authors' have besieged. The devised technique computes the saliency map and as a result of which the salient pixels of the image are generated. The less salient pixels are the areas where the secretive data is to be embedded. Through repeated investigations, it was found out that the saliency map of a medical image on most occasions fail to highlight the minor areas of abnormal distortions present in the original image. These distortions can be anything like protruded out tissues, tumours, or equivalent medical syndromes. To erode this problem, phase congruency map was thought of as an additional method of implementation. Phase congruency is a robust way of detecting features of any image. It is a function of the frequency domain and it was found out that features of an image lie in the same frequency. This ideology is the backbone of the phase congruency map. This advanced version of object feature recognition goes hand in hand with the besieged area of concern of the authors. Hence the phase congruency map was used as a way of fine tuning of the saliency map. It could eliminate the problem raised by the saliency mapped image. Thus, the authors' worked on generating a binary masked image combining both the saliency map and the phase congruency map. The generated binary mask served as an excellent copy of the original medical image, prominently distinguishing the more noticeable pixels of the image from the unnoticeable obscure ones. These obscure pixels served as the region of interest of the image for hiding the sensitive data pertaining to the patient. For further security, the subtle text data was encrypted before implementing it as the desired watermark. The generated watermark was barely visible. This technique served as a fragile watermarking technique owing to the fact that when the watermark was tried to be extracted or attacked against the prescribed method, the watermark or the embedded data was completely damaged. Thus, it made the process of retrieval of the watermark by any unrelated user difficult. This ensured the protection of copyright information of the image and thereby provided a suitable solution to the problem of copyright protection as mentioned in an earlier section.

Before exploring the embedding and extraction processes as proposed by the authors' in the preceding section, it is worthwhile to have an understanding of the associated works in the domains of saliency and phase congruency. L. Itti, C. Koch and E. Niebur (1998) worked on combining multi scale image features into a single topographical saliency map. Behaviour and the neuronal architecture of the early primate visual system were the reasons for the creation of this dynamic neural network which selected the attended locations in order of decreasing saliency. Dongjian He, Yongmei Zhang and Huaibo Song (2010) proposed a saliency mapping technique different from the Itti's model and it involved three steps: extraction of visual features like intensity, colour and orientation from image, based on these features three conspicuity maps are generated and the combination of these maps into a saliency map non linearly. According to D. Lai, B. Xiong and G. Kuang (2017), the feature maps of a synthetic aperture radar (SAR) images including local variance, frequency of intensity values and global contrast based on Itti visual saliency model. The final saliency map is generated by merging the feature maps using a non-linear strategy at the original image scale, preceding to which Gaussian blurring and normalization is performed. The model designed by G. Han and Y. Jiao (2016) was used to detect pulmonary nodules based on the visual attention of the Itti's model. In this method, only some primary features like corner point, gray, edge, local entropy and direction were selected to create the saliency map. A. Borji and L. Itti (2012) prescribed a model performing a list of functions: measuring patch rarities in each colour space and combining them in a final map, the input image being segregated into non-overlapping patches and representing each patch by a vector of coefficients that linearly reconstruct it, local and global measures of saliency being fused after calculation and finally normalizing and fusing these two saliency maps of all channels from both colour systems. Thus, it can be said that it based on the consideration that local and global image patch rarities as two complementary processes. Moving onto the concept of phase congruency, a distinct methodology of combining phase congruency (PC) and guided filter was published by N. Dhengre, K. P. Upla, H. Patel and V. M. Chudasama (2017). In this method, the bio-medical was divided into low and high frequency sub-bands by non-subsampled contourlet transform (NSCT) and then the features were extracted from the low frequency bands by further processing it using PC. Similarly, the high frequency image features were extracted using the guided filter method after which both the types of features were combined using the inverse NSCT to obtain fused image in spatial domain. Based on dimensionality reduction, feature detection method using phase congruency in ultrasound images was delivered by Q. Xu, L. Wang and Z. Wang (2016). To generate exactly congruent corner features which are invariant to illumination and rotation with regards to corner detection found within the arrangements of iris patterns in the domain of iris recognition, G. Mabuza-Hocquet and F. Nelwamondo (2015) fused the phase congruency and Harris algorithm.

WATERMARK EMBEDDING

The block diagram for the process of watermark embedding is shown in Figure 1. The sensitive text information pertaining to a specific patient was encrypted, based on a user defined key, for improved security. This encrypted text was the desired watermark for the medical image. The original medical image is a RGB image (since the images were downloaded from open database, the images initially had RGB values) that is each pixel of the image has a red, green and blue component. For the embedding process, it was converted into its corresponding grayscale image. The grayscale image was operated upon by two different algorithms: phase congruency by Peter Kovesi (1996, 1997, 1999, 2002 and 2003) and saliency implementation (also referred as simpsal) by Jonathan Harel. Firstly, the saliency implementation of the grayscale image is undertaken. Simpsal is a simplified version of only the Itti algorithm by L. Itti, C. Koch, & E. Niebur (1998) and hence its output is not similar to that of the Itti algorithm. A mask was generated as a result of this. The generated mask was compared with the phase congruency map. As per the features of the phase congruency map, the mask was modified. This newly generated mask served as the intended mask for watermarking. It distinctly separated the region of interest (ROI) from the areas of the image where observable human organ information was present. Through the method of adaptive bit replacement and by comparing the original medical image with the ultimate generated mask, the watermark was embedded into the ROI of the original medical image. In the method of adaptive bit replacement, bit at certain positions of the pixel in the region of interest of the image were converted

Figure 1. Block diagram for watermark embedding

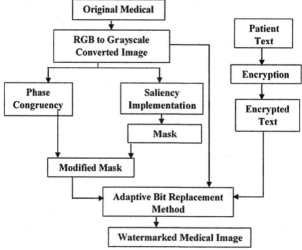

according to the bits of the encrypted text watermark so as to store the watermark in the image without it being distinctly visible to the human visual system model.

Considering the function Simpsal, the intended saliency technique used by the authors here, is a simplified version of Itti's algorithm (1998), therefore it is worthwhile to mention the generalized architectural model of Itti's algorithm which is a primarily a bottom up approach.

The equations involved in the mentioned algorithm are hereby discussed.

$$I = \frac{r + g + b}{3} \qquad (1)$$

where I is the intensity of image, r is the red channel of image, g is the green channel of image, and b is the blue channel of the image.

I is used to create a Gaussian pyramid which is expressed as

Figure 2. Itti's saliency architecture model

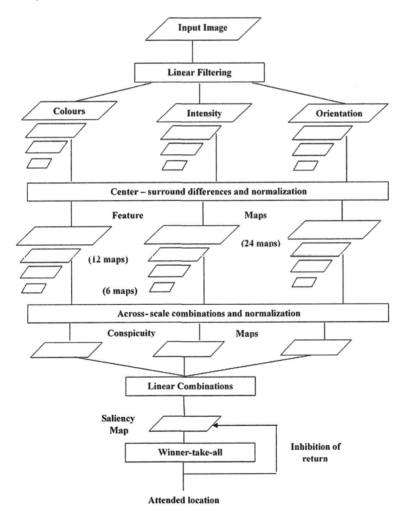

$$I(\sigma), where \, \sigma \in [0.8]. \tag{2}$$

Four broadly tuned colour channels are created.

$$G = g - \frac{r+b}{2} \, for \, green \tag{3}$$

$$B = b - \frac{r+g}{2} \, for \, blue \tag{4}$$

$$Y = \frac{r+g}{2} - \frac{|r-g|}{2} - b \, for \, yellow \tag{5}$$

$R(\sigma), G(\sigma), B(\sigma) \, and \, Y(\sigma)$ are created.

Then the feature maps are created. $\ominus$ refers to center-surround difference where c denotes the "center" fine scale and s denotes the "surround" coarse scale.

$$I(c,s) = |I(c) \ominus I(s)| \, where \, c \in \{2,3,4\}, s = c + \delta, \delta \in \{3,4\} \tag{6}$$

Thus, maps for colour channels are created.

$$RG(c,s) = |(R(c) - G(c)) \ominus (G(s) - R(s))| \tag{7}$$

$$BY(c,s) = |(B(c) - Y(c)) \ominus (Y(s) - B(s))| \tag{8}$$

Orientation feature maps are created using Gabor pyramids

$$O(\sigma, \theta) \, where \, \sigma \in [0.8] \, and \, \theta \in \{0°, 45°, 90°, 135°\}.$$

$$O(c,s,\theta) = |O(c,\theta) \ominus O(s,\theta)| \tag{9}$$

The generated feature maps are combined into the conspicuity maps $\overline{I}, \overline{C} \, and \, \overline{O}$ of intensity, colour, and orientation, respectively.

$$\bar{I} = \overset{4}{\underset{c=2}{\oplus}} \; \overset{c=4}{\underset{s=c+3}{\oplus}} \; N\Big(I\big(c,s\big)\Big) \tag{10}$$

$$\bar{C} = \overset{4}{\underset{c=2}{\oplus}} \; \overset{c+4}{\underset{s=c+3}{\oplus}} \; \Big[N\big(RG(c,s)\big) + N\big(BY(c,s)\big)\Big] \tag{11}$$

$$\bar{O} = \sum_{\theta \in \{0°,45°,90°,135°\}} N \left(\overset{4}{\underset{c=2}{\oplus}} \; \overset{c+4}{\underset{s=c+3}{\oplus}} \; N\big(O(c,s,\theta)\big) \right) \tag{12}$$

where N (.) is the normalization operator.

These three conspicuity maps result in the formation of the saliency map.

$$S = \frac{1}{3}\Big(N\big(\bar{I}\big) + N\big(\bar{C}\big) + N\big(\bar{O}\big)\Big) \tag{13}$$

According to Peter Kovesi's model (1999), features are perceived at points of maximum phase congruency in an image. A distinctly perceived feature is produced due to the congruency of phase at any angle.

$$B\big(x\big) = \sum_{0}^{n} \frac{1}{\big(2n+1\big)} \sin\Big[\big(2n+1\big)x + \varnothing\Big] \tag{14}$$

where $\varnothing$ is the offset at which congruence of phase occurs and it is varied from 0 to $\pi/2$. The phase congruency function was defined by Morrone and Owens (1987). It is in terms of the Fourier series expansion of a signal at some location x as

$$PC\big(x\big) = \max_{\bar{\phi}(x) \in [0,2\pi]} \frac{\sum_n A_n \cos\big(\varnothing_n\big(x\big) - \bar{\varnothing}\big(x\big)\big)}{\sum_n A_n} \tag{15}$$

where A_n is the amplitude of nth Fourier component, $\varnothing_n(x)$ is the local phase of the Fourier component at position x and $\varnothing(x)$ is the amplitude weighted mean local phase angle of all the Fourier terms at the point being considered.

It was observed that the localization of phase congruency remains poor on blurred features. So, Peter Kovesi derived the phase deviation function as

$$\Delta\Phi\left(x\right) = \cos\left(\phi_n\left(x\right) - \bar{\phi}\left(x\right)\right) - \left|\sin\left(\phi_n\left(x\right) - \bar{\phi}\left(x\right)\right)\right| \tag{16}$$

Ultimately, the new measure of phase congruency was suggested as

$$PC_2\left(x\right) = \frac{\sum_n W\left(x\right)A_n\left(x\right)\Delta\Phi_n\left(x\right) - T}{\sum_n A_n\left(x\right) + \varepsilon} \tag{17}$$

where ε is a small constant to avoid division by zero and T is the estimated noise influence.

The above mentioned equations vividly portray the saliency and phase congruency algorithms. These algorithms have to be applied on the concerned medical image and thereby undergo requisite modifications to generate the fragile watermark.

The input medical cover image is denoted by the following equation:

$$I_{original} = h\left(a,b\right); 0 \leq a \leq X, 0 \leq b \leq Y, h\left(a,b\right) \in \left\{0,\ldots,255\right\} \tag{18}$$

where I is the Medical Image with size X * Y.

The saliency map of the given image is computed and the subsequent mask is generated.

$$S_{map} = S\left(I_{original}\right) \tag{19}$$

$$I_{mask} = g\left(I_{original}, S_{map}\right); g\left(I_{original}, S_{map}\right) = \begin{cases} 0, & < t_l \\ 1, & otherwise \end{cases} \tag{20}$$

where t_l is the thresholding level.

The phase congruency map of the given image is shown by the following equation.

$$I_{PC} = PC_2\left(I_{original}\right) \tag{21}$$

Finally, the modified mask is generated to embed the watermark into the image.

$$I_M = f\left(I_{original}, I_{PC}, I_{mask}\right); f\left(I_{original}, I_{PC}, I_{mask}\right) \in \left\{0,1\right\} \tag{22}$$

$$f\left(I_{original}, I_{PC}, I_{mask}\right) = 0 \, if \, < t_h \, else \, 1$$

t_h is the threshold limit

The information of the patient (Text) is encrypted and then encoded into the area of interest of input image.

$$Text_{Encrypted} = Encrypt\left(Text\right) \tag{23}$$

$Text_{Encrypted}$ is the encrypted text

Applying adaptive bit replacement method, the encrypted text is embedded into the original image $I_{original}$.

$$I_{watermark} = Embed\left(I_M, Text_{Encrypted}\right) \tag{24}$$

$I_{watermark}$ is the watermarked image.

Until now, the analytical methodology to the proposed technique has been projected under this section of watermark embedding. But for a better understanding, a qualitative approach in line with the technological applicability of saliency map and phase congruency on medical images is hereby illustrated and explained. Medical images, precisely radiology images, are required to diagnose a patient before/after any worrying symptoms appear and also to investigate the health conditions post diagnosis or after the treatment of syndromes. X-rays, MRI, CT scan, ultrasound and nuclear medicine imaging are certain common examples of medical imaging. These radiology images are mostly grayscale images, meaning each pixel will have a shade of black or white. Since such sensitive images are the matter of interest, hence it is important to understand which portions of the image will be chosen to embed the watermark without tampering any data related to the internal body structure of a patient. In the technique of medical imaging, radiations are passed through the body of the patient and the observations are recorded on a computer or a film. Dense structures such as bones, tissues block the radiations to pass through and therefore appear white. On the other hand, structures containing air, muscles and fat will all appear black. Thus, it is understood that the radiology images are designed to emphasise on the white portions and these are the portions of importance to the medical fraternity. Considering the presence of black portions in the images which are of negligible significance to patients and doctors alike, these emerge as the Region Of Interest (ROI) to the authors. These areas can be well utilized for the implementation of the ideology of watermarking. As mentioned by W. J. Oosterkamp and G. M. Ardran (1955), a detailed explanation of image intensification in radiology is presented. This understanding lays the foundation to the concept of generation of a saliency map, which is the segmentation of an image based on its colour, intensity or texture. Saliency map represent the original image in a different way, such that it simplifies the process of clear demarcation of the region of interest from the medical information on the image. Pixels are categorised and thereby similar pixels are represented in a certain way to assist image recognition which mostly helps in finding out the boundaries. The generation of a saliency map can be analysed from another view point. Colour, orientation, texture, movement are some of the stimuli related to the perception of images. Information overload is one of the significant problems of the Human Visual System model (HVS model). For perception, the selected stimuli need to be prioritized, with the nervous system deciding on which part of the available information will be selected for further detailed processing and which parts are to be eliminated. Also, the selective stimuli need to be ordered for subsequent treatment. Thus, arises the importance of a single topographically oriented saliency map which is a combination of the different visual features related to the attentive selection of a stimulus, into one global measure of conspicuity. This clearly helps in perceiving the region of interest on the medical image under investigation for watermarking. With this being the initial approach, the technique was investigated on multiple images. Thereby, it was understood that the saliency map fails to highlight certain minor but significant medical information present on the images. This could be something like protruded tissues, organs. It was realised that a watermark might get embedded onto these minor areas of medical content, and thus they should be discarded from the ultimate region of interest on the image. Therefore, the need for a sharper image feature detection mechanism was required. This directed the authors towards the usage of phase congruency map. The phase congruency model signifies that the image pixels shouldn't be redundant and aim at having a high content of information. A. V. Oppenheim and J. S. Lim (1981) highlighted the importance of phase to the perception of image features and thus the phase congruency model is defined for patterns of order in the phase component of the Fourier transform. Instead of the changes in intensity, human visual system retorts to uniform phase component features, as remarked by M. C. Morrone and D. C. Burr (1988). It has been found out that gradient based algorithms are sensitive to noise, scale change and illumination change, as noted by Burlacu, A & Lazar, Corneliu (2008) and thereby laid the foundation to the importance of feature detection using the phase congruency model. The phase congruency model highlights that the edges of an image are of the highest phase order in the frequency based domain and thus the sharp edges of the image components are the constituents of the phase congruency map. These sharp points phase coherent points are points of maximum local energy. The phase congruency singular values/moments are in the range of 0-1 and are dimensionless. This is the reason why they are invariant to illumination change and contrast. Considering a wide variety of features can be detected and the amalgamation of data generated from edge and corner information using the phase congruency model, features for extended sequences can be tracked more accurately and reliably and thus it emerges as the trust worthy mechanism to be applied alongside the saliency map in the suggested methodology. From the saliency map, a binary masked image was generated based on the salient feature segregation of the image. This masked image, after being brought into a comparison with the phase congruency map of the original medical image, was remoulded as the features from the phase congruency map were sharply defined. Since the phase congruency map defined image features as points with high phase order, therefore the masked image which was ultimately generated was a one wherein all the significant medical information pertaining to the patient were discarded and only the region of interest was totally brought into consideration for the watermark to be embedded over there. Combining the saliency map and the phase congruency map is integral to the devised technique as both the results are dependent on each other for the successful segregation of the region of interest of the image. It must be understood that the proposed method can only be effective if no part of the actual information content of the original medical image, which has importance to the doctors and physicians, is lost or tampered. At the same time, preserving its copyright is also of importance to avoid identity theft. Realising the actual region of interest is of immense importance. Leaving any one of the methods of saliency and phase congruency will ultimately lead to the loss of different image features which are satisfied by both the methods differently and thereby result in the generation of a faulty mask. This would lead to the penetration of the region of interest of the image into the portions where internal body related information is stored and thus would lead to the loss and tampering of original information stored in the pixels. The above explanation clearly justifies the importance of having a sharp region of interest for watermark embedding, which can be effectively established using both the above mentioned methods. To clarify better, the ultimate generated binary masked image consist of pixel values having the value either 0 or 1, 0 representing black and 1 representing white. Hereby it can be clearly understood that the pixels with value as 0 on the binary masked image serve as the region of interest and the pixels with 1 as value are practically to be left untouched. Using the method of adaptive bit replacement watermarking, the watermark is embedded with the idea of it being visually not perceptible to the human eye. In simpler words, bits from the watermark are implanted into certain bit positions of the individual pixels in the region of interest of the mask and this is referred to as embedding. While doing so, the authors had to keep in mind that the information hiding capacity of each pixel is also quite significant for data transmission of copyright information. After embedding the watermark at its requisite positions, the mask which appears to be visually unchanged to the human visual system, it is superimposed on the original image. To improve the efficiency of the proposed method, the watermark was encrypted to ensure better security of the copyright information. The watermark over here served as a text or a sequence of characters which uniquely identifies a patient and other details pertaining to the patient. The plain text was encrypted, in simpler words altered with respect to a secret key, and this was used as the watermark of interest which was finally incorporated into the region of interest of the image. Decryption and retrieval of the watermark without the secret key was practically impossible. Finally, the watermarked image could ensure that the encrypted watermark was practically not visible to the human visual system and at the same data pertaining to the medical health condition of the patient was unaltered and not tampered. This resulting watermarked image thus completely validated the usage of saliency map, phase congruency map and the adaptive bit replacement method as the three pillars on which the entire architecture of the proposed technique was laid on. Considering that these three well illustrated methods was implemented in a coherent manner, elimination of any of the above principles could totally bring down the entire foundation of the devised technique. Generating this hand in hand relation between the above mentioned principles ensured that the watermarked image was created as desired by the authors. Hence, the bigger utility of copyright protection could be initiated using the watermark embedding aspect of the given technique.

WATERMARK EXTRACTION

In the extraction process, the original medical image having RGB value (since the images were downloaded from open database, the images initially had RGB values) was converted to its grayscale form and then its saliency map was found out. A primary mask was created on the basis of the saliency map, which was then again modified on the basis of the comparison with the phase congruency map highlighting the features of the image. Both these principles were integral to the generation of the final mask because of their contribution to distinctly highlighting all the necessary features of the image that were needed for watermark embedding. This was similar to what was implemented in embedding to distinguish the area or region of interest of the image from the non-area of interest. Using the secondary mask and the watermarked medical image as the inputs to the decoder of the adaptive bit replacement method, the watermark was decoded. This decoded watermark, after decryption, yields the original text which was embedded. The decryption was only possible because of the availability of the secret key that was initially used for encryption in the watermark embedding section. The entire method is well portrayed in Figure 3. Hence, in this way the copyright information can be stored in the image, the image can be transmitted over cloud for better treatment and diagnosis and the watermark can be decoded and decrypted from the image as and when the need arises to verify copyright credentials of the patient.

The modified mask is generated using equation (22).

$$I_M = f\left(I_{original}, I_{PC}, I_{mask}\right); f\left(I_{original}, I_{PC}, I_{mask}\right) \in \{0,1\} \, using \, (22)$$

$$f\left(I_{original}, I_{PC}, I_{mask}\right) = 0 \, if < t_h \, else \, 1$$

t_h is the threshold limit

Decoding is achieved through the following equation.

Figure 3. Block diagram for watermark decoding

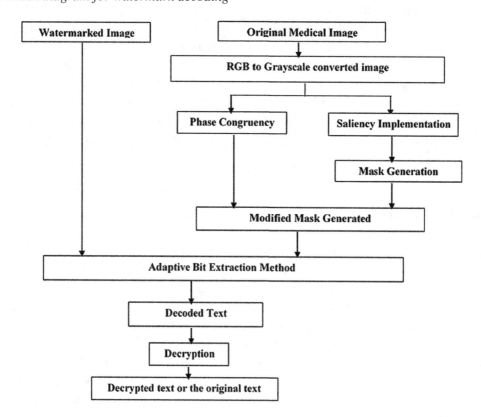

$$I_{Decoded} = Decoding\left(I_{watermark}, I_{M}\right) \tag{25}$$

$$Text_{Decrypted} = Decryption\left(I_{Decoded}\right) \tag{26}$$

The decrypted text is obtained from equation (26) and then it is compared with the original text encoded. It is found out that both the texts are completely identical.

RESULTS AND DISCUSSION

This section validates the results of the proposed algorithm by displaying the different observations. Initially, medical images were downloaded from open database spread over the internet. To be specific, these were some radiology images, like X-Ray, MRI and USG images, of image size 256 x 256. These served as the testing images. Before the algorithm could be employed, the watermark that is the encrypted text was developed. Figure 4a represents the encrypted watermark, where '*XYZ*' and '*Patient Id: 6234*' refer to the Patient Name and the unique identity number for the patient, respectively. This unique identity number is sufficient information to explore cloud storage and thereby to find out the complete identity of the patient.

With this watermark, the proposed algorithm is implemented on the testing images. Figure 4b distinctly demonstrates the original image, saliency map, primary binary mask image, phase congruency map, modified binary mask image and the watermarked image for five images. Also, the other test images are represented in Figure 5. The watermark over here is intended to be invisible in the image. But it has to be kept in mind that the perceptual quality of the image isn't degraded by any means so as to be evident to the human eye. Hence, this imperceptibility test results against various measure, as given by Abhishek Basu et al (2016), are formulated in Table 1. Table 1 also specifies the information hiding capacity in the images using the suggested method.

The imperceptibility performance and information hiding capacity of the images given in Figure 5 are well illustrated graphically in Figure 6(a), 6(b), 6(c), 6(d), 6(e) and 6(f).

The proposed algorithm remarks on the fragile nature of the watermark. Hence, it is tested against different image processing attacks like Poisson and Gaussian noise addition, filtering, cropping and rotation and the experimental results are provided in Figure 7 and Table 2. The decoded output column of Table 2 is representing the outcome of encoder and decoder after applying encryption and decryption accordingly.

The imperceptibility results offered by the projected algorithm are fairly acceptable. It is also to be noted that this method provides a reasonable information hiding capacity in the pixels of the image,

Figure 4a. Encrypted watermark

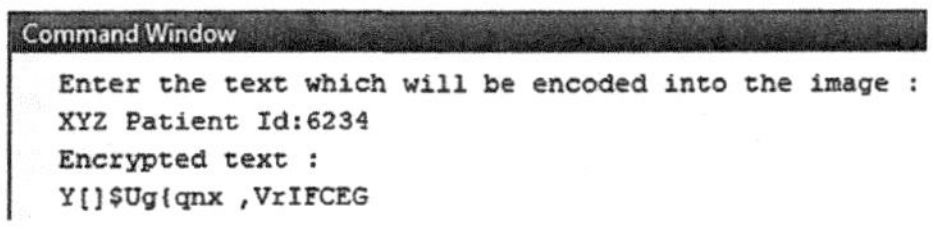

```
Command Window
    Enter the text which will be encoded into the image :
    XYZ Patient Id:6234
    Encrypted text :
    Y[]$Ug{qnx ,VrIFCEG
```

Figure 4b. Proposed technique applied on two X-Ray images (a) and (b), one MRI image (c) and two USG images (d) and (e).

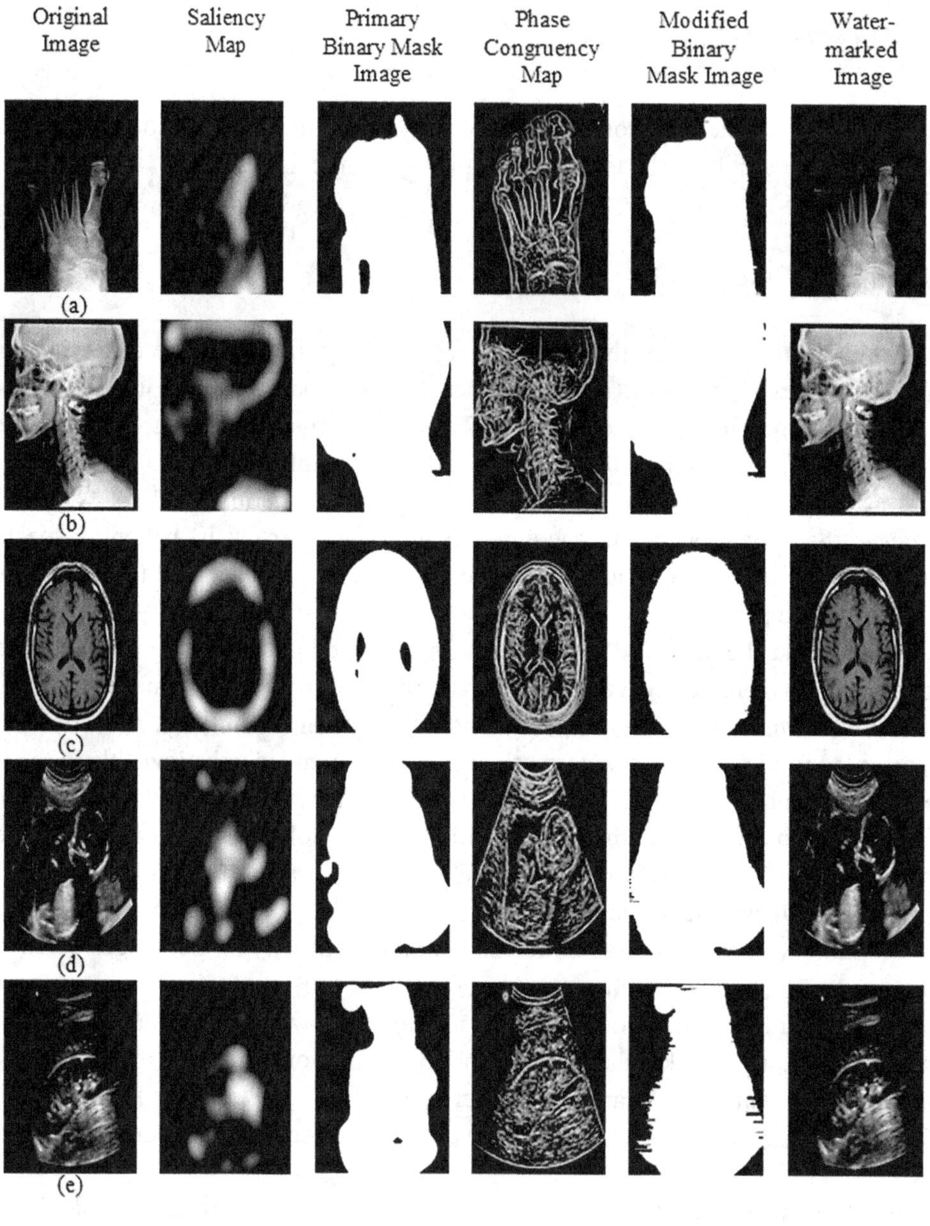

without causing any perceivable change in the image. The aim of the authors was to generate a fragile watermark. Since the test for fragility condition of the watermark indicate that under different image processing attacks, the decoder fails to decrypt the original encoded watermark, so it can be safely considered that the projected method has led to the generation of a fragile watermark for medical images.

Table 3 portrays the comparison of the proposed technique against some other state of the art techniques. In Table 3, for the proposed scheme, the average of the PSNR values and bits per pixel values are computed for all the test images respectively which are considered for implementing this method.

Figure 5. Remaining test images comprising of eight X-Ray images (a), (b), (c), (d), (e), (f), (g) and (h), four MRI images (i), (j), (k) and (l) and three USG images (m), (n) and (o).

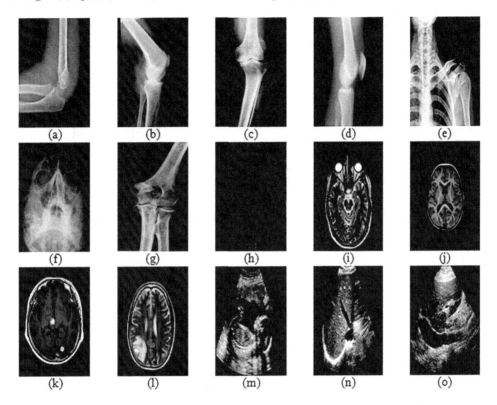

Table 1. Imperceptibility results with bit hiding capacity

Image	4b (a)	4b (b)	4b (c)	4b (d)	4b (e)	Average
PSNR(dB)	54.7756	74.2077	54.0528	63.6298	57.5169	60.8366
UIQI	0.6352	0.8482	0.6776	0.7446	0.6818	0.7175
SSIM	0.9279	0.9650	0.9473	0.9520	0.9274	0.9439
IF	0.9982	0.9999	0.9979	0.9998	0.9992	0.9990
Time(sec)	7.5790	2.6762	6.5067	5.1271	6.9737	5.7725
Bits per pixel	0.7998	0.2813	0.6943	0.5186	0.7207	0.6029

The comparison results are flawlessly appropriate and suitable.

Thus, all the earlier drawn results signify that the desired fragile medical image watermarking algorithm has been successfully achieved. Moreover, the performance comparison in terms of imperceptibility and hiding capacity with state of the art techniques ensure the supremacy of the proposed scheme.

Over here it is worthwhile to mention that the watermarking technique used incorporates a fragile watermark which has a fairly significant imperceptibilty result and bit hiding capacity. Usually, there is a trade-off between the imperceptibilty results and the hiding capacity. But the results clearly signify that the watermark is practically not visible to the human visual system model and the calculations also

Figure 6a. PSNR results for different images.

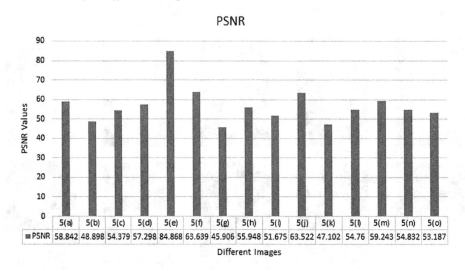

Figure 6b. SSIM values for different images.

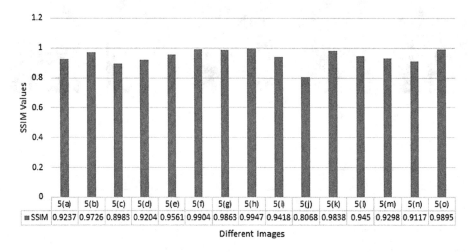

Figure 6c. UIQI values for different images.

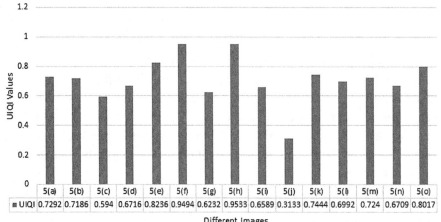

Figure 6d. Image Fidelity (IF) values for different images.

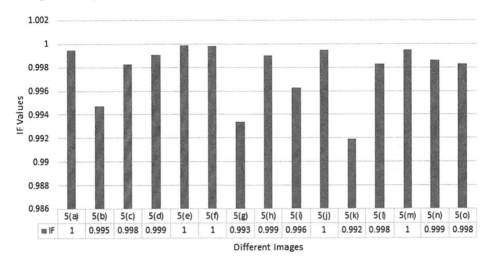

	5(a)	5(b)	5(c)	5(d)	5(e)	5(f)	5(g)	5(h)	5(i)	5(j)	5(k)	5(l)	5(m)	5(n)	5(o)
▪ IF	1	0.995	0.998	0.999	1	1	0.993	0.999	0.996	1	0.992	0.998	1	0.999	0.998

Different Images

Figure 6e. Time taken for encoding the watermark in different images by the proposed algorithm

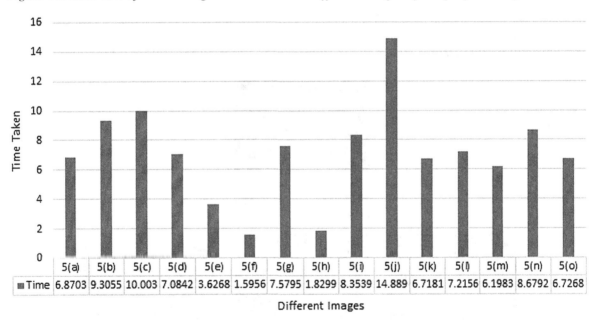

	5(a)	5(b)	5(c)	5(d)	5(e)	5(f)	5(g)	5(h)	5(i)	5(j)	5(k)	5(l)	5(m)	5(n)	5(o)
▪ Time	6.8703	9.3055	10.003	7.0842	3.6268	1.5956	7.5795	1.8299	8.3539	14.889	6.7181	7.2156	6.1983	8.6792	6.7268

Different Images

reveal that sufficient information is hidden into the watermarked image pixels. So, the trade-off has somewhat been diluted by the proposed method. Practically speaking, it is quite impossible for a single watermarked image to survive all the different kinds of image processing attacks that are relevant in the modern digital age. But it is expected that the watermarking mechanism can survive some of the common methods of spatial domain attacks and transform domain attacks. The watermark could not survive some of the significant image processing attacks in the sense that it was designed to be fragile which ensures that the copyright information would not be gathered by any user who is not entitled to have it. When the given medical image was attacked by different image processing measures, the method failed to extract, decode and decrypt the original watermark that was embedded into the medical image

Figure 6f. Information hiding capacity in the different images

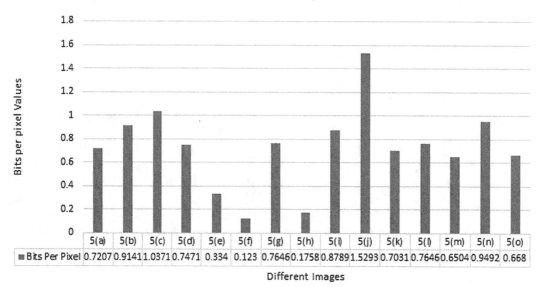

Different Images	5(a)	5(b)	5(c)	5(d)	5(e)	5(f)	5(g)	5(h)	5(i)	5(j)	5(k)	5(l)	5(m)	5(n)	5(o)
■ Bits Per Pixel	0.7207	0.9141	1.0371	0.7471	0.334	0.123	0.7646	0.1758	0.8789	1.5293	0.7031	0.7646	0.6504	0.9492	0.668

Figure 7. (a), (b), (c), (d), (e), (f) and (g) represent No Attack Image, Poisson Noise Attack Image, Gaussian Noise Attack Image, Erode Attack Image, Median Filtering Attack Image, Crop Attack Image and Rotated Image respectively.

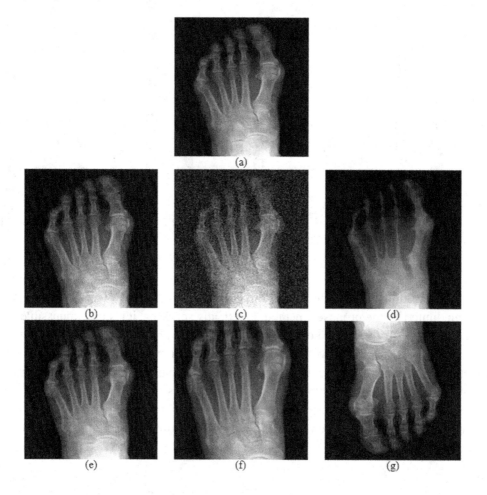

Table 2. Test for fragility condition of watermark.

Condition of Image	Observed Image	Decoded Output
No Attack	Figure 7(a)	Decoded encrypted text: Y[]$Ug{qnx, VrIFCEG Decrypted text: XYZ Patient Id: 6234
Poisson Noise	Figure 7(b)	Decoded encrypted text: (The corresponding binary bits are all 0) Decrypted text: (Nothing to be displayed)
Gaussian Noise	Figure 7(c)	Decoded encrypted text: (The corresponding binary bits are all 0) Decrypted text: (Nothing to be displayed)
Erode	Figure 7(d)	Decoded encrypted text: (The corresponding binary bits are all 0) Decrypted text: (Nothing to be displayed)
Median Filtering	Figure 7(e)	Decoded encrypted text: ? □_w _ zyo Decrypted text: >}□[ryxwvutSrqpoig\
Crop	Figure 7(f)	Decoded encrypted text: (The corresponding binary bits are all 0) Decrypted text: (Nothing to be displayed)
Rotation	Figure 7(g)	Decoded encrypted text: □ 0 (□□□ 8@ D1@ Decrypted text: □ * □ * 1 3□-

Table 3. Performance comparison result

Method	Average PSNR Value	Average Bits Per Pixel Value
Proposed Method	57.9140	0.6987
H-GAWM by Amine Mestiri et al. (2017)	47.587	0.55
Xuan Approach by Guorong Xuan et al. (2005)	41	0.55
Companding based RIWA by M. Arsalan et al. (2012)	41.1	0.55
EAP by Sunil Prasad Jaiswal et al. (2013)	46	0.55
Secured Medical Image Watermarking Method by Abhishek Basu et al. (2015)	46.923	0.043
Robust Reversible Watermarking by H. K. Maitya, S. P. Maity (2012)	45.063	0.497

and the watermark itself got damaged as shown in the results. This is when a watermark is termed as fragile, that is, it becomes non detectable under any slight modifications or changes. It can be extracted only by the predefined mechanisms elaborated in this technique that is by providing the detection side information to the decoder. They are capable to validate content authentication rather than copyright ownership. At the same time, if it is found to be tampered, edited, damaged or altered it can be realised that some modifications has happened to the watermarked image while transmission. This method ensures the detection of minute alterations to the watermarked image with considerably high probability. The fragile watermarks thereby provide an appropriate answer as being evidences when the credibility of the image content is questioned. So, it can be confirmed that the watermark cannot be extracted by any user using malicious methods of extraction. Also, technical aspect of the watermark embedding and extraction parts of the proposed method ensure that the embedded watermark cannot be removed and subsequently a different watermark cannot be added onto the watermarked image as it will lead to severe visual distortions which can be easily perceived by the human visual system model.

CONCLUSION

Here the authors proposed a fragile medical image watermarking technique using saliency and phase congruency. Both are used to find out the area of interest of the medical image that will be used for embedding the watermark based on the mentioned algorithm. The results of imperceptibility and information hiding capacity are noteworthy. Moreover, the fragility of the scheme is also ensured and implemented by means of encryption. To test the superiority of the scheme, the results of imperceptibility and hiding capacity are tested against some other state of the art techniques and the comparison results are trustworthy.

In future, in spite of using bit replacement, reversible technology may be used to implement medical image watermarking.

REFERENCES

Ahmad, M., Shahid, A., Qadri, M. Y., Hussain, K., & Qadri, N. N. (2017). Fingerprinting non-numeric datasets using row association and pattern generation. *2017 International Conference on Communication Technologies (ComTech)*, 149-155. 10.1109/COMTECH.2017.8065765

Ajili, S., Hajjaji, M. A., & Mtibaa, A. (2015). Hybrid SVD-DWT watermarking technique using AES algorithm for medical image safe transfer. *2015 16th International Conference on Sciences and Techniques of Automatic Control and Computer Engineering (STA)*, 69-74. 10.1109/STA.2015.7505164

Amin, M. M., Salleh, M., Ibrahim, S., Katmin, M. R., & Shamsuddin, M. Z. I. (2003). Information hiding using steganography. *4th National Conference of Telecommunication Technology, 2003. NCTT 2003 Proceedings*, 21-25. 10.1109/NCTT.2003.1188294

Arsalan, M., Malik, S. A., & Khan, A. (2012). Intelligent reversible watermarking in integer wavelet domain for medical images. *Journal of Systems and Software*, 85(4), 883–894. doi:10.1016/j.jss.2011.11.005

Assini, I., Badri, A., Safi, K., Sahel, A., & Baghdad, A. (2017). Hybrid multiple watermarking technique for securing medical image using DWT-FWHT-SVD. *2017 International Conference on Advanced Technologies for Signal and Image Processing (ATSIP)*, 1-6. 10.1109/ATSIP.2017.8075569

Baeth, M. J., & Aktas, M. (2015). On the Detection of Information Pollution and Violation of Copyrights in the Social Web. *2015 IEEE 8th International Conference on Service-Oriented Computing and Applications (SOCA)*, 252-254. 10.1109/SOCA.2015.27

Bamgbade, B. J., Akintola, B. A., Agbenu, D. O., Ayeni, C. O., Fagbami, O. O., Abubakar, H. O., ... Škaron, K. (2013). Cyber crime and violation of copyright. *36th International Convention on Information and Communication Technology, Electronics and Microelectronics (MIPRO)*, 1127-1130.

Basalla, G. (1988). *The evolution of technology*. Cambridge University Press.

Basu, A. (2015). On the implementation of a secure medical image watermarking. *National Conference on Frontline Research in Computer, Communication and Device (FRCCD)*.

Basu, A. (2016). Some Studies on Quality Metrics for Information Hiding. *National Conference on Recent Innovations in Computer Science & Communication Engineering*.

Bender, Gruhl, Morimoto, & Lu. (1996). Techniques for data hiding. *IBM Systems Journal, 35*(3-4), 313-336. doi: 10.1147j.353.0313

Berbecel, G., Cooklev, T., & Venetsanopoulos, A. N. (1997). A Multiresolution Technique For Watermarking Digital Images. *1997 International Conference on Consumer Electronics*, 354-355. 10.1109/ICCE.1997.625997

Biermann, C. J. (1996). *7. In Handbook of Pulping and Papermaking* (2nd ed.; p. 171). San Diego, CA: Academic Press.

Boney, L., Tewfik, A. H., & Hamdy, K. N. (1996). Digital watermarks for audio signals. *Proceedings of the Third IEEE International Conference on Multimedia Computing and Systems*, 473-480. 10.1109/MMCS.1996.535015

Borji, A., & Itti, L. (2012). Exploiting local and global patch rarities for saliency detection. *2012 IEEE Conference on Computer Vision and Pattern Recognition*, 478-485.10.1109/CVPR.2012.6247711

Brummer, M. E., Mersereau, R. M., Eisner, R. L., & Lewine, R. R. J. (1993, June). Automatic detection of brain contours in MRI data sets. *IEEE Transactions on Medical Imaging, 12*(2), 153–166. doi:10.1109/42.232244 PMID:18218403

Burlacu, A & Lazar, C. (2008). *Image Features Detection using Phase Congruency and Its Application in Visual Servoing*. Academic Press. .10.1109/ICCP.2008.4648353

Candes & Wakin. (2007). An Introduction To Compressive Sampling. *IEEE Signal Processing Magazine, 25*(2), 21-30. doi: 10.1109/MSP.2007.914731

Chae, J. J., Mukherjee, D., & Manjunath, B. S. (1998). A robust data hiding technique using multidimensional lattices. *Research and Technology Advances in Digital Libraries, 1998. ADL 98. Proceedings. IEEE International Forum on*, 319-326. 10.1109/ADL.1998.670432

Chawla, Saini, & Kamaldeep. (2012). Classification of Watermarking Based upon Various Parameters. *International Journal of Computer Applications & Information Technology, 1*(2).

Chung, T.-Y., Hong, M.-S., Oh, Y.-N., Shin, D.-H., & Park, S.-H. (1998, August). Digital watermarking for copyright protection of MPEG2 compressed video. *IEEE Transactions on Consumer Electronics, 44*(3), 895–901. doi:10.1109/30.713211

Cox, I. J., Kilian, J., Leighton, T., & Shamoon, T. (1996). Secure spread spectrum watermarking for images, audio and video. *Proceedings of 3rd IEEE International Conference on Image Processing*, 243-246. 10.1109/ICIP.1996.560429

Desai, H. V. (2012, December). Steganography, Cryptography, Watermarking: A Comparative Study. *Journal of Global Research in Computer Science*, 3(12). doi:10.1109/ICAETR.2014.7012790

Dhengre, N., Upla, K. P., Patel, H., & Chudasama, V. M. (2017). Bio-medical image fusion based on phase-congruency and guided filter. *2017 Fourth International Conference on Image Information Processing (ICIIP)*, 1-5.10.1109/ICIIP.2017.8313792

Diffie, W., & Hellman, M. (1976, November). New directions in cryptography. *IEEE Transactions on Information Theory*, 22(6), 644–654. doi:10.1109/TIT.1976.1055638

Dillon, T., Wu, C., & Chang, E. (2010). Cloud Computing: Issues and Challenges. *2010 24th IEEE International Conference on Advanced Information Networking and Applications*, 27-33. 10.1109/AINA.2010.187

Divecha, N. H., & Jani, N. N. (2015). Reversible Watermarking Technique for Medical Images Using Fixed Point Pixel. *2015 Fifth International Conference on Communication Systems and Network Technologies*, 725-730. 10.1109/CSNT.2015.287

Eswaraiah, R., & Reddy, E. S. (2014). A Fragile ROI-Based Medical Image Watermarking Technique with Tamper Detection and Recovery. *2014 Fourth International Conference on Communication Systems and Network Technologies*, 896-899. 10.1109/CSNT.2014.184

Gaba, J., & Kumar, M. (2013). Implementation of steganography using CES technique. *2013 IEEE Second International Conference on Image Information Processing (ICIIP-2013)*, 395-399. 10.1109/ICIIP.2013.6707622

Girdhar, A., & Kumar, V. (2018). Comprehensive survey of 3D image steganography techniques. IET Image Processing, 12(1), 1-10. doi:10.1049/iet-ipr.2017.0162

Hamed, G., Marey, M., El-Sayed, S. A., & Tolba, M. F. (2016). Comparative study for various DNA based steganography techniques with the essential conclusions about the future research. *2016 11th International Conference on Computer Engineering & Systems (ICCES)*, 220-225. 10.1109/ICCES.2016.7822003

Hamid, N., Yahya, A., Ahmad, R. B., & Al-Qershi, O. (2012). Characteristic region based image steganography using Speeded-Up Robust Features technique. *2012 International Conference on Future Communication Networks*, 141-146. 10.1109/ICFCN.2012.6206858

Han, G., & Jiao, Y. (2016). Feature selection and regional labeling of significant detection for pulmonary nodules in CT images. *2016 IEEE International Conference on Signal and Image Processing (ICSIP)*, 60-63. 10.1109/SIPROCESS.2016.7888224

Hartung, F., & Kutter, M. (1999, July). Multimedia watermarking techniques. *Proceedings of the IEEE*, 87(7), 1079–1107. doi:10.1109/5.771066

He, D., Zhang, Y., & Song, H. (2010). A novel saliency map extraction method based on improved Itti's model. *2010 International Conference on Computer and Communication Technologies in Agriculture Engineering*, 323-327. doi: 10.1109/CCTAE.2010.5544608

Hernandez, J. R., Amado, M., & Perez-Gonzalez, F. (2000, January). DCT-domain watermarking techniques for still images: Detector performance analysis and a new structure. *IEEE Transactions on Image Processing*, *9*(1), 55–68. doi:10.1109/83.817598 PMID:18255372

Hong, I., & Potkonjak, M. (1998). Techniques for intellectual property protection of DSP designs. *Acoustics, Speech and Signal Processing, 1998. Proceedings of the 1998 IEEE International Conference on*, 3133-3136. 10.1109/ICASSP.1998.678190

Hsu, C.-T., & Wu, J.-L. (1999, January). Hidden digital watermarks in images. *IEEE Transactions on Image Processing*, *8*(1), 58–68. doi:10.1109/83.736686 PMID:18262865

Itti, L., Koch, C., & Niebur, E. (1998, November). A model of saliency-based visual attention for rapid scene analysis. *IEEE Transactions on Pattern Analysis and Machine Intelligence*, *20*(11), 1254–1259. doi:10.1109/34.730558

Izquierdo, E., & Macq, B. (2003, August). Introduction to the special issue on authentication, copyright protection, and information hiding. *IEEE Transactions on Circuits and Systems for Video Technology*, *13*(8), 729–731. doi:10.1109/TCSVT.2003.817838

Jaiswal, S. P., Au, O. C., Jakhetiya, V., Guo, Y., Tiwari, A. K., & Yue, K. (2013). Efficient adaptive prediction based reversible image watermarking. *IEEE International Conference on Image Processing*, 4540-4544. 10.1109/ICIP.2013.6738935

Jouini, M., & Latifa, B. A. R. (2016). Comparative Study of Information Security Risk Assessment Models for Cloud Computing systems. *Procedia Computer Science*, *83*, 1084–1089. doi:10.1016/j.procs.2016.04.227

Jouini, Rabai, & Aissa. (2014). Classification of security threats in information systems. *ScienceDirect 5th International Conference on Ambient Systems, Networks and Technologies (ANT-2014)*. doi: 10.1016/j.procs.2014.05.452

Kamstra, L., & Heijmans, H. J. A. M. (2005, December). Reversible data embedding into images using wavelet techniques and sorting. *IEEE Transactions on Image Processing*, *14*(12), 2082–2090. doi:10.1109/TIP.2005.859373 PMID:16370461

Kothari, L., Thakkar, R., & Khara, S. (2017). Data hiding on web using combination of Steganography and Cryptography. *2017 International Conference on Computer, Communications and Electronics (Comptelix)*, 448-452. 10.1109/COMPTELIX.2017.8004011

Kovesi. (1999). Image Features From Phase Congruency. *Videre: A Journal of Computer Vision Research, 1*(3).

Kovesi, P. (1996). *Invariant Measures of Image Features From Phase Information* (PhD Thesis). The University of Western Australia.

Kovesi, P. (1997). Symmetry and Asymmetry From Local Phase. *AI'97, Tenth Australian Joint Conference on Artificial Intelligence. 2 - 4 December 1997. Proceedings - Poster Papers*, 185-190.

Kovesi, P. (2002). Edges Are Not Just Steps. *Proceedings of ACCV2002 The Fifth Asian Conference on Computer Vision*, 822-827.

Kovesi, P. (2003). Phase Congruency Detects Corners and Edges. *The Australian Pattern Recognition Society Conference: Digital Image Computing: Techniques and Applications DICTA 2003*, 309-318.

Kumar, S., & Dutta, A. (2016). A study on robustness of block entropy based digital image watermarking techniques with respect to various attacks. *2016 IEEE International Conference on Recent Trends in Electronics, Information & Communication Technology (RTEICT)*, 1802-1806. 10.1109/RTEICT.2016.7808145

Kundur, D., & Hatzinakos, D. (1997). A robust digital image watermarking method using wavelet-based fusion. *Proceedings of International Conference on Image Processing*, 544-547. 10.1109/ICIP.1997.647970

Kundur, D., & Hatzinakos, D. (1999, July). Digital watermarking for telltale tamper proofing and authentication. *Proceedings of the IEEE, 87*(7), 1167–1180. doi:10.1109/5.771070

Lach, J., Mangione-Smith, W. H., & Potkonjak, M. (1998). Signature hiding techniques for FPGA intellectual property protection. *1998 IEEE/ACM International Conference on Computer-Aided Design. Digest of Technical Papers*, 186-189. 10.1145/288548.288606

Lai, C. C., & Tsai, C. C. (2010, November). Digital Image Watermarking Using Discrete Wavelet Transform and Singular Value Decomposition. *IEEE Transactions on Instrumentation and Measurement, 59*(11), 3060–3063. doi:10.1109/TIM.2010.2066770

Lai, D., Xiong, B., & Kuang, G. (2017). Weak target detection in SAR images via improved itti visual saliency model. *2017 2nd International Conference on Frontiers of Sensors Technologies (ICFST)*, 260-264. 10.1109/ICFST.2017.8210515

Letaba, P., Pretorius, M. W., & Pretorius, L. (2015). Analysis of the intellectual structure and evolution of technology roadmapping literature. *2015 Portland International Conference on Management of Engineering and Technology (PICMET)*, 2248-2254. 10.1109/PICMET.2015.7273147

Lin, C.-Y., & Chang, S.-F. (2001, February). A robust image authentication method distinguishing JPEG compression from malicious manipulation. *IEEE Transactions on Circuits and Systems for Video Technology, 11*(2), 153–168. doi:10.1109/76.905982

Luo, L., Chen, Z., Chen, M., Zeng, X., & Xiong, Z. (2010, March). Reversible Image Watermarking Using Interpolation Technique. *IEEE Transactions on Information Forensics and Security, 5*(1), 187–193. doi:10.1109/TIFS.2009.2035975

Mabuza-Hocquet, G., & Nelwamondo, F. (2015). Fusion of Phase Congruency and Harris Algorithm for Extraction of Iris Corner Points. *2015 3rd International Conference on Artificial Intelligence, Modelling and Simulation (AIMS)*, 315-320. 10.1109/AIMS.2015.57

Maes, M. J. J. J. B., & van Overveld, C. W. A. M. (1998). Digital watermarking by geometric warping. *Proceedings 1998 International Conference on Image Processing. ICIP98*, 424-426. 10.1109/ICIP.1998.723408

Maitya, H. K., & Maity, S. P. (2012). Joint Robust and Reversible Watermarking for Medical Images. *2nd International Conference on Communication, Computing & Security*. 10.1016/j.protcy.2012.10.033

Marvel, L. M., Boncelet, C. G., & Retter, C. T. (1999, August). Spread spectrum image steganography. *IEEE Transactions on Image Processing, 8*(8), 1075–1083. doi:10.1109/83.777088 PMID:18267522

Mashalkar, A. M. S. D., & Shirgan, S. S. (2017). Design of watermarking scheme in medical image authentication using DWT and SVD technique. *2017 International Conference on Computing Methodologies and Communication (ICCMC)*, 955-960. 10.1109/ICCMC.2017.8282609

Mathur, E., & Mathuria, M. (2017). Unbreakable digital watermarking using combination of LSB and DCT. *2017 International conference of Electronics, Communication and Aerospace Technology (ICECA)*, 351-354. 10.1109/ICECA.2017.8212832

McCay-Peet, Toms, & Marchionini. (2017). Researching Serendipity in Digital Information Environments. *Researching Serendipity in Digital Information Environments, 1*, 91. doi: 10.2200/S00790ED-1V01Y201707ICR059

Mestiri, A., Kricha, A., Sakly, A., & Mtibaa, A. (2017). *Watermarking for integrity, authentication and security of Medical Imaging. 2017 14th International Multi-Conference on Systems, Signals & Devices*.

Mintzer, F., Braudaway, G. W., & Yeung, M. M. (1997). Effective and ineffective digital watermarks. *Proceedings of International Conference on Image Processing*, 9-12. 10.1109/ICIP.1997.631957

Mohanty, S. P. (1999). *Digital watermarking: a tutorial review. Report*. Bangalore, India: Department of Electrical Engineering, Indian Institute of Science.

Morrone, M. C., & Burr, D. C. (1988). Feature detection in human vision: A phase-dependent energy model. *Proceedings of the Royal Society of London. Series B, Biological Sciences, 235*(1280), 221–245. doi:10.1098/rspb.1988.0073 PMID:2907382

Morrone, M. C., & Owens, R. A. (1987). Feature detection from local energy. *Pattern Recognition Letters, 6*(5), 303–313. doi:10.1016/0167-8655(87)90013-4

Nair, U. R., & Birajdar, G. K. (2016). Audio watermarking in wavelet domain using Fibonacci numbers. *2016 International Conference on Signal and Information Processing (IConSIP)*, 1-5. 10.1109/ICONSIP.2016.7857479

Namdev, D., & Bansal, A. (2015). Frequency Domain Analysis for Audio Data Forgery Detection. *2015 Fifth International Conference on Communication Systems and Network Technologies*, 702-705. 10.1109/CSNT.2015.168

Negroponte, N. (1995). The digital revolution: Reasons for optimism. *The Futurist, 29*(6), 68.

Nguyen, T. H., & Duong, D. M. (2015). Reversible Medical Image Watermarking Technique Based on Choosing Threshold Values in Histogram Shifting. *2015 Seventh International Conference on Knowledge and Systems Engineering (KSE)*, 204-209. 10.1109/KSE.2015.75

Oosterkamp, W. J., & Ardran, G. M. (1955, November). Discussion on image intensification in radiology. *Proceedings of the IEE - Part B: Radio and Electronic Engineering, 102*(6), 845–849. doi:10.1049/pi-b-1.1955.0169

Oppenheim, A. V., & Lim, J. S. (1981). The importance of phase in signals. *Proceedings of the IEEE, 69*(5), 529–541. doi:10.1109/PROC.1981.12022

Patel, R., & Patel, M. (2014). Steganography over video file by hiding video in another video file, random byte hiding and LSB technique. *2014 IEEE International Conference on Computational Intelligence and Computing Research*, 1-5. 10.1109/ICCIC.2014.7238343

Pathak, Y., & Dehariya, S. (2014). A more secure transmission of medical images by two label DWT and SVD based watermarking technique. *2014 International Conference on Advances in Engineering & Technology Research (ICAETR - 2014)*, 1-5. 10.1109/ICAETR.2014.7012790

Petitcolas, F. A. P., Anderson, R. J., & Kuhn, M. G. (1999, July). Information hiding-a survey. *Proceedings of the IEEE, 87*(7), 1062–1078. doi:10.1109/5.771065

Piva, A., Barni, M., Bartolini, F., & Cappellini, V. (1997). DCT-based watermark recovering without resorting to the uncorrupted original image. *Proceedings of International Conference on Image Processing*, 520-523. 10.1109/ICIP.1997.647964

Podilchuk, C. I., & Delp, E. J. (2001, July). Digital watermarking: Algorithms and applications. *IEEE Signal Processing Magazine, 18*(4), 33–46. doi:10.1109/79.939835

Podilchuk, C. I., & Zeng, W. (1998, May). Image-adaptive watermarking using visual models. *IEEE Journal on Selected Areas in Communications, 16*(4), 525–539. doi:10.1109/49.668975

Potdar, V. M., Han, S., & Chang, E. (2005). A survey of digital image watermarking techniques. *INDIN '05. 2005 3rd IEEE International Conference on Industrial Informatics*, 709-716. 10.1109/INDIN.2005.1560462

Prashanti, G., Jyothirmai, B. V., & Chandana, K. S. (2017). Data confidentiality using steganography and cryptographic techniques. *2017 International Conference on Circuit, Power and Computing Technologies (ICCPCT)*, 1-4. 10.1109/ICCPCT.2017.8074276

Provos, N., & Honeyman, P. (2003, May-June). Hide and seek: An introduction to steganography. *IEEE Security and Privacy, 1*(3), 32–44. doi:10.1109/MSECP.2003.1203220

Qiao, L., & Nahrstedt, K. (1998). Watermarking methods for MPEG encoded video: towards resolving rightful ownership. *Proceedings. IEEE International Conference on Multimedia Computing and Systems*, 276-285. 10.1109/MMCS.1998.693656

Qu, G., & Potkonjak, K. (1998). Analysis of watermarking techniques for graph coloring problem. *1998 IEEE/ACM International Conference on Computer-Aided Design. Digest of Technical Papers*, 190-193. 10.1145/288548.288607

Rayachoti, E., & Edara, S. R. (2014). A novel medical image watermarking technique for detecting tampers inside ROI and recovering original ROI. *2014 IEEE International Symposium on Signal Processing and Information Technology (ISSPIT)*, 321-326. 10.1109/ISSPIT.2014.7300608

Ruanaidh, J. J. K. O., Dowling, W. J., & Boland, F. M. (1996). Phase watermarking of digital images. *Proceedings of 3rd IEEE International Conference on Image Processing*, 239-242. 10.1109/ICIP.1996.560428

Sandaruwan, G. W. R., & Ranathunga, L. (2017). Robust and adaptive watermarking technique for digital images. *2017 IEEE International Conference on Industrial and Information Systems (ICIIS)*, 1-6. 10.1109/ICIINFS.2017.8300387

Sarani, N., & Amudha, K. (2015). A security technique based on watermarking and encryption for medical image. *2015 International Conference on Innovations in Information, Embedded and Communication Systems (ICIIECS)*, 1-4. 10.1109/ICIIECS.2015.7192934

Saturwar, J. H., & Chaudhari, D. N. (2017). Review of models, issues and applications of digital watermarking based on visual cryptography. *2017 International Conference on Inventive Systems and Control (ICISC)*, 1-4. 10.1109/ICISC.2017.8068588

Sharma, S., Gupta, A., Trivedi, M. C., & Yadav, V. K. (2016). Analysis of Different Text Steganography Techniques: A Survey. *2016 Second International Conference on Computational Intelligence & Communication Technology (CICT)*, 130-133. 10.1109/CICT.2016.34

Silvestre, G. C. M., & Dowling, W. J. (1997). Image watermarking using digital communication techniques. *1997 Sixth International Conference on Image Processing and Its Applications*, 443-447. 10.1049/cp:19970933

Singh, A., Nigam, J., Thakur, R., Gupta, R., & Kumar, A. (2016). Wavelet Based Robust Watermarking Technique for Integrity Control in Medical Images. *2016 International Conference on Micro-Electronics and Telecommunication Engineering (ICMETE)*, 222-227. 10.1109/ICMETE.2016.103

Singla, D., & Juneja, M. (2014). *An analysis of edge based image steganography techniques in spatial domain. In 2014 Recent Advances in Engineering and Computational Sciences* (pp. 1–5). Chandigarh: RAECS; doi:10.1109/RAECS.2014.6799604

Su, Zhang, Yue, Chang, Jiang, & Yao. (2018). SNR-Constrained Heuristics for Optimizing the Scaling Parameter of Robust Audio Watermarking. *IEEE Transactions on Multimedia*. doi: 10.1109/TMM.2018.2812599

Suganya, G., & Amudha, K. (2014). Medical image integrity control using joint encryption and watermarking techniques. *2014 International Conference on Green Computing Communication and Electrical Engineering (ICGCCEE)*, 1-5. 10.1109/ICGCCEE.2014.6922265

Sujatha, C. N., & Satyanarayana, P. (2016). Analysis of robust watermarking techniques: A retrospective. *International Conference on Communication and Signal Processing (ICCSP)*, 336-341. 10.1109/ICCSP.2016.7754151

Sumathi, C. P., Santanam, T., & Umamaheswari, G. (2013, December). A Study of Various Steganographic Techniques Used for Information Hiding. *International Journal of Computer Science & Engineering Survey*, 4(6). doi:10.5121/ijcses.2013.4602

Surse, N. M., & Vinayakray-Jani, P. (2017). A comparative study on recent image steganography techniques based on DWT. *2017 International Conference on Wireless Communications, Signal Processing and Networking (WiSPNET)*, 1308-1314. 10.1109/WiSPNET.2017.8299975

Tang, W., & Aoki, Y. (1997). A DCT-based coding of images in watermarking. *Proceedings of ICICS, 1997 International Conference on Information, Communications and Signal Processing. Theme: Trends in Information Systems Engineering and Wireless Multimedia Communications*, 510-512. doi: 10.1109/ICICS.1997.647150

Tirkel, A. Z., Rankin, G. A., Van Schyndel, R. M., Ho, W. J., Mee, N. R. A., & Osborne, C. F. (1993). Electronic Water Mark. In *DICTA 93* (pp. 666–673). Macquarie University.

Trithemius, J. (1499). *Steganographia, a treatise on cryptography and steganography*. Retrieved from Jonathan Harel, A Saliency Implementation in MATLAB: http://www.klab.caltech.edu/~harel/share/gbvs.php and http://www.klab.caltech.edu/harel/share/simpsal.zip

Tyagi, S., Singh, H. V., Agarwal, R., & Gangwar, S. K. (2016). Digital watermarking techniques for security applications. *2016 International Conference on Emerging Trends in Electrical Electronics & Sustainable Energy Systems (ICETEESES)*, 379-382. 10.1109/ICETEESES.2016.7581413

van Schyndel, R. G., Tirkel, A. Z., & Osborne, C. F. (1994). A digital watermark. *Proceedings of 1st International Conference on Image Processing*, 86-90. doi: 10.1109/ICIP.1994.413536

Venkateswarlu, L., Rao, N. V., & Reddy, B. E. (2017). A Robust Double Watermarking Technique for Medical Images with Semi-fragility. *2017 International Conference on Recent Advances in Electronics and Communication Technology (ICRAECT)*, 126-131. 10.1109/ICRAECT.2017.40

Venkateswarlu, L., Reddy, B. E., & Rao, N. V. (2016). Arnold - wavelet based robust watermarking technique for medical images. *2016 International Conference on ICT in Business Industry & Government (ICTBIG)*, 1-5. 10.1109/ICTBIG.2016.7892689

Verhelst, M., & Bahai, A. (2015, Summer). Where Analog Meets Digital: Analog?to?Information Conversion and Beyond. *IEEE Solid-State Circuits Magazine*, 7(3), 67–80. doi:10.1109/MSSC.2015.2442394

Vidal, J., & Sayrol, E. (1998). Optimum watermark detection and embedding in digital images. *1998 IEEE Second Workshop on Multimedia Signal Processing*, 285-290. 10.1109/MMSP.1998.738948

Wong, K. K., Tse, C. H., Ng, K. S., Lee, T. H., & Cheng, L. M. (1997, November). Adaptive water marking. *IEEE Transactions on Consumer Electronics*, *43*(4), 1003–1009. doi:10.1109/30.642365

Xu, Q., Wang, L., & Wang, Z. (2016). Ultrasound Image Features Detection Using Phase Congruency Based Dimensionality Reduction. *2016 6th International Conference on Digital Home (ICDH)*, 68-73. 10.1109/ICDH.2016.024

Xuan, G., Yang, C., Zhen, Y., Shi, Y. Q., & Ni, Z. (2005). Reversible data hiding using integer wavelet transform and companding technique. In Lecture Notes in Computer Science: Vol. 3304. *Digital Watermarking* (pp. 115–124). Berlin: Springer. doi:10.1007/978-3-540-31805-7_10

Yeh, C. H., & Kuo, C. J. (1999). Digital watermarking through quasi m-arrays. *1999 IEEE Workshop on Signal Processing Systems. SiPS 99. Design and Implementation*, 456-461. doi:10.1109/SIPS.1999.822351

Yeung, M. M., & Mintzer, F. (1997). An invisible watermarking technique for image verification. *Proceedings of International Conference on Image Processing*, 680-683. 10.1109/ICIP.1997.638587

Yeung, M. M., Mintzer, F. C., Braudaway, G. W., & Rao, A. R. (1997). Digital watermarking for high-quality imaging. *Proceedings of First Signal Processing Society Workshop on Multimedia Signal Processing*, 357-362. 10.1109/MMSP.1997.602661

Chapter 4
Exploring Recent Advances in Digital Video Steganography and Future Scope

Barnali Gupta Banik

St. Thomas' College of Engineering and Technology, India

ABSTRACT

In this digital era, with the advent of technology like 4G network and VOIP, video calling is the most cost effective and cutting-edge communication technique. Simultaneously, video sharing through social networking sites is very popular, as it can reach a wider public domain in seconds. This enormous use of video motivates the fact that as digital medium video can be effectively utilized for secret sharing. Using video steganography, any kind of secret data like text, image, audio, even a short video can be hidden inside another video object, which can be securely transmitted to the recipient over the internet. In this chapter, an effort has been made to relate various techniques of video steganography under a single header to identify future scope of research. Also, all possible quality metrics for videos and for measuring robustness have been studied, and different steganalysis attacks on video have been analyzed. The broad mission of this chapter is to be a quick reference to future researchers of video steganography.

INTRODUCTION TO VIDEO STEGANOGRAPHY

In this era of internet, communication through postal mail or through PSTN are out dated. In near future, talking over cellular phone or sending e-mail may become obsolete, as VOIP call and video chats are developing into cheapest and most innovative communication channel. In recent times, one of the trendy way of communication is video sharing in social networking sites, through which within a minute, it is possible to reach a wider domain of public. Those videos are created for literally all kind of subjects like movies, songs, animations, advertisements, recipes, lectures, handcrafts etc., and can be easily shared through social networking sites like YouTube, Facebook, Twitter, Instagram, LinkedIn, Reddit etc. As per recent press release of the most popular video sharing website YouTube, they have over 1,300,000,000 users and each day those users watch a billion hours of video; In every minute, ap-

DOI: 10.4018/978-1-5225-7107-0.ch004

proximately 300 hours of videos are uploaded to YouTube. All these facts reveal that video is grabbing almost 80% of digital data now-a-days.

As communication using video becomes prevalent, it turns into necessary to protect video communication from tampering. Video can also be used as carrier of secret data, which can be transmitted over the globe to the intended recipient without any obstacles from the network administrator or the intruder, as no one can anticipate existence of secret data, hidden inside video. Steganography is very primeval technique of data hiding where except sender and intended recipient, no one is aware of presence of hidden data even beyond their presumption. With the arrival of internet, digital steganography replaces the primitive ways of steganography. In steganography, there are three objects –

- **Cover:** The object where the secret data would be hidden
- **Secret:** The object to be hidden
- **Stego:** The object created after data hiding is completed

Gupta Banik, B., & Bandyopadhyay, S. K. (2015) have shown that in digital steganography, the cover and secret can be any digital objects like text, image, audio, and video. The stego object is similar to cover object in format and up to human perception.

In Video Steganography, cover object is chosen as video, where secret data is hidden. A video is collection of frames and a frame is similar to a still image. If motion is created by arranging sequential frames one after another, then video is generated. Since the size of the video is bigger than any other digital cover media (like image, text, audio etc.), hence it is possible to hide large amount of data in a video. With the advent of computer technology, there are plenty of video compression techniques available (like MPEG-7 or H.264/AVC), which reduces the overall video size keeping duration of the video intact. Even such compressed videos can also be used as carrier of secret data. The general block diagram of video steganography to create stego video has been shown in Figure 1.

Figure 1. Stego video creation technique in video steganography

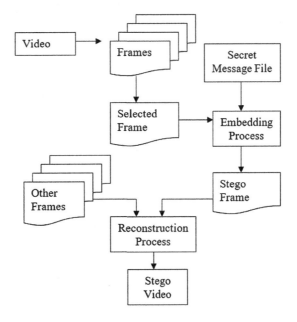

In this article, various techniques of video steganography are studied along with their quality metrices and different steganalysis attacks on video have been performed, using which the robustness of the steganography method can be determined. At last, the discussed approaches are compared to unveil the future prospect of video steganography.

INTRODUCTION TO VIDEO

A sequence of images used to compose a moving picture is called video, whereas those individual images are known as frames. Therefore, to hide any secret, at first video needs to be broken into frames. Then by Scene Change Detection process, one/few particular frames are selected where secret data can be hidden.

The frequency at which frames are displayed known as frame rate. Read, P., & Meyer, M.-P. (2000) states generally human visual system can process 10-15 frames per second. Videos are saved in compressed format otherwise it could have taken bulk memory space. There are different formats available in Video, among those, MPEG format is most popular; hence it has been discussed here.

To process video easily each video frame is evenly partitioned into smaller chunks which are called Macroblocks. Haskell, B. G., & Puri, A. (2012) proposed that Macroblock composed of a 16x16 block of luma and chroma. Chroma or Chrominance (C) is the color information of the picture. Luma or Luminance (Y) is the brightness of the light. Chrominance and Luminance collectively define the color of interest. In High Efficiency Video Coding (HEVC, one of the video compression standards; e.g. H.265, MPEG-H Part 2 etc.), a concept of Coding Tree Block has been introduced, which splits the Macroblocks into multiple Coding Blocks. B. Bing. (2015) shows simultaneously CB can be partitioned into transform blocks which can be used as input to linear block transform DCT in Video Codec, using which video compression is done.

A video can be composed of three types of frames:

- **Intra-Coded Frame or I-Frame:** This frame is popularly known as key frame. This frame is self-referential and doesn't use information of any other frame. These are largest frame amongst the three types of frames and possess high quality but less efficient in compression perspective.
- **Predicted Frame or P-Frame:** This frame is forward predicted from last P-frame or previous I-Frame. P-Frames are more efficient than I-Frame but not than B-Frame. This is inter-coded frame.
- **Bi-Directional Predicted Frame or B-Frame:** This is the most efficient frame among three; it looks forward and backward for redundant picture information. This is also inter-coded frame.

This prediction means to provide a motion vector to move the content of the frame one position to other in due course of the video stream. Motion vector can have a positive value which inclines to right or down ward motion and can have negative value which incline to left or upward motion.

Furht, B. et al. (1995) states that the prediction of macroblock in current frame depending on previous frame is called forward prediction and depending on future frame is known as backward prediction. A macroblock in current frame, F (m, n) is predicted by following expression:

$$F_P\left(m,n\right) = G\left(m + dx, n + dy\right) for \left(m,n\right) = \left\{8, -8\right\} \tag{1}$$

Figure 2. MPEG display order

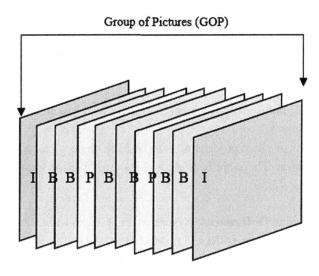

where, $F_P(m,n)$ is predicted current macroblock, $G(m,n)$ is the same macroblock in previous/future frame and (dx, dy) is estimated motion vector. For prediction, each Macroblock can be divided into one or multiple Prediction Block (PB).

There are two types of compression techniques: inter-frame and intra-frame. The inter-frame or temporal compression defines that a video is composed of group of frames that references each other. It requires more processing power to look back neighbor frames to display one frame. In case of intra-frame compression each frame is self-contained doesn't require looking back its neighbors. Group of pictures (GOP) specifies how inter-frame and intra-frames are arranged in a video. The below figure 2 reflects how different types of frames can compose a Group of Pictures (GOP).

The GOP pattern in a MPEG sequence is arbitrary. The intra-frames store all the information of a single image. There are in addition Predicted and Bidirectional frames. These P and B frames are the most of a GOP, but they do not take much space. Because they contain no independent image information, but only show changes to previous and subsequent frames.

SCENE CHANGE DETECTION

To hide secret data using video steganography process, a specific frame needs to be chosen by scene change detection method. A scene is collection of shots. In other words, a scene is unit of video which takes place at specific location in same time whereas a shot results from one continuous recording by a single camera. The gap between two shots is called shot boundaries. There are broadly two types of shot boundary detection method:

- **Abrupt Transition:** In this transition sudden transition from one shot to another happens. This is sometimes called hard cut or simply cut.
- **Gradual Transition:** This transition is correlated by spatial-chromatic effect which means one shot gradually replaces another one. This soft transition can be of different types like:

    ○   **Fade:** This can be fade-in or fade-out. The fade-in happens when the image is displayed from a black image and fade-out when an image fades to a black screen.

    ○   **Dissolve:** When fade-in and fade-out occurs one after another.

    ○   **Wipe:** When one frame wipes another frame, means during transition a virtual line going across the frame clearing the old one and displaying the new screen.

For illustration, a video from discovery channel has been taken and analyzed to show the abrupt and gradual scene change in Figure 3.

One of the important parts of video processing is to find the place where scene change happens. This is called scene change detection. There are four algorithms available for scene change detection, which are discussed as follows –

- **By Mean Absolute Frame Differences:** Xiaoquan Yi, & Nam Ling. (2005). tested the frames are by mean absolute frame differences (MAFD). MAFD provides dissimilarity measure between two consecutive frames. MAFD of nth frame can be given by:

$$MAFD^n = \frac{1}{xy} \sum_{p=0}^{x-1} \sum_{q=0}^{y-1} \left| f_n(p,q) - f_{n-1}(p,q) \right| \tag{2}$$

where x and y are the width and height of the frame, $f_n(p, q)$ is the intensity of pixel (p, q).

After MAFD test, other non-change frames are normalized through histogram equalization process and three other features are calculated like, signed difference of MAFD (SDMAFD), absolute difference of frame variance (ADFV), and mean absolute frame differences (MAFD') which are given by:

$$SDMAFD^n = MAFD^n - MAFD^{n-1} \tag{3}$$

$$ADFV^n = \left| \sigma_n - \sigma_{n-1} \right| \tag{4}$$

where, $\sigma_n = \frac{1}{xy} \sum_{p=0}^{x-1} \sum_{q=0}^{y-1} \left| f_n(p,q) - MAFD'^n \right|$ and σ_n known as Frame variance

Figure 3. Frame 399 – 404; the abrupt scene change detected at Frame 401 and 402 and gradual scene change occurs between Frame 399-401 or 402-404

In the second phase, after histogram equalization MAFD' calculated with equation (2).

- **By Likelihood Function:** Canagarajah, C. N. et al. (2001) have described a new method of abrupt scene change using likelihood function through the following formula

$$\lambda = \frac{\left[\frac{\sigma_i + \sigma_{i+1}}{2} + \left(\frac{\mu_i - \mu_{i+1}}{2} \right)^2 \right]^2}{\sigma_i \sigma_{i+1}} \tag{5}$$

where μ_i and μ_{i+1} are mean of intensities of two consecutive frames, σ_i and σ_{i+1} are corresponding variances, if λ exceeds certain threshold then an abrupt scene change can be considered.

- **By Histogram Correlation:** Radwan, N. I. et al. (2012) computes correlation between histogram of reference frame and all other frames. If change is sharp, then the correlation factor is high and for no scene change the factor is zero.
- **By Edge Change Ratio:** Zabih, R. et al. (1995). have used Edge change ratio (ECR) based cut detection. Let α_n is the number of edge pixels of frame n, C_n^{in} is the number of entering edge pixels of frame n and C_n^{out} is the number of exiting edge pixels of frame n,

$$ECR = \max \left(\frac{C_n^{in}}{\alpha_n}, \frac{C_{n-1}^{out}}{\alpha_{n-1}} \right) \tag{6}$$

RECENT WORKS ON VIDEO STEGANOGRAPHY

Spatial Domain Techniques

Least Significant Bit (LSB) approach is traditional spatial domain approach of steganography. In this approach, the cover video is decomposed into number of frames and a designated frame where data hiding will take place, has been converted to an image. Now the Least Significant Bit of each byte of that image is modified depending on the secret bit to be embedded. Figure 4 demonstrates the result of implementation of video steganography using 4 Least Significant Bit substitution method. The PSNR and SSIM between original secret and extracted secret have been calculated as 48.95 dB and SSIM 0.91 respectively.

Hash Based Least Significant Bit (LSB) Method

The most popular technique of steganography is Least Significant Bit (LSB) modification technique. This LSB technique has been also utilized in video steganography by different approaches. Deshmukh P. R., Rahangdale B. (2014) described a hash-based technique of LSB which is popularly abbreviated as HLSB technique. Riasat, R., Bajwa, I. S., & Ali, M. Z. (2011) have described that the hash function can be used to find out LSB position where the secret data will be stored.

Hash function is a function $h : P \rightarrow Q$ where the domain $P = \{0,1\}^*$ and $Q = \{0,1\}^n$ for some $n \geq 1$.

Sobti R., Geetha G. (2012) stated that, hash function compresses any arbitrary length numerical input to a fixed length numerical output as shown in figure 5.

There are broadly two types of hash functions keyed hash function and un-keyed hash function shown in figure 6. Keyed hash function requires a secret key and it is mainly used to create message digest. It has enormous application in message authentication. Popular hash functions are Message Digest (MD5) and Secure Hash Function (SHA).

Figure 4. Result of LSB substitution in Video

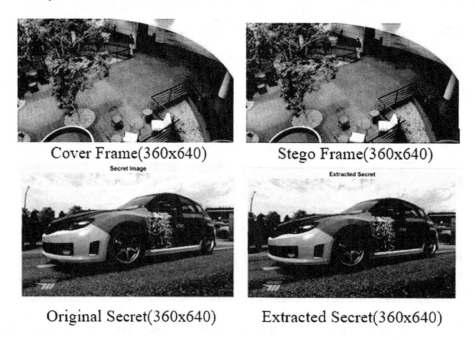

Cover Frame(360x640)   Stego Frame(360x640)

Original Secret(360x640)   Extracted Secret(360x640)

Figure 5. Hash Function

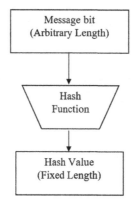

The hash function used in HLSB is called un-keyed hash function as it does not require any secret key. Specifically, One Way Hash Function is used here as it can be defined independently so far it meets the definition of hash function. Deshmukh P. R., Rahangdale B. (2014) have described hash function as:

$$h = m\%n \qquad (7)$$

where h is the LSB position where the hidden bit will be stored, m is the position of hidden bit in the message byte, n is the number of LSB used to hide data

Chaudhary, A., & Vasavada, J. (2012) have calculated R by a random number generator algorithm and skip R number of byte to select the message byte to be hidden next.

Random Number Generator Based LSB Method

In Bhole, A. T., & Patel, R. (2012) and Patel, R., & Patel, M. (2014) have discussed an approach called 'Random Byte Hiding' where a random number N is chosen to select the byte of a frame to be embedded. If the highest pixel value of each line of the specific frame is X, then it will select X+N position to store the secret information. In other case N-Y can be chosen for information hiding, in that case N will be higher than 256 so that N-Y not goes to negative. This random number is shared with intended recipient so that the message can be extracted from the stego object. Bhole, A. T., & Patel, R. (2012) used the secret is in text format and Patel, R., & Patel, M. (2014) used message is in video format.

Gosalia, S., Shetty,S. A. Revathi, S. (2016) have taken the secret as audio. Here a random number generator is required to select the frame of the video where the secret data will be stored. Once the frame is selected, secret data is embedded in the red component of selected video frame using LSB modification technique.

Figure 6. Different types of hash functions

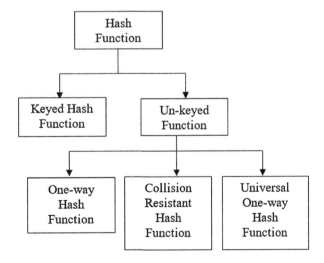

Symmetric Key Encryption Technique Using LSB

Yadav, P., Mishra, N., & Sharma, S. (2013) has encrypted the secret message which is in image format using Symmetric Key Encryption technique. In symmetric key encryption technique, a single key is used for encryption and decryption. Therefore, here author has decided one encryption key which has been shared with intended recipient for decryption as well. Here XOR is used as symmetric key encryption technique. First secret message is encrypted through XOR using encryption key. Then encoded in LSB of the selected frame in BGRRGBGR pattern where R, G, B are Red, Green, Blue color value of the pixel. This algorithm demonstrated in figure 7. The advantage of LSB method is the capacity and perceptual quality which are very high. Moreover, the security of this method is poor as LSB steganography is very prone to RS Steganalysis attack.

Using Artificial Neural Network

Neural Networks or Artificial Neural Networks (ANN) resembles the methods that are based on mathematical model of human brain. Schmidhuber, J. (2015) stated a standard ANN is composed of many connected processors called neurons. A Neural Network can be thought of as a network of Neurons arranged in layers. There is an input layer which is also known as predictor and output layer which is known as forecast. Each predictor attached to some coefficients known as 'weight'. These weights are adjustable

Figure 7. Block diagram of Symmetric Key Encryption technique in LSB Approach

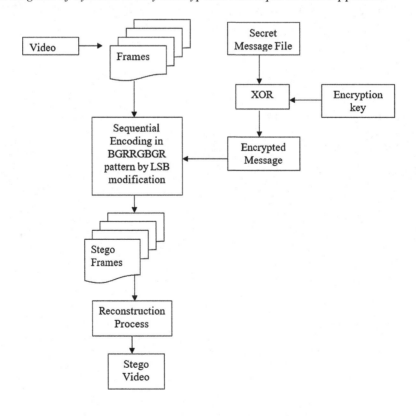

parameters. The weighted sum of input comprises activation of the neurons. This is called linear regression of ANN. If a new intermediate hidden layer is introduced which would work as transfer function, then the system becomes non-linear. According to Agatonovic-Kustrin, S., & Beresford, R. (2000). the activation signal passes through transfer function and produces a single output. The general diagram of a neural network is shown in figure 8. To configure the ANN such that it can produce intended set of output from given set of input, one must train the ANN through feeding teaching rule. After training it should perform accordingly. This is called supervised learning if the training set specifies the mechanism of what to perform upon getting what type of data. Otherwise if the teacher or supervisor is not available, only sample inputs are available and ANN itself discovers the pattern that is called unsupervised learning. Khare, R.et al. (2014). have used ANN for embedding and extraction of data in a video file. Here NN is trained to perform XOR, select the symmetric key and bit position.

Motion Vector Based Techniques

Motion Vectors are used to represent the Macroblock in a picture which is in another position of another reference picture. it is a key element of motion estimation of a video. Motion vectors can have different attributes like amplitude, phase angle etc.

Local Optimality

Cao, Y., et al. (2015b) have been described a method of video steganography where secret message embedded in motion vector by perturbing their motion estimation process. Here the author has utilized the fact that the local optimality is an important quality of motion vector which ensures block-based motion estimation. According to Pardalos, P. M., & Schnitger, G. (1988) it is known that local optimality is the solution to the local optimization problem which chooses either maximal or minimal values among the neighboring set of optimal solutions. Zhang, H., et al. (2016). described another approach of using local optimality through creating a search area composed of all candidate motion vectors. Then evaluating whole search area to select least contributing motion vector to hide the secret data.

Figure 8. General Block diagram of ANN

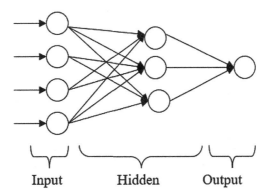

Using Motion Characteristic, Local Optimality, and Statistical Distribution

Wang, P., et al. (2016) defined a distortion function is using Motion Characteristic, Local Optimality and Statistical Distribution of motion vectors which is applied to macro block's motion to embed secret data onto cover video. It exploits the fact that the modifications in rich motion areas are less sensitive to draw human attention. This technique also uses two layered syndrome-trellis codes (STC) to reduce embedding impact on practical embedding implementation.

Using Linear Block Codes

Pan, F., et al. (2010) stated that linear block codes are used to embed secret data in motion vectors of cover video. Linear block codes are linear in nature, means the summation of any two linear codeword is also a codeword. This reduces the medication rate of motion vectors.

Uncertainty of Motion Estimation

Motion vectors can have some uncertainty in estimating motion. If the uncertainty is higher it is more suitable for modification as the distortion cannot make perceivable difference in human vision. Cao, Y., et al. (2015a) have utilized this fact. Let h and v denotes the horizontal and vertical component of motion vectors, then the embedding of data can be performed by equation (8).

$$\alpha\left(M_v\right) = LSB\left(h + v\right) \tag{8}$$

where $\alpha\left(M_v\right)$ returns all the motion vectors and LSB stands for Least Significant Bit.

Matrix Encoding

Motion vectors have some exceptional features of robustness, security, and blind detection. Hao-Bin, et al. (2011) have utilized this fact to conceal the data in the optimal component of motion vector using matrix encoding technique. Optimal component can be horizontal or vertical component. Motion vectors can be divided into two components: horizontal and vertical component, as shown in equation (9)

$$M_V = \sqrt{M_{V\_H}^2 + M_{V\_V}^2} \tag{9}$$

where, M_{V_H} and M_{V_V} represent horizontal component and vertical component of motion vector M_V respectively.

If the value of horizontal component is zero that incur the direction of movement of Macroblock is vertical, vice versa. Horizontal component of motion vector is very sensitive. It induces perceivable difference in slight modification. Therefore, in this paper secret message is embedded in motion vector by using phase angle (θ).

$$\theta = \tan^{-1}\left|\frac{M_{V\_V}}{M_{V\_H}}\right| \tag{10}$$

Macroblock Component

Jue, W., et al. (2011) have find out the luminance component of each Macroblock of P and B frames and embed the secret information in the luminance differences of each Macroblock of cover video.

Motion Histogram

Jose, J. A., & Titus, G. (2013) have described a method of creating motion histogram using PCRM (Pixel Change Ratio Map) and embedding secret data in the motion histogram. PCRM demonstrates the intensity of motion in a video sequence. It exploits the fact that human can only perceive the motion if the motion intensity is high and it persist for long time as stated by Yi, H., et al. (2005).

Motion Search Technique

Zhang, M., & Guo, Y. (2014) have proposed a method of hiding message data in a best possible motion vector when $M_V > T$, T is the threshold value. Kamp, S., et al. (2007) have defined following Lagrangian cost function to estimate the cost of the motion to choose the best possible motion vector.

$$Motion_{Cost} = SAD + \lambda \cdot r \tag{11}$$

Olivares, J., et al. (2004) defines the sum of Absolute Differences (SAD) is a quality measure of video. It is used for block matching and motion vector calculations. This adds up absolute differences between the candidate and reference block elements.

$$SAD = \sum_{p=1}^{N}\sum_{q=1}^{N}\left|C_{p,q} - Ref_{p,q}\right| \tag{12}$$

where, $C_{p,q}$ is the element of candidate block; $Ref_{p,q}$ is the element of reference block;

The variable λ is a dummy variable called a "Lagrange multiplier" used to find maxima and minima of a multivariate function $f(x_1, x_2, \ldots x_N)$. Here λ allows for a trade-off between motion vector rate and texture rate. r is the motion rate to encode the motion information.

The best motion vector is determined by minimizing the motion cost function in eq.(a) for all unique vectors of the final set. Rezagholipour, K., & Eshghi, M. (2016) have modified the above-mentioned approach using mean shift algorithm for motion object detection. Here the algorithm of secret embedding is same, but the embedding is done only on moving objects. These objects are tracked by mean shift algorithm. Yanming Xu. (2013) defined Mean shift algorithm which is a popular pattern matching algorithm. Here metric coefficient is used to measure similarity between target and reference. At every step object shifts and that is tracked by to detect moving object.

Perturbed Macroblock Partition

In this approach each macroblock is partitioned into smaller partitions which is called partition mode (PM). PMs can be 1st level and 2nd level. 1st level PM contains blocks of size 16×16, 16×8or 8 × 16and 2nd level PM contains block sizes equal to or less than 8×8.

$$\mathbb{P} = Partition\left(\mathbb{F}\right) = \left(P_1.P_2...P_n\right) \tag{13}$$

Where $\mathbb{F}$ is an inter-frame containing n inter-macroblocks

Zhang, H., et al. (2014) have applied Syndrome Trellis Code (STC) to embed secret message. STC is binary linear convolution code represented by parity–check matrix. Every codeword of STC, $C = \left\{z \in \left\{0,1\right\}^n \mid \mathbb{H}z = 0\right\}$ where the parity-check matrix $\mathbb{H} \in \left\{0,1\right\}^{m \times n}$, n is the length of STC and m is co-dimension

Filler, T., et al. (2011) stated that the application of STC in steganography is very useful as it minimizes the additive noise improving the stego quality as well as increase the embedding rate. This method is called perturbed because Macroblock partitioning is perturbed during inter-frame coding.

FREQUENCY DOMAIN TECHNIQUES

Thakur, V., & Saikia, M. (2013) have discussed a method of video steganography where DCT (Discreet Cosine Transform) has been performed on all the frames of the video and secret data is embedded in the higher order coefficient of the DCT. Moreover Mstafa, R. J., & Elleithy, K. M. (2015) have used DWT (Discreet Wavelet transform) to embed secret data which is BCH encoded before embedding. BCH ((Bose, Chaudhuri, and Hocquenghem) is a cyclic error correcting binary code. Jasim Mohammed, S. (2013) defines that an (n,k) BCH code encodes k bits message into n bits code word. Suppose the message is denoted by m(x), and then a polynomial g(x) can be created by $L.C.M\left(m_1\left(x\right), m_2\left(x\right)..., m_t\left(x\right)\right)$ where $t = 2^{p-1} \, and \, n = 2^p - 1$

Now the m(x) can be divided by g(x) and remainder is stored in r(x). Now the whole BCH encoded message will be, E(x) = m(x) +r(x). Mstafa, R. J., & Elleithy, K. M. (2015) also have used DWT to embed secret data which is BCH encoded only in face region of the frames of the cover video. This face region is detected by Kanade-Lucas-Tomasi (KLT) tracker which searches Harris Corners in the facial regions. Mstafa, R. J., & Elleithy, K. M. (2016a) and Mstafa, R. J., & Elleithy, K. M. (2016b) have used same algorithm demonstrated by Jasim Mohammed, S. (2013). However, they have embedded BCH encoded secret data in DCT coefficient of YUV space of cover video.

VARIOUS OTHER METHODS

Niu Ke, & Zhong Weidong. (2013) have utilized the Context Adaptive Variable Length Coding (CAVLC) which is used in H.264. Here the parity of trailing ones is checked, if found even then the codeword is 0 otherwise 1. In this algorithm, the data embedding is done using the codeword.

Munasinghe, A., et al. (2013) uses a method where message is converted into bytecode and then embedded into the carrier video file which is an uncompressed AVI file.

Moon, S. K., & Raut, R. D. (2013) have used 1 LSB,2 LSB and 4 LSB method to hide image and text behind a cover video file using authentication key. Moreover, they have done forensic check to enhance data security.

Abbas, S. A., et al. (2015) have proposed an innovative idea of video steganography utilizing Cuckoo Search (CS) Algorithm which is motivated by breeding behavior of cuckoos. Authors have chosen RGB values of cover frame by CS optimization algorithm and then using 3-3-2 LSB approach secret bit is embedded in cover frame. The first 3 bits of secret byte is embedded in least 3 significant bits of R component, next three bits of secret byte embedded in the 3 significant bits of G component and remaining 2 bits of secret byte embedded in least 2significant bits of B component.

Kaur, R., Pooja, & Varsha. (2016) have first encrypted the secret message using RSA algorithm. For first 4 bits of encrypted secret message embedded in the edge pixel of randomly selected video frame using 4LSB modification algorithm. The remaining 4 bits of secret message is embedded in non-edge pixel of randomly selected video frame using 7pair based identical match technique. This 7pairs based identical match technique says if there are 7 pair of identical bits among secret message byte and cover frame byte then author just keeping note of it otherwise using 2 LSB is used to hide bits of secret message.

Singh, D; Kanwal N. (2016) have used Local Binary pattern (LBP) to embed secret message in the chosen cluster of cover frame of the video. The fundamental idea of LBP is to sum up the local structure in an image by comparing each pixel with its neighborhood. For this purpose, authors have first created cluster of cover frame. Clustering is a method of partitioning group of data points into a small number of clusters. This has been done by k-means clustering algorithm. It is an unsupervised learning algorithm specifically used in data mining and machine learning purposes. The first step of this algorithm is to determine the number of cluster k and assume the centroid of these clusters. Then in the next step determine the distance of each object from the centroid. At the final step, one need to group the objects based on minimum distance.

Umadevi R. (2016) has proposed a joint approach (JA) for video steganography using irreversible and reversible methods. In irreversible methods of data hiding original cover is unavailable once data hiding is done whereas in reversible method cover can be recovered from the stego after extracting the secret message. Selvigrija, P., & Ramya, E. (2015) have embedded a video inside a video using linked list method. The linked list method is used by embedding the byte of information inside one 3*3pixel, the address of the location of next byte of information should be embedded next to it. Qian, L., et al. (2016) have used EMD – efficient modular arithmetic to propose a new technique of embedding namely Improved Matrix Embedding (IME). Seema, & Chaudhary, J. (2014) embedded secret through traditional LSB approach but frame selection is done through a novel approach of entropy evaluation. Entropy is evaluated by following equation:

$$E = -\sum_{i=1}^{GL} P(i) \log_2 \left(P(d_i) \right) \tag{14}$$

where, GL is gray level of the frame, P (d) is the probability of existence of gray level.

Seema, & Chaudhary, J. (2014) have identified N high entropy valued frame and split the secret in N parts. After that data embedding is done. Song, G., et al. (2014) have discussed a new technique of data hiding in video to reduce distortion drift using Multi-view coding video. Multi-view coding video is a video compression standard that includes efficient encoding.

Firmansyah, D. M., & Ahmad, T. (2016). have used neighboring similarity method for video steganography. First the frames are generated then the histograms of those frames are drawn, and peak point is identified. From original frames prediction error is calculated. By using peak point and prediction error secret message is embedded in the specific frame. Hu, S. D., & U, K. T. (2011) have used a non-uniform rectangular portioning algorithm to embed a secret video of same size into a cover video.

Mstafa, R. J., & Elleithy, K. M. (2015c) proposed an interesting method than the previous ones. Here the secret is encoded using Hamming codes (n, k). Then by using object tracking algorithm Region of Interest (ROI) which is motion object is identified. At last the encoded message is embedded in 1st and 2nd LSB of RGB pixel components for all motion objects in the cover video.

Sharifzadeh, M., & Schonfeld, D. (2015) worked in video steganography in accordance with video watermarking scheme. de Carvalho, et al. (2008) have used existing methods of video steganography used for integrity, privacy, and version control of confidential documents.

Idbeaa, T. F., Samad, S. A., & Husain, H. (2015) have used traditional pixel value differencing technique of steganography. They also improvised this technique by Enhanced pixel value differencing (EPVD) and try-way pixel value differencing (TPVD) techniques. In traditional PVD method, cover image is partitioned into two non-overlapping blocks of pixels. Then pixel value differences are calculated between two sets of pixels. The blocks with small differences locate in the smooth region and big differences lies in the sharp edge area. As per human visual perception, eyes can tolerate changes at sharp areas rather than smooth areas. So, the embedding is done in the high differences in the range table of PVD.

Hanafy, A. A., et al. (2008) segmented the secret message into blocks. Then the blocks are embedded in the pseudo-random locations of cover video frame generated by re-ordering of secret keys. Acharya, A. K., et al. (2013) have embedded secret data using LSB technique at the frame where scene changes take place. Histogram difference technique detects scene changes.

Liu, B., Liu, F., Yang, C., & Sun, Y. (2008) has proposed a compressed video secure steganography (CVSS) technique where secret data is embedded in the DC coefficient of the scene change point. Job, D., & Paul, V. (2016) have used Elliptic Curve Cryptography to encrypt secret data. Then this encrypted data is hidden in the cover object using Sudoku Matrix by Genetic Algorithm. Zhang, Y., et al. (2015) have performed Discrete Cosine Transform (DCT) on cover frame then the trailing coefficient of each quantized DCT block is obtained to embed secret information.

QUALITY ANALYSIS

'Quality Analysis' is a process of assuring quality. Here quality means degree of excellence of the proposed method. This quality can be determined through comparing a new object with a standard object. There are different types of method available for video steganography. To compare these algorithms, one needs some measures. There are two kinds of approach for measuring video quality: objective and subjective.

Objective Methods

Objective method of quality analysis measures the quality of new method against an existing method. These methods are repeatable and are not subject to human variation. The goal of objective methods is to model a mathematical formula that can predict the quality of an image accurately and automatically. An ideal objective method should be capable of mimicking the quality predictions of an average human observer. Based on the availability of a reference image which should be distortion-free and have perfect quality, the objective quality assessment methods can be classified into three categories. The first category is full-reference (FR) model where the undistorted, perfect quality reference image is fully available. The second category is reduced-reference(RR) model where the reference image is not fully available. The third category is no-reference(NR) model in which there is no access to the reference image.

Sarkar, A., Sullivan, K., & Manjunath, B. S. (2008) stated in objective testing, source and processed signal is mathematically compared and convey a score. In this approach quality of video steganography is analyzed by traditional full reference (FR) based quality measures like signal-to-noise ratio (SNR) and peak signal-to-noise ratio (PSNR). Full reference model is shown in Figure 9.

SNR (Signal-to-Noise Ratio)

The SNR also often written as S/N is a measure of signal strength relative to background noise. According to Poobathy, D., & Chezian, R. M. (2014) SNR can be given by:

$$SNR = \frac{Magnitude\,of\,Signal}{Variance\,of\,Noise} \tag{15}$$

The magnitude of the signal can be given by mean or average value of the signal. This can be formulated as:

$$\mu = \frac{1}{N}\sum_{i=1}^{N-1} x_i \tag{16}$$

where μ is the mean, N is the number of samples, i is the index in each sample x_i

The variance of noise can be given by standard deviation of the noise signal and can be formulated as:

Figure 9. Full Reference (FR) model

$$\sigma^2 = \frac{1}{N-1}\sum_{i=0}^{N-1}\left(x_i - \mu\right)^2 \tag{17}$$

where σ is the standard deviation.

PSNR (Peak-Signal-to-Noise Ratio)

PSNR is the ratio between the maximum possible power of a signal and power of corrupted signal. This can be derived by using Mean Squared Error (MSE). MSE can be calculated by original and distorted signal which depends on following formula according to Chikkerur, S., et al. (2011):

$$MSE = \frac{1}{Size\ of\ the\ video}\left[Original\ video - stego\ video\right]^2 \tag{18}$$

$$PSNR = 20\log_{10}\left(\frac{255}{\sqrt{MSE}}\right) \tag{19}$$

Other methods of objective testing are Structural Similarity Index for Video (VSSIM) and Video Quality Matrix (VQM).

Video Structural Similarity Metric (VSSIM)

Smith, S. W. (1997). states the philosophy behind SSIM is that Human Visual System(HVS) is very efficient in extracting structural information from viewing field. For an image structural information are attribute that reflect the structure of the objects in the scene which is independent of average luminance and contrast of the image. If the compared signals are m and n, then SSIM can be given by:

$$SSIM\left(m,n\right) = \frac{\left(2\mu_m\mu_n + C_1\right)\left(2\sigma_{mn} + C_2\right)}{\left(\mu_m^2 + \mu_n^2 + C_1\right)\left(\sigma_m^2 + \sigma_n^2 + C_2\right)} \tag{20}$$

where, μ_m is the mean of signal m and μ_n is the mean of signal n; σ_m is standard deviation of signal m and σ_n is standard deviation of signal n; σ_{mn} is cross correlation of m and n after removing their means, C_1 and C_2 are two constants and can be defined by:

$$C_1 = \left(k_1 L\right)^2 \text{ and } C_2 = \left(k_2 L\right)^2 \tag{21}$$

where k_1 and k_2 are very small two constants and L =255 for 8 bits/ pixel grayscale images.

Kaur, H., & Kaur, V. (2016) defines the VSSIM metric measures the quality of distorted video in three different levels like local region level, frame level and sequence level and given by equation (22):

$$SSIM\left(p,q\right) = W_Y SSIM^y\left(p,q\right) + W_{Cb} SSIM^{Cb}\left(p,q\right) + W_{Cr} SSIM^{Cr}\left(p,q\right) \tag{22}$$

where W_Y, W_{Cb} and W_{Cr} are weights for Y(Luminance), Cb (Chroma Blue) and Cr (Chroma Red) color components. The block diagram of SSIM algorithm has been shown in figure 10.

Video Quality Metric (VQM)

Wang, Z., Lu, L., & Bovik, A. C. (2004) defines VQM. VQM is a FR based objective metric to measure video quality of digital video system. This tool estimates how people perceive video quality. This draws correlation between objective and subjective approach where VQM purely treated as objective approach. Pinson, M. H., & Wolf, S. (2004) states the VQM algorithms compare the processed video (output) with the original video (input) using perceptual effects like blurring, jerky/unnatural motion, global noise, block distortion and color distortion.

The Table 1 provides comparison of aforesaid objective measures.

Figure 10. Block diagram of the SSIM algorithm as shown in Wang et al., 2004

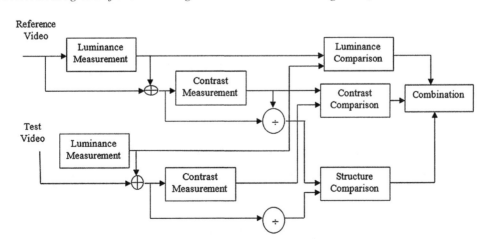

Subjective Methods

Subjective methods or psychophysical experiments are the most accurate method of measuring video quality. Here many subjects or observers are asked to watch the set of input video signals and give their judgment depending on their quality of perceived annoyance. The judgments are collected and averaged to get the Mean Opinion Score (MOS) which is key output of subjective testing as described by Q. Farias, M. C. (2010).

Scales for Different Subjective Methods

There are different subjective methods available, like DSIS, DSCQS, SSCQE etc., the scales of those respective methods have been shown in Table 2, Table 3 and Table 4.

Table 1. Comparison of objective measures

Quality Metric	Mathematical Complexity	Correlation With Subj. Methods	Accessibility
SNR	Simple	Poor	Easy
PSNR	Simple	Poor	Easy
VSSIM	Complex	Fair	Available
VQM	Very Complex	Good	Available as a tool

Table 2. Double stimulus impairment scale (DSIS)

Scale	The Presentation Structure
5 imperceptible, 4 perceptible, but not annoying, 3 slightly annoying, 2 annoying, 1 very annoying.	(reference video sequence, processed video sequence, Vote)

Table 3. Double stimulus continuous quality scale (DSCQS)

Scale	The Presentation Structure
• excellent (80–100) • good (60–79) • fair (40–59) • poor (20–39) • bad (10–19)	(reference video sequence, processed video sequence, reference video sequence, processed video sequence, vote)

Table 4. Single stimulus continuous quality evaluation (SSCQE)

Scale	The Presentation Structure
• 5 excellent, • 4 good • 3 fair • 2 poor • 1 bad	(processed video sequence, vote)

Quality Metrics

There are different metrics available for quality analysis. Metrics means a standard of measurement. This metrics provides different quality criteria of a proposed algorithm. For video steganography, several quality metrics are used, which are discussed as follows:

Hiding Data Ratio (per Frame)

The hiding ratio can be defined by:

$$Hiding\ Ratio = \frac{Hidden\ Bytes}{Frame\ size} \tag{23}$$

This ratio gives how much secret byte can be hidden in a cover frame.

Capacity

Steganographic capacity is the maximal message length that can be embedded without producing perceptually or statistically detectable distortions in the stego object. Shannon Channel Capacity can formulate this as follows:

$$C = B_w \log_2 \left(1 + \frac{S}{N} \right) \tag{24}$$

where C is the steganographic capacity, B_w is the bandwidth of the channel, S is the signal power of secret message and N is the signal power of the noise.

Error Bit Rate (EBR)

The performance of extraction of secret message in video steganography is measured by Error Bit rate. The received bits may be modified due to interference, noise, and distortion. EBR is a given by following formula,

$$EBR = \frac{No.\ of\ modified\ Bits\ received}{Total\ Number\ of\ transferred\ bits} \tag{25}$$

EBR has no dimension and measured in percentage decreases with the decrease of steganography payload capacity. When payload is less than channel capacity EBR is moderately low as given in Uhrina, M., Hlubik, J., & Vaculik, M. (2013).

Changes in Bit Rate (Encryption Time and Decryption Time)

Time required embedding secret data in cover object known as Encryption Time and time required to decrypt secret data from stego object.

False Positive Rate (FPR)

In video steganography, a video is divided into number of frames and one of those frames is chosen to hide secret data. FPR denotes the ratio of incorrectly classifying a frame as stego, which is given by Umadevi R. (2016):

$$FPR = \frac{Incorrectly\ Classified\ as\ stego}{No.\ of\ Frames} \times 100 \tag{26}$$

ROBUSTNESS MEASUREMENT: STEGANALYSIS ATTACKS ON VIDEO

Steganalysis is a method of detecting presence of covert or secret data in a stego object. These methods are also known as steganalysis attack, by which robustness of the steganography methods can be determined. Generally, there are 7 different types of attacks applied on video, discussed as follows:

- **Cropping:** Cropping is removal of part of Video Frame. This can be done by rectangular area which has top, bottom, left and right coordinate specified. This is required for improving framing, accentuate subject matter or change aspect ratio.
- **Rotation:** Rotation is rotating a Video Frame in θ angle about its origin. It can be performed by computing the inverse transformation for every pixel. This is to improve the visual appearance of a Video Frame.
- **Resizing:** Resizing or scaling of an Video Frame is changing size of the image either increasingly or decreasingly. The number of pixels doesn't change in this case. The difference between pixels either increased or decreased respective to requirement. That is why it is much easier to downsize a Video Frame than larger size. If it is not captured with high resolution is not possible to enlarge the image.
- **Histogram Equalization:** An histogram is a depiction of tonal distribution of a Video Frame. Histogram equalization is a technique of adjusting image intensities. It is used to enhance the contrast.
- **JPEG Compression:** Compression means reducing volume. JPEG (Joint Photographic Experts Group) is a standard of compressing Video Frame.
- **Gaussian Noise:** Adding Gaussian noise to a Video Frame.
- **Gaussian Low Pass and Median Filter:** Filters are used to remove noise and reduce the contrast. Various tests have proved that Gaussian filter is faster than Median filter.

Figure 11 demonstrates all these attacks are performed on a frame.

Figure 11. Attacks on video frame (a) Random cropping (b) Rotation(c) Resize (d) Adding White Gaussian Noise (e) Filtering (f) Histogram equalization

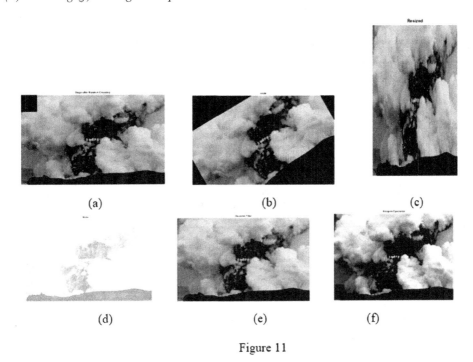

Figure 11

SUGGESTED FUTURE WORK

Depending on the existing literature and comparison results as shown in Table 5, few future scopes of work in video steganography has been suggested as below:

- Video Steganography work can be done in Macroblock as this technique ensures better steganographic capacity. Not only that if transform domain is used for data embedding then perceptual transparency can be better maintained.
- Moreover, there are very less work done using Elliptical Curve Cryptography and Genetic Algorithm.
- Another topic discussed as Joint Approach which can be more explored for novel techniques of video steganography.
- Frequency domain can be more practiced to evolve new ideas.
- New methods for scene change detection or key frame identification can be applied to existing method of video steganography.
- Background subtraction technique can be explored which is recent area in video steganography.
- There is very less work who have encrypted secret before embedding which can be done using Arnold Transform, Lorenz chaotic encryption, Fibonacci encryption and many more.
- Moreover, the robustness test has not been performed for all discussed methods. This could be a future work to make the existing methods more robust. Other than these, no work has been performed till now in HD Video (High Definition) which can be a significant practical work in this domain.

Table 5. Comparative Analysis of few Video Steganography Methods

Methods as per Reference	Secret Embedding Capacity	Quality Result	Robustness Against Steganalysis Attacks	Method Features
Bhole et al. (2012)	Low embedding capacity (0.2%)	PSNR 36.17 dB	Not robust against noise addition and compression attack	Cover/Secret Pre-processing not required
Hanafy, A. A., et al. (2008)	Low embedding capacity (0.65%)	PSNR 51.45 dB	Not robust against noise addition and compression attack	Cover and Secret has been randomized
Hu et al. (2011)	Moderate embedding capacity (1.5%)	PSNR 29.13 dB	Not robust against noise addition and compression attack	Secret has been partitioned non-uniformly
Jue, W., et al. (2011)	Low embedding capacity (~0.16%)	PSNR 36.57 dB	Robust against compression attack	Cover/Secret Pre-processing not required
Liu et al. (2008)	Low embedding capacity (~0.12%)	PSNR 36.27 dB	Robust against compression attack	Secret has been encrypted
Moon et al. (2013)	High embedding capacity (12.5%)	PSNR 31.03 dB	Not robust against noise addition and compression attack	Secret has been encrypted
Pan et al. (2010)	Low embedding capacity (~0.12%)	PSNR 37.25 dB	Robust against compression attack	Cover/Secret Pre-processing not required
Patel et al. (2014)	High embedding capacity (12.3%)	PSNR 31.53 dB	Not robust against noise addition and compression attack	Secret has been encrypted by Rijndael 256
Yanming Xu. (2013).	Low embedding capacity (~0.14%)	PSNR 34.41 dB	Robust against compression attack	Cover/Secret Pre-processing not required
Wang et al. (2004)	Low embedding capacity (0.57%)	PSNR 37.25 dB	Robust against compression attack	Cover/Secret Pre-processing not required

CONCLUSION

This article is a review of existing methods of video steganography. There are various approaches in video steganography. Here only significant works has been considered for discussion. This work reveals the probable areas of work done and not done which opens scopes of novel future works of video steganography. In this current article different spatial and frequency domain techniques are analyzed. Other than that, intra frame prediction, inter-frame prediction, motion vector-based techniques also have been discussed. The paper organized thee recent work in video steganography into spatial domain techniques, motion vector-based techniques and frequency domain technique. Not only that, discussion about scene change detection also has been made with few available and popular techniques. This open up the way to invent new scene change detection techniques. Although most of the specific work has been discussed, the compressed domain of video is not explored in this paper. There a future work can be carried out only on the compressed domain.

REFERENCES

Abbas, S. A., El Arif, T. I. B., Ghaleb, F. F. M., & Khamis, S. M. (2015). *Optimized video steganography using Cuckoo Search algorithm.* IEEE. doi:10.1109/IntelCIS.2015.7397279

Acharya, A. K., Paul, R., Batham, S., & Yadav, V. K. (2013). *Hiding large amount of data using a new approach of video steganography.* Institution of Engineering and Technology. 10.1049/cp.2013.2338

Agatonovic-Kustrin, S., & Beresford, R. (2000). Basic concepts of artificial neural network (ANN) modeling and its application in pharmaceutical research. *Journal of Pharmaceutical and Biomedical Analysis*, *22*(5), 717–727. doi:10.1016/S0731-7085(99)00272-1 PMID:10815714

Bhole, A. T., & Patel, R. (2012). *Steganography over video file using Random Byte Hiding and LSB technique.* IEEE. doi:10.1109/ICCIC.2012.6510230

Bing, B. (2015). *Video Coding Fundamentals, Next-Generation Video Coding and Streaming.* Hoboken, NJ: John Wiley & Sons, Inc.; doi:10.1002/9781119133346.ch2

Canagarajah, C. N., Faernando, W. A. C., & Bull, D. R. (2001). Scene change detection algorithms for content-based video indexing and retrieval. *Electronics & Communication Engineering Journal*, *13*(3), 117–126. doi:10.1049/ecej:20010302

Cao, Y., Zhang, H., Zhao, X., & Yu, H. (2015a). Covert Communication by Compressed Videos Exploiting the Uncertainty of Motion Estimation. *IEEE Communications Letters*, *19*(2), 203–206. doi:10.1109/LCOMM.2014.2387160

Cao, Y., Zhang, H., Zhao, X., & Yu, H. (2015b). *Video Steganography Based on Optimized Motion Estimation Perturbation.* ACM Press. doi:10.1145/2756601.2756609

Chaudhary, A., & Vasavada, J. (2012). *A hash based approach for secure keyless image steganography in lossless RGB images.* IEEE. doi:10.1109/ICUMT.2012.6459795

Chikkerur, S., Sundaram, V., Reisslein, M., & Karam, L. J. (2011). Objective Video Quality Assessment Methods: A Classification, Review, and Performance Comparison. *IEEE Transactions on Broadcasting*, *57*(2), 165–182. doi:10.1109/TBC.2011.2104671

de Carvalho, D. F., Chies, R., Freire, ·A. P., Martimiano, L. A. F., & Goularte, R. (2008). *Video steganography for confidential documents: integrity, privacy and version control.* ACM Press. doi:10.1145/1456536.1456578

Deshmukh, P. R., & Rahangdale, B. (2014). Hash Based Least Significant Bit Technique For Video Steganography. *Int. Journal of Engineering Research and Applications, 4*(1), 44-49.

Farias, Q. M. C. (2010). Video Quality Metrics. In F. De (Ed.), Digital Video. InTech. doi:10.5772/8038

Filler, T., Judas, J., & Fridrich, J. (2011). Minimizing Additive Distortion in Steganography Using Syndrome-Trellis Codes. *IEEE Transactions on Information Forensics and Security*, *6*(3), 920–935. doi:10.1109/TIFS.2011.2134094

Firmansyah, D. M., & Ahmad, T. (2016). *An improved neighbouring similarity method for video steganography*. IEEE. doi:10.1109/CITSM.2016.7577528

Furht, B., Smoliar, S. W., & Zhang, H. (1995). *Video and Image Processing in Multimedia Systems*. Boston, MA: Springer US. doi:10.1007/978-1-4615-2277-5

Gosalia, S., Shetty, S. A., & Revathi, S. (2016). Embedding Audio inside a Digital Video Using LSB Steganography. *3rd IEEE International Conference on Computing for Sustainable Global Development (INDIACom)*, 2650 – 2653.

Gupta Banik, B., & Bandyopadhyay, S. K. (2015). Review on Steganography in Digital Media. *International Journal of Science and Research, 4*(2), 265–274. doi:10.21275/SUB151127

Hanafy, A. A., Salama, G. I., & Mohasseb, Y. Z. (2008). *A secure covert communication model based on video steganography*. IEEE. doi:10.1109/MILCOM.2008.4753107

Hao-Bin, Li-Yi, & Wei-Dong. (2011). *A novel steganography algorithm based on motion vector and matrix encoding*. IEEE. 10.1109/ICCSN.2011.6013622

Haskell, B. G., & Puri, A. (2012). MPEG Video Compression Basics. In L. Chiariglione (Ed.), *The MPEG Representation of Digital Media* (pp. 7–38). New York, NY: Springer New York. doi:10.1007/978-1-4419-6184-6_2

Hu, S. D., & U, K. T. (2011). *A Novel Video Steganography Based on Non-Uniform Rectangular Partition*. IEEE. 10.1109/CSE.2011.24

Idbeaa, T. F., Samad, S. A., & Husain, H. (2015). *An adaptive compressed video steganography based on pixel-value differencing schemes*. IEEE. doi:10.1109/ATC.2015.7388379

Jasim Mohammed, S. (2013). Implementation of Encoder for (31, k) Binary BCH Code based on FPGA for Multiple Error Correction Control. *International Journal of Computers and Applications, 76*(11), 23–28. doi:10.5120/13291-0815

Job, D., & Paul, V. (2016). *An efficient video Steganography technique for secured data transmission*. IEEE. doi:10.1109/SAPIENCE.2016.7684125

Jose, J. A., & Titus, G. (2013). *Data hiding using motion histogram*. IEEE. doi:10.1109/ICCCI.2013.6466269

Jue, W., Min-qing, Z., & Juan-li, S. (2011). *Video steganography using motion vector components*. IEEE. doi:10.1109/ICCSN.2011.6013642

Kamp, S., Heyden, D., & Ohm, J.-R. (2007). *Inter-temporal vector prediction for motion estimation in scalable video coding*. IEEE. doi:10.1109/ISPACS.2007.4445955

Kaur, Pooja, & Varsha. (2016). *A hybrid approach for video steganography using edge detection and identical match techniques*. IEEE. 10.1109/WiSPNET.2016.7566255

Kaur, H., & Kaur, V. (2016). *Invisible video multiple watermarking using optimized techniques*. IEEE. doi:10.1109/GET.2016.7916675

Ke, N., & Zhong, W. (2013). *A video steganography scheme based on H.264 bitstreams replaced.* IEEE. doi:10.1109/ICSESS.2013.6615345

Khare, R., Mishra, R., & Arya, I. (2014). *Video Steganography Using LSB Technique by Neural Network.* IEEE. doi:10.1109/CICN.2014.189

Liu, B., Liu, F., Yang, C., & Sun, Y. (2008). *Secure Steganography in Compressed Video Bitstreams.* IEEE. doi:10.1109/ARES.2008.140

Moon, S. K., & Raut, R. D. (2013). *Analysis of secured video steganography using computer forensics technique for enhance data security.* IEEE. doi:10.1109/ICIIP.2013.6707677

Mstafa, R. J., & Elleithy, K. M. (2015). *A high payload video steganography algorithm in DWT domain based on BCH codes (15, 11).* IEEE. doi:10.1109/WTS.2015.7117257

Mstafa, R. J., & Elleithy, K. M. (2015). *A novel video steganography algorithm in the wavelet domain based on the KLT tracking algorithm and BCH codes.* IEEE. doi:10.1109/LISAT.2015.7160192

Mstafa, R. J., & Elleithy, K. M. (2015c). *A New Video Steganography Algorithm Based on the Multiple Object Tracking and Hamming Codes.* IEEE. doi:10.1109/ICMLA.2015.117

Mstafa, R. J., & Elleithy, K. M. (2016a). *A DCT-based robust video steganographic method using BCH error correcting code.* IEEE. doi:10.1109/LISAT.2016.7494111

Mstafa, R. J., & Elleithy, K. M. (2016b). *A novel video steganography algorithm in DCT domain based on hamming and BCH codes.* IEEE. doi:10.1109/SARNOF.2016.7846757

Munasinghe, A., Dharmaratne, A., & De Zoysa, K. (2013). *Video steganography.* IEEE. doi:10.1109/ICTer.2013.6761155

Olivares, J., Hormigo, J., Villalba, J., & Benavides, I. (2004). Minimum Sum of Absolute Differences Implementation in a Single FPGA Device. In J. Becker, M. Platzner, & S. Vernalde (Eds.), *Field Programmable Logic and Application* (Vol. 3203, pp. 986–990). Berlin: Springer Berlin Heidelberg. doi:10.1007/978-3-540-30117-2_112

Pan, F., Xiang, L., Yang, X.-Y., & Guo, Y. (2010). *Video steganography using motion vector and linear block codes.* IEEE. doi:10.1109/ICSESS.2010.5552283

Pardalos, P. M., & Schnitger, G. (1988). Checking local optimality in constrained quadratic programming is NP-hard. *Operations Research Letters*, *7*(1), 33–35. doi:10.1016/0167-6377(88)90049-1

Patel, R., & Patel, M. (2014). *Steganography over video file by hiding video in another video file, random byte hiding and LSB technique.* IEEE. doi:10.1109/ICCIC.2014.7238343

Pinson, M. H., & Wolf, S. (2004). A New Standardized Method for Objectively Measuring Video Quality. *IEEE Transactions on Broadcasting*, *50*(3), 312–322. doi:10.1109/TBC.2004.834028

Poobathy, D., & Chezian, R. M. (2014). Edge Detection Operators: Peak Signal to Noise Ratio Based Comparison. International Journal of Image. *Graphics and Signal Processing*, *6*(10), 55–61. doi:10.5815/ijigsp.2014.10.07

Qian, L., Li, Z., Zhou, P., & Chen, J. (2016). *An Improved Matrix Encoding Steganography Algorithm Based on H.264 Video*. IEEE. doi:10.1109/CSCloud.2016.8

Radwan, N. I., Salem, N. M., & El Adawy, M. I. (2012). Histogram Correlation for Video Scene Change Detection. In D. C. Wyld, J. Zizka, & D. Nagamalai (Eds.), *Advances in Computer Science, Engineering & Applications* (Vol. 166, pp. 765–773). Berlin: Springer Berlin Heidelberg; doi:10.1007/978-3-642-30157-5_76

Read, P., & Meyer, M.-P. (2000). *Restoration of Motion Picture Film*. Burlington: Elsevier. Retrieved from http://www.123library.org/book_details/?id=36001

Rezagholipour, K., & Eshghi, M. (2016). *Video steganography algorithm based on motion vector of moving object*. IEEE. doi:10.1109/IKT.2016.7777764

Riasat, R., Bajwa, I. S., & Ali, M. Z. (2011). *A hash-based approach for colour image steganography*. IEEE. doi:10.1109/ICCNIT.2011.6020886

Sarkar, A., Sullivan, K., & Manjunath, B. S. (2008). Steganographic capacity estimation for the statistical restoration framework. Academic Press. doi:10.1117/12.767841

Schmidhuber, J. (2015). Deep learning in neural networks: An overview. *Neural Networks*, *61*, 85–117. doi:10.1016/j.neunet.2014.09.003 PMID:25462637

Seema, & Chaudhary, J. (2014). *A Multi Phase Model to Improve Video Steganography*. IEEE. 10.1109/CICN.2014.158

Selvigrija, P., & Ramya, E. (2015). *Dual steganography for hiding text in video by linked list method*. IEEE. doi:10.1109/ICETECH.2015.7275018

Sharifzadeh, M., & Schonfeld, D. (2015). *Statistical and information-theoretic optimization and performance bounds of video steganography*. IEEE. doi:10.1109/ALLERTON.2015.7447179

Singh, D., & Kanwal, N. (2016) Dynamic video steganography using LBP on CIELAB based K-means clustering. *International Conference on Computing for Sustainable Global Development (INDIACom)*, 2684 – 2689.

Smith, S. W. (1997). *The scientist and engineer's guide to digital signal processing* (1st ed.). San Diego, CA: California Technical Pub.

Sobti, R., & Geetha, G. (2012). Cryptographic Hash Functions: A Review. *International Journal of Computer Science Issues, 9*(2).

Song, G., Li, Z., Zhao, J., Tu, H., & Cheng, J. (2014). *A video steganography algorithm for MVC without distortion drift*. IEEE. doi:10.1109/ICALIP.2014.7009893

Thakur, V., & Saikia, M. (2013). *Hiding secret image in video*. IEEE. doi:10.1109/ISSP.2013.6526892

Uhrina, M., Hlubik, J., & Vaculik, M. (2013). Correlation between Objective and Subjective Methods Used for Video Quality Evaluation. *Advances in Electrical and Electronic Engineering*, *11*(2). doi:10.15598/aeee.v11i2.775

Umadevi, R. (2016). Joint Approach For Secure Communication Using Video Steganography. *3rd International Conference on Computing for Sustainable Global Development (INDIACom)*, 3104 – 3106.

Wang, P., Zhang, H., Cao, Y., & Zhao, X. (2016). *A Novel Embedding Distortion for Motion Vector-Based Steganography Considering Motion Characteristic, Local Optimality and Statistical Distribution.* ACM Press. doi:10.1145/2909827.2930801

Wang, Z., Lu, L., & Bovik, A. C. (2004). Video quality assessment based on structural distortion measurement. *Signal Processing Image Communication*, *19*(2), 121–132. doi:10.1016/S0923-5965(03)00076-6

Xu, Y. (2013). *An improved mean-shift moving object detection and tracking algorithm based on segmentation and fusion mechanism.* IEEE. doi:10.1109/SPC.2013.6735136

Yadav, P., Mishra, N., & Sharma, S. (2013). *A secure video steganography with encryption based on LSB technique.* IEEE. doi:10.1109/ICCIC.2013.6724212

Yi, H., Rajan, D., & Chia, L.-T. (2005). A new motion histogram to index motion content in video segments. *Pattern Recognition Letters*, *26*(9), 1221–1231. doi:10.1016/j.patrec.2004.11.011

Yi, X., & Ling, N. (2005). *Fast Pixel-Based Video Scene Change Detection.* IEEE. doi:10.1109/ISCAS.2005.1465369

Zabih, R., Miller, J., & Mai, K. (1995). *A feature-based algorithm for detecting and classifying scene breaks.* ACM Press. doi:10.1145/217279.215266

Zhang, F., & Zhang, X. (2014). EBR Analysis of Digital Image Watermarking. In S. Patnaik & X. Li (Eds.), *Proceedings of International Conference on Computer Science and Information Technology (Vol. 255, pp. 11–18)*. New Delhi: Springer India. 10.1007/978-81-322-1759-6_2

Zhang, H., Cao, Y., & Zhao, X. (2016). Motion vector-based video steganography with preserved local optimality. *Multimedia Tools and Applications*, *75*(21), 13503–13519. doi:10.100711042-015-2743-x

Zhang, H., Cao, Y., Zhao, X., Zhang, W., & Yu, N. (2014). *Video steganography with perturbed macroblock partition.* ACM Press. doi:10.1145/2600918.2600936

Zhang, M., & Guo, Y. (2014). *Video steganography algorithm with motion search cost minimized.* IEEE. doi:10.1109/ICIEA.2014.6931298

Zhang, Y., Zhang, M., Niu, K., & Liu, J. (2015). *Video Steganography Algorithm Based on Trailing Coefficients.* IEEE. doi:10.1109/INCoS.2015.47

Chapter 5
Reversible Data Hiding:
An Active Forensic Framework for Digital Images

Mehul S. Raval
Ahmedabad University, India

ABSTRACT

The chapter presents an application of reversible data hiding for the authentication of image travelling over a hostile and insecure communication channel. The reversible data resides in the image and tracks any changes done to it on a communication channel. The extraction of data and any modification to its structure reveals changes in the image. This allows the use of data hiding for forensic purpose. The reversible data hiding provides an additional advantage along with active forensics. The image regains original form after removal of the embedded data. However, reversible data hiding is an interplay between the image quality and watermarking capacity. The chapter presents the generic framework for data hiding and discusses its special case reversible data hiding. It presents capacity-behavior analysis of the difference expansion scheme. It performs in-depth analysis on the type of predictor and its impact on the capacity of the reversible data hiding scheme. Finally, the chapter presents a case study to showcase the use of reversible data hiding for image authentication.

INTRODUCTION

Digital forensics deals with the idea of investigating and analysing digital data (Popescu, Farid, 2004; Farid, Lyu, 2003). The process involves data collection, preservation, analysis, and present an evidence in the suitable forum. The digital forensics is useful in variety of applications like network vulnerability testing, fraud detection, crime detection, counterintelligence, law enforcement, and intrusion detection (Watson, Dehghantanha, 2016; Franke et al., 2018). One of the prime requirement during forensic process is to prevent a change in the evidence.

The domain of digital forensics can be broadly categorized into:

1. Active forensics
2. Passive forensics

DOI: 10.4018/978-1-5225-7107-0.ch005

Figure 1. Domain of digital forensics

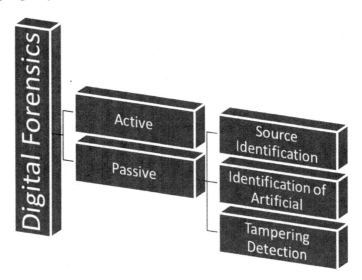

The active forensic is a proactive measure while the passive forensic is a retroactive measure. In case of active forensic an attack is anticipated, and data is prepared to negate the attack (Conti et al., 2018). A countermeasure to thwart the attack is built into the forensic framework. The example of the active forensics is a digital watermarking. It supports the application of copyright protection and authentication. The active forensics requires an explicit knowledge about the host signal and it can be made stronger by exploiting the information about the host. The classification of digital forensics is shown in Figure 1.

Passive Forensics

On another hand, the passive forensic establish the tell-tale after the manipulation is applied to the data. It is based on the primary assumption that digital content has a native statistical flavour, which remains consistent. Such statistical patterns are very closely related to the physical process generating the content (Sommer, 2018; Dilijonaite et al. 2017). Passive forensics, believes that any tampering will change statistical fidelity of the content. Even-though changes are perceptually invisible, but they can be tracked by performing statistical analysis of the content. The analysis is independent of any side information about the content. Therefore, this type of forensics is termed as passive as it does not need any information about the content.

The passive forensics is mainly divided into three broad categories as shown in Fig.1. The categories are as follows:

1. Image source identification.
2. Classifying computer generated and natural images.
3. Tampering detection.

Image source identification (Wang et al. 2017) is based on the premise that device captures and leave the tell-tale pattern in the image. This pattern can be used as a fingerprint or signature for the device and it links device with the image. Each device has unique fingerprint; therefore, it can be used to establish one to one relationship between signature and the image (Pomponiu, Cavagnino, & Botta, 2018).

The second category of passive forensics deals in segregating natural and computer-generated images. A sophistication in software and hardware has enables generation of near real images. With the digital domain penetrating the social life misuse of computer-generated fake images can wreak havoc for the individual. Therefore, it is utmost necessary to develop a mechanism to separate real and computer-generated images. Usually, this is a very good application of the machine learning which is based on using statistical features present in natural images or acquisition device characteristics.

The third type of passive forensic discovers tampering in the digital content. Again, with the sophistication of tools, an image can change without leaving any perceptual trail. However, addition or deletion of the digital portion significantly affect statistics of the image. The idea is to detect such changes and localize tampering in the image. Many interesting methods are available but they all pertain to a specific solution. The universal framework for detection of artefacts is yet to evolve.

Challenges in Digital Forensics

The digital forensics mechanism faces several challenges (Franke et al., 2018; Hamm et al. 2018).

- The design should be robust against the anti-forensic measures and it should not allow evidence tampering.
- It may have a predictive mechanism to anticipate attacks and provide feedback to the system.
- It should collect and process the evidence cleanly and mechanism should not be spoofed by misleading information.
- Forensic measures must reduce the investigation time and facilitate early detection.
- It must be able to present the evidence in the court of law for enforcement and facilitate speedy trial.

The law enforcement based on digital forensics is concerned with two important aspects. The integrity of the digital evidence and its authenticity; which is an ability to confirm the former. Authenticity and integrity are important aspects as digital data can be duplicated easily in a modern era. The integrity ensures that evidence has not been modified during the forensic process. The authenticity, on the other hand, is a guarantee that integrity is preserved while travelling from a crime scene, through analysis phase and finally when it reaches court. Usually, data hiding methods are seen as an anti-forensic measure (Pomponiu, Cavagnino, & Botta, 2018). Conventionally it is seen as a measure to spoof the digital forensic mechanism. However, this chapter present data hiding technique as a pro-forensic measure. It investigates the use of reversible data hiding technique for checking integrity and authenticity. The data hiding can be applied to any digital content but in this chapter digital images are used as a host signal. The broad objectives of the chapter are:

- Introduce generic framework of data hiding.
- Motivate use of reversible data hiding technique as an active forensic tool.
- Discuss process to implement reversible data hiding scheme for authentication.
- Show means to improve forensic ability of the reversible data hiding technique.

Goals of Data Security

The goals of data security are confidentiality, integrity, and availability. The measure of confidentiality relates to the protection of data against unauthorised access. The integrity protection ensures data consistency on the channel. Its preservation means received data is same as the transmitted one. The authenticity guarantees the integrity preservation. The availability means that system is available for use as and when required by the authorised user. The hacker may exploit a vulnerability and threatens data security. The attacks like snooping on a channel, measuring traffic flow and its analyses cause the significant threat to the confidentiality. The attacks like masquerading, replay, repudiation, and modification of content pose a significant threat to integrity. The masquerading means impersonating an authorised user to gain access to the data or system resources. The replay attack involves capturing data sent by an authorised user and use it later to gain access to the system. The denial of service attack (DoS) poses a significant threat to availability. This attack disrupts the normal communication and even disrupt the network. Data hiding can be used as a tool to overcome many of the above security threats specifically to confidentiality and data integrity on a transmission channel.

DATA HIDING

Secure transmission of information has always been very important to mankind. Secret writing is traced back to ancient China, India, and Greece. Interesting discussions on the history of data hiding is available in (Swanson, Kobayashi, & Tewfik, 2009; Petitcolas, Anderson, & Kuhn, 1999). Ancient Chinese rulers were known to communicate secretly by writing the messages in thin sheets of silk or paper. Several ancient Indian texts (for example, Kautilya's Artha-Shastra, which dates back to 321-300 BCE) discusses in detail the art of covert communication. There is the historical evidence that covert communication is as old as the civilization itself. Trithemius, in 1500 A.D., defined the term steganography (secret writing) in his book Steganographia (Tanaka, Nakamura, & Matsui, 1990). There are several examples of secret communication in history, such as the use of invisible inks, or writing a message on a shaved head and then growing the hair.

Usually, data hiding is useful for the following:

- Protecting important information
- Keeping information secret
- Setting up a trap

As pertinent, one of the goals of the data hiding is to protect important information in an image. Since it is believed that image will travel over a hostile channel, prior data is inserted for its protection. By looking at a state of recovered data at the end of communication channel one can either select or reject the image. Such a form of data hiding anticipates manipulations and take countermeasures before its occurrence. Therefore, it can be used for setting up the active forensic framework in images.

Hierarchy of Data Hiding Techniques

Data hiding, or information hiding is the general term encompassing a wide range of problems. Figure 2 shows a hierarchy of various data hiding techniques. "Steganography" is one form of data hiding. Steganography is derived from the Greek words *Steganos*, which means, "covered" and *Graphien* means "writing" (Celik, Sharma, Tekalp, & Saber, 2005; Raval, 2009). Literally, "Steganography" means hidden writing and it is widely used for covert communication. The modern steganography is divided into a problem of finding a presence of the message in the content (message detection) and its subsequent decoding (message decoding).

Copyright protection of intellectual property is another dimension of data hiding. A copyright regime uses digital watermarking for proving content ownership. Digital watermarking embeds data into the content and it has two basic flavours: non-reversible and reversible watermarking. Non-reversible watermark permanently changes the content to which it is added and generates high distortion. The watermark is robust to manipulations.

Content authentication is another application area for data hiding. A fragile watermark is lost, or it changes if the cover image undergoes any manipulations. The change in the watermark is an indication of the image tampering. The exact recovery of the watermark is established authenticity and integrity of the image. However, some manipulations are non-malicious e.g., lossy image compression in the storage. Such manipulations should not be flagged as loss of the image integrity and therefore, the watermark should survive some innocuous manipulation. This category of data hiding is known as semi-fragile watermarking. It also requires that watermark is sensitive to malicious manipulations and it should change structure after the image manipulation.

In reversible watermarking case, the image recovers its original structure after removal of the watermark. Structural fidelity of the watermark indicates whether the image has been manipulated or not. Such reversible data hiding technique is under focus in this chapter. It is also important to understand general principles of data hiding especially interplay amongst different properties. Therefore, the next section describes the general principle applicable to data hiding process.

Figure 2. Hierarchy of data hiding techniques

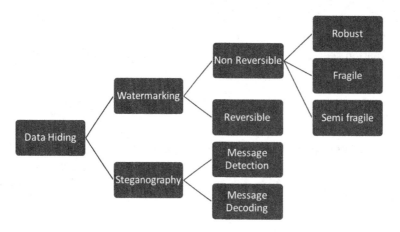

General Principles of Data Hiding

Several issues or requirements are involved in the design of data hiding systems. Some of the key requirements are as follows:

1. **Perceptual Transparency:** Almost all applications require that the distortion induced in the cover image remains imperceptible, or in other words, the composite signal (watermark + image) is perceptually transparent.
2. **Robustness:** The composite signal must survive several intentional or unintentional attacks that might attempt to remove the embedded data.
3. **Capacity:** This represents the number of bits embedded by a given system while satisfying the other design constraints (such as robustness). Depending on the application capacity should be very high while satisfying other constraints.
4. **Security:** This means the ability of the system to resist any attempt of removing the watermark or nullifying its effect. For example, the attacker may attempt to override the receiver decision or remove the watermark from the content.
5. **Statistical Transparency:** This refers to the change in statistics of the cover image after data insertion. Embedding is done in a way minimise the change in the statistics of the image (statistical transparency). This is required when the data-hiding system is employed for secret communication.
6. **Computational Complexity:** In many applications, it is important to have fast encoding, decoding, or both. Low computational complexity is a requirement for applications where data recovery happens in real-time.

Perceptual transparency, robustness, and capacity are three main axes of data hiding space. The watermark decoder may use original image, side information about the image and watermark. Such systems are known as non-blind or semi-blind methods. A blind system will use original image for detection.

Generic Framework for the Data Hiding Problem

The data hiding embeds some information in the image. Mostly this information remains perceptually invisible. The block diagram representing general data hiding scheme is shown in Figure 3. It shows a typical data hiding scenario in which message W is embedded in image $A \in \mathbb{R}^N$ and generate watermarked image $A_w \in \mathbb{R}^N$. The received signal A_w' is corrupted by noise n due to attacks, from which the decoder estimates the message, W^*.

In invisible data hiding it is mandatory that data insertion should not cause any change in perceptual transparency of the image. This perceptual change is limited by amount of the allowable distortion to the image. It is modeled as constraint on amount of distortion that can be made to the host. An attacker is also limited by the amount of distortion that can be induced in the image. It is necessary to maintain usability of the image and over distortion by an attacker may render the image useless for any purpose. The distortion constraints are complex functions and they are based on human visual perception.

The most common distortion measure is Mean Square Error (MSE) which is given as follows:

Figure 3. General frame work of data hiding technique

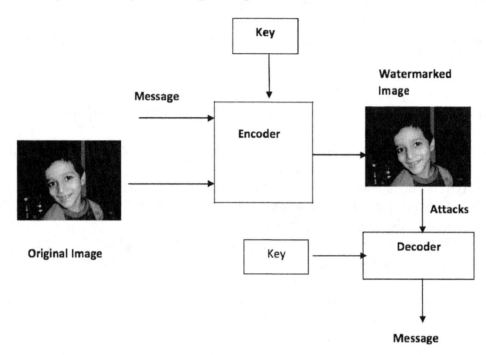

$$D\left(A, A_W\right) = \frac{1}{N}\sum_{n=1}^{N}\left(A_W - A\right)^2 \tag{1}$$

The maximally allowable distortion is D_1, i.e., $D\left(A, A_W\right) < D_1$, and the attacker can induce a maximum distortion of D_2 i.e., $D\left(A, A_w'\right) < D_2$. The watermark embedding function ε takes the image A, the watermark signal W, and a key K to generates the watermark image A_W.

$$\varepsilon\left(A, W, K\right) = A_W \tag{2}$$

The definition $\varepsilon\left(\cdot\right)$ may use pixels or transform coefficients giving rise to spatial or transform domain watermarking methods respectively.

Types of Data Hiding Receivers

The watermarking receiver has two different forms as shown in Figure 4a and 4b.

According to Figure 4a, the detector reads A_w' (received watermarked image), a watermark W and checks for it in A_w'. Optionally it may use key K. The detector is termed as non-blind in case it compares A_w' and A for watermark detection. In case detector makes decision without A it is termed blind detec-

Figure 4. (a) Detectable watermarking; (b) Readable watermarking

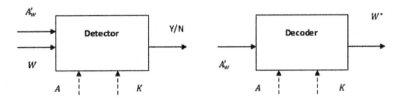

tion. In Figure 4a data can be detected, i.e., the data can only be revealed if its content is known in advance. This extraction of *detectable* data is classified as data *detection.*

The detector ε_d for blind detectable data hiding has three arguments. It accepts A'_w, W, K. Then it decides whether A'_w has W or not, i.e.,

$$\varepsilon_d\left(A'_w, W, K\right) = \frac{yes}{no} \qquad (3)$$

The image A can also be used for detection in ε_d i.e.,

$$\varepsilon_d\left(A'_w, W, K, A\right) = \frac{yes}{no} \qquad (4)$$

Alternatively, as in Figure 4b, the aim is to get W^* from A'_w. It may use A and K. This extraction of readable data is classified as *data decoding.*

In blind, readable data hiding, the decoder function takes as inputs a digital image A'_w, key K and gives as output string of bits W^*.

$$\varepsilon_d\left(A'_w, K\right) = W^* \qquad (5)$$

This obviously assumes the form for non-blind data hiding as follows

$$\varepsilon_d\left(A'_w, K, A\right) = W^* \qquad (6)$$

In the readable data hiding (cf. Figure 4b), the decoding process generates bits irrespective of the fact that image has watermark or not. In case image is not watermarked than bit stream is neglected. Such detectable data codes are also known as one-bit data hiding techniques, as output of detector is just one or zero bit.

REVERSIBLE DATA HIDING

Broadly data hiding is segregated by type of distortion it causes to the image. The non-reversible technique causes permanent distortion to the image even after watermark removal. Therefore, intuitively Reversible Data Hiding (RDH) is a technique in which the image regains its original structure after watermark removal. Reversible data hiding techniques are broadly classified as follows and it is also shown in Figure 5.

1. Lossless compression based (Goljan, Fridrich, & Du, 2001; Celik, Sharma, Tekalp, & Saber, 2005).
2. Histogram modification based (Lin, Tai, & Chang, 2008; Wu, Duglelay, & Shi, 2015; Ni, Shi, Ansari, & Su, 2006; Tsai, Hu, & Yeh, 2009; Luo, Chen, Chen, Zeng, & Xiong, 2010).
3. Difference expansion based (Tian, 2003; Alattar, 2004; Thodi, & Rodriguez, 2004; Coltuc, 2011).

Lossless Compression Based RDH

The lossless compression based RDH approach works on the principle of squeezing some part of an image. The method uses a host space which offers maximum redundancy. For example, the least significant bits (LSBs) are useful for the purpose of data hiding. The total payload i.e., the compressed image part, the watermark and related side information is embedded back into space created by compressing the host. A RDH scheme requires an excellent perceptual quality, therefore, payload is usually placed in the LSBs. During recovery, the payload is extracted and LSB's are decompressed. Many times, a hash of 128 bits is computed from the most significant energy portion of the image and stored in the space created by the lossless compression. The concatenated hash and the compressed image are encrypted to provide additional security. The hash is separated out at the decoder and data is decrypted. On decompression, the original image is available from which the hash is recomputed which is compared with the extracted hash. The image under review is declared authentic if both match than else the image is rejected.

Histogram Based RDH Schemes

The histogram shifting RDH schemes are more efficient than lossless compression methods. Usually, image features like pixel difference, gray level, the prediction error are used to create the histograms. A histogram shifting will use either a zero or peak bin(s) for data embedding. Typically, a histogram bin is selected, its adjacent bin vacated, and the data is embedded into it. For example, let x be the selected bin then $x + 1$ bin is used for watermark insertion. This is achieved by shifting bins greater than x by one position i.e., by adding 1 to the gray value of the pixel. Many schemes embed data in bin x with the purpose of maximizing capacity. Depending on the bit the pixel is left unchanged or positioned in x

Figure 5. Types of reversible data hiding techniques

+ 1 bin. In this case, the bins are shifted right during the process of data embedding. By following the similar procedure, one can also embed data in bins less than *x* i.e., *x* - 1 bin onwards.

By embedding in the bin with the highest number and second ranking bin (Hong, Chen, & Shiu, 2009) capacity shows improvement. The double bin insertion can double the capacity when compared to single run embedding in a maximum bin. However, embedding in first and second ranking bins significantly increase the distortion. An efficient multiple round histogram-based scheme is shown in (Wang, Li, & Yang, 2010). Depending on required embedding capacity, scheme selects two smallest bins on the left and right side of the *x*. This causes only a small change in the histogram as smallest bins are situated towards tail and therefore distortion is minimal. If higher embedding capacity is required more bins are selected iteratively. However, with increase in number of iterations and bins, the distortion also increases.

Difference Expansion RDH Scheme

The most efficient solution for capacity - distortion paradigm is obtained through Difference Expansion (DE) (Tian, 2003) based RDH schemes. Introduced by (Tian, 2003) the basic difference expansion scheme generates and then expands the difference between neighbouring pixels. A data bit is added to this expanded difference after checking for the underflow or overflow. Mostly, the expansion is a by a factor of two as LSB of the difference is replaced by the data bit. The pixels during embedding are also indexed. This is done by marking a bit for every pixel pair. The mark is set to "1" if the difference is expanded else it is set to "0". The mark pattern is known as location map and it is inserted with another payload in the image. At the receiver, pixel pair is identified from the location map. Original pixel values are restored using LSB of the difference. The scheme has embedding capacity of 0.5 bits per pixel (bpp) with single embedding.

In recent years several variants of basic DE scheme have been proposed which aims at increasing the embedding capacity. The basic capacity enhancement is achieved by forming *n* pixels group and then inserting *n* - 1 bits per group (Alattar, 2004). This increases the capacity to 0.6 bpp. The bits for location map shrinks as *n* increases because only one bit per group is required for representation. The bit rate for embedding has improved to 0.75 bpp for *n* = 4 in (Alattar, 2004).

A simple example will help to understand the basic mathematics behind the basic difference expansion scheme. Assume working with 8 bits, so pixel range will span [0, 255]. Let sample pixels in the pair be 203, 194 and the watermark bit is b = 1. The average l and difference h are computed as follows:

$$l = \frac{194 + 203}{2} = 198; h = 2 - 3 - 194 = \left(9\right)_{10} = \left(1001\right)_2$$

Now concatenate *b* after the LSB of *h* to generate $h' = \left(1001b\right)_2 = \left(10011\right)_2 = \left(19\right)_{10}$

This is equivalent to $h' = 2 * h + b = 2 * 9 + 1 = 19.$. Now compute new values of pixels i.e., *x'* and *y'*. The embedding operation of $h' = 2 * h + b$ is known as Difference expansion and it should not cause underflow or overflow.

$$x' = l + \frac{h'+1}{2} = 198 + 10 = 208; y' = l - \frac{h'}{2} = 189$$

The inverse operation is as follows

$$l' = \frac{x' + y'}{2} = 198; h' = x' - y' = 19$$

Extract the LSB of h', i.e., 1, leaving the original difference $h = 9$.. The operation can now be inverted as follows.

$$l = y' + \frac{h'}{2} = 198; x = l + \frac{h+1}{2} = 203; y = l - \frac{h}{2} = 194$$

The reversible operation is also known as S transform.

Distortion Reduction in DE Schemes

In recent years emphasis of DE schemes is on reducing the embedding distortion. The earliest of the approach suggested histogram shifting techniques (Thodi, & Rodriguez, 2007) in lieu of location map. The core idea is to change the non-embeddable pixels in such that they have the greater difference at the receiver as compared to embedded pixels. These non-embeddable pixels are indexed using underflow / overflow map which is very efficiently compressed. It has been shown that DE with histogram shifting is more efficient than DE with the location map for embedding capacity up to 1 bpp (Thodi, & Rodriguez, 2007). However, for embedding capacity, greater than 1 bpp performance of DE with histogram shifting deteriorates. This is due to the fact that histogram shifting distorts both embeddable and non-embeddable pixel set.

As highlighted in Table 1, difference expansion-based techniques provide highest data hiding capacity with lower distortion. Another way of creating the difference is to generate pixel estimate using an interpolation technique and subtract it from original value. The interpolation error i.e., the difference between the actual and the predicted value is expanded to the embed the data. One may note that this is similar to DE scheme. But it uses interpolation error instead of expanding the differences in neighbouring pixels. Also, it expands the difference with addition instead of shifting bits. Authors (Wu, Duglelay, & Shi, 2015; Ni, Shi, Ansari, & Su, 2006; Tsai, Hu, & Yeh, 2009; Luo, Chen, Chen, Zeng, & Xiong, 2010) have shown use of prediction error expansion which depends on correlation among neighbouring pixels for data embedding. The performance of the prediction error-based expansion methods is poor for high-frequency image region due to large prediction error.

Improving the predictor can also control the distortion hence in (Wu, Duglelay, & Shi, 2015; Ni, Shi, Ansari, & Su, 2006; Tsai, Hu, & Yeh, 2009; Luo, Chen, Chen, Zeng, & Xiong, 2010), authors use different predictors to reduce the embedding distortion. In general, all reversible data hiding techniques have a trade-off between distortion and capacity. Another approach for minimizing the embedding distortion is to expand smaller differences. This can be achieved by replacing pixel difference with the prediction error (Thodi, & Rodriguez, 2007). A basic prediction error expansion scheme is as follows.

Assume that pixel is represented by 8 bits, let e be the difference between the original pixel value (X) and its estimate $\hat{X}$.

$$e = X - \hat{X} \tag{7}$$

Let $d \in \{0,1\}$ be the data for embedding, then the prediction error expansion is given as follows:

$$\ddot{e} = 2e + d\hat{X} \tag{8}$$

The watermarking is done is as follows:

$$\ddot{X} = X + e + d\hat{X} \tag{9}$$

The pixels are selected such that after watermarking; 1. They remain distinctive; 2. Error is less than predefined threshold; 3. do not cause overflow and underflow. The pixels satisfying above criteria forms an expandable set. Using Eq. 7 in Eq. 9 results into.

$$\ddot{X} = X + X - \hat{X} + d\hat{X}$$

Therefore,

$$\ddot{X} + \hat{X} = 2X + d\hat{X} \tag{10}$$

Eq. 10 reveals that difference between expanded pixel and its estimate is an even multiple of sample pixel with d as LSB. Therefore, at the receiver d can be recovered as per Eq. 11.

$$d = \left(\ddot{X} - X \right) mod 2 \tag{11}$$

where, mod is a modulus operator and original X is generated as per Eq. 12,

$$\dot{X} = \ddot{X} - d; X = \dot{X} - \left(\frac{\dot{X} - \hat{X}}{2} \right) \hat{X} \tag{12}$$

Other interesting ideas in (Ou, Li, Zhao, Ni, & Shi, 2011; Sachnev, Kim, Nam, Suresh, & Shi, 2009; Li, Yang, & Zeng, 2011; Kamstra, & Heijmans, 2005) for minimizing the distortion is to sort the pixels based on the smoothness and then embed in the pixel pair with small differences. The ideas can be combined by embedding more bits into smooth region and less into high frequency region of the image. Such approaches have low prediction error and they provide high capacity.

Summary of RDH Schemes

Some of the pros and cons of RDH techniques covered above are summarized in following Table 1.

Capacity of the reversible data hiding technique can be increased by improving predictor. It minimizes interpolation error which is used for data embedding. The following section discusses various predictors to improve performance of reversible data hiding scheme.

Predictors for Reversible Data Hiding Technique

The improvement in predictor can significantly increase the RDH scheme performance. It is based on simple premise that improved predictor means low prediction error, minimizing the embedding distortion. The median edge detector predictor (MED) used in (Hu, Lee & Li, 2009; Thodi, & Rodriguez, 2007) is one such improved predictor. It is also one of the predictor used in JPEG - lossless compression (JPEG-LS) and shown in Figure 6.

The three pixels "A", "B" and "C" are used to estimate center pixel X. The Table 2 shows eight possible combination of the predictor.

It can be seen that predictors are combination of one dimensional (0 - 3) or two dimensional (4 - 7) values. The JPEG - LS also use MED or LOCO - I predictor (Weingerberm Seroussi, & Sapiro, 2000). It uses the horizontal or vertical edge detection by examining the neighbouring pixels of X as shown in Fig. 6. In case of vertical edge, pixel used for prediction is "C" and for horizontal edge it is "A". The prediction is made based on following rules

Table 1. Summary of RDH schemes

Data Hiding Technique	Advantages	Disadvantages
Lossless compression based	It is simple to implement as LSBs are used for embedding payload. The security of the scheme is poor or at most equals security of the encryption algorithm used to encrypt the image. It can be used for authentication of the compressed media as well.	The lossless compression scheme does not provide high compression ratio as LSBs have high entropy. The noisy image may force embedding in the most significant bits increasing perceptual distortion of the image.
Histogram shifting based	The perceptual quality of the watermarked image is good with high peak signal to noise ratio (PSNR). It has a low computational complexity and provides fast execution for single run of algorithm. The embedding and decoding process is simple.	The capacity is limited to number of elements in the single bin for one -time embedding run of the algorithm. In multiple runs algorithm needs an exhaustive search within an image. This increases the computation time.
Difference expansion based	The interpolation technique generates low magnitude in expansion error. It can use lossless compression as additional step for data embedding. High embedding rate is possible by using each image pixel and it has good perceptual quality. It suits audio and video modality due to high embedding capacity. Additional step of encrypting the compressed location map along with *changeable* bits increases the security. Multiple iterations embedding can be applied while maintaining high PSNR.	The decoder must know the differences used during expansion. The size of location map is large. Computational complexity is high. There is rounding effect due to division by two at encoder and decoder. Basic difference expansion does not exploit the inherent correlation in the neighboring pixels in an image. The best results can be obtained if the image has large proportion of flat or low frequency regions.

Figure 6. JPEG-LS predictor template

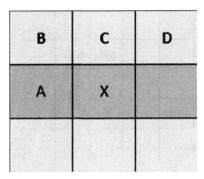

Table 2. Predictors selection

Value	Prediction
0	No prediction
1	A
2	C
3	B
4	A + C – B
5	A + C - B / 2
6	C + A - B / 2
7	(A + C) / 2

$$X = \begin{cases} \min(A,C) & if\ B \geq \max(A,C) \\ \max(A,C) & if\ B \leq \min(A,C) \\ A + C - B & otherwise \end{cases} \qquad (13)$$

These selection is based on the type of edge detected. It selects "C" in case vertical edge is present in the left of X, "A" in case there is a horizontal edge above X, and A + C – B when an edge is absent. The gradient adjusted predictor (GAP) (Coltuc, 2011) is based on the gradient estimation around X and when combined with predefined thresholds results into final prediction. The GAP predictive template is shown in Figure 7.

GAP identifies three types of edges: 1. strong; 2. simple; 3. soft edge and works on the context of seven pixels around X. The GAP is used as a predictor in context adaptive lossless image compression (CALIC) codec (Wu, Memon, & Sayood, 1995). It is a simple adaptive predictor and adjust itself to the gradient near candidate pixel. The gradient estimation is given as;

$$G_v = |W - NW| + |N - NN| + |NE - NNE|.$$

Figure 7. GAP predictive template

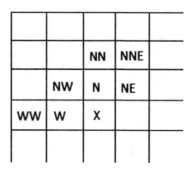

$$G_h = \left| W - WW \right| + \left| N - NW \right| + \left| N - NE \right|$$

The GAP adjust the predictors based on the local gradient and prediction is made context sensitive. The schemes (Coltuc, 2011) based on GAP outperforms MED based scheme.

The lower prediction error can be achieved by using the simple average of four horizontal and four vertical neighbors of X. However, watermarking pixels in raster scan order cause a problem in prediction. This is because prediction uses two original and two modified pixels. The context of the neighborhood also plays a very important role in improving the prediction. For example, a simple averaging on a context of a rhombus yields very good result. It is simply due to the fact that large neighborhood has been used for prediction.

The adaptive predictors (Dragoi, & Coltuc, 2011) can also reduce the embedding distortion. The approach involves computing a predictor coefficient such that prediction error is minimized. One of the popular approaches is to use the least square error (LSE). Using such predictor on the rhombus of MED is better than simple MED approach. Other optimization techniques like genetic algorithms are also used for the prediction. The image statistics varies from region to region; therefore, multiple local predictors can also be used. For example, an image is divided into blocks and LS predictor can be computed on each one of them. It can be observed that small blocks yield better prediction as compared to one large ones. However, the amount of side information increases significantly as block size becomes smaller. The data hiding will change the pixel values and therefore exact prediction at the receiver cannot be obtained. Thus, predictors are also inserted in the image.

RESULTS, OBSERVATIONS, AND DISCUSSIONS

The section covers three important results and a case study as follows:

1. Capacity - PSNR behaviour for standard DE scheme.
2. Increasing the capacity with improved predictor
3. Use of reversible data hiding for authentication

Basic Difference Expansion Scheme

The results and observations for basic difference expansion scheme as proposed in (Tian, 2003) is discussed in this section. Table 3 shows statistics for a basic difference expansion scheme (Tian, 2003). The experimentation is shown for gray scale image 'Lena' with size 256 x 256. It can be observed from the Table 3 that as threshold τ on the difference increases, number of watermark #bits i.e., capacity increases, but perceptually quality of the image is degrading. The perceptual quality is measured in peak signal to ratio with units in decibels (dB). The last column measures capacity in bits per pixel which is computed as $bpp = \dfrac{\#\,bits}{Total\,image\,pixels}$

The perceptual quality of image with respect to various threshold values is captured in Figure 8.

On very careful observation one can find that perceptual quality degrades as embedding capacity rises. There is an increase in image blockiness from Figure 8a to 8d (Please observe the region near the left eye in an image carefully in Figures 9a and 9b). Figures 8c and 8d has large embedding capacities of 0.34 and 0.43 bpp respectively but they have degraded image quality.

Capacity Increase Due to Improved Predictor

The results of one such improved predictor based reversible data hiding technique (Jaiswal, Au, Jakhetiya, Guo, Tiwari, & Yue, 2013) is shown in Table 4. The results are shown for 8-bit grayscale image Lena with size 512 x 512. It can be seen that as number of iteration increases embedding capacity increases. The PSNR in dB degrades on the other hand. However, when compared to simple DE scheme of (cf. Table 3) embedding capacity of this scheme is very high with comparable PSNR. For example, in simple DE scheme, 0.47 bpp capacity results in PSNR of 32.8 dB. The comparable PSNR of 32.45 dB results in embedding capacity of 0.84 bpp for the improved predictor based RDH scheme. These facts are also highlighted in Figure 10 and Figure 11.

Table 3. Basic difference expansion scheme

τ	PSNR dB	# bits	bpp
7	43.60	1354	0.020
8	42.96	3737	0.057
9	42.36	5671	0.086
10	41.86	7346	0.11
11	41.41	8955	0.14
12	40.92	10383	0.16
15	39.89	13659	0.20
25	37.20	20944	0.32
50	34.22	28254	0.43
100	32.80	30655	0.47

Tian, 2003.

Figure 8. Watermarked images with different threshold

a) $\tau = 7, bpp = 0.020$ b) $\tau = 12, bpp = 0.16$

c) $\tau = 25, bpp = 0.32$ d) $\tau = 50, bpp = 0.43$

Figure 9. Expanded view of watermarked images

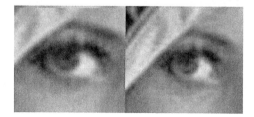

It can be seen from Figure 10 that capacity in bits and PSNR which indicates the signal strength are two contrasting parameters. They are inversely related which means that increase in embedding capacity will decrease the peak signal to noise ratio. The PSNR also represents perceptual quality and it will degrade with an injection of more data hiding bits.

One of the advantage in the method proposed by (Jaiswal, Au, Jakhetiya, Guo, Tiwari, & Yue, 2013) is the use of improved predictor (Zhang, Hu, Li, & Yu, 2013). The basic intuition is that with the improved predictor the perceptual degradation will decrease gracefully. This allows data embedding

Table 4. Results of improved predictor scheme

#Iterations	Capacity in Bits	PSNR dB	Time in Sec	bpp
1	49948	48.57	0.064	0.19
2	93630	42.97	0.066	0.36
3	128994	39.82	0.079	0.49
4	157425	37.65	0.070	0.60
5	179718	35.99	0.066	0.69
6	196833	34.63	0.068	0.75
7	209727	33.47	0.071	0.80
8	219809	32.45	0.065	0.84
9	227384	31.53	0.064	0.87
10	233117	30.71	0.066	0.89

Figure 10. PSNR: Capacity in Bits. X Axis: Capacity in Bits; Y Axis: PSNR in dB

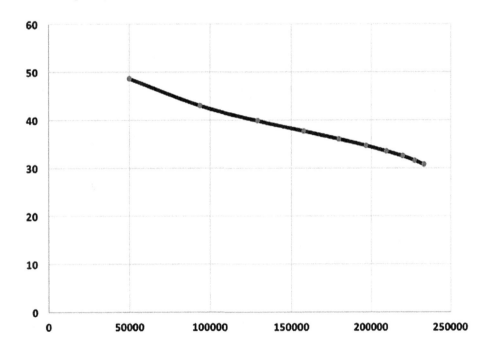

cycle to run multiple times increasing the embedding capacity significantly. This variation is shown in Figure 11 which captures an increase in embedding capacity with respect to the number of iterations. It is interesting to note that initially the embedding capacity increases exponentially and then it tapers off after many iterations.

One can also perceptually compare simple difference expansion and the improved predictor based RDH. The results are collocated in Figure 12. At 0.43 bpp perceptual quality of the watermarked image is poor in Figure 12a. It contains blockiness in the high-frequency regions e.g., near the eye region. On the other hand, Figure 12b shows better perceptual quality with an absence of blockiness in the high-

Figure 11. No. of Iterations: Capacity in Bits. X Axis: Iterations; Y Axis: Capacity in Bits

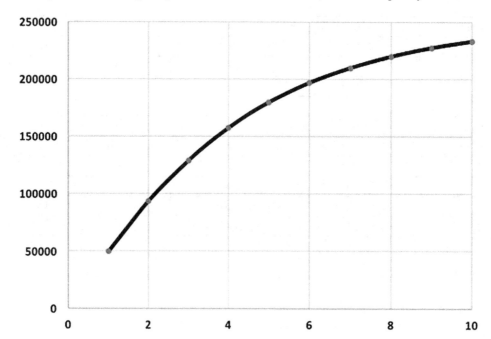

Figure 12. Comparison of Simple DE and Improved Predictor Outputs a. Simple DE PSNR 34.22, bpp 0.43 b. Improved Predictor PSNR 34.63. bpp 0.73

frequency region. The embedding capacity of watermarked image in Figure 12b is also higher; i.e., 0.73 bpp. However, there is a presence of high-frequency noise in Figure 12b e.g., observe the dots in flat image regions. This effect can be controlled by reducing the embedding capacity.

Data Authentication Using Reversible Data Hiding Technique

By looking at the general framework for data hiding (cf. Figure 3) one may note that data security is vulnerable on the transmission channel. The data could be subjected to variety of manipulations on the channel. The malicious purpose of such manipulations is to get an access to the data for unauthorized usage. Therefore, it is utmost important to maintain data consistency on the channel and place a checking mechanism to sense breach of the data integrity. The reversible watermark can be used to check the authenticity or integrity of the image in which it is embedded. It can be used as a fragile watermark i.e., it will change if the image is changed or irremediably altered. Such a loss in an image can be global i.e., affects the whole image, or local i.e., changes some image parts. The reversible watermark must change with the global or local change in an image. Therefore, reversible data hiding is used for data authentication.

Potential benefits of using the watermark in the image authentication are as follows:

- Watermark removes any need to store separate data.
- Watermark undergoes same change as the cover image in which it is embedded.

A fragile watermark (Raval, & Rege, 2005; Raval, Joshi, Rege & Parulkar, 2011; Joshi, Raval, Gupta, Rege, & Parulkar, 2016) has exactly opposite requirements to that of a robust watermark, thereby, it finds its use in tamper detection applications like medical and military imaging. The desirable features of the fragile watermarking systems are:

1. Better perceptual quality
2. Detection of tampering

It is mandatory for some of the applications to restore the image. It is shown that the methods can securely embed personal signatures or copyright logos into an image as fragile watermarks and track any changes to the host. The watermark must be sensitive to any manipulation. In a most conservative form of the security requirement, a single bit change in the watermark is intolerable and a host is declared unauthentic. The image authentication is tested by applying following manipulations on grayscale image. The image is watermarked using the method proposed in (Jaiswal, Au, Jakhetiya, Guo, Tiwari, & Yue, 2013).

1. Histogram equalization
2. Laplacian filtering ($\alpha = 0.2$)
3. Low pass filtering (3 x 3 mask)
4. Gaussian noise addition with zero mean and 0.01 variance.
5. Cropping and filling 25% of an image with other content

The binary watermark is extracted from the image and compared bit by bit with the recomputed watermark. The frequency of bit difference with respect to the total number of bits is computed which is known as bit error rate (BER). The results of this experimentation are shown in Table 5.

Table 5. BER against different attacks

Attacks	Bit Error Rate (BER)
Histogram equalization	0.49
Laplacian filtering ($\alpha = 0.2$)	0.49
Low pass filtering (3 x 3 mask)	0.50
Gaussian noise addition with zero mean and 0.01 variance	0.51
Cropping and filling 25% of image with other content	0.39

It can be observed from Table 5 that watermark is sensitive to manipulations. The recovered watermark is severely degraded when the image is subjected to manipulations. Since watermark resides in an image, any change to watermark structure flags an event that image has lost its integrity and it is no longer structurally and semantically safe to believe in the image. One may note that the above approach is extremely conservative as it does not differentiate between the malicious and non-malicious manipulations. However, for the applications which demand the strict level of integrity, reversible data hiding provides an active forensic framework.

CONCLUSION

The chapter presents a use of reversible data hiding for establishing the authenticity and integrity of the image travelling over a hostile communication channel. It is an active forensic measure because the watermark is inserted in the image as the precautionary measure with a belief that it will be subjected to hostile attack on the channel. This assumption makes reversible data hiding an active forensic measure. It is different from passive forensics where the content is deciphered after the changes have been made to it. The alteration in the watermark is an indication of the change in the image when it is traversing communication channel. This is a valid observation as watermark resides in the image covertly. The reversible data hiding provides an additional advantage along with active forensics. In case image consistency is established at the receiver it regains its original form after the watermark removal.

The chapter also establishes the fact that reversible data hiding is an interplay between the image perceptual quality and the number of watermark bits. A modern RDH technique requires a high capacity paving the way to find an optimal point between the PSNR and capacity space. It can be observed that increasing the capacity lowers PSNR of an image. The perceptual quality can also be measured by the PSNR; however, it has a subjectivity around it i.e., higher PSNR image does not guarantee the best perceptual fidelity. One of the ways to improve PSNR and perceptual quality simultaneously is to improve type of the predictor used in RDH. It has been shown in the literature that predictor difference expansion-based scheme has the capability to increase the embedding capacity with lower perceptual distortion. This is attained by lowering the difference between the sample and non-sample pixel set used in setting up the predictor. This phenomenon also allows multiple rounds of data insertion increasing the data capacity to 1 bpp.

The chapter presents zero error tolerance authentication measure. It means that single bit change in watermark will render an image to be unauthentic. This strict measure is necessary for secure communication in domains like military or medical. However, many situations do not demand such strict measure of tolerance on authenticity check. For example, a friendly communication between two friends. It is also possible that many manipulations are unintentional e.g., saving an image to lossy compression format (Joshi M., Raval, Dandawate, Joshi K., Metkar, 2014). However, the present authentication mechanism does not segregate between the malicious and non-malicious manipulations.

In future, the RDH can be contextualized for an application. It must be able to segregate between the malicious and non-malicious attempts on the image. One can obtain this segregation by putting a threshold on the tolerable distortion. Any value above the threshold can be flagged off as a malicious attempt. However, the challenge is to find a correct value of the threshold. Also, the forensic value of the RDH scheme can be enhanced by incorporating the following capabilities:

1. Localization of the changes in the manipulated image.
2. Filling up the localized changes with the original or predicted content.

The above two capabilities will localize the change and attempts to fill up the holes with the predicted or original content. The success of the fill-ups is dependent on the amount of damage done to the image. The advance forensic process using RDH will then have three basic steps.

- Authentication.
- Localization of the manipulations.
- Fill up the holes (localized regions) with predicted or original content.

A complete and universal forensic method using RDH is a matter of future research and it opens up many new research vistas.

REFERENCES

Alattar, A. (2004). Reversible Watermark Using the Difference Expansion of a Generalized Integer Transform. *IEEE Transactions on Image Processing*, *13*(8), 1147–1156. doi:10.1109/TIP.2004.828418 PMID:15326856

Celik, M., Sharma, G., Tekalp, A., & Saber, E. (2005). Lossless generalized-LSB data embedding. *IEEE Transactions on Image Processing*, *14*(2), 253–266. doi:10.1109/TIP.2004.840686 PMID:15700530

Coltuc, D. (2011). Improved Embedding for Prediction-Based Reversible Watermarking. *IEEE Transactions on Information Forensics and Security*, *6*(3), 873–882. doi:10.1109/TIFS.2011.2145372

Conti, M., Dehghantanha, A., Franke, K., & Watson, S. (2018). *Internet of Things security and forensics: Challenges and opportunities*. Academic Press.

Dilijonaite, A., Flaglien, A., Sunde, I. M., Hamm, J., Sandvik, J. P., Bjelland, P., & Axelsson, S. (2017). Digital Forensic Readiness. *Digital Forensics*, 117-145.

Dragoi, I., & Coltuc, D. (2014). Local-Prediction-Based Difference Expansion Reversible Watermarking. *IEEE Transactions on Image Processing*, *23*(4), 1779–1790. doi:10.1109/TIP.2014.2307482 PMID:24808346

Farid, H., & Lyu, S. (2003, June). Higher-order wavelet statistics and their application to digital forensics. In *Computer Vision and Pattern Recognition Workshop, 2003. CVPRW'03. Conference on* (Vol. 8, pp. 94-94). Academic Press. 10.1109/CVPRW.2003.10093

Franke, K., Årnes, A., Flaglien, A., Sunde, I. M., Dilijonaite, A., Hamm, J., & Axelsson, S. (2018). Challenges in Digital Forensics. *Digital Forensics*, 313-317.

Goljan, M., Fridrich, J., & Du, R. (2001). Distortion-free data embedding for images. *Information Hiding*, *2137*, 27–41. doi:10.1007/3-540-45496-9_3

Hamm, J., Flaglien, A., Sunde, I. M., Dilijonaite, A., Sandvik, J. P., Bjelland, P., & Axelsson, S. (2018). Computer Forensics. *Digital Forensics*, 147-190.

Hong, W., Chen, T., & Shiu, C. (2009). Reversible data hiding for high quality images using modification of prediction errors. *Journal of Systems and Software*, 82(11), 1833–1842. doi:10.1016/j.jss.2009.05.051

Hu, Y., Lee, H., & Li, J. (2009). DE-Based Reversible Data Hiding with Improved Overflow Location Map. *IEEE Transactions on Circuits and Systems for Video Technology*, 19(2), 250–260. doi:10.1109/TCSVT.2008.2009252

Jaiswal, S., Au, O., Jakhetiya, V., Tiwari, A., & Yue, K. (2013). Efficient adaptive prediction based reversible image watermarking. In *International conference on Image Processing* (pp. 4540–4544). Academic Press. 10.1109/ICIP.2013.6738935

Joshi, M., Raval, M. S., Dandawate, Y., Joshi, K., & Metkar, S. (2014). *Image and video compression* (1st ed.). Boca Raton, FL: CRC Press, Taylor and Francis. doi:10.1201/b17738

Joshi, V., Raval, M. S., Gupta, D., Rege, P., & Parulkar, S. (2015). A multiple reversible watermarking technique for fingerprint authentication. *Multimedia Systems*, 22(3), 367–378. doi:10.100700530-015-0465-6

Kamstra, L., & Heijmans, H. (2005). Reversible data embedding into images using wavelet techniques and sorting. *IEEE Transactions on Image Processing*, 14(12), 2082–2090. doi:10.1109/TIP.2005.859373 PMID:16370461

Lin, C., Tai, W., & Chang, C. (2008). Multilevel reversible data hiding based on histogram modification of difference images. *Pattern Recognition*, 41(12), 3582–3591. doi:10.1016/j.patcog.2008.05.015

Luo, L., Chen, Z., Chen, M., Zeng, X., & Xiong, Z. (2010). Reversible Image Watermarking Using Interpolation Technique. *IEEE Transactions on Information Forensics and Security*, 5(1), 187–193. doi:10.1109/TIFS.2009.2035975

Ni, Z., Shi, Y., Ansari, N., & Su, W. (2006). Reversible data hiding. *IEEE Transaction on Circuits Systems And Video Technology*, 16(3), 354–362. doi:10.1109/TCSVT.2006.869964

Ou, B., Li, X., Zhao, Y., Ni, R., & Shi, Y. (2013). Pairwise Prediction-Error Expansion for Efficient Reversible Data Hiding. *IEEE Transactions on Image Processing*, 22(12), 5010–5021. doi:10.1109/TIP.2013.2281422 PMID:24043388

Petitcolas, F., Anderson, R., & Kuhn, M. (1999). Information hiding-a survey. *Proceedings of the IEEE*, 87(7), 1062–1078. doi:10.1109/5.771065

Pomponiu, V., Cavagnino, D., & Botta, M. (2018). Data Hiding in the Wild: Where Computational Intelligence Meets Digital Forensics. In *Surveillance in Action* (pp. 301–331). Cham: Springer. doi:10.1007/978-3-319-68533-5_15

Popescu, A. C., & Farid, H. (2004, May). Statistical tools for digital forensics. In *International Workshop on Information Hiding* (pp. 128-147). Springer. 10.1007/978-3-540-30114-1_10

Raval, M. S. (2009). A Secure Steganographic Technique for Blind Steganalysis Resistance. In *Seventh International Conference on Advances in Pattern Recognition* (pp. 25-28). Kolkata: Academic Press.

Raval, M. S., Joshi, M., Rege, P. P., & Parulkar, S. (2011). Image tampering detection using compressive sensing based watermarking scheme. In *National Conference on Machine Vision and Image Processing* (pp. 5-9). Pune: IET.

Raval, M. S., & Rege, P. P. (2005). Scalar Quantization Based Multiple Patterns Data Hiding Technique for Gray Scale Images. *ICGST Journal of Graphics, Vision and Image Processing, 5*(9), 55–61.

Sachnev, V., Kim, H. J., Nam, J., Suresh, S., & Shi, Y. Q. (2009). Reversible Watermarking Algorithm Using Sorting and Prediction. *IEEE Transactions on Circuits and Systems for Video Technology, 19*(7), 989–999. doi:10.1109/tcsvt.2009.2020257

Sommer, P. (2018). *Accrediting digital forensics: What are the choices?* Academic Press.

Swanson, M., Kobayashi, M., & Tewfik, A. (1998). Multimedia data-embedding and watermarking technologies. *Proceedings of the IEEE, 86*(6), 1064–1087. doi:10.1109/5.687830

Tanaka, K. (2011). Embedding of computer-generated hologram in a dithered image. *Applied Optics, 50*(34), H315. doi:10.1364/AO.50.00H315 PMID:22193023

Thodi, D., & Rodriguez, J. (2004). Prediction-error based reversible watermarking. In *International Conference on Image Processing* (pp. 1549-1552). IEEE.

Thodi, D., & Rodriguez, J. (2007). Expansion Embedding Techniques for Reversible Watermarking. *IEEE Transactions on Image Processing, 16*(3), 721–730. doi:10.1109/TIP.2006.891046 PMID:17357732

Tian, J. (2003). Reversible data embedding using a difference expansion. *IEEE Transactions on Circuits and Systems for Video Technology, 13*(8), 890–896. doi:10.1109/TCSVT.2003.815962

Tsai, P., Hu, Y., & Yeh, H. (2009). Reversible image hiding scheme using predictive coding and histogram shifting. *Signal Processing, 89*(6), 1129–1143. doi:10.1016/j.sigpro.2008.12.017

Wang, C., Li, X., & Yang, B. (2010). Efficient reversible image watermarking by using dynamical prediction-error expansion. In *International conference on Image processing* (pp. 3673–3676). Academic Press. 10.1109/ICIP.2010.5652508

Wang, J., Li, T., Shi, Y. Q., Lian, S., & Ye, J. (2017). Forensics feature analysis in quaternion wavelet domain for distinguishing photographic images and computer graphics. *Multimedia Tools and Applications, 76*(22), 23721–23737. doi:10.100711042-016-4153-0

Watson, S., & Dehghantanha, A. (2016). Digital forensics: The missing piece of the Internet of Things promise. *Computer Fraud & Security, 2016*(6), 5–8. doi:10.1016/S1361-3723(15)30045-2

Weinberger, M., Seroussi, G., & Sapiro, G. (2000). The LOCO-I lossless image compression algorithm: Principles and standardization into JPEG-LS. *IEEE Transactions on Image Processing, 9*(8), 1309–1324. doi:10.1109/83.855427 PMID:18262969

Wu, H., Dugelay, J., & Shi, Y. (2015). Reversible Image Data Hiding with Contrast Enhancement. *IEEE Signal Processing Letters*, 22(1), 81–85. doi:10.1109/LSP.2014.2346989

Wu, X., Memon, N., & Sayood, K. (1995). *A context- based, adaptive, lossless/nearly-lossless coding scheme for continuous-tone images*. ISO.

Zhang, W., Hu, X., Li, X., & Yu, N. (2013). Recursive Histogram Modification: Establishing Equivalency Between Reversible Data Hiding and Lossless Data Compression. *IEEE Transactions on Image Processing*, 22(7), 2775–2785. doi:10.1109/TIP.2013.2257814 PMID:23591495

Chapter 6
Commutative Watermarking– Encryption of Multimedia Data Based on Histograms

Roland Schmitz
Stuttgart Media University, Germany

Shujun Li
University of Kent, UK

Christos Grecos
Central Washington University, USA

Xinpeng Zhang
Shanghai University, China

ABSTRACT

Histogram-based watermarking schemes are invariant to pixel permutations and can thus be combined with permutation-based ciphers to form a commutative watermarking-encryption scheme. In this chapter, the authors demonstrate the feasibility of this approach for audio data and still image data. Typical histogram-based watermarking schemes based on comparison of histogram bins are prone to desynchronization attacks, where the whole histogram is shifted by a certain amount. These kind of attacks can be avoided by synchronizing the embedding and detection processes, using the mean of the histogram as a calibration point. The resulting watermarking scheme is resistant to three common types of shifts of the histogram, while the advantages of previous histogram-based schemes, especially commutativity of watermarking and permutation-based encryption, are preserved. The authors also report on the results of testing robustness of the still image watermark against JPEG and JPEG2000 compression and on the possibility of using histogram-based watermarks for authenticating the content of an image.

DOI: 10.4018/978-1-5225-7107-0.ch006

INTRODUCTION

Encryption and watermarking are both important tools in protecting digital contents, e.g. in digital rights management (DRM) systems. While encryption is used to protect the contents from unauthorized access, watermarking can be deployed for various purposes, ranging from ensuring authenticity of content to embedding metadata, e.g. copyright or authorship information, into the contents. Heterogeneous end-to-end media distribution scenarios, where the ultimate receiver of the media data may be unknown to the sender, call for protection schemes in which both watermarking and encryption need to be combined in a flexible way.

The concept of commutative watermarking-encryption (CWE) was first discussed in (Herrera-Joancomarti et al., 2005) with a special emphasis on watermarking in the encrypted domain. Four properties about watermarking in the encrypted domain are formulated in Sec. 2.2 of Herrera-Joancomarti et al.'s report:

Property 1: The marking function M can be performed in the encrypted domain.
Property 2: The verification function V is able to reconstruct a mark in the encrypted domain when it has been embedded in the encrypted domain.
Property 3: The verification function V is able to reconstruct a mark in the encrypted domain when it has been embedded in the clear domain.
Property 4: The decryption function does not affect the integrity of the watermark.

All four properties should hold without the marking and verification functions having access to the encryption key, and without the encryption and decryption functions having access to the watermarking key. The four properties can be fulfilled in the most natural way if the encryption operation and the watermarking operation commute, meaning that the outcome is the same no matter whether the encrypted media are watermarked or if the watermarked media are encrypted (see also Sec. 4).

In this chapter, histogram-based watermarking schemes which are capable of being integrated into a CWE scheme are described. For still images, it is well known that histogram-based watermarking schemes are resistant to permutations of image pixels. In particular, using histograms implies robustness against rotation, scaling and translation (RST) of images. In (Schmitz, 2012) this fact has been utilized to devise a commutative watermarking-encryption (CWE) scheme by choosing a permutation cipher for encryption and a histogram-based scheme for watermarking.

In (Schmitz & Gruber, 2017) it has been demonstrated that the basic approach also works for audio data. Here, the permutation cipher is applied to discrete sample values obtained from sampling the analogous audio signal. Likewise, the histogram is computed from the amplitude values of the sample values.

Typical histogram-based watermarking schemes like those proposed in (Schmitz et al., 2012) and (Chrysochos et al., 2007) work by comparing selected histogram bins, where the selection process is controlled by a watermarking key. If the whole histogram is shifted by a small amount, i.e. by adding a small number to each pixel value, the detector will use completely different bin pairs for extracting the embedded watermark and will produce wrong results. To overcome this problem, a synchronization process between embedder and detector is employed that is based on the global mean of the histogram.

The rest of the chapter is organized as follows. In Sec. 2 previous approaches to CWE along with other histogram-based watermarking algorithms are briefly summarized. Section 3 describes three types of histogram shifts which may be used to attack histogram-based watermarking algorithms. Sec.

4 describes the proposed watermarking algorithm for image data, which is robust against these shifts, in greater detail. In Sec. 5 experimental results for this algorithm are investigated, especially its robustness against histogram shifts and lossy compression. In Sec. 6 a qualitative comparison between the watermarking scheme proposed here and previous histogram-based schemes is provided. Section 7 reports on extending the proposed CWE scheme to audio data and to image authentication. Section 8 concludes the chapter and gives directions for further work. The present chapter is an extension of the earlier journal article (Schmitz et al., 2014).

RELATED WORK

Commutative Watermarking-Encryption (CWE)

While encryption algorithms are evaluated mainly according to their security and run-time performance, in watermarking there are more and often conflicting requirements (Cox et al., 2007): *Watermarking security* normally refers to the difficulty for an attacker to remove/manipulate a watermark that he does not have access to or to insert a watermark of his own, while *robustness* is the ability of a watermark to withstand compression or other image-procession operations. Further evaluation criteria for watermarks are *fidelity* (the degree of imperceptibility) and *capacity* (the number of bits that may be embedded by a watermarking scheme).

As confidentiality provided by encryption and authenticity provided by watermarking are both important security services in the transmission of multimedia data, it is often proposed to combine them in a single security system (see (Dagadu & Li, 2018) for a recent example). While watermarking first, then encrypt is straightforward to do using existing algorithms for watermarking and encryption, it is quite a different matter to combine them in a commutative way, so that the watermark may be extracted in the cipher domain and in the plaintext domain. A more formal way to express this relationship is the equation

$$M(E_k(I), m) = E_k(M(I, m)),$$

where E is the encryption function, k is the encryption key, I is the plaintext media data, M is the watermarking function and m is the mark to be embedded (see also section 4).

One possible way to combine watermarking and encryption in a commutative way is provided by deploying so called homomorphic encryption techniques (Fontaine & Galand, 2007). They are characterized by the property that some basic algebraic operations such as addition and multiplication on the plaintexts can be transferred onto the corresponding ciphertexts, i.e., they are transparent to encryption (cf. (Lagendijk et al., 2013) and Sec. 2.1 of (Herrera-Joancomarti et al., 2005)). Now, if both the encryption and the watermarking processes use compatible homomorphic operations, one gets a commutative watermarking-encryption scheme. Examples of compatible homomorphic operations are exponentiation modulo n (being compatible with multiplication modulo n), multiplication modulo n (being compatible with multiplication modulo n) and addition modulo n (being compatible with addition modulo n), which includes the bitwise XOR operation. One drawback of using addition modulo n for encryption and watermarking is that the modular addition operation may cause overflow/underflow pixels that have to be handled separately, thus making the system "quasi-commutative" (see (Lian, 2009)). The XOR operation does not suffer from the overflow/underflow problem, though. On the other hand, the watermark's robustness is limited by the encryption operation.

Subramanyam et al. (2012) have used this approach to watermark images in the compressed-encrypted domain. More specifically, they encrypt the JPEG2000 – codestream of an image using the stream cipher RC4. The cipher generates a pseudorandom byte stream. The encryption process itself is bytewise addition modulo 255 in order to avoid artificial JPEG2000 headers due to the encryption process. Thereafter, a watermark generated by a robust watermarking scheme is added to the encrypted codestream modulo 255. While watermark detection in the encrypted domain is straightforward using this approach, for reliable detection in the decrypted domain the encryption key, and depending on the watermarking scheme being used, the unmarked original cipherstream are needed. Pappa et al. (2017) basically repeat this approach, but use a more secure variant of RC4 called MRC4.

In partial encryption based CWE schemes, the plaintext multimedia data is partitioned into two disjoint parts, where one part is encrypted and the other part is watermarked. Since the encryption part is independent of the watermarking part, they are naturally commutative. To take a typical example, in (Lian et al., 2006), the multimedia data is partitioned into two parts after a four-level discrete wavelet transformation. The lowest-level coefficients are fully encrypted, while for the medium- and high-level coefficients only the signs are encrypted. In this case, the unencrypted absolute values of medium-level coefficients can be watermarked either before or after encryption.

Another more recent example of a partial encryption based CWE scheme is the CEWoD (CWE based on Orthogonal Decomposition) scheme (Xu et al., 2014). In this scheme, the media data are organized as an n-dimensional vector X. If B is an orthogonal transformation matrix, X can be written in the form $X = B \cdot Y$, where $Y = B^{-1} \cdot X$. By choosing sub-matrices R and S so that $B = (R \quad S)$, X gets decomposed into two independent parts $X = B \cdot Y = R \cdot Y_1 + S \cdot Y_2$. Encryption and watermarking are applied to the orthogonal decomposition coefficients Y_1 and Y_2, respectively.

In (Boho et al., 2013) a partial encryption scheme is used to protect an H.264/AVC & HEVC video stream: Sign bits of DCT coefficients, motion vector differences and prediction modes of I-, B- and P-frames are encrypted, while the residual DCT coefficients are watermarked by Quantized Index Modulation (QIM, see (Chen & Wornell, 2001)).

Generally, in a partial encryption based CWE scheme, there is a trade-off between security of the encryption part and robustness of the watermarking part. The more visually important data are encrypted, the less quality distortion can be introduced due to the process of watermark removal by an attacker.

The third approach to CWE as introduced in (Schmitz et al., 2012) is to encrypt all media data, but to use a cipher that leaves a feature space invariant. This feature space can be used to embed a watermark. This approach is called invariant encryption in (Boho et al., 2013). As an example, a permutation cipher is used for encryption and a histogram-based algorithm is used for watermarking in (Schmitz et al., 2012). The advantage of the invariant encryption approach is that all media data are encrypted (and not just a subset)

Possible Attacks on CWE Schemes

Generally speaking, it is hard to devise a robust watermarking algorithm that can work in the encrypted domain because there are no perceptually important features to use for embedding in this case. This fact limits the robustness of all CWE schemes presented in this section.

In homomorphic schemes which are able to act in the encrypted domain, the position for watermark embedding must be carefully selected so that small modifications of the encrypted data do not lead to large quality deteriorations of the decrypted data (cf. Subramanyam et al. (2012)). Therefore, in the example CWE scheme presented in chapter 9 of the book (Lian, 2008), the watermark only affects the least significant bitplane of the image data. Subramanyam et al. (2012) take a similar approach by embedding the mark into less significant bitplanes of middle resolutions in the Discrete Wavelet Transform (DWT). This placement makes the watermarks vulnerable to malicious attackers, which can heavily modify the affected bitplanes in order to remove the watermark without deteriorating image quality too much.

In partial encryption schemes, there are always unencrypted, watermarked data, and on the other hand, encrypted, unmarked data. While the unencrypted, watermarked data are supposed to be perceptibly unimportant, there is certainly some information leakage through these data. The fact that only perceptibly unimportant data are marked, limits the robustness of these schemes against attacks aiming to remove the mark.

In the invariant encryption approach, by suitable operations in the invariant feature space of the cipher, the watermark may be removed or manipulated. Examples of this kind of operations are provided by the histogram shifts described in Sec. 3.

Histogram-Based Watermarking

As in this contribution the histogram-based watermarking algorithm presented in (Schmitz et al., 2012) will be developed further towards higher robustness, a review of earlier common histogram-based watermarking algorithms is presented here.

The most widely studied approach to histogram-based watermarking is so-called exact histogram specification (Coltuc & Bolon, 1999; Roy & Chang, 2004; Lin et al., 2006), where the histogram of the original image or a (randomly and secretly selected) sub-region of it is modified toward a target histogram, which is then used as the signature for watermark detection. However, exact histogram specification does not involve a secret embedding/detection key, and there are few other histogram-based watermarking algorithms without this problem.

For example, the video watermarking scheme by (Chen et al., 2009) first computes the mean value of luminance values for each frame in the video sequence, then computes a histogram for the temporal sequence of the mean values and embeds the watermark by comparing and modifying neighbouring histogram bins. A watermark key is not used for embedding.

The scheme proposed by (Xiang et al., 2008) represents the histogram shape as the ratios of population between groups of two neighbouring bins and then modifies the ratios to carry a key-based pseudo-random sequence. Only histogram bins in the range $[(1-\lambda)\overline{A},(1+\lambda)\overline{A}]$ are used in the process, where $\overline{A}$ is the global mean of the histogram and $\lambda \in [0.5, 0.7]$ is a public parameter (note that λ must be a multiple of $1/\overline{A}$). In order to withstand scaling and cropping attacks on the image that will also affect the histogram and the mean, the extraction algorithm uses a search process based on the mean $\overline{A}'$ of the histogram of the marked image: Different ranges $[(1-\lambda)(\overline{A}'+s),(1+\lambda)(\overline{A}'+s)]$, where s is an integer running through some search space, are tried, until the correlation between the extracted sequence and the known embedded sequence reaches a maximum. The resulting scheme is very robust against geometric image modifications and lossy compression, but it suffers from two severe limitations: The parameter λ may be seen as a watermarking key if kept secret, but as λ is taken from the interval

$[0.5, 0.7]$, this interval can searched through for candidate values of λ using a stepsize of $1 / \bar{A} \approx 1 / 128$. Thus, there are only $(0.7 - 0.5) \times 128 \approx 26$ possibilities for λ, and the correct value of λ can be verified by an attacker by matching the detected watermark to the embedded watermark, if the latter is known. The effective capacity of the scheme is only 20-30 bits. Moreover, as this scheme calculates the image histogram only after filtering out high-frequency information using a Gaussian kernel low-pass filter (and writing this information back into the image after watermarking), it cannot be used in a CWE scheme because encrypted and unencrypted images will contain different high-frequency information.

Two other histogram-based watermarking schemes do use a longer watermarking key, but are by construction prone to histogram shift attacks: The scheme proposed by (Chrysochos et al., 2007) is based on the idea of (selectively) swapping two selected histogram bins a and b containing the pixels with values a and b, respectively. In this scheme, the distance $|b - a|$ between a and b is a fixed number $d < 10$. A message bit is encoded by the relative heights of the bins (denoted by $hist(a)$ and $hist(b)$: a 1-bit is encoded by $hist(a) > hist(b)$ and a 0-bit by $hist(a) < hist(b)$. Here, swapping two histogram bins a and b means changing all pixel values a to b and vice versa.

In (Schmitz et al., 2012), the scheme described in (Chrysochos et al., 2007) was extended and integrated into an invariant encryption based CWE scheme. Histogram bins a and b are randomly selected from the 256 available bins under the condition that their relative distance d is smaller than 10. This leads to a significant enlargement of the key space. As this scheme also forms the basis for the present watermarking algorithm it is described in greater detail in Sec. 4.

HISTOGRAM SHIFT ATTACKS

Most histogram-based watermarking algorithms work by analyzing the image histogram at certain location defined by a watermarking key. If an attacker manages to de-synchronize embedder and detector such that they analyze different parts of the histogram, the watermark cannot be detected anymore. In this section simple histogram modification attacks are described, where the histogram as a whole is shifted along the horizontal axis by adding a (positive or negative) fixed amount to each pixel value. As mentioned above, in principle these attacks are relevant for all histogram-based watermarking algorithms that rely on manipulating certain pre-defined histogram bins. This fact is demonstrated for the earlier schemes by (Chrysochos et al., 2007) and (Schmitz et al., 2012) in Sec. 5.

Three different types of histogram shifting may be identified, where the discussion is focussed on gray-scale images with a bit-depth of 256 for the sake of simplicity. The basic principle can be easily generalized to colour images and images with a higher bit depth.

Cyclic Histogram Shifting

In a cyclic shift, each pixel value $P(i,j)$ is shifted by a certain amount x modulo 256:

$$P_{attacked}(i, j) = (P(i, j) + x) \bmod 256 ,$$

where x is a positive or negative integer. Due to the wrap-up at both edges of the histogram, cyclic histogram shifting may lead to severe degradation of image quality (see Fig. 1(b)). Cyclic histogram shifts therefore constitute practically less relevant attacks. Moreover, cyclic shifts are invertible if the amount of shift is known. This fact will be used later, when it is tried to approximate non-cyclic shifts by suitable cyclic shifts.

Accumulated Non-Cyclic Histogram Shifting

A more relevant attack leading to less degradation of image quality is accumulated non-cyclic histogram shifting. Here, the wrap-up in cyclic shifting is avoided as the shift is only applied to those pixels whose gray values are sufficiently small or large. For example, a rightward shift can be defined by

$$P_{attacked}(i,j) = \begin{cases} P(i,j) + x, if\ P(i,j) < 256 - x, \\ \qquad P(i,j) else, \end{cases}$$

where x is a positive integer chosen by an attacker. Analogously, a leftward shift may be defined by using a negative integer x. This kind of histogram modification leads to an accumulation of pixels at the start or the end of the histogram. Nevertheless, the amount of image distortion remains small, if $|x|$ is sufficiently small. Note that this kind of histogram shift normally cannot be fully reverted, unless sufficient information about the original histogram is known.

Histogram Cropping

In a histogram cropping attack, the bins are shifted to the left (or to the right), where bins are dropped if their corresponding pixel value exceeds 255 or falls below zero. To be specific, a rightward shift-and-crop operation can be defined by the new histogram

$$H_{attacked}(i) = \begin{cases} 0, if\ 0 \leq i \leq x - 1, \\ \quad H(i - x), else. \end{cases}$$

The parameter x can be seen as a measure for the amount of shift, before the cropping takes place. The resulting histogram for small $|x|$ is similar to the original one (see Fig. 1(d)), but contains less pixels and therefore does not constitute a valid histogram for the original image. However, after rescaling the attacked histogram, the attacked image can be reconstructed from the attacked histogram by exact histogram specification (Coltuc & Bolon, 1999).

Comparing the Shifts

Figure 1 shows the visual influence of the three kinds of histogram shift on an example image. In all cases, the blue channel histogram has been shifted by an amount of 20. Note the visible artifacts in the case of a cyclical shift, while the other two shifts do not have any visible effect.

Although the different visual influence, the three kinds of shifts can behave very similarly up to a certain amount of shift, depending on the histogram shape. Figure 2 shows the effects of the various kinds of shifts on the same example histogram (the blue channel histogram of the baboon image, see Fig. 2(a)).

Figure 1. Effects of a histogram shift by the amount of 20: (a) Original image; (b) Cyclical shift (PSNR: 34.22); (c) Non-cyclical shift (PSNR: 41.09); (d) Shifted and cropped blue channel histogram (PSNR: 42.46).

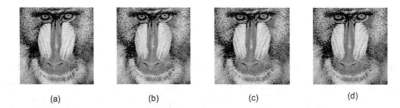

The amount of distortion caused by each type of histogram shift can be verified by calculating the PSNR (Peak Signal-to-Noise-Ratio) between the blue channel of the original image P and the blue channel of the attacked image $P_{attacked}$ computed from the shifted blue channel histogram. The PSNR is for monochromatic images consisting of $(m \times n)$ pixels defined by

$$PSNR = 10 \log_{10} \left(\frac{\left(\max\limits_{1 \le i \le m, 1 \le j \le n} P(i,j) \right)^2}{MSE} \right), where\ MSE = \frac{1}{m \cdot n} \sum_{i=1}^{m} \sum_{j=1}^{n} \left(P(i,j) - P_{attacked}(i,j) \right)^2$$

is called the Mean Squared Error. In Fig. 3 the resulting PSNR is plotted against the amount of shift for the three types of shift and for two different test images. Figure 3(b) shows a very similar behaviour of all three shift types, while in Figure 3(a) there is a marked difference between the graph of the cyclic shift (shown in red) and the other two types. Shifting the right graph horizontally, however, will bring

Figure 2. Effects of a histogram shift by the amount of 20: (a) Original histogram; (b) Cyclically shifted histogram; (c) Non-cyclically shifted histogram; (d) Shifted and cropped histogram.

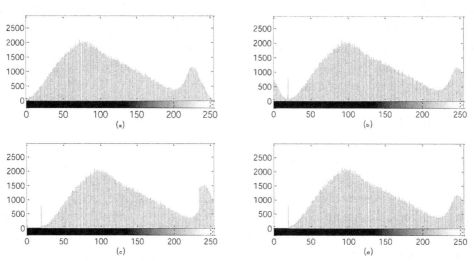

it very close to the other two graphs, meaning that the non-cyclic shifts and histogram crops can be approximated by cyclic shifts of a slightly different amount.

As cyclic shifts can be reverted, it seems reasonable to assume that the effects of non-cyclic shifts and histogram crops on the watermarked image can be approximately reverted by a suitably chosen cyclic histogram shift at the detector side. The optimal cyclic shift amount is found when the linear correlation of the detected mark and the reference mark reaches the maximum (see Sec. 4).

PROPOSED CWE ALGORITHM

The design goal of the presented algorithm is to improve the robustness of previous histogram-oriented CWE algorithms against simple histogram shifts, while retaining the original advantages, especially commutativity of watermarking and permuation-based encryption. Moreover, the algorithm should be able to use a watermarking key that is long enough to withstand brute-force attacks.

Embedding

In order to embed a given bipolar N-bit watermark $W = \{w_i\}, 1 \leq i \leq N$ (i.e. $w_i \in \{-1, 1\}$), a single watermark bit w_i is embedded by pseudo-randomly selecting two histogram bins that have not been selected before if their distance is smaller than some parameter d and if they are not of equal height. Here, bipolar watermarking bits were chosen in order to facilitate watermark detection via linear correlation. The heights of the two selected bins a_i and b_i encode w_i as follows: if $w_i = 1$, hist(a_i) < hist(b_i) should hold, and if $w_i = -1$, hist(a_i) > hist(b_i) should hold, where hist(x) denotes the height of bin x. If this is not the case, the two bins a_i and b_i are swapped. The selection process for the bin pairs is governed by a watermark key W_K. The theoretical maximum capacity that can be achieved by this scheme is 128 bits and can be further extended by using more than one colour channel and/or subdividing the image.

Figure 3. The amounts of distortion caused by histogram shifts: (a) Blue channel of Baboon image; (b) Blue channel of Lenna image.

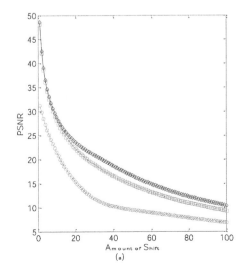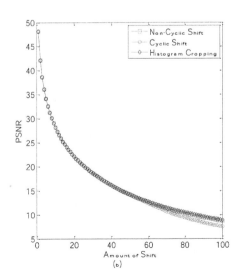

In order to speed up the search for the optimal amount of cyclic shift during extraction, a a calibration process was devised that uses the global mean value $\bar{A}$ of the image as a calibration point. More specifically, before selecting the histogram bins for embedding, all bins are cyclically shifted by an amount of $x = 256 - \bar{A}$ as described in Sec. 3 so that the bin corresponding to $\bar{A}$ becomes the first bin in the calibrated histogram. After calibrating, the embedding process proceeds as described above.

Detection

Basically, the detector works by comparing the histogram bins as specified by the watermarking key. For this to work the embedder and the detector need to be synchronized, i.e. they need to use the same ordering of histogram bins. As a histogram shift will change the global mean gray value of the watermarked image, the detector searches for the correct calibration point by cyclically shifting the histogram of the watermarked image by an amount of $x = 256 - \bar{A'} - s$, where $\bar{A'}$ is the mean value of the marked shifted image, and s runs through the search space $S = \{s \mid -\bar{A'}/4 \le s \le \bar{A'}/4\}$. If needed, this search space may be enlarged until it covers the complete range $0 \le s \le 255$ (see also Sec. 5). The detector then computes the linear correlation of the extracted watermark $W_{\text{ex}} = \{\tilde{w}_i\}$ with the reference watermark $W = \{w_i\}$ for each s. The detector response is

$$\max_{-\bar{A'}/4 \le s \le \bar{A'}/4} \left(\frac{1}{N} \sum_{i=1}^{N} \tilde{w}_i w_i \right).$$

As usual in correlation based detection, the watermark is detected if the detector response exceeds a certain previously chosen threshold T. A larger T means a lower false positive probability and a higher false negative probability (see below). While the synchronization process proposed by (Xiang et al., 2008) is very similar to the calibration process described here, the present approach has a much larger key space and a higher capacity.

Keyspace and False Positive Probability

As the calibration process prior to selecting the histogram bin pairs does not affect the number of available bin pairs, the key space size $K(N)$, where N is the length of the watermark, stays the same as in the earlier scheme (Schmitz et al., 2012). In order to get a lower bound on $K(N)$, the 256 histogram bins are partitioned into N disjoint parts, each containing bins.

In order to embed a single bit, a bin pair from each part is chosen. The members of the bin pair must not be further than d apart. As there may be less than d bins in each part, there are possibilities to define a bin pair. Repeating this for each watermarking bit and noticing that the N bits may be arbitrarily permuted, gives an upper bound of

$$K(N) > N! \left(\frac{256}{N} \times \min \left\{ d, \frac{256}{N} - 1 \right\} \right)^{N}.$$

For $N = 32$ and $d = 10$, the key length is already well beyond 200 bits.

In order to simplify the analysis of the false positive probability, it is assumed that the bipolar bits of W_{ex} are evenly distributed in the set $\{-1, 1\}$. Then, the probability that two single bits of W and W_{ex} agree is 1/2. Now let $\tilde{W}$ be a mark extracted from an unmarked image I_U. If $\tilde{W}$ agrees with W at k positions, their linear correlation is $\dfrac{2k - N}{N}$. Therefore, the mark is wrongly detected if $k > \dfrac{N}{2}(T + 1)$. Therefore, the false positive probability for a single detection step becomes

$$p(\textit{False Positive}) = q = \left(\frac{1}{2}\right)^N \cdot \sum_{k = \left\lceil \frac{N}{2}(T+1) \right\rceil}^{N} \binom{N}{k}.$$

For example, if $N = 64$, choosing the detection threshold $T = 0.7$ and evaluating the formula above leads to a false positive probability $q \leq 1.77 \times 10^{-9}$, while choosing a lower bound $T = 0.3$ gives $q \leq 0.0084$. If the detection process is carried out by running through a search space of size $|S|$, the false positive probability becomes

$$p(\textit{False Positive}) = 1 - (1 - q)^{|S|} \approx q \, |S| \; \textit{for small } q.$$

On the other hand, false negative probabilities in general are highly dependent on what happens to the watermarked image between the time the watermark was embedded and the time it is detected. The watermark can be distorted by lossy compression and other image processing operations, resulting in an increased probability of a false negative (cf. (Cox et al., 2007)). It is therefore very difficult to give an analytical estimation of the false negative probability in general. Instead, the robustness of the proposed watermarking algorithm against histogram shifts and lossy compression is experimentally assessed in Sec. 5. A higher robustness of the watermark automatically results in a lower false negative probability.

Commutativity With Permutation-Based Encryption

As the presented algorithm is completely histogram-based and the histogram is invariant to permutations, the commutativity property

$$M(E_k(I), m) = E_k(M(I, m))$$

holds, where E is the encryption function, k is the encryption key, I is the plaintext media data, M is the watermarking function and m is the mark to be embedded. Figure 4 shows an example encryption-watermarking process. In the upper row, the plaintext image I is first encrypted by using the iterations of the Cat Map and watermarked afterwards. The result (Figure 4(c)) is $M(E_k(I), m)$. In the lower row, on the other hand, the plaintext image is watermarked first and then encrypted, resulting in $E_k(M(I, m))$ (see Fig. 4(e)). Finally, Fig. 4(f) shows the difference image of $M(E_k(I), m)$ and $E_k(M(I, m))$ where all pixels have colour values zero.

Figure 4. Commutative Watermarking-Encryption process for the baboon image: (a) Plaintext Image; (b) Encrypted Image; (c) Watermarked Encrypted Image; (d) Watermarked Plaintext Image; (e) Encrypted Watermarked Image; (f) Difference Image of (c) and (e).

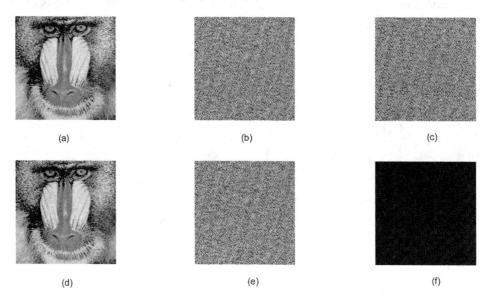

In the prototype implementation, a permutation generated by the repeated application of a discrete two-dimensional chaotic map, the so-called Cat Map is used (see (Schmitz et al., 2012) and (Chen et al., 2004) for details) for encryption.

EXPERIMENTAL RESULTS

In the experiments described here, 64 random bits are embedded into the blue channel of all the 24 images from the Kodak image database (see http://r0k.us/graphics/kodak) and three additional standard images from the SIPI image database (a collection of digitized images hosted at the Signal and Image Processing Institute of the University of Southern California, see http://sipi.usc.edu/database/). The amount of visual distortion is measured for two different maximum step sizes d and robustness against histogram shifts and JPEG/JPEG2000 compression is investigated.

Visual Distortion

The main difference between the present algorithm and the algorithm proposed in (Schmitz, 2012) consists in the calibration step performed before embedding and detecting, which has no impact on the amount of distortion. Therefore, results on visual distortion basically carry over from (Schmitz et al., 2012).

In order to assess the overall visual quality, the Structural Similarity Index (SSIM, cf. (Wang et al., 2004)) was chosen as metric, because SSIM correlates better to the human visual system than the traditionally more used Peak Signal-to-Noise Ratio (PSNR). Figure 5 shows the SSIM values for the 24 images from the Kodak database after embedding 64 random bits, where embedding was carried out

Figure 5. Visual quality comparison of embedding 64 bits into 24 test images with maximum stepsizes $d = 10$ (blue bars) and $d = 15$ (red bars).

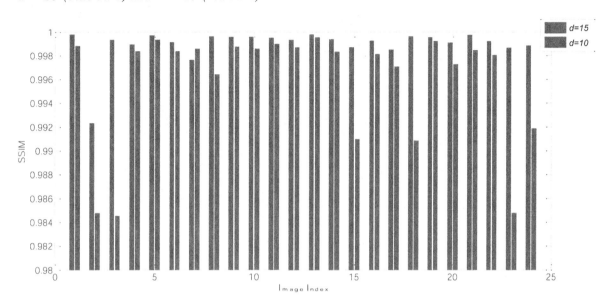

with two different maximum step sizes $d = 10$ and $d = 15$, respectively. Clearly, visual distortions are higher for the greater stepsize, but they remain low for both stepsizes.

Figure 6 shows the visual effect of embedding 64 random bits into the blue channel of three standard images from the SIPI database with a maximum stepsize $d = 10$. Only the marked images are shown.

Robustness Against Histogram Shifts

First, the robustness of two earlier algorithms (Chrysochos, 2007) and (Schmitz, 2012) against histogram shifts was tested. As expected, the watermark is completely destroyed in most cases, resulting in a correlation value around or even below zero (see Fig. 7).

Figure 6. Embedding 64 random bits into three standard test images: (a) Watermarked baboon image (PSNR: 50.55 dB); (b) Watermarked sailboat image (PSNR: 58.86 dB); (c) Watermarked Lenna image (PSNR: 58.60 dB).

(a)   (b)   (c)

Figure 7. Robustness of previous histogram-based watermarking algorithms against histogram shifts: (a) Algorithm by Chrysochos et al. (2007); (b) Algorithm by Schmitz et al. (2012).

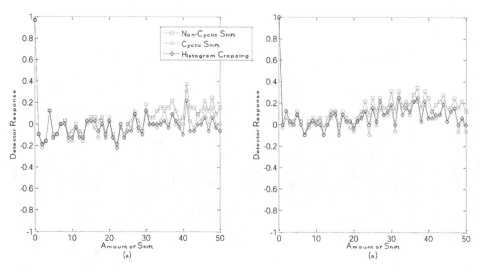

When testing the improved algorithm described in Sec. 4, it turned out that the three standard images from the SIPI database (Baboon, Sailboat and Lenna) show a rather prototypical behaviour with respect to robustness against the three kinds of histogram shift attacks. Figures 8(a) and 8(b) show a very good robustness for the sailboat and Lenna image, due to the fact that the corresponding histograms behave very similarly for the three kinds of shift and the shifts may thus be reversed by a suitable cyclic shift quite accurately. The relevant histogram for Figs. 8(c) and 8(d) is the blue channel histogram of the baboon image (see Fig. 2(a)), which behaves less favourably. In this case, the results can be significantly improved by enlarging the search space, e.g. to $S = \{s \mid -\overline{A}' / 2 \leq s \leq \overline{A}' / 2\}$ as Fig. 8(d) shows.

Figure 8. Robustness results against histogram shifts: (a) Sailboat image; (b) Lenna image; (c) Baboon image; (d) Baboon image with an enlarged search space.

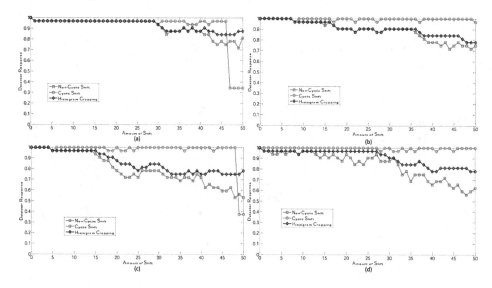

All other tested images behaved in a similar way. Thus, a robust detection strategy consists in enlarging the search space successively if the mark is not detected using a smaller search space. The resulting increase of the false positive probability is negligible (see Sec. 4).

In order to get an overall impression of the robustness against histogram shifts, Figure 9 gives the average results of the tests with the 24 images in the Kodak database. Even with a shift amount of 50, the watermark can still be reliably detected with a threshold value of $T = 0.7$.

Robustness Against Compression

In this part of the section the robustness of the proposed watermarking algorithm against JPEG and JPEG2000 compression is reported. As Fig. 10 shows, the histograms are affected even by mild compression in a quite serious way that is similar to adding random noise to the image. Different from histogram shifts, there is no connection to cyclic shifts and the calibration process described above will not have an effect. Therefore, it can be expected that the robustness against compression of watermarking algorithms based on comparing histogram bins is not very high.

Figure 11 shows the detector results when an uncompressed image (the Lenna image) is watermarked and afterwards compressed using JPEG and JPEG 2000 with varying quality degrees. Watermarking was done with the previous algorithms (Chrysochos, 2007) and (Schmitz, 2012). While the later algorithm gives better detector responses, it is clear from these results that neither algorithms are robust with respect to JPEG / JPEG2000 compression.

Figure 12, on the other hand, shows the corresponding results for the algorithm proposed in the present chapter. Here, watermarking was done with two different stepsizes to see if increasing the step size can improve robustness against lossy compression.

As the results in Fig.12 show, there is some improvement compared to the earlier algorithms (Chrysochos, 2007) and (Schmitz, 2012), leading to a modest degree of robustness against JPEG/JPEG2000 compression. The robustness against JPEG2000 compression can be slightly increased if a bigger stepsize for embedding is used, i.e. the maximum difference between histogram bin pairs for embedding is

Figure 9. Robustness results against histogram shifts averaged over 24 test images.

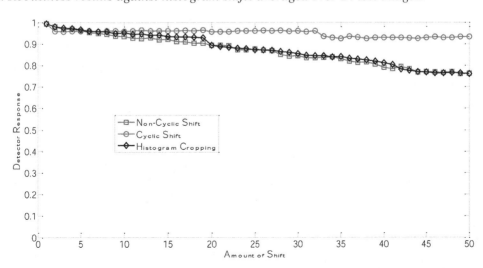

Figure 10. Effects of JPEG and JPEG2000 compression on the blue channel histogram of the Lenna image: (a) uncompressed image; (b) JPEG compression with quality factor 90 (PSNR 40.78); (c) JPEG2000 compression with compression ratio 10.72 (PSNR 41.70).

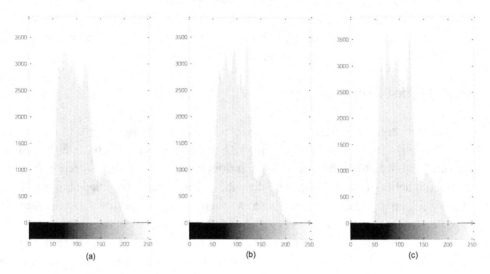

Figure 11. Robustness of earlier histogram-based watermarking algorithm in Lenna image against JPEG and JPEG 2000 compression (a) JPEG compression; (b) JPEG 2000 compression.

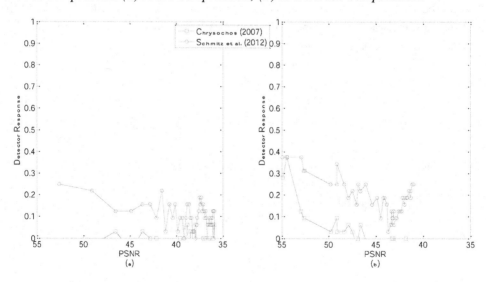

enlarged. Other than for the older algorithms, for detection a threshold value of $T = 0.3$ may be used, corresponding to a false positive probability of 0.84% (cf. Sec. 4). This claim is confirmed by Fig. 13 showing the averaged robustness results against compression for the 24 images of the Kodak database.

Figure 12. Robustness of proposed CWE algorithm applied to Lenna image: (a) JPEG compression and (b) JPEG 2000 compression.

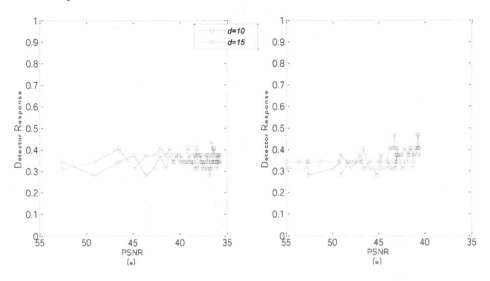

Figure 13. Robustness against JPEG and JPEG2000 compression averaged over 24 test images: (a) JPEG compression; (b) JPEG2000 compression.

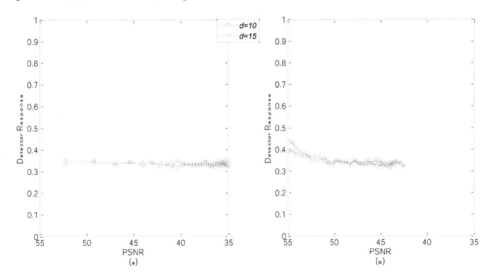

COMPARISON OF RELATED WATERMARKING SCHEMES FOR IMAGE DATA

Table 1 provides a qualitative overview of the merits of four histogram-based watermarking algorithms, including the one proposed here. The four algorithms were chosen due to the fact that they all base embedding and detection on comparing selected watermarking bins. Robustness against histogram shifts was not tested for the algorithm in (Xiang et al., 2008), but due to the reported high robustness against lossy compression and the fact that it uses similar techniques to the one proposed here, good robustness against histogram shifts can be expected for that algorithm.

Table 1. Qualitative Comparison of histogram based watermarking algorithms.

Algorithm	Robustness Against Histogram Shifts	Robustness Against Lossy Compression	Key Length	Capacity	Suitable for CWE
Chrysochos (2007)	low	low	~ 11 bits	~ 128 bits	yes
Schmitz et al. (2012)	low	low	> 200 bits	~ 128 bits	yes
Xiang et al. (2008)	not tested	high	~ 5 bits	20- 30 bits	no
Proposed	high	moderate	> 200 bits	~ 128 bits	yes

EXTENSIONS OF THE ORIGINAL CWE SCHEME

In this section two extensions of the original CWE scheme for still image data are reported. The first of these extensions is an adaption of the scheme for audio data, which was first presented in (Schmitz & Gruber, 2017). The second extension is concerned with using the watermark for authenticating the content of an image (Schmitz et al., 2015).

CWE for Audio Data

An analogue audio signal is transferred into the digital domain by sampling the time-continuous signal at a certain discrete sampling rate. At the same time, the obtained samples are quantized according to the bit depth available, the result being a set of N sample values $F = \{f(i) \mid 0 \leq i \leq N - 1\}$ where the index i can be seen as a discrete time coordinate. Common bit depths for representing audio are 16, 20 or 24 bit. The general idea is to permute the discrete points in time, while leaving the sample values untouched. In order to generate the permutations, as in section 4, the discrete version of Arnold's Cat Map was used.

Because the Cat Map is a two-dimensional map, in order to apply it on a discrete audio signal of length N, the audio signal is rearranged into a square grid of size $\sqrt{N}$. If is N not a square number, the signal is padded with random sample values having the same probability distribution (i.e. the same histogram) as the original signal. Figure 14 shows the effect of encrypting the first three seconds of an example audio file.

Figure 14. Effect of Encrypting an Example Audio File of Three Seconds Length: (a) Plaintext Audio; (b) Permuted Audio

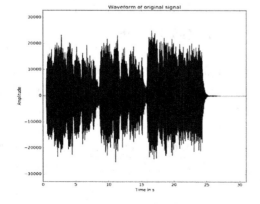
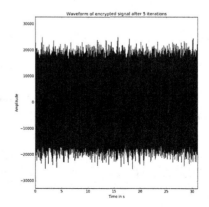

It was possible to embed an histogram-based watermark into the audio file while retaining the CWE property. Figure 15 shows the PSNR between original file and watermarked file for increasing watermark length and seven different example soundfiles.

CWE for Image Authentication

The contents of an image can be authenticated by so called *content-fragile* (or *semi-fragile*) watermarks. In these watermarks, one tries to strike the middle ground between exact authentication as provided by cryptographic hash functions or digital signatures, and robust watermarks that are hard to destroy by any image modification. They are supposed to survive benign operations like compression, but should be destroyed by modifications of the image content. In the most common way of content-fragile watermarking, the first step is to compute a content-fragile signature value, which is a numerical value representing the semantics of the image. The content-fragile signature is then embedded by some robust watermarking scheme. In the verification process, the watermark is extracted from the marked image and compared to the signature value computed from the marked image. Therefore, care must be taken that the watermarking process does not influence the signature value. Very often, these watermarks are applied separately to small image parts, so that unauthorized content modifications can be localized.

At first glance, it seems to be paradoxical to search for a content-fragile watermark that is commutative with encryption. After all, the encryption process is supposed to destroy the visual information from an image, so how can a content-related watermark survive this operation? However, in the past, there have been attempts to define content-fragile signatures which only involve first-order statistics of the image, but no localization information, like the mean histogram value (Schneider and Chang, 1996) and the pixel entropy (Thiemert et al., 2006). Obviously, this kind of signatures will be invariant under permutation ciphers. The same is true for watermarking strategies that are purely histogram based. In order to be able to combine these two approaches, the watermarking process must not change the histogram in such a way that the content-fragile signature is affected.

More specifically, in (Schmitz et al., 2015) the pixel entropy defined as

Figure 15. Fidelity over Capacity Graph for Seven Soundfiles

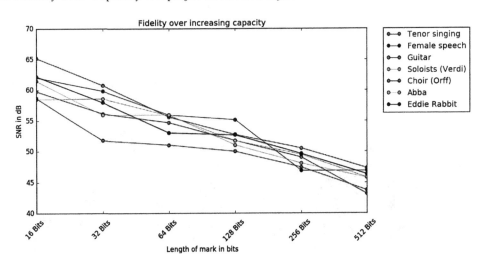

$$PE(I,c) = -\sum_{k=0}^{L} p_k \log_2(p_k)$$

is used as a content-fragile signature, where p_k is the probability of the grey value k within the colour channel c and L is the maximum grey value.

The pixel entropy has some interesting properties which make it useful for content-related commutative watermarking-encryption. Obviously, it is invariant under pixel permutations, meaning it does not change if the image undergoes a permutation-based cipher. Moreover, it is also invariant under permutations of the histogram bins of a colour channel, because permuting the histogram bins will permute the order of summation in the above equation, but will not change the value of the pixel entropy. This implies that the pixel entropy is invariant under the watermarking process described in section 4.

Following this reasoning, in (Schmitz et al., 2015) a CWE scheme for image authentication has been devised. The scheme can be localized, meaning it is capable of showing the location of image modifications, if it is applied to different rectangular image regions separately. Figure 16 shows the results of embedding, modifying the marked image and trying to verify the mark after the modification, respectively.

In a variant of the localized scheme, the region which is authenticated by the watermark is randomized by using an additional secret key. While this version is not able to localize modifications, the randomization makes it harder for an attacker to construct collisions (variants of image regions having the same content-fragile signature as the original region).

CONCLUSION

In this chapter a way to combine watermarking and encryption of multimedia data in a commutative way has been presented, meaning the watermark can be embedded (and extracted) in the cleartext domain and the encrypted domain. The general watermarking scheme can be used e. g. for annotation or copyright protection of still images, audio and even video data. An extension of the general watermarking scheme can be used for image authentication in the encrypted domain. The guiding idea here is to use a cipher which leaves a certain feature space of the media data invariant and to use this feature space for embedding the watermark, the so-called invariant encryption approach.

Figure 16. From left to right: (a) Original image; (b) Marked image (PSNR 43.82 db, SSIM 0.98); (c) Modified marked original image (note the black dots below the nose); (d) Verified original image showing the modified region.

Generally speaking, it is hard to devise a robust watermarking algorithm that can work in the encrypted domain because there are no perceptually important features to use for embedding in this case. Therefore, in the present chapter, extended an earlier algorithm that is commutative with encryption has been extended by deploying a synchronization process between the embedder and the detector, making it robust against simple histogram shifts and modestly robust against lossy compression. While Commutative Watermarking-Encryption schemes based on partial encryption have the advantage of higher robustness against lossy compression, the invariant encryption approach proposed here has the advantage of full encryption of the media data. Furthermore, unlike previous more robust histogram-based watermarking algorithms, it is able to use a watermarking key that is long enough to withstand brute-force attacks. Further work in this area will focus on improving robustness of the presented algorithm against lossy compression and other types of common multimedia processing operations.

REFERENCES

Boho, A., van Wallendael, G., Dooms, A., de Cock, J., Braeckman, G., Schelkens, P., ... Van de Walle, R. (2013). End-to-end security for video distribution. *IEEE Signal Processing Magazine*, *30*(2), 97–107. doi:10.1109/MSP.2012.2230220

Chen, B., & Wornell, G. W. (2001). Quantization Index Modulation: A class of provably good methods for digital watermarking and information embedding. *IEEE Transactions on Information Theory*, *47*(4), 1423–1443. doi:10.1109/18.923725

Chen, C., Ni, J., & Huang, J. (2009). Temporal statistic based video watermarking scheme robust against geometric attacks and frame dropping. *Digital Watermarking: 8th. International Workshop IWDW 2009, Guildford, UK, August 24-16, 2009, Proceedings*, 81-95.

Chen, G., Mao, Y., & Chui, C. K. (2004). A symmetric image encryption scheme based on 3D chaotic cat maps. *Chaos, Solitons, and Fractals*, *21*(3), 749–761. doi:10.1016/j.chaos.2003.12.022

Chrysochos, E., Fotopoulos, V., Skodras, A. N., & Xenos, M. (2007). Reversible image watermarking based on histogram modification. *Proc. 11th Panhellenic Conf. Informatics*, 93-104.

Coltuc, D., & Bolon, P. (1999). Robust watermarking by histogram specification. *Proc. Int. Conf. Image Processing*, 2, 236-239.

Cox, I. J., Miller, M., Bloom, J., Fridrich, J., & Kalker, T. (2007). *Digital Watermarking and Steganography*. Morgan Kaufman.

Dagadu, J. C., & Li, J. (2018). (2018). Context-based watermarking cum chaotic encryption for medical images in telemedicine applications. *Multimedia Tools and Applications*. doi:10.100711042-018-5725-y

Fontaine, C., & Galand, F. (2007). A survey of homomorphic encryption for nonspecialists. EURASIP Journal on Information Security.

Herrera-Joancomarti, J., Katzenbeisser, S., Megias, D., Minguillon, J., Pommer, A., Steinebach, M., & Uhl, A. (2005). *First summary report on hybrid systems*. EU project ECRYPT (European Network of Excellence in Cryptology), Deliverable D.WVL.5.

Lagendijk, R.-L., Erkin, Z., & Barni, M. (2013). Encrypted signal processing for privacy protection. *IEEE Signal Processing Magazine, 30*(1), 82–105. doi:10.1109/MSP.2012.2219653

Lian, S. (2008). *Multimedia Content Encryption: Techniques and Applications*. CRC Press, Auerbach Publications.

Lian, S. (2009). Quasi-commutative watermarking and encryption for secure media content distribution. *Multimedia Tools and Applications, 43*(1), 91–107. doi:10.100711042-008-0258-4

Lian, S., Liu, Z., Zhen, R., & Wang, H. (2006). Commutative watermarking and encryption for media data. *Optical Engineering (Redondo Beach, Calif.), 45*(8), 080510. doi:10.1117/1.2333510

Lin, C. H., Chan, D. Y., Su, H., & Hsieh, W. S. (2006). Histogram-oriented watermarking algorithm: Colour image watermarking scheme robust against geometric attacks and signal processing. *IEE Proceedings. Vision Image and Signal Processing, 153*(4), 483–492. doi:10.1049/ip-vis:20050107

Pappa, C. K., Vijayaraj, M., & Subbulakshmi, M. (2017). (2017), An optimal approach for watermarking using MRC4 encryption scheme. *Cluster Computing*. doi:10.100710586-017-1349-7

Roy, S., & Chang, E. C. (2004). Watermarking color histograms. *Proc. 2004 Int. Conf. Image Processing*, 2191-2194.

Schmitz, R., & Gruber, J. (2017). Commutative Watermarking Encryption of Audio Data with Minimum Knowledge Verification. *Advances in Multimedia, 2017*, 5879257. doi:10.1155/2017/5879257

Schmitz, R., Li, S., Grecos, C., & Zhang, X. (2012). A new approach to commutative watermarking-encryption. *Communications and Multimedia Security: 13th IFIP TC 6/TC 11 International Conf., CMS 2012, Canterbury, UK, September 3-5, 2012. Proceedings*, 117-130.

Schmitz, R., Li, S., Grecos, C., & Zhang, X. (2013). Towards more robust commutative watermarking-encryption. *Proceedings of 2013 IEEE International Symposium on Multimedia*, 283-286. 10.1109/ISM.2013.54

Schmitz, R., Li, S., Grecos, C., & Zhang, X. (2014). Towards Robust Invariant Commutative Watermarking-Encryption based on Image Histograms. *International Journal of Multimedia Data Engineering and Management, 5*(4), 36–52. doi:10.4018/ijmdem.2014100103

Schmitz, R., Li, S., Grecos, C., & Zhang, X. (2015). Content-Fragile Commutative Watermarking-Encryption Based on Pixel Entropy. *Lecture Notes in Computer Science, 9386*, 474–485. doi:10.1007/978-3-319-25903-1_41

Schneider, M., & Chang, S. F. (1996): A robust content based digital signature for image authentication, *Proc. International Conference on Image Processing*, 3, 227–230. 10.1109/ICIP.1996.560425

Subramanyam, A. V., Emmanuel, S., & Kankanhalli, M. S. (2012). Robust watermarking of compressed and encrypted JPEG2000 images. *IEEE Transactions on Multimedia, 14*(3), 703–716. doi:10.1109/TMM.2011.2181342

Thiemert, S., Sahbi, H., & Steinebach, M. (2006). Using entropy for image and video authentication watermarks. *Proceedings of the Society for Photo-Instrumentation Engineers, 6072*, 607218–1, 607218–10. doi:10.1117/12.643053

Wang, Z., Bovik, A. C., Sheikh, H. R., & Simoncelli, E. P. (2004). Image quality assessment: From error visibility to structural similarity. *IEEE Transactions on Image Processing, 13*(4), 600–612. doi:10.1109/TIP.2003.819861 PMID:15376593

Xiang, S., Kim, H. J., & Huang, J. (2008). Invariant image watermarking based on statistical features in the low-frequency domain. *IEEE Transactions on Circuits and Systems for Video Technology, 18*(6), 777–790. doi:10.1109/TCSVT.2008.918843

Xu, Z., Xiong, L., & Xu, Y. (2014). On the provably secure CEW based on orthogonal decomposition. *Signal Processing Image Communication, 29*(5), 607–617. doi:10.1016/j.image.2013.10.007

Chapter 7
De–Noising of Binary Image Using Accelerated Local Median–Filtering Approach

Amit Khan
RCC Institute of Information Technology, India

Dipankar Majumdar
RCC Institute of Information Technology, India

ABSTRACT

In the last few decades huge amounts and diversified work has been witnessed in the domain of de-noising of binary images through the evolution of the classical techniques. These principally include analytical techniques and approaches. Although the scheme was working well, the principal drawback of these classical and analytical techniques are that the information regarding the noise characteristics is essential beforehand. In addition to that, time complexity of analytical works amounts to beyond practical applicability. Consequently, most of the recent works are based on heuristic-based techniques conceding to approximate solutions rather than the best ones. In this chapter, the authors propose a solution using an iterative neural network that applies iterative spatial filtering technology with critically varied size of the computation window. With critical variation of the window size, the authors are able to show noted acceleration in the filtering approach (i.e., obtaining better quality filtration with lesser number of iterations).

INTRODUCTION

In real life often images are found within a noisy perspective, whether it is a camera shot image or printed image of old books, newspapers or posters or even micro or distant vision instruments like microscope or binoculars. In every case the human brain is able to filter the noise and extract out the object under probe with spectacular efficiency may be with certain limitations. When the scale of the input rises abruptly, human error tends to creep into the performance. Consequently, the authors resort to computational technologies in order to handle such problems. The computer obviously performs the execution

DOI: 10.4018/978-1-5225-7107-0.ch007

faster than that of the human brain but unfortunately when people expect accuracy of the level of that of the human brain, they land up in an undesired output and hence our despair. Therefore the authors feel the need for intelligent computer vision for the accomplishment of such objective. Recent years have already witnessed growth in usage of digital images in dramatic proportions and as a result they play an important role in many image processing applications such as content-based retrieval.

Needless to mention that several classical techniques have evolved over the years aimed towards addressing the above. For instance there are some graph theoretic approaches presented in (Bhattacharyya S.et. al., 2014) that employs energy function optimization technology to solve image extraction problem. While (Bhattacharyya S.et. al., 2011) presents a graph cuts based active contours (GCBAC) approach to object segmentation, (Perlovsky L.I. et al. 1997) presents ratio contour as a novel graph-based method for extracting salient closed boundaries of interesting objects from noisy images. Although these methodologies seem to give satisfactory performances in some cases, but they clearly show their inefficiency in solving the image extraction problems in the case of complicated image conditions such as in cluttered image or noisy images etc. On the other hand human visual capabilities go far ahead in its efficiency of executing the same task.

RELATED WORK

Among various extraction approaches the ones that perform better are the ones that behave in accord with human visual perceptions. Itti et al. (Bhattacharyya S.et. al., 2014) presented an approach in which Multi-scale image features are combined into a single topographical saliency map and thereafter a dynamical neural network selects the attended locations in order of decreasing saliency. Ma and Zhang (Ma Y. and Zhang H.,2003) proposed a feasible and fast approach to attention area detection in images based on contrast analysis. The main contributions are generation of a new saliency map through a method based on local contrast analysis followed by simulation of human perception as a fuzzy growing method to extract attended areas or objects from the saliency map; and finally a practicable framework has been presented for image attention analysis.

Achanta et al. (Achanta R.et. al., 2009) introduced a method for salient region detection that outputs full resolution saliency maps with well-defined boundaries of salient objects. Their method exploits features of color and luminance, which is simple to implement, and is computationally efficient. Hou and Zhang (Hou X.and Zhang L., 2007) presented a model that is independent of features, categories, or other forms of prior knowledge of the objects. By analyzing the log-spectrum of an input image, they have extracted the spectral residual of an image in spectral domain, and proposed a fast method to construct the corresponding saliency map in spatial domain. However, nearly all existing saliency-based approaches suffer from the integrity problem, viz., the extracted result is either a small part of the object (referred to as sketch-like) or a large region that contains some redundant part of the background (referred to as envelope-like). Yu et al. (Yu H. et. al., 2010) have proposed a novel object extraction approach by integrating two kinds of "complementary" saliency maps (i.e., sketch-like and envelope-like maps). In the said approach, the extraction process is decomposed into two sub-processes, one used to extract a high-precision result based on the sketch-like map, and the other used to extract a high-recall result based on the envelope-like map. They have also proved experimentally that their approach outperforms six state-of-art saliency-based methods remarkably in automatic object extraction, and is even comparable to some interactive approaches. Other efforts in this direction demonstrate the usage of wavelets for image de-noising and compression (Achanta R.et. al., 2009), (Hou X.and Zhang L., 2007), (Yu H.et. al., 2010) .

Among the other filtering approaches Smolka et al. in (Smolka B.et. al., 2012) presents an approach to the problem of impulsive noise removal in colored digital images using switching filter which is based on the rank weighted, cumulated pixel dissimilarity measures, which are used for the detection of image samples contaminated by impulsive noise process. Neural networks have often been employed by researchers for dealing with the daunting tasks of extraction (Wang S.et. al., 2005), (Yu H.et. al., 2010), (Pham D.T. and Bayro-Corrochano E.J., 1998),(Kamgar-Parsi B.,1995), (Ghosh A. et. al., 1993), (Shiozaki A,1986) for classification (Pham D.T. and Bayro-Corrochano E.J., 1998), (Lippmann R.P., 1987), (Haykin S., 1999) of relevant object specific information from redundant image information bases and identification and recognition of objects from an image scene (Abdallah M.A. et. al., 1995), (Antonucci M.et. al., 1994),(Scott P.D. et. al., 1997), (Narendra K. C.and Satyanarayana S.,2016).

Several neural network architectures, both self-organized and unsupervised, are reported in the literature, which have been evolved to produce outputs in real time. Kohonen's self-organizing feature map (Kohonen T. 1984) is centered on pre-serving the topology in the input data by subjecting the output data units to certain neighborhood constraints. The Hopfield's network (Hopfield J.J.,1984) proposed in 1984, is fully connected network architecture with capabilities of auto-association. A photonic implementation of the Hopfield network is also reported in (Scott P.D.et. al., 1997), where a winner-take-all algorithm is used to emulate the state transitions of the network. Bhattacharyya et al. in (Bhattacharyya S.et. al., 2014) presented a quantum version of the MLSONN architecture, which is similar to the MLSONN architecture, the proposed quantum multilayer self-organizing neural network (QMLSONN) architecture for extracting a binary image from a noisy background. (Bhattacharyya S.et. al., 2011) further proposes a collection of adaptive thresholding approaches to multilevel activation functions. The proposed thresholding mechanisms incorporate the image context information in the thresholding process using a self-supervised multilayer self-organizing neural network (MLSONN) and a supervised pyramidal neural network (PyraNet).

SCOPE OF THE CHAPTER

This chapter presents an approach towards eliminating the noise from a set of binary images which are inflicted with a constant intensity of i.e. 50% noise level. Our technique employs metric based iterative noise filtering technology harnessing the power of the artificial neural network that happens to be one of the premier soft computing technologies till date. In the first stage, the size of the working window is set to its default initial value and thereafter, the same is enhanced or maintained the same with each iteration. The following sections of the chapter elaborate the same for ease of understanding.

The Chapter in organized as follows. Sub-section 3.1 and 3.2 presents a brief overview of the filtering approaches available and applicable for de-noising operation in the current context. It enlists the options available accomplishing the objective. The proposed work for the implementation of the filter is described in Section 4. The section firstly presents the diagrammatic overview of the proposed work and thereafter presents the methodology from the theoretical perspective. The application of various technologies applied and their justifications for feature based clustering of images. The Sections 5 and 6 present the usage of the Multi-Layer Self Organizing Neural Network (MLSONN) that has been used for the filtering operation.

De-Noising of Images Problems

Removal of noise from an image has been quite a perplexing yet fundamental problem for a good span of time. There have been several approaches suggested with their own assumption, benefits and limitations. Although spatial filtering approaches have been pioneering in the domain in early days of research on de-noising, transform based de-noising operations have been in the spotlight for the last few decades. Fourier Transforms have been leading the domain for about a decade followed by other variations, which have come up in recent years. Wavelets transforms have been found to yield better results in image de-noising process owing to its inherent properties namely sparsity and multi-resolution structure. As Wavelet Transform acquires reputation in the last decade, several algorithms for de-noising have been introduced utilizing the potential of the wavelet transform. Consequently the attention of the research community seems to have been shifted from the Spatial and Fourier domain to the Wavelet transform domain. In the presented chapter the authors have shown an Image de-noising approach that employs wavelet transforms for edge content estimation and performs the execution of the filtration operation on spatial domain. Generically image de-noising approaches as mentioned by Motwaniet. al. (Motwani M C.et. al., 2010) has been classified in the following sections.

Prevalent Approaches for De-Noising of Images

As a reference for readers unfamiliar with the domain we shall preset overview on the prevalent approaches for de-noising of images. As mentioned in Section 3.1 approaches for de-noising of images has been broadly classified under the following heads which are explained in the following subsections.

- Spatial Filtering Approach
- Transform Based Filtering Approach

Spatial Filtering Approaches

A regular way to remove noise from an image is to utilize spatial filters. Spatial filtering is a term that is used to refer to filtering operations that are performed directly on the pixels of an image. The process consists simply of moving the filter window from pixel to pixel in an image. At every pixel the response of the filter is calculated using a predefined relationship. The resultant value of the current pixel after computation at spatial level mainly depends on itself and neighboring pixels. Spatial filters can be further categorized into non-linear and linear filters. This class of filters accomplishes the removal of noise devoid of any attempt to identify or categorizing the same. A spatial filter utilizes a low pass filtering strategy on groups (window) of pixels. The process is executed with the assumption that the noise occupies the higher bandwidth of frequency spectrum while the data occupies the lower side. Although the spatial filters have been able to remove noise to an acceptable level but the objective has been accomplished at the cost of blurring the images which in turn makes the edges in pictures considerably blurred and leads to the image losing its luster. Researchers of contemporary times have come up with a good number of nonlinear median type filters such as mentioned below aiming at overcoming the said drawback.

- Weighted median filter
- Rank conditioned rank selection filter

- And relaxed median filter

Linear Filters

Linear filters attempt to modify an image by replacing the value at each pixel with some linear function of the values of nearby pixels. For instance if the working window is of size 3x3, the number of neighboring pixels amounts to 9 or 8 inclusive of the pixel under consideration (or not inclusive as per the choice of the algorithm designer). Consequently if the pixel under consideration is at [i, j]th index of the image, then the modified value will be

$$pixel[i, j] = flinear(\{pixel[x, y]\}) \mid x \, \varepsilon \, [i - 1, i + 1] \, AND \, y \, \varepsilon \, [j - 1, j + 1] \tag{1}$$

The function flinear({pixel[x, y]}) mentioned above may be modeled as any linear function as described below. The said function is assumed to be independent of the pixel's location (i, j), where (i, j) indexes the pixels within the image, which is represented as an m x n matrix. This kind of operation can be expressed as convolution or correlation function. For spatial filtering, it's often more intuitive to work with correlation. For example as shown in equation (1), suppose the programmer wants to use an average or mean function that works on taking average intensity of neighboring pixels that lies on a 3 x 3 window, the Equation (1) boils down to equation (1.1) as mentioned below.

$$pixel[i, j] = average(pixel[x, y]) \mid x \, \varepsilon \, [i - 1, i + 1] \, AND \, y \, \varepsilon \, [j - 1, j + 1] \tag{1.1}$$

where (i,j) indicates current pixel position and I(i,j) indicates the intensity value of a pixel at position (i,j).

Non-Linear Filters

A nonlinear filter is any filter that does not meet the criteria of linearity. Linear filter is the filtering in which the value of an output pixel is a linear combination of neighborhood values, which can produce blur in the image. Thus a variety of smoothing techniques have been developed that are nonlinear. Median filter (MF) is the one of the most popular non-linear filter. When considering a small neighborhood, it is highly efficient but for large window and in case of high noise it gives rise to more blurring to image. A median filter is specified by giving some form of neighborhood shape, which can significantly affect the behavior of the filter. This neighborhood is passed over the image as in convolution, but instead of taking a weighted sum of elements within the neighborhood, the median can be taken. Calculation of Median is done as first sorting all the pixel values from the surrounding neighborhood (either ascending or descending order) and then replacing the pixel being considered with the middle pixel value. Analogous to the equation (1) the design for the mathematical equation for the non-linear filter and median filter can be accomplished as follows:

$$pixel[i, j] = fnonlinear(\{pixel[x, y]\}) \mid x \, \varepsilon \, [i - 1, i + 1] \, AND \, y \, \varepsilon \, [j - 1, j + 1] \tag{2}$$

$$pixel[i, j] = median(\{pixel[x, y]\}) \mid x \, \varepsilon \, [i - 1, i + 1] \, AND \, y \, \varepsilon \, [j - 1, j + 1] \tag{2.1}$$

Transform Domain Filtering Approaches

This class of filtering approaches resort to noise-removal based on transforms applied on the input image. The objective behind applying noise removal filters on transform domains is the variety of noises. Noises may be Uniform, Localized, Gaussian or of other categories. Therefore varied technologies suitable for varied noise patterns need to be applied for acquiring satisfactory results. Some of the ones that worth mentioning may be enlisted as follows:

Fourier Transform Based Filtering Approaches

This category of filters, work on the basic assumption that noises differ from the information by virtue of their frequency. Consequently, if the frequency band of the noises can be identified and eliminated, the noise of the image shall be removed yielding the de-noised clear image. The same can be mathematically expressed as follows:

img(f), where the |f| < µ indicates noise and |f| > µ indicates information

A low-pass filter of the form lpfilter(f) may be defined as

```
lpfilter(f) = 1:        |f| > µ
            = 0:        otherwise
```

Similarly a high-pass filter of the form hpfilter(f) may be defined as follows:

```
hpfilter(f) = 1:        |f| < µ
            = 0:        otherwise
```

And the filtered image may be acquired using the following equation.

```
filtered_image(f) = hpfilter(f) * img(f)
```

Hartley Transform Based Filtering Approaches

In mathematics, the Hartley transform (HT) is an integral transform closely related to the Fourier transform (FT), but which transforms real-valued functions to real-valued functions only. It was proposed as an alternative to the Fourier transform by Ralph V. L. Hartley in (Hartley and Ralph V. L. 1942) in the year 1942 and is one of many known Fourier-related transforms. Compared to the Fourier transform, the Hartley transform has the advantages of transforming real functions to real functions (as opposed to requiring complex numbers) and of being its own inverse. A discrete Hartley transform (DHT) is the discrete orientation of the basic Hartley transform and has been successful applied to correlation filter designing technologies for processing of images (Narendra K. C.and Satyanarayana S., 2016). A 2-D Discrete Hartley transform is given by

$$H(u,v) = \sum_{x=0}^{N-1}\sum_{y=0}^{N-1} f(x,y)cas(ux+vy)$$

where *cas(ux+vy) = cos(ux+vy)+sin(ux+vy)*, *f(x; y)* is the image under consideration.

Wavelet Transform Based Filtering Approaches

Wavelets are basically mathematical functions that analyses data according to scale or resolution. In Fourier transform a user can get information about the frequencies present in a signal but not where and when the frequencies occurred. Wavelets transform signals in the time domain to a joint time-frequency domain. Signals with sharp spikes or signals having discontinuities, wavelet transform will provide efficient result than Fourier transform (Kanithi A. K., 2011). Wavelet transform can be discrete or continuous. Recently, Discrete Wavelet Transform (DWT) has attracted more and more interest in image de-noising. The same may be mathematically represented as follows where X(t) represents the noisy signal with I(t) as the information inflicted with N(t) noise and W (t) represents wavelet domain output that consist wavelet coefficients.

X (t) = I (t) + N (t), W (t) = wavelet_transform (X (t)),

The presented work contributes in the former category i.e. in the domain of spatial filtering approaches. The said domain, although happens to be a very old and an already established one, yet needs certain tuning for better performance. The chapter demonstrates a methodology through which a user can accelerate the de-noising procedure so as to get the desired response with lesser number of iterations and hence a faster result without compromising on the accuracy of the performance.

PROPOSED WORK

The proposed work is a contribution in the non-linear spatial filtering domain. In the presented work, the median filtering approach is applied iteratively. The enhancement proposed in the said work is reducing the number of iterations for achieving a better output in terms of noise removal. The objective is to achieve a de-noising operation of binary images inflicted with uniform salt and pepper noise with the application of iterative filtration process. The overview of the concept is presented in Fig-1 for the sake of clarity.

Figure 1. Overview of the Iterative Noise Filtration Process

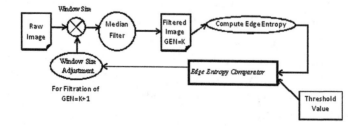

In the current context the authors have used binary images with logical pixel values i.e. 0 or 1. Using binary images both the mean filter as well as the median filter is found to perform in the same manner. The justification may be provided as follows. As shown in equation (1.1), the mean filtering expression may be expressed as:

$$mean(\{pixel[x, y]\}) = [\Sigma\{pixel[x, y]\}] / |\{pixel[x, y]\}|$$

Now for an n x n window size, the Σ {pixel[x, y]} may be expressed as $\{\delta*0 + (n-\delta)*1\}$, where δ may be referred to as the count of the black pixels in the n x n window (n-δ) amounts the number of white pixels. In the above situation, the mean value amounts to be as follows.

$$mean = (n-\delta)/n = 1 - (\delta/n)$$

For a given distribution of {pixel[x, y]} let us assume ε as a small finite quantity deviating from the 0.5. Then the following can be obtained.

if $\delta > n/2$: mean = 1- $\{(n/2)+ \varepsilon\}/n = 1 - (1/2 + \varepsilon/n) = 0.5 - \varepsilon/n =>$ mean = 0

else if $\delta < n/2$: mean = 1- $\{(n/2)- \varepsilon\}/n = 1 - (1/2 - \varepsilon/n) = 0.5 + \varepsilon/n =>$ mean = 1

In the former case for a binary distribution, mean has been approximated to a value = 0 i.e. a black pixel and on the other hand for the latter case, it has been approximated to a value = 1 i.e. a white pixel. Now let us examine the case for a median filtering technology. Here the central tendency (median) is not computed but selected out of a sorted list. For example as in the case of any unknown distribution, the following can be said.

Σ {pixel[x, y]} may be expressed as $\{\delta*0 + (n-\delta)*1\}$.

If the list of pixel values are sorted, then a selection of the (n/2+1)th element from the list shall result in the following.

```
if δ > n/2: the (n/2 + 1)th element of the sorted list always is a 0.
Therefore median = 0
else if δ < n/2: the (n/2 + 1)th element of the sorted list always is a 1.
Therefore median = 1
```

Consequently, it may be told that both the mean as well as the median noise filtering element behaves in the same manner in case of binary images as shown in Fig-2. As a result the authors claim to have failed to crisply categorize their work either under linear or non-linear filtering strategy. Therefore, the authors categorize it solely as a spatial filtering operation without any remark on its linearity.

In the current scenario, the Raw Image i.e. noisy image is fed to the system for noise filtration. The input image initially undergoes a process of 3x3 Window Median Filtering. The filtered image so generated may be categorized as GEN = 1 i.e. the filtered image of the 1st generation, where generation signifies the iteration count of the noise filtering process.

Figure 2. Characteristics of Mean Filter and Median Filter for Binary Images

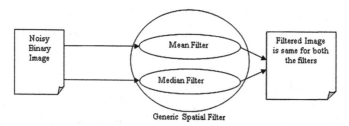

As the image of the GEN=1 is generated, a decision has to be taken as to whether it is essential for the user to go for filtration of next iteration or not. This decision is solely governed by the user, whether he/she stays satisfies with the current level of filtering or he/she wants to go for the next level of iteration. The said problem is beyond the scope of the chapter and is left solely at the desire and satisfaction level of the user. But for the sake of completion of the presented work the authors have presented a methodology to determine the effectiveness of the filtered image obtained at the last iteration. Therefore as a parameter for proving the efficacy of the filtration achieved, the authors have projected a comparison of the last filtered image to the original noise free image using Peak Signal to Noise Ratio (PSNR) Value.

If it is assumed that the user wishes to proceed for next level of iteration, thereafter comes the question as to what should be the size of the working window. Should it be maintained at the level 3x3 or can it be enhanced to 5x5 level? In the current chapter, the authors propose that this decision be taken based on the quantity of high frequency edges present in the image. In order to have a quantified value of the said feature the authors have resorted to (Shiozaki A, 1986) estimating the entropy of the edges presents in the image and authors accomplished the same using Wavelet transform. The authors have computed the aggregate of the entropy values of the coefficient matrices of the Wavelet transform and shall refer to as *edge-entropy.*

Significance of Features

The feature that the authors have identified is based on several works that has been proposed on edge identification using wavelet transform. The authors have observed that if the quantity of edges present in the image is sufficiently high, then they term the image to be highly informative and consequently the entropy of information content should be high. In the current context, the information is the quantity of edges, which the authors propose to measure using the entropy value of the same. As recommended in (Zhang Z, SiliangMa, HuiLiu, YuexinGong, 2009), (Porwik, et al. 2004), the authors have resorted to wavelet transforms for finding the edges. The significance of the chosen feature for the current context is elaborated as follows.

Edge Entropy Estimation

Median filtering process has 'window size' as a vital parameter. While working with variable 'window-size' the authors had the following observation that urged us to investigate the wavelet transform domain for the images under consideration.

Observation-1: As the size of the window is enhanced with higher generations of median filtering, the result converges faster than with constant window size in certain cases.

Observation-2: If there is significant quantity of edges available in the image then enhancement of window size leads to decline in performance and consequently, the window size has to be maintained constant.

In generic terms it can be mentioned that the performance does differ for different cases. The authors believe that this must be based on certain qualitative or quantitative features of the images that cause the filtering process to behave differently under different conditions. Therefore, in order to quantify the above proposal into a formal hypothesis the authors have used Haar Wavelet Transforms for estimating the quantity of high frequency edges in an image so as to propose a correlation between the enhancement of window size and performance of filtering. The justification of the selection of Haar Wavelet Transform for the above purpose may be presented as follows.

Haar Wavelet Transform for Edge-Entropy of an Image

The standard 2D wavelet transform (WT) has already been identified as an effective tool in image processing in (Zhang Z et al., 2009), (Porwik, et al., 2004). It is basically a time-frequency analysis method that selects appropriate frequency band on the characteristics of the signal. The application of the transform is most frequently based on a separable transform (Zhang Z et al., 2009), i.e. rows and columns of an image are treated independently. The wavelet analysis method stands highly appropriate on the removal of noise from the image. According to the features of the multi-scale edge of the wavelet transforms, the de-noising methods of the orthogonal wavelet transform is based on soft and hard threshold values. These threshold values are adjusted and used for filtering the information off the noisy perspective. The wavelet transforms emit 4 distinct matrices namely,

- The approximation coefficient matrix,
- The horizontal detail coefficient matrix,
- The vertical detail coefficient matrix and
- The diagonal detail coefficient matrix.

Out of the above, the approximation coefficient matrix has not been found empirically useful in the current scenario. Consequently the other 3 matrices namely, the horizontal detail coefficient matrix, the vertical detail coefficient matrix and the diagonal detail coefficient matrix have been used for identifying the quantity of high frequency edges present in the image. In order to estimate the quantity, the authors have found the entropy value suitable for the application and consequently, the wavelet transform coefficient matrices are augmented and the entropy of the same is taken for identifying the quantity of edge content of an image. Once the amount of edge present in the image has been quantified, the authors have clustered them under two different categories as follows:

1. **CAT-1 [Having Lower Edge Content]:** If the entropy of the augmented wavelet-transform coefficient matrix amounts to a value lesser than the cluster boundary, they have been categorized as CAT-1.

2. **CAT-2 [Having Higher Edge Content]:** If the entropy of the augmented wavelet-transform coefficient matrix amounts to a value higher than the cluster boundary, they have been categorized as CAT-2.

The cluster boundary as mentioned above have been obtained through empirical values as mentioned in the subsequent sections. The position of the quantified feature element allows us to decide on the execution methodology of the noise filtering process.

As shown in Fig-1, the characteristic parameter mentioned above is evaluated against the reference values obtained from the k-means clustering. If the value is found permissible then the filtered image generated at kth generation is forwarded for filtration at k+1th level (generation) iterative noise filtration process with enhanced window size or else the window size is maintained constant. The logic is formally presented as follows.

```
if (Entropy(Wavelet Coefficient Matrices) > threshold-point)
                Maintain the Last Window Size
else
                Enhance the Window Size of the Filter
```

Setting of the Threshold Values

The authors have conducted experiments for median filtering operation on 20 set of binary images. As mentioned in Section 4.1, the entropy of the constituent edges has been identified as a feature for analysis of the iterative filtering operation. Again mentioned in Section 4.1.2 that for the said analysis the authors have used Haar Wavelet Transform Coefficient Matrices and performed a clustering operation. This is done for separating the images with values of Haar Wavelet Transform Coefficient Entropy on the higher side from the ones that have the value on the lower side. The authors have used the most popular K-Means clustering approach for accomplishing the above objective. For the sake of the reader's reference, a small note on K-Means Clustering approach has been presented in section 4.3. Following the above, the authors have attempted to identify a threshold value above which they would be regarded as the ones with higher edge entropy and below which can be identified as the ones with low edge entropy. The implementation of the above is presented in Section 5 and 6.

K Means Clustering

This type of clustering happens to be one of the simplest types of clustering and hence the simplest to implement under the constraint that the distribution of data for a cluster should be of convex type. In the current context, the authors have conducted experiments with 20 sets of images and have found that the clusters are typically of convex type with no evidence of concave clusters. Consequently, the authors have indisputably applied the K Means clustering approach for locating the separation boundary between the two clusters namely the ones with low edge-entropy and the ones with high edge-entropy values. K-means clustering is a method of vector quantization, originally from signal processing, that is popular for cluster analysis in data mining. K-means clustering aims to partition n observations into k clusters in which each observation belongs to the cluster with the nearest mean, serving as a prototype of the cluster. This results in a partitioning of the data space into Voronoi (Aurenhammer, F. and Klein, R. 2000) cells.

Given a set of observations *(x1, x2, ..., xn)*, where each observation is a d-dimensional real vector, k-means clustering aims to partition the n observations into *k (≤ n) sets S = {S1, S2, ..., Sk}* so as to minimize the within-cluster sum of squares (i.e. variance). Formally, the objective is to find:

$$\arg \min \Sigma i \ \Sigma x \ \varepsilon \ Si \parallel x - \mu i \parallel$$

where μi is the mean of points in *Si*. This is equivalent to minimizing the pairwise squared deviations of points in the same cluster. The results obtained have been checked for validation against the original image using the PSNR Value obtained on comparison between the last filtered image and the original noise free image. The values have been shown plotted graphically in Figure 8.

IMPLEMENTATION

In order to implement the above concept the authors have used an iterative neural network suitable for noise filtering of binary images. The authors have implemented our approach using 20 sets of binary images which have been deliberately inflicted with salt and pepper noise of 50% uniformity. The proposed work employs the multi-layer self-organizing neural network architecture as proposed in (Ghosh A. et al, 1993). The proposed network consists of 3 layers. The input layer accepts the inputs which are in the form of pixel values in binary forms. The hidden layer works on the logic and functional aspects i.e. the computation of new pixel value devoid of the inflicted noise and finally the output layer producing the output in the form of de-noised image. The 3 layers together works on our sample images inflicted with Uniform Noise of level: 50%. The authors have used Adobe Photoshop 7.0 to artificially inflict the noise on the clear image as mentioned before. Thereafter they have used them for their experimentation for noise removal. In order to estimate the correctness of our algorithm, each time i.e. at each generation of the filtered image they have shown a comparison between the obtained image and the original (clear) image so as to validate our observations mentioned in Section 4. The next section presents a brief outline on Multi-Layer Self Organizing Neural Network (MLSONN) and its application for De-noising of Binary images.

Multi-Layer Self Organizing Neural Network

The Multi-Layer Self organizing Neural Network (MLSONN) happens to be a self-supervised form of structure that emulates the architecture of that of the human brain which has its own self supervising system. It comprises of multiple layers viz. Input Layer (IL), Hidden Layer (HL) and the Output Layer (OL). The presented network follows a forward propagation strategy in a case that the incident information is accepted at the input layer and subsequent processing is executed at the hidden layers and result produced at the output layer. The efficiency of the execution is calculated at the output layers using Peak Signal to Noise Ratio (PSNR). These errors are used to decide whether or not to repeat the same execution or adjust the size of the window by adjusting the interconnection weights for possible acceleration in the de-noising process. Details regarding the operation and dynamics of the system are presented in the subsequent sections of the chapter.

Using MLSONN for De-Noising Binary Image

The presented form of MLSONN takes input as a binary vector of size a^2, $(a+d)^2$, $(a+2*d)^2$, ... {a + $(n-1)*d)^2$, viz. 9, 25, 49, 81 for the window sizes 3x3, 5x5 or 7x7 and so on. The values of the vector can be either 0 or 1. This binary vector as fed to the input layer is multiplied with again a binary matrix to generate a new vector to be fed to the hidden layer. The median filtering operation is executed at the hidden layer and the output is projected at the concerned pixel of the output layer image. The image generated is examined based on the metric value as presented in Section 4.1.1. If the value of the metric is below a permissible limit, the authors enhance the window size accelerating the image filtering process.

EXECUTION OF THE OPERATION

In this section the authors shall take the opportunity to demonstrate the actual operation that is executed for achieving the de-noising operation. As mentioned in the prior sections, the user shall initially try to identify the threshold which will mark as the partition between the two clusters. Below this value the images may be said to have low edge-entropy and above which the images may be said to have high edge-entropy. Thereafter the authors shall describe the dynamics of the MLSONN so as to complete the de-noising operation. The following subsections shall elaborate the mathematical and operations details.

Clustering of Edge Entropy Values

As mentioned in Section 3.3, the authors have used K-Means clustering algorithm in order to accomplish the desired distinct and mutually exclusive clusters one that for high edge-entropy and the other that for low edge-entropy values. The authors have executed our experiment on 20 sets of noisy binary images as shown below in Fig: 3-I through Fig: 3-XX and at each instance of the filtered image obtained, they have computed the edge entropy value using Haar Wavelet Transforms as mentioned in section 3.1.2 and attempted for clustering the same as mentioned in section 3.3 and 5.1.

The authors have used the following formula for calculating the partition threshold.
Let us consider:

```
Mean of Cluster-1: meanCluster-1
Mean of Cluster-2: meanCluster-2
```

Mean of the distance of all the points of Cluster-1 from the mean point of Cluster-1: *mdistCluster-1*
Mean of the distance of all the points of Cluster-2 from the mean point of Cluster-2: *mdistCluster-2*
Threshold Point or Partition Point

```
= {meanLOWER-VALUE CLUSTER + mdistLOWER-VALUE CLUSTER}
+ {|(meanCluster-1 - meanCluster-2)| - (mdistCluster-1 + mdistCluster-2)}/2
```

The same could also be derived from the higher value cluster as follows:
Threshold Point or Partition Point

Figure 3.

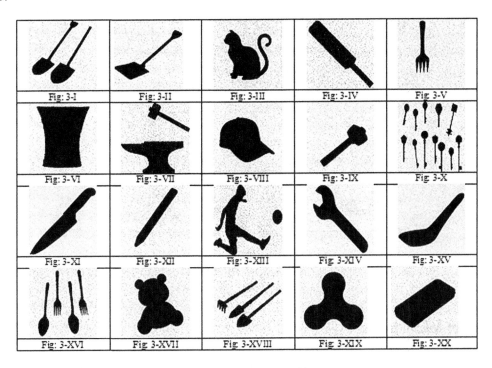

Fig: 3-I	Fig: 3-II	Fig: 3-III	Fig: 3-IV	Fig 3-V
Fig: 3-VI	Fig: 3-VII	Fig: 3-VIII	Fig: 3-IX	Fig 3-X
Fig: 3-XI	Fig: 3-XII	Fig: 3-XIII	Fig 3-XIV	Fig: 3-XV
Fig: 3-XVI	Fig 3-XVII	Fig 3-XVIII	Fig 3-XIX	Fig: 3-XX

```
= {meanHIGHER-VALUE CLUSTER - mdistHIGHER-VALUE CLUSTER}
- {|(meanCluster-1 - meanCluster-2)| - (mdistCluster-1 + mdistCluster-2)}/2
```

The same can be diagrammatically depicted as follows:

The mean values of each of the k-mean clusters obtained are 0.0485 and 0.1112 and the inter cluster partition or threshold point obtained is 0.0804. Consequently the user may set the partition threshold at the said point i.e. at 0.0804. Images with edge-entropy value above the point may be regarded as one with higher edge content and the ones with value less than the point may be regarded as the ones with low edge content.

As mentioned before the user shall promote the ones with higher edge content for spatial filtering with constant window size while for the ones with lower edge content, the user shall forward them for spatial filtering with enhanced window size. The obtained distribution for our case is shown graphically in Fig 5.

Figure 4. Clustering and Threshold Finding Strategy

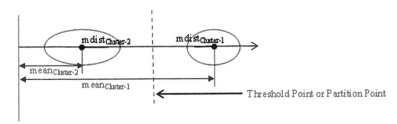

Figure 5. Graphical plot of the distribution of edge entropy values

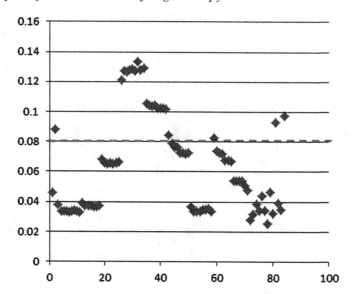

Dynamics of MLSONN

As mentioned before, our MLSONN consists of 3 layers viz. the Input Layer, Hidden Layer and the Output Layer. The input data i.e. the pixel values of the noisy image is fed into the input layer. At the initial stage, the user shall restrict the size of the window to 3x3. Consequently, the user shall feed a 3x3 matrix of pixel values, which amounts to a vector of (3*3=) 9 pixel values to the input layer.

But as mentioned previously, the user also have an option of enhancing the window size as and when required for faster de-noising process i.e. with lesser number of iterations and hence the user need to maintain a provision for the same. In order to cater for this issue, the weight matrix needs to be dynamic (or changeable) with each iteration. The whole principle in depicted in the following Fig-6.

Fig-1(a), (b) and (c) shows the input matrices with window sizes *3x3*, *5x5* and *7x7*. The same may scale up to $[(2*i+1) \times (2*i+1)]$ for any value of $i >= 1$ if the problem at its current state demands. The noisy image pixel matrix is fed to the input layer in the form of a vector of size $= [(2*i+1) * (2*i+1)]$. The weight matrix that functions intermediary to the input layer and the hidden layer happens to be a column matrix of size same as the size of the input vector. This result in the hidden layer getting the data from input layer operated with certain filtering strategy.

```
Input = [input_i],
input_i = pixel_ij
Weight = [w_i = 1]
wi        = [w_i / |[w_i]|]^T
```

With enhancement in the size of the window, the user finds the following change. *[input_i]* increases its span from n x n to *(n+2) x (n+2)* i.e. the l[input_i]l rises from n^2 to $n^2 + 2n + 1$. $[w_i / |[w_j]|]^T$ will change from *[1/ n²]* to *[1/(n² + 2n + 1)]*

Figure 6. MLSONN for de-noising of binary images

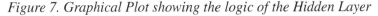

Figure 7. Graphical Plot showing the logic of the Hidden Layer

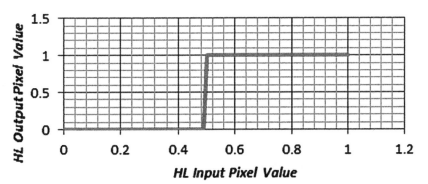

The input to the hidden layer (HL) is of the form $h_i = [input_i] * [w_i]$ and the behavioral pattern of the layer shall have the following pattern, which may be mathematically represented as follows:

$$h_{output} \quad = 0: h_{input} <= 0.5$$
$$= 1: h_{input} > 0.5$$

As the output is produced the user estimates the feature value, namely the edge-entropy. If the value is found below the threshold or the inter cluster partition point as mentioned in Section 4.1 and 4.3, the user shall go for the next level iteration with enhanced window size i.e. a 5x5 window.

Each time the user have two options either to maintain the window-size same as the previous iteration or enhance it to a larger window-size. The user shall arrive at the decision using the feature as mentioned above. The filtered output images has been shown in Fig 8-I through Fig 8-XX. The validation of the legitimacy of the decision has been demonstrated through empirical results in the following Sections.

Iterative Filtration With Critical Window Size Adjustment: A Comparative Study

In this section we shall demonstrate the results obtained in the execution of the iterative filtration. As mentioned and depicted in Section 6.1, the authors have conducted an investigation on 20 sets of images, passing them through the proposed noise filtration procedure. For each of the images two different study were conducted and it has been found that for images with lesser edge-entropy value, the window size can be safely enhanced to accelerate the filtration while for the ones with higher image entropy values the enhancement results in fall in the accuracy of filtration. For the sake of brevity the demonstration of the results obtained have been restricted to two images of either from the lower-edge-entropy and two from the higher-edge-entropy categories.

As previously mentioned in Section 4, the PSNR Values in comparison with the original noise-free image has been considered as a parameter for assessment of the process. The performance of the iterative filtration for two images from the cluster of lower edge-entropy values have been shown in Figs: 9a and 9b. The blue curve showing the performance with constant window size, while the red curve showing the performance with enhanced window size.

The performance of the iterative filtration for two images from the cluster of higher edge-entropy values have been shown in Figs: 9c and 9d. The blue curve showing the performance with constant window size, while the red curve showing the performance with enhanced window size.

DISCUSSION AND CONCLUSION

The chapter presents a de-noising methodology applicable to binary images. Although de-noising of binary images is an age old phenomena and the spatial filtering and iterative filtering approaches are quite established in the domain, the critical adjustment of the size of the window in order to bring about early converging filtration operation is an unprecedented fact.

Figure 8.

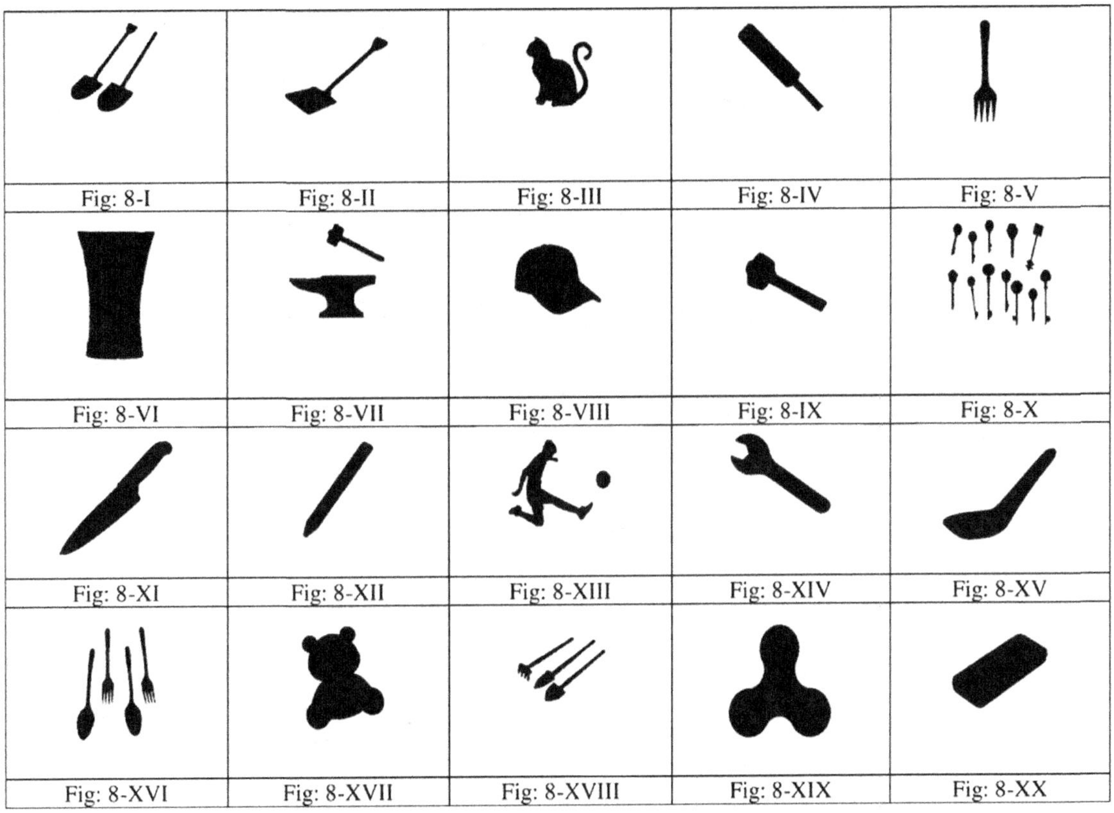

Fig: 8-I
Fig: 8-II
Fig: 8-III
Fig: 8-IV
Fig: 8-V
Fig: 8-VI
Fig: 8-VII
Fig: 8-VIII
Fig: 8-IX
Fig: 8-X
Fig: 8-XI
Fig: 8-XII
Fig: 8-XIII
Fig: 8-XIV
Fig: 8-XV
Fig: 8-XVI
Fig: 8-XVII
Fig: 8-XVIII
Fig: 8-XIX
Fig: 8-XX

The chapter presents a discussion on implementation of MLSONN in order to accomplish the desired objective. Generally, the network weights are adjusted based on errors computed at the output layer so as to bring about better filtration in the next iteration. But in contrast to that, the current chapter presents a deviation from the concept. It recommends the window size to be adjusted i.e. either enhanced or to remain the same and consequently the adjustment of the weight matrix will be accordingly as demonstrated. Although some initial results have been shown achieved in the current domain, yet a closer and more exhaustive probe is necessary to investigate the matter further. The authors are currently engaged in the direction.

Figure 9a. Graph showing the increase in performance with enhanced window size.

PSNR Values
30
20
10
0
1
2
3
Iterations of Noise Filtration

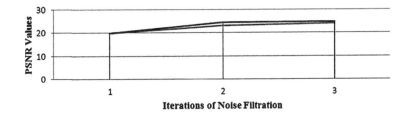

Figure 9b. Graph showing the increase in performance with enhanced window size.

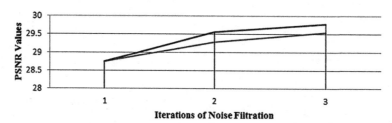

Figure 9c. Graph showing the fall in performance with enhanced window size.

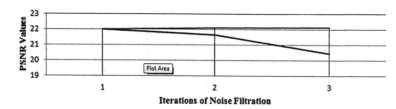

Figure 9d. Graph showing the fall in performance with enhanced window size.

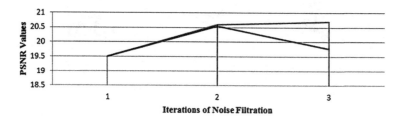

FUTURE ASPECTS

The study and analysis of the current chapter is limited to the investigation of 20 binary images with uniform noise level i.e. 50%. Sincere effort is necessary for the investigation of the same with varying noise levels, followed by the same investigation with grey scale as well as color images. The authors are currently engaged in the said investigation taking the presented work further ahead.

REFERENCES

Abdallah, M. A., Samu, T. I., & Grisson, W. A. (1995). Automatic target identification using neural networks. *SPIE Proceedings Intelligent Robots and Computer Vision XIV, 2588,* 556–565.

Achanta, R., Hemami, S., Estrada, F., & Susstrunk, S. (2009). Frequency-tuned salient region detection. *IEEE CVPR.*

Antonucci, M., Tirozzi, B., Yarunin, N. D., & Dotsenko, V. S. (1994). Numerical simulation of neural networks with translation and rotation invariant pattern recognition. *International Journal of Modern Physics B, 8*(11–12), 1529–1541. doi:10.1142/S0217979294000658

Atkinson, L., Kamalabadi, F., & Jones, D. (2003). Wavelet-based hyperspectral image estimation. *Proc. IGARSS, 2,* 743–745.

Aurenhammer, F., & Klein, R. (2000). Voronoi Diagrams. In J.-R. Sack & J. Urrutia (Eds.), *Handbook of Computational Geometry* (pp. 201–290). Amsterdam: North-Holland. doi:10.1016/B978-044482537-7/50006-1

Ben Hamza, A., Luque, P., Martinez, J., & Roman, R. (1999, October). Removing noise and preserving details with relaxed median filters. *Journal of Mathematical Imaging and Vision, 11*(2), 161–177. doi:10.1023/A:1008395514426

Bhattacharyya, S., Maulik, U., & Dutta, P. (2011). Multilevel image segmentation with adaptive image context based thresholding. *Applied Soft Computing, 11*(1), 946–962. doi:10.1016/j.asoc.2010.01.015

Bhattacharyya, S., Pal, P., & Bhowmick, S. (2014). Binary image denoising using a quantum multilayer self-organizing neural network. *Applied Soft Computing, 24,* 717–729. doi:10.1016/j.asoc.2014.08.027

Chang, G., Yu, B., & Vetterli, M. (2000). Adaptive wavelet thresholding for image denoising and compression. *IEEE Transactions on Image Processing, 9,* 1532–1546. doi:10.1109/83.862633 PMID:18262991

Chang, S., & Vetterli, M. (1997). Spatial adaptive wavelet thresholding for image denoising. *Proc. of the IEEE-ICIP,* 374–377. 10.1109/ICIP.1997.638782

Egmont-Petersen, M., de Ridder, D., & Handels, H. (2002). Image processing using neural networks – a review. *Pattern Recognition, 35*(10), 2279–2301. doi:10.1016/S0031-3203(01)00178-9

Ghosh, A., Pal, N. R., & Pal, S. K. (1993). Self organization for object extraction using a multilayer neural network and fuzziness measures. *IEEE Transactions on Fuzzy Systems, 1*(1), 54–68. doi:10.1109/TFUZZ.1993.390285

Hardie, R. C., & Barner, K. E. (1994, March). Rank conditioned rank selection filters for signal restoration. *IEEE Transactions on Image Processing, 3*(2), 192–206. doi:10.1109/83.277900 PMID:18291919

Hartley, R. V. L. (1942). A More Symmetrical Fourier Analysis Applied to Transmission Problems. *Proceedings of the IRE., 30*(3), 144–150. doi:10.1109/JRPROC.1942.234333

Haykin, S. (1999). *Neural Networks: A Comprehensive Foundation* (2nd ed.). Upper Saddle River, NJ: Prentice Hall.

Hopfield, J. J. (1984). Neurons with graded response have collective computational properties like those of two state neurons. *Proceedings of the National Academy of Sciences of the United States of America, 1984*(10), 3088–3092. doi:10.1073/pnas.81.10.3088 PMID:6587342

Hou, X., & Zhang, L. (2007). Saliency detection: a spectral residual approach. *IEEE Conference on Computer Vision and Pattern.*

Itti, L., Koch, C., & Niebur, E. (1998). A model of saliency-based visual attention for rapid scene analysis. *IEEE Pattern Anal. Mach. Intell., 20*(11), 1254–1259. doi:10.1109/34.730558

Kamgar-Parsi, B. (1995). Automatic target extraction in infrared images. *NRL Review*, 143–146.

Kanithi, A. K. (2011). *Study of Spatial and Transform Domain Filters for Efficient Noise Reduction* (Master's thesis). NIT Rourkela, India.

Kohonen, T. (1984). *Self-organization and Associative Memory*. London: Springer-Verlag.

Kother Mohideen, S., Arumuga Perumal, S., & Mohamed Sathik, M. (2008). Image De-noising using Discrete Wavelet transform. *International Journal of Computer Science and Network Security, 8*(1).

Li, E., Xu, C., Gui, C., & Fox, M. D. (2005). *Level set evolution without re-initialization: a new variational formulation*. IEEE CVPR.

Lippmann, R. P. (1987). An introduction to computing with neural nets. *IEEE ASSP Magazine*, 3–22.

Ma, Y., & Zhang, H. (2003). Contrast-based image attention analysis by using fuzzy growing. *ACM Trans. Multimedia*.

Motwani, M. C., Gadiya, M. C., & Motwani, R. C. (2010). *Survey of Image Denoising Techniques*. Retrieved from https://www.cse.unr.edu/~fredh/papers/conf/034-asoidt/paper.pdf

Narendra, K. C., & Satyanarayana, S. (2016). Hartley transform based correlation filters for face recognition. *Proc of the International Conference on Signal Processing and Communications (SPCOM)*. 10.1109/SPCOM.2016.7746699

Neelima, M., & Mahaboob Pasha, M. (2014). Wavelet Transform Based On Image Denoising Using Thresholding Techniques. *International Journal of Advanced Research in Computer and Communication Engineering, 3*(9).

Perlovsky, L. I., Schoendor, W. H., & Burdick, B. J. (1997). Model-based neural network for target detection in SAR images. *IEEE Transactions on Image Processing, 6*(1), 203–216. doi:10.1109/83.552107 PMID:18282889

Pham, D. T., & Bayro-Corrochano, E. J. (1998). Neural computing for noise filtering, edge detection and signature extraction. *J. Syst. Eng., 2*(2), 666–670.

Porwik, P., & Lisowska, A. (2004). The Haar-wavelet transform in digital image processing: Its status and achievements. *Machine Graphics and Vision, 13*(1-2).

Scott, P. D., Young, S. S., & Nasrabadi, N. M. (1997). Object recognition using multilayer hop-field neural network. *IEEE Transactions on Image Processing, 6*(3), 357–372. doi:10.1109/83.557336 PMID:18282932

Shiozaki, A. (1986, October). Edge extraction using entropy operator. *Elsevier Journal of Computer Vision, Graphics, and Image Processing, 36*(1), 1–9. doi:10.1016/S0734-189X(86)80025-1

Smolka, B., Malik, K., & Malik, D. (2012). Adaptive rank weighted switching filter for impulsive noise removal in color images. *Journal of Real-Time Image Processing*, 1–23.

Wang, S., Kubota, T., Siskind, J.M., & Wang, J. (2005). Salient closed boundary extraction with ratio contour. *IEEE Pattern Anal. Mach. Intell., 27*, 546–561.

Xu, N., Bansal, R., & Ahuja, N. (2003). Object segmentation using graph cuts based active contours. *IEEE CVPR.*

Yang, R., Yin, L., Gabbouj, M., Astola, J., & Neuvo, Y. (1995, March). Optimal weighted median filters under structural constraints. *IEEE Transactions on Signal Processing, 43*(3), 591–604. doi:10.1109/78.370615

Yu, H., Li, J., Tian, Y., & Huang, T. (2010). Automatic interesting object extraction from images using complementary saliency maps. Proc. of the MM'10. doi:10.1145/1873951.1874105

Zhang, Z., Ma, S., Liu, H., & Gong, Y. (2009, April). An edge detection approach based on directional wavelet transform. *Elsevier Journal of Computers and Mathematics with Applications, 57*(8), 1265–1271. doi:10.1016/j.camwa.2008.11.013

Chapter 8

Analysis of Human Gait for Designing a Recognition and Classification System

Jayati Ghosh Dastidar
St. Xavier's College, India

Debangshu Chakraborty
St. Xavier's College, India

Soumen Mukherjee
RCC Institute of Information Technology, India

Arup Kumar Bhattacharjee
RCC Institute of Information Technology, India

ABSTRACT

Identification and recognition of a human subject by monitoring a video/image by using various biometric features such as fingerprints, retina/iris scans, palm prints have been of interest to researches. In this chapter, an attempt has been made to recognize a human subject uniquely by monitoring his/her gait. This has been done by analyzing sampled frames of a video sequence to first detect the presence of a human form and then extract the silhouette of the subject in question. The extracted silhouette is then used to find the skeleton from it. The skeleton contains a set of points that retains the connectivity of the form and maintains the geometric properties of the silhouette. From the skeleton, a novel method has been proposed involving the neighborhood of interest pixels to identify the end points representing the heel, toe, etc. These points finally lead to the calculation of gait attributes. The extracted attributes represented in the form of a pattern vector are matched using cosine distance with features stored in the database resulting in identification/rejection.

DOI: 10.4018/978-1-5225-7107-0.ch008

INTRODUCTION

Human walking is a complicated motion. However, there is a rhythm which can be easily observed in the walk of a person. Human gait refers to the manner in which one walks and achieves translator motion through the movement of his/her limbs. Studying human gait helps one understand how different people move in a complex way. We can also identify different human beings by observing their style of walking. Gait based recognition systems try to identify entities on the basis of human gait. The objective is to develop an automated system which would not require human intervention to study the gait of an individual and uniquely identify him/her. The topic is extremely relevant in the current volatile scenario, both nationally as well as internationally. Such a system may be used in military bases, airports, parks, etc. Some researchers have been involved in researching this, as yet nascent field and have had a mixed success rate.

The recent times have intensely felt the need for video analysis. It has been observed that security has become an integral issue in our society. Be it the finance sector like banks and ATMs or residential locations or offices, security is a serious issue everywhere. Hence, there crept in the concept of live footages of a wholesome timeframe being recorded since that helps in keeping a check on the regular activities. In the recent times of research dealing with image and video processing, an immense concentration has been put in the field of analysing human behavior from videos. Understanding human activity has been a prospective area of research for years since it has got a lot of applications in virtual reality, automated surveillance systems, biomechanical analysis for sports and medicines etc.

As explained before, that human gait refers to the manner in which one walks and that there is a systematic, co-ordinated rhythm and periodicity to this walk. Let us start by considering the gait/walk cycle of a person and identify the rhythm in it. The gait cycle is formed by a repetition of two major movements – the step and the stride. The step-and-stride sequence can be further expanded to be composed of six basic stages. The Figure 1 shows the gait cycle of a human being.

The six stages (Durward, et. al., 1999) in the cycle are Heel Strike (HS), Foot Flat (FF), Mid Stance (MS), Heel Off (HO), Toe Off (TO) and Mid Swing (MSW). These six stages are followed by a Heel Strike again to continue with the subsequent cycle. Using gait as a biometric technique involves measuring and analysing various aspects of the gait cycle such as the time taken between two successive heel strikes, distance between the front foot toe and the back foot heel in the heel strike stage, distance of the back heel from the ground in the toe off stage, etc. However, of all of these various measures, any one of them may not be capable of representing the complete dynamics of human gait uniquely. Instead, two or more of these measures may have to be combined together to uniquely represent the gait characteristics of an individual (mason, et. al., 2016).

Use of gait as a biometric tool for identification purposes is increasingly becoming popular. One of the major reasons for that is other biometrics such as finger prints, retinal scans, palm images, etc.

Figure 1. Gait cycle of a human being

all require the use of a machinery of sorts to acquire the biometric information. As for example, finger prints need finger print scanners. So do retina and iris scans. It is not possible to acquire biometric data from an individual without him/her coming in close proximity with the device and thus becoming aware of the entire process of biometric authentication. Use of such devices often invites unwarranted attention of a purported miscreant. Using gait as a biometric authentication medium can be done in an unobtrusive manner. As for example, the corridor leading up to a secured enclosure may be monitored with the help of CCTV cameras. The gait of a person walking up to the enclosure may be captured on video and analysed to find out whether he/she should be given an entry or not. All of this may be done while the person is walking, and by the time the enclosure is reached a decision may be arrived at. The subject thus did not have to make any contact with any scanning device. Such unobtrusive monitoring at times proves to be a psychological edge over intruders.

In this chapter we intend to discuss a method that may be used to uniquely identify human beings by analysing their gaits. Amongst other things, edge detection schemes for foreground object extraction will be discussed. The next section of the chapter will be devoted to extract features of human gait. In order to do so, features involving the Skeleton of the intruded object will be considered. After the computation of the features from the skeleton, they will then be used for Classification by the calculation of the Cosine Distance.

BACKGROUND STUDY AND LITERATURE REVIEW

The first step in trying to designing a Gait-based identification system is to study and understand the dynamics of human gait. The authors in their insightful work (Durward, et. al., 1999) explained the stages involved in ones gait as well as the kinematics associated in each of the stages in laymen's language without going into the complexities of medical jargon. Comprehensive assessment techniques were proposed in (Loudon, et. al., 2008) to accurately assess and obtain functional information about normal and abnormal static and dynamic motions. The fact that the step lengths, stride times, velocity, etc. varies from person to person was highlighted by the author in his work (Charalambous, 2014). (Charalambous, 2014) observed that there was similarity in the duration of successive phases of stance and swing, during the same walking trial and during repeated trials of the same subject. Step and stride length and stride width showed the same striking similarity. Foot angles, however, showed greater individual variability. In his work, (Whittle, 2013) made similar observations and objectively defined three important gait parameters – cadence, velocity and stride length. The cadence is the rate at which an individual's feet contacts the ground. It is measured in steps per minute. The velocity is the distance the whole body moves forward in a given time and is measured in meters per second. The stride length is the distance between the two heels in the heel strike stage. This attribute is dependent on a person's height.

Different approaches to identify a person by studying their gait have been studied and researched upon. For the purpose of automatic recognition and analysis of gait, one of two broad techniques may be used. These two techniques comprise analysis using wearable systems and analysis using non-wearable systems.

Wearable systems are convenient and precise techniques for gait analysis (Tao, et. al., 2012). In this technique wearable sensors are attached to body parts and data are gathered and then analysed. These sensors can measure various gait characteristics as signals, which can be analysed. The popular wearable sensors are inertial sensors, strain gauges, goniometers, force sensors, inclinometers, ultrasonic sensors, etc. (Tao, et. al., 2012).

Inertial sensors are used to calculate temporal characteristics of gait. These sensors combine accelerometers and gyroscopes to measure acceleration of body parts along with angular velocity (Muro-de-la-Herran, et. al., 2014).

Strain gauges are used to calculate the strain on the body part with which it is attached. It works by converting the various parameters such as force, weight, tension, pressure into varying electrical resistance which is measured and analysed (Muro-de-la-Herran, et. al., 2014).

Goniometers can be used to measures the angles for knees, angles, etc. These may be used in gait analysis for measurement of human posture and spatial motion.

Non-wearable systems can be implemented using two approaches Image processing and floor sensors. The floor sensors would be fitted into the surface on which the subject would walk.

Typical image processing systems that are used for gait analysis consists of a set of digital cameras that captures gait data of the subject under examination and it is fed into a system that processes the image, calculates gait attributes that later can be analysed. (Mason, et. al., 2016) explained that a single measure may not fully represent the complex set of dynamics involved in human gait. They further explained that multiple techniques may be employed to study and analyse human gait. Such techniques may include cameras and sensor approaches.

A comprehensive survey on different gait Analysis techniques has been done by the authors in (Soni & Singh, 2016).

The authors in (Benbakreti & Benyetto, 2012) obtained a gait signature based on the angle and the contour of the silhouette. Principal component analysis (PCA) was then applied to this dataset in order to reduce the dimensionality.

The proposal of incorporation of HOG (Histogram of Oriented Gradients) to Gait Gaussian Image for visibly improved results in gait recognition has been discussed by the authors in (Arora, et. al., 2015). This new spatial-temporal representation, called Gradient Histogram Gaussian Image (GHGI) is almost similar to Gait Energy Image (GEI) but the usage of Gaussian function and further application of HOG considerably increases efficiency and reduces amalgamation of noise.

(Das & Sarat Saharia, 2014) explored the basic concept of Point Light animation along with machine vision and machine learning techniques to analyse and classify gait patterns by using Support Vector Machines Modelling.

(Bora and Gupta, 2014) studied in depth various techniques such as K-Means, Euclidean Distance, Cosine Distance, etc. to calculate the distance between two arbitrary data sets.

OVERVIEW OF THE PROPOSED SYSTEM

The main objective of the proposed system is to:

1. Develop a method capable of performing recognition of individuals derived from an image sequence of a person walking.
2. Automatic extraction of relevant gait feature points should be available from an image sequence in order to automate the classification process.

The proposed system can be viewed as having two sub-systems – Entity Registration and Claimant Verification. The Entity Registration sub-system is used to register the attributes of a known subject in a database. This stored data is later on used in the Claimant Verification phase to match the attributes of the claimant to the ones stored in the database for a possible recognition.

The process can be broken down into three main sections.

1.   **Segmentation:** this module will take the image sequence as an input, then perform processing in order to determine which pixels are part of the foreground and which are part of the background. The process essentially makes use of Background Subtraction.
2.   **Feature Extraction:** once the model has been fitted to the image, features, which can be used to create a gait signature, will be derived from the model parameters i.e. variation in heel distances, heel height from floor, etc.
3.   **Recognition:** the recognition engine will take data from either a newly captured subject via the feature extraction module, or a previously stored signature, and perform recognition based on a database of test subjects.

Of these sections, the Recognition section would be of use only in the Claimant Verification Subsystem. Thus, the major steps to be followed in this system are as follows:

1.   Video feed containing human gait is stored as a stream of images.
2.   Static background information is collected and stored as media.
3.   Dynamic foreground information is generated – The foreground object is extracted by using a combination of edge detection algorithms along with background subtraction.
4.   Features of object causing change in foreground are extracted – this is done by sketching the skeleton of the subject and then computing identifying attributes (features) such as distance between left and right heels, angle formed by a feet with the ground, etc.

Comparison of the extracted features with the stored feature set of human beings is done by the computation of Cosine Distance.

DETAILED DESIGN

As explained in the previous section, that the entire system may be viewed as having two subsystems, each of which have been explained in Figure 2 and Figure 3 diagrammatically:

Figure 2. Entity Registration

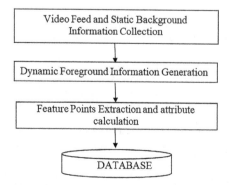

Figure 3. Claimant Verification

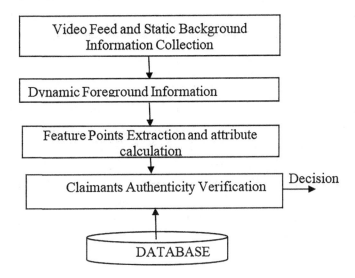

Video Feed and Static Background Information Collection

This process starts by recording a video containing human gait with a camera that records video in at least 30 frames per second rate. This requirement of 30 fps is important because if the camera shoots video in less than 30 fps then the frames will have a ringing effect, i.e., the edges of the feet will be blurred. This blurring will cause problem during the background subtraction phase. The recorded video is fed into the system. Now the frames from the video are extracted to convert the video into a stream of images. From this stream of images or frames the first frame will be selected as the initial frame. This frame will be a blank frame i.e. the subject will not be present in the frame; it will contain only the background. The first intermediate frame is defined as the frame in which the entire body of the subject appears for the first time. We will apply a frame selection algorithm to select the first intermediate frame.

Intermediate Frame Selection Algorithm

Step 1: The first frame is the initial frame.
Step 2: First frame is denoted by i and the next frame is denoted by j.
Step 3: j is subtracted from i. If the number of non-black pixels in the result of the subtraction is above a certain threshold then j is the frame containing human gait.

Return j.

Step 4: Consider the next frame and denote it by j.
Step 5: Goto step-3.

Since in all the areas of j except the portion occupied by the subject is same in pixel value as I; hence on subtraction of j from I, all the background pixels become zero except the pixels on the subject. These non-black pixels are counted. As the subject enters the frame with each incrementing frame more area of the subject's body will enter the frame and the number of non-black pixels also increases. When it crosses a certain threshold it is assumed that the subject has completely entered the frame and the frame is returned.

With increasing resolution of the image the number of total pixel increases. Thus incrementing j by 1 will make this algorithm very slow, as the high number of pixels require more computation time. If the video is recorded in high fps then to observe a noticeable change more number of frames has to be passed. The subject will enter the frame after more number of frames than in a video with less fps thus resulting in increasing time. Suppose the subject has completely entered the frame after 3 seconds then if the camera had shot the video in 60 fps then 180 frames has to be considered to get the intermediate frame. If the camera shot the video in 30 fps then the number of frame becomes 90. To solve this problem instead of increasing j by 1 we will increase it by 20. Thus instead of considering all the frames in the video, only a sample of a few frames are chosen. A sampling rate of 20 implies that every 20th. frame is chosen to find out if it is an intermediate frame or not. Thus we only have to compute 9 frames making the algorithm efficient in terms of time.

Shown in Figure 4 is the walk of a subject in sequence of time (anticlockwise direction).

Dynamic Foreground Information Generation

This step extracts the foreground that is the subject. By background subtraction (Ghosh Dastidar & Biswas, 2015) the resultant image will contain the subject in the foreground with a black featureless background. From the previous step we got two frames an initial frame and an intermediate frame obtained by the frame selection algorithm. The intermediate frame is subtracted from the initial frame. As we can see in the fig the background pixel remains same in both the frames so after subtraction it will became zero but the pixel value in the subject's body is different in pixel value from the background so it will result in non-zero pixels (Figure 5).

Figure 4. Walk of a subject

Figure 5. Foreground silhoutte

Feature Point Extraction and Attribute Calculation

Human gait have two types of attributes, temporal and spatial. Temporal attributes include time taken for each step, stride time etc. Here we are identifying entities on the basis of spatial attributes. To recognize and measure these spatial attributes first the feature points have to be recognized and based on these feature points the attributes are calculated and finally based on these attributes an entity is authenticated. The background subtracted image of the previous phase is used to generate a skeleton (Kundu, et. al., 2014) of the foreground as shown in Figure 6. Since skeletonization is a morphological operation first the image is binarized. We use the MATLAB function, *bwmorph()* to achieve this task.

Now from the skeleton, the feature points are extracted. Here we are only interested in two feature points, the toe of the front foot and the heel of the back foot. For identifying these feature points a neighbourhood algorithm is used. Neighbourhood of a pixel at i^{th} row and j^{th} column of an image is a 3X3 sub-matrix of the entire image centered at the pixel at location (i,j) shown in Table 1.

The feature points are in fact the end points of the skeleton. The proposed method for extracting the feature points has been described as follows:

The feature points will contain only two white pixels in its neighbourhood while all other points will contain more than two white pixels in its neighbourhood as shown in the Figure 7.

Figure 6. Skeleton of the subject's silhouette in the frame

Table 1. Neighbourhood of a pixel (i, j)

i-1, j-1	i-1, j	i-1, j+1
i, j-1	i, j	i, j+1
i+1, j-1	i+1, j	i+1, j+1

Figure 7. (a) part of a skeleton containing a foot, (b) intermediate point, (c-e) feature points

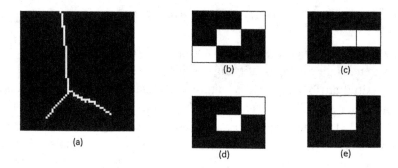

Algorithm to Find Feature Point

Step 1: Repeat the following steps for the skeleton image starting from bottom-right corner until four feature points are found

Step 2: Examine the neighbourhood

Step 3: If it has only two white pixels consider it as a feature point, and add it to the feature point matrix (FPM).

As we loop through the skeleton image from bottom right corner whenever a non-black pixel is found its neighbourhood will be examined as shown in the above figures if it is not a feature point then it will be connected to two other non-black pixels otherwise if it's a feature point then it will be the end point of the skeleton thus it will connected to only one non-black pixel thus the neighbourhood will have only two non-black pixels.

The Figure 8 illustrates the discovery of two feature points using the method just described.

Figure 8. Discovery of feature points

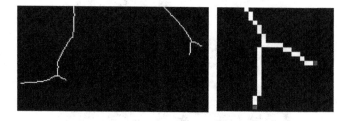

The Feature Point Matrix (FPM) is a 4X2 matrix where each row corresponds to a feature point and the two columns corresponds to location (row, column) of the feature point. When we loop from the bottom right corner the feature points we encounter will be in the order toe of front foot which will be the first row of FPM followed by the heel of front foot whose location will be in the second row of the FPM. Similarly, we then encounter toe followed by the heel of the back foot which will be in the third and fourth row of the FPM. As stated earlier we are only interested in the toe of the front foot and the heel of the back foot so we will only use the values from first and fourth row from the FPM. Let us assume that the toe of the front foot is at the co-ordinate (x,y) and the heel of the back foot is at the co-ordinate (x',y'). The three attributes we are considering here are discussed below:

Distance Between Heel and Floor (dbhf)

This is calculated by the length of the straight line connecting the floor and the heel of the back foot. The attribute *dbhf* is calculated by subtracting the y axis value of the heel of the back foot and the y axis value of the toe of the front foot as illustrated in Figure 9.

dbhf=(y-y')

As the first and fourth row of FPM respectively contains the spatial co-ordinates of the toe of the front foot and the heel of the back foot dbhf can be calculated as follows:

dbhf = FHM(1,2)-FHM(4,2)

Distance Between Two Feet (dbtf)

This Attribute is calculated by subtracting the x coordinate of the back foot from the x co-ordinate of the front foot.

dbtf=(x-x')

From FPM the value of dbtf is calculates as follows:

dbhf = FHM(1,1)-FHM(4,1)

The calculation of dbtf has been demonstrated in the Figure 10.

Figure 9. Calculation of dbhf

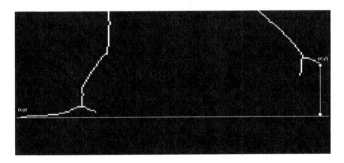

Figure 10. Calculation of dbtf

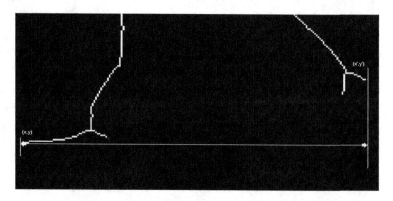

Angle Between Foot and Floor (abhf)

This attribute is the angle between the floor and the straight line connecting the heel of the back foot and the toe of the front foot. We have already calculated dbtf and dbhf now let us assume that abhf is is θ. The tan of the θ will be equal to $\dfrac{dbtf}{dbhf}$. Thus abhf can be calculated as follows in equation (1).

$$\tan\theta = \frac{dbtf}{dbhf} \tag{1}$$

$$\theta = \tan^{-1}\frac{dbtf}{dbhf} \tag{2}$$

The angle computation has been shown in Figure 11.

Now we can construct a vector AV which will contain all 3 attribute of the natural gait of the subjected obtained from the Skeleton

$$AV = \begin{bmatrix} dbhf \\ dbtf \\ abhf \end{bmatrix}$$

We repeat this process 10 times and construct 10 AVs and collect them together into a pattern class. And this class is stored in the database. This process is called entity registration.

Claimant's Authenticity Verification

In this phase the extracted features of the claimant is compared with the existing feature sets to authenticate the entity. Ten vectors calculated during ten iterations in the entity registration phase forms a pattern class. For each authentic entity there will be a pattern class in the database. When a claimant will demand verification the pattern class, containing its attribute will be generated and compared with each of the stored pattern classes to find a match (Gonzalez & Woods, 2009).

Figure 11. Calculation of abhf

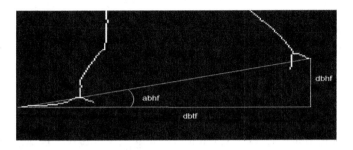

The function we use for measuring the similarity is Cosine Distance (Bora and Gupta, 2014), which is the complement of cosine similarity. Cosine similarity measures the similarity between two vectors. The cosine distance between two vectors is one minus the cosine of the included angles between two vectors. This cosine distance value will be used for identifying the claimant. For two vectors, the attribute vector of the claimant, AVCM and mean vector of ith. pattern class, AVM the Cosine Distance can be calculated by equations (3) and (4).

$$AVCM.AVM = \|AVCM\| . \|AVM\| \cos \theta . \tag{3}$$

$$\text{Cosine Distance} = 1 - \frac{AVCM.AVM}{\|AVCM\| \|AVM\|} \tag{4}$$

For two vectors A and B with n attributes. If ith. attribute of vector A is A_i and ith. attribute of B is B_i then cosine similarity between A and B vector are calculated as shown in equation (5).

$$\text{Cosine Distance} = 1 - \frac{\sum_{i=1}^{n} A_i B_i}{\sqrt{\sum_{i=1}^{n} A_i^2} \sqrt{\sum_{i=1}^{n} B_i^2}} \tag{5}$$

The procedure of claimant verification is as follows:

Step 1: The mean of pattern class of the claimant is calculated and stored in vector AVCM.
Step 2: Each pattern class corresponding to one entity is fetched from database into a 3X10 matrix where each row represents the attributes and columns represent the value of the attributes.
Step 3: Mean of each of the pattern class is calculated and stored in a vector AVM.
Step 4: Cosine distance between AVM and each of the AVCM's is calculated.
Step 5: For the pair of vector for which the distance will be lowest is considered as a match and the claimant will be identified as the corresponding entity.

A greater Cosine Distance implies that the similarity is less for the pair. Thus the least cosine distance implies the highest similarity.

RESULTS AND DISCUSSION

The process described above has been implemented using MATLAB and a comprehensive set of relevant data has been collected. The gait of a person has been monitored and during each walk 10 pattern vectors have been collected. A subject goes through 10 such walk sequences each of which gives 10 vectors. Thus the pattern class representing a subject has a total of 100 vectors.

In some problems where the number of features is very large, it is useful to reduce the feature dimension to increase the classification accuracy. In this problem there are only 3 features, so reduction of feature dimension is not so much necessary, but for finding which feature is the most effective one, two popular supervised feature ranking algorithms are used. The first one is the ReliefF (Kononenko, 1997) and the second one is the Concave Minimization (Bradley & Mangasarian, 1998). The ReliefF algorithm has ranked abhf, dbhf and dbtf as 1, 2 and 3 respectively. The Concave Minimization algorithm has ranked abhf, dbtf and dbhf as 1, 2 and 3 respectively. It is worth noting that both of the algorithms have ranked abhf as the best. This is not a surprising outcome, considering the fact that abhf is an attribute that considers both dbhf and dbtf to be computed. Hence the effectiveness of abhf is the maximum.

Below is a table (Table 2) that shows the mean vectors calculated from three different pattern classes representing three different subjects.

The Cosine Distances for matches with the three different subjects at different times has been shown in Table 3. For the first claimant a match with Subject3 is the maximum.

A similar matching was also done by calculating the Euclidean distances for the subjects. However, the results obtained were more precise by using the Cosine Distance.

Table 2. Mean vectors of three pattern classes

dbtf	dbhf	abhf
13.81	76.38	1.04
22	135.9	1.11
13.57	102.2	1.21

Table 3. Cosine distances for different claimants

Claimant	Subject1	Subject2	Subject3
1	0.0043	0.0047	0.008
2	0.0001	0.0002	0.0013
3	0.0023	0.0026	0.0052
4	0.2895	0.1808	0.2237
5	0.688	0.1731	0.6343
6	0.0018	0.0015	0.0003
7	0.0027	0.0024	0.0008
8	0.0012	0.001	0.0001

(Murat, 2006) in his work used a similar approach for matching. The author calculated Mahalanobis distances between the test cases and the training cases (stored in the database). For same styles of walking he achieved 100% match results for the top 3-4 records.

CONCLUSION

The analysis done in this work has considered just three attributes. The precision of the method may be increased by considering more attributes and then subjecting them to a meta heuristic feature optimisation or principal component analysis (PCA) for finding a subset of the most effective attributes. Computation of the Cosine Distance is a step ahead of the Minimum Distance Classifier that makes use of the Euclidean distance. This method may be further improved upon by using other classification schemes such as the Support Vector Machine or an algorithm such as K-Means.

Identification and Authentication techniques using Gait Analysis, particularly the methods which do not use wearable sensors are perhaps the most unobtrusive ones. Such techniques do not require retina/iris scanners for biometric authentication involving ones' eyes. Neither does this method require precise cameras for capturing features for the purpose of face recognition nor does this method require finger print sensors for doing finger print matching. However, one big drawback of this method is that gait is an acquired trait and thus subject to copying. This drawback may be overcome by combining gait analysis with other authentication techniques. Moreover, at crowded places a purported intruder may be caught unawares.

REFERENCES

Arora, P., Srivastava, S., Arora, K., & Bareja, S. (2015). Improved Gait Recognition using Gradient Histogram Gaussian Image. *Procedia Computer Science*, *58*, 408–413. doi:10.1016/j.procs.2015.08.049

Benbakreti, S., & Benyettou, M. (2012). Gait Recognition Based on Leg motion and Contour Of Silhouette. *International Conference on Information Technology and e-Services*. 10.1109/ICITeS.2012.6216626

Bora, D. J., & Gupta, A. K. (2014). Effect of Different Distance Measures on the Performance of K-Means Algorithm: An Experimental Study in Matlab. *International Journal of Computer Science and Information Technologies*, *5*(2), 2501–2506.

Bradley, P. S., & Mangasarian, O. L. (1998). Feature Selection via Concave Minimization and Support Vector Machines. *ICML - Proceedings of the Fifteenth International Conference on Machine Learning*, 82-90.

Charalambous, C. P. (2014). Walking Patterns of Normal Men. In P. Banaszkiewicz & D. Kader (Eds.), *Classic Papers in Orthopaedics* (pp. 393–395). Springer. doi:10.1007/978-1-4471-5451-8_99

Das, D., & Saharia, S. (2014). Human Gait Analysis and Recognition using Support Vector Machines. *ICCSEA, SPPR, VLSI, WiMoA, SCAI, CNSA, WeST, 2014*, 187–195.

Durward, B. R., Baer, G. D., & Rowe, P. J. (1999). *Functional Human Movement* (3rd ed.). Edinburgh, UK: Elsevier Science Ltd.

Ghosh Dastidar, J., & Biswas, R. (2015). Tracking human intrusion through a CCTV. In IEEE conference CICN. IEEE. doi:10.1109/CICN.2015.95

Gonzalez, R. C., & Woods, R. E. (2009). Digital Image Processing (3rd ed.). Pearson Education.

Kononenko, I. (1997). Overcoming the myopia of inductive learning algorithms with RELIEFF. *Applied Intelligence*, *7*(1), 39–55.

Kundu, M., Sengupta D., & Ghosh Dastidar, J. (2014). Tracking direction of human movement – an efficient implementation using skeleton. *International Journal of Computer Applications*, *96*(13), 27-33.

Loudon, J., Swift, M., & Bell, S. (2008). *The clinical orthopedic assessment guide* (2nd ed.). Human Kinetics.

Mason, E. J., Traore, I., & Woungang, I. (2016). Gait Biometric Recognition. In *Machine Learning Techniques for Gait Biometric Recognition*. Springer.

Murat, E. I. (2006). *Human Identification using Gait* (Vol. 14). Turkey Journal of Elec. Engg.

Muro-de-la-Herran, A., Garcia-Zapirain, B., & Mendez-Zorrilla, A. (2014). Gait Analysis Methods: An Overview of Wearable and Non-Wearable Systems, Highlighting Clinical Applications. *Sensors (Basel)*, *14*(2), 3362–3394. doi:10.3390140203362 PMID:24556672

Soni, K., & Singh, A. (2016). A Survey Paper on Human Gait Recognition Techniques. *International Journal of Science Technology & Engineering, 2*(10).

Tao, W., Liu, T., Zheng, R., & Feng, H. (2012). Gait Analysis Using Wearable Sensors. *Sensors (Basel)*, *12*(2), 2255–2283. doi:10.3390120202255 PMID:22438763

Whittle, M. W. (2013). *Gait analysis. In The Soft Tissues* (pp. 187–199). Elsevier. doi:10.1016/B978-0-7506-0170-2.50017-0

Chapter 9
Implementation of a Hybrid Classification Method for Diabetes

Dilip Kumar Choubey
National Institute of Technology Patna, India

Sanchita Paul
Birla Institute of Technology Mesra, India

Kanchan Bala
Birla Institute of Technology Mesra, India

Manish Kumar
Birla Institute of Technology Mesra, India

Uday Pratap Singh
Madhav Institute of Technology and Science, India

ABSTRACT

This chapter presents a best classification of diabetes. The proposed approach work consists in two stages. In the first stage the Pima Indian diabetes dataset is obtained from the UCI repository of machine learning databases. In the second stage, the authors have performed the classification technique by using fuzzy decision tree on Pima Indian diabetes dataset. Then they applied PSO_SVM as a feature selection technique followed by the classification technique by using fuzzy decision tree on Pima Indian diabetes dataset. In this chapter, the optimization of SVM using PSO reduces the number of attributes, and hence, applying fuzzy decision tree improves the accuracy of detecting diabetes. The hybrid combinatorial method of feature selection and classification needs to be done so that the system applied is used for the classification of diabetes.

DOI: 10.4018/978-1-5225-7107-0.ch009

INTRODUCTION

In the current scenario, there are certain factor such as an environmental factor, sedentary life style, genetically (hereditary) producing several diseases most popularly known as 'diabetes', which has become the most leading chronic diseases. So the primary need of this generation is to become the state of art healthcare. The main motto of this work is to provide a indigenous efficient diagnostic tool of detection of diabetes, even though there are already several established existing technique, which have been used for the diagnosis of diabetes.

Diabetes is a disease which increases the blood glucose known as hyperglycemia to a level which affects the body to a greater extent (http://www.who.int/diabetes). The main reason for the coming of symptoms of hyperglycemia is the deficiency of insulin where the production of insulin in the pancreas fails by the beta cells. This type of category generally known as diabetes-1. The other form of diabetes is the diabetes-2 where the production of insulin can't be effected by the body cells (Brussels, Belgium: International Diabetes Federation, 2007). Due to these orders of Diabetes chances of blindness, heart disease, blood pressure, kidney disease increases. This disease is of the form type-1 and type-2 (Temurtas et al., 2009). The Pima Indians of Arizona considered being the most prevalence of diabetes incidence of type-2 (Temurtas et al., 2009). Since with the increase of medical progress the diagnosis of type-2 patients are unaware and hence take more years for the recovery from such disease(http://www.diabetes.org/diabetes-basics).

The researchers provides a new and efficient technique for the medical diagnosis by integrating the feature selection using Support Vector Machine (SVM)(Brank et al., 2002) optimized with the Particle Swarm Optimization (PSO)(Mandal and N, 2012) and rule generation using Fuzzy based Decision Tree (FDT) hence the approach is the selection of features so that classification is done for the diabetes mellitus patients (Dash and Liu, 1997).

Feature Selection is a technique of identifying the selecting the most relevant features as possible (Liu and Sentino, 1998). By selecting the most relevant features from the dataset and removing the irrelevant features the high dimensionality data size can be reduces and allows the process to apply efficiently and quickly (Abraham et al., 2007). Particularly in the classification of diabetes dataset the number of features used increases the accuracy of predicting diabetes patients.

A Decision Tree (DT) is a recursive form of the tree used for the classification of uncertain data or huge data. A DT consists of root nodes and leaves which shows the dataset dependent attributes and their respective values. In Data mining there are several decision tree such as using ID3 (Iterative Dichotomiser), CART (Classification & Regression Tree), Random Forest, J48graft DT (J48 graft Decision Tree), etc.

The advantages of decision tree are: Easy to understand and generate rules, Reduce problem complexity, Tree creates all possible outcome, Easy to run and relatively fast, Automatic variable selection and good at missing value handling, Highlight possibilities yet not considered, Improve result, Simpler and more compact representation, Easily created, State is recorded in memory, Decision tree can be learned, Inexpensive to construct and okay for noisy data, Handle both continuous and symbolic data, No requirement of distance function; and disadvantages are: Training time is expensive, Mistake made at higher level leads to any sub tree wrong, Continuous variable and numeric data can't handled, May suffer from over fitting, Large pruning is needed, Tree is complex for numeric data, Process can be time consuming, and unmanageable for complex decision, Real time data problem, Need many example as possible, Probabilities only estimated, Requirement for qualitative input for complete picture, High CPU cost, Reliability depends upon accuracy of data used; and application are Predicting library books, Agriculture, Astronomy, Biomedical engineering, control system, Financial analysis, Manufacturing and production, Medicine, Molecular biology, Object recognition, Pharmacology, physics, plant diseases, Power system, Remote sensing, Software development, Text processing, Real option analysis, Corporate analysis. This is also mentioned in literature review (Choubey et al., 2014; Choubey and Paul, 2016).

The example of decision tree is shown in Figure 1.

The manuscript is distributed under following headings: Background is present in section 2, Motivation is devoted to section 3, Literature Review section is discussed in section 4, Proposed approach in detail is introduced in section 5, Results and Discussion of proposedapproach are present in section 6, in the end conclusion and future work are devoted to section 7.

BACKGROUND

Vladimir N. Vapnik (Vapnik, 1995) firstly proposed SVM in the 1995. SVM are supervised machine learning approach that are associated with learning algorithms which analyze data, recognize patterns and are used for classification as well as regression analysis. SVM constructs hyper plane or decision surface that classifies the data with a largest margin. The decision surface that maximizes the margin of the training set will reduce the generalization error. It operates on the finding of hyper plane which uses an interclass distance or margin width for the separation of positive and negative samples. For the unequal misclassification cost a coefficient factor of $C+$ & $C-$ denoted as 'J' is used for the generation of errors can be outweighs both positive and negative examples (Morik et al., 1998). Hence the optimization problem of SVM becomes (Kennedy and Eberhart, 1995):

$$minimize \frac{1}{2}\|w\|^2 + C_+ + \sum_{i|y_i=1} \aleph_i + C_- \sum_{j|y_j=-1} \aleph_j \qquad (1)$$

This satisfies the condition,

$$y_k\left(wx_k + b\right) \geq 1 - \aleph_k, \aleph_k \geq 0 \qquad (2)$$

Figure 1. An Example of Decision Tree

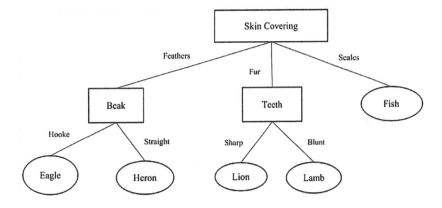

Table 1. Notations used in SVM

Parameters	Explanation
y_i	Class labels used in the training dataset
W	Normal to the hyper plane
$\left| b \right| l \left\| w \right\|$	Perpendicular distance from origin (b) to the hyper plane (w)
$\left\| w \right\|$	Euclidean norm of w
C	Regularization parameter used to find the tradeoff between training error and margin width d
$\aleph_i$	Slack variable that allows error in classification [8].

The Table 1 describes the used notations of SVM.

SVM is fulfilled in linear and non-linear way, the non-linear form or Radial bias kernel are used for the non-linearly separable data with lagrangemultiplier α_i, Hence optimization problem becomes:

$$\text{minimize } w\left(\alpha\right) = \sum_{i=1}^{l} \alpha_i - \frac{1}{2} \sum_{i=1,j=1}^{l} \alpha_i y_i \alpha_j y_j K\left(x_i . y_j\right) \tag{3}$$

where,

$$C \geq \alpha_i \geq 0 \forall_i, \sum_{i=1}^{l} \alpha_i y_i = 0 \tag{4}$$

For the classification of medical diabetes mellitus a final decision is crucial requirement by the end users (Ye and Johnson, 1995; Chen et al., 2007; Wyatt and Altman, 1995). Hence Feature Extraction is executed for the exact working of the SVM (Barakat, 2007). The Figure 2 represents the basic architecture of Linear SVM.

The advantages of SVM are: Training is relatively easy, Scales well to high dimensional data, Error can be Controlled explicitly; disadvantages are: Need for a good kernel function, Not able to provide Comprehensible justification for the classification decisions they make; and application of SVM are: Pattern recognition Problems, Hand writing analysis, Face analysis, Text and hypertext categorization, Classification of images.This is also mentioned in literature review (Choubey et al., 2014; Choubey and Paul, 2016).SVM classifies the linearly separable data.

Linear SVM was developed to separate the two classes that belong to either one side of the margin of hyper plane or the other side.

Given labeled training data as data points of the form:

Figure 2. Basic Architecture of Linear SVM

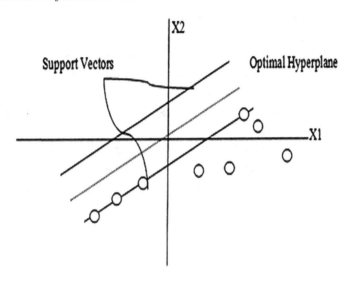

$$M = \left\{ \left(u_1, v_1 \right), \left(u_2, v_2 \right), \dots\dots\dots\dots\dots\dots\dots\dots, \left(u_n, v_n \right) \right\} \tag{5}$$

where, $v_n = 1 / -1$, this constant denotes the class which will belongs to the point u_n, n = Number of data sample.

Each u_n, is a p-dimensional real vector or is a set of training tuples with associated class labels v_n. The SVM classifier first maps the input vectors into a decision value, and then performs the classification using an appropriate threshold value.

If the data is non-linear, SVM is not suited to achieve the classification tasks. To overcome this limitation, these support vectors are transformed into higher dimensional feature space, which is introduced by kernel functions (Chen et al., 2007). Here by support vectors means the training points that are nearest to the separating function are called support vectors. For a domain expert a kernel is a similarity function provide to a machine-learning algorithm. Kernel makes linear models in nonlinear settings. Kernel is used for non-separable problem in to separable and map data into better representational space. A Kernel function is defined as a function that corresponds to a dot product of two feature vectors in some expanded feature space:

$$K\left(u, v \right) = D(u)' D\left(v \right) \tag{6}$$

The motivation for this extension is that a SVM with nonlinear decision surface can classify nonlinear separable data.

Eberhart and Kennedy developed PSO in 1995 (Kennedy and Eberhart, 1995; Eberhart and Kennedy, 1995). PSO is a heuristic search algorithm which is inspired by the social behavior of a flock of birds or school of fish. It is swarm intelligence or evolutionary technique.

The advantages of PSO techniques are: No overlapping and mutation calculation, Seed of researching fast, Calculation very simple and bigger optimization ability, Adopt real number code and decided the solution directly, Derivative - free technique, Concept and coding is easy, Less sensitive to objective function as compare to conventional mathematical approaches, Few algorithm parameter, Faster convergence, Simple implementation, Insensitive for design variable, Generate high quality solution within shorter calculation time, Easier researching for large problem space, Concurrent processing can easily parallelized, Less dependent on initial point set; disadvantages of PSO techniques are: Suffer from partial optimization, Not work out the problem of scattering, Optimization and non coordinate system, Lacks the mathematical foundation for analysis, Limitation for real time ED application, Require longer computational time than mathematical approach, Fast and premature convergence in mid optimum point, Weak local search ability; and applications are: Robotics, Antenna design, Biomedical, Signal processing, Design and Modelling, Image and Graphics, Networking, Electronics and Electromagnetic, Prediction and Forecasting, Optimization, Neural network training, Fuzzy system, Clustering, Data mining, Power generation and controlling, Solved constrained problem, Electric machinery, Sensor network, Security and military, Metallurgy.This is also mentioned in literature review (Choubey et al., 2014; Choubey and Paul, 2016).

Typically, a flock of birds have no leaders and they find food for them by collaborative trial and error. They follow one of the members of the group that has the closest position with a food source. Others update their position simultaneously by communicating with members who already have a better position. This needs to be done repeatedly until the best food source is found. PSO algorithm finds the optimal values by following the same process. PSO consists of a population of individuals called swarm, and each individual is called a particle which represents a location or possible candidate solution in a multidimensional search space.

Initially, the particles are placed at various positions randomly and perform search for the optimal value of a given objective function by exploration and exploitation. The value of the objective function at that position or the fitness value is also stored. Each particle records the position in the search space at which the best solution was obtained by it till now and calls it as personal best or *pbest* . Along with the *pbest* value, a global best or *gbest* position is also stored by each particle. *gbest* is the best solution found till now in the topological neighborhood of that particle. The movement of particles in a swarm depend on three factors namely *pbest, gbest* and velocity. The first factor is called the cognitive component and the second denotes the social component. The third factor is the velocity of each particle which is updated towards the *pbest* and *gbest* positions using some random component. In each iteration, the *pbest* and *gbest* are also updated for each particle. Based on these three values, each particle updates its position if it is more fit. Iteratively, the process continues until the termination criteria met. The termination criteria may be the number of function evaluations or number of runs or minimum acceptable error.PSO is easier to implement and it is easy the parameters of PSO. PSO is also used for maintaining the variety of swarm (Engelbrecht, 2006).

The Basic form of PSO consists of the moving velocity of the form:

$$V_i(K+1) = V_i(K) + \gamma_{1i}(P_i - X_i(k)) + \gamma_{2i}(G - X_i(k)) \tag{7}$$

And accordingly its position is given as:

$$X_i(K+1) = X_i(K) + V_i(K+1) \tag{8}$$

where,

The Table 2 describes the basic notations used in PSO.

The Figure 3 represents the basic several variants of PSO.

MOTIVATION

It is well known that till some years back physicians diagnosed diabetes solely on the basis of experience and with the aid of raw clinical data of the patient which mainly constituted laboratory test reports. These laboratory test reports varied depending on meals, exercise, sickness, stress, small changes in temperature, different equipment used, and ways of sample handling. So, this kind of diagnosis of the disease is not only time consuming but also depends entirely on the availability and the experience of the physician who has to deal with imprecise and uncertain clinical data of the patient. Thus, to improve and expedite the decision ability using only readily available clinical data, an efficient (intelligent) diagnosis system is very much needed.

The present study answers as to how by analyzing the input data (patient's data i.e., PIDD) and developing an accurate description or model for each class using the features in the dataset which is further easily based on the same concept, diagnosis system may be developed.

The main problems behind any misdiagnosis of disease are stated below:

- **Lack of Proper Communication:** Patients does not communicate effectively with the physician which means not revealing the right symptoms from which they suffer.
- **Lack of Experience:** If the physician lacks the experience or ability to diagnose the disease correctly.

Table 2. Basic Notations of PSO

Parameter	Summary
i	Particle Index
K	Discrete time index
V_i	Velocity of the ith particle
X_i	Position of ith particle
P_i	Best position found by ith particle
G	Best position found by swarm
$\gamma_{1i,2i}$	Random numbers on the interval [0,1] applied to ith particle.

Figure 3. PSO Variants
Imran et al., 2012.

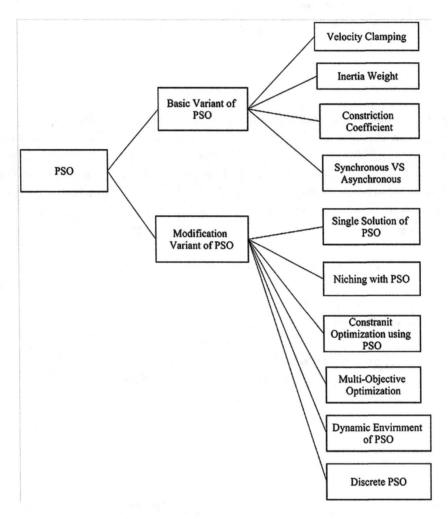

- **Lack of Pathological or Laboratory Tests:** Unavailability of well-established equipment, chemicals, experienced pathologist etc. In developing countries also if well-equipped laboratories are found, they are available only in some few big cites or metropolitans.

LITERATURE REVIEW

There are already several existed techniques, which have been implemented for classification of diabetes and popular dataset is Pima Indian Diabetes Dataset. The Pima Indian Diabetes Dataset (PIDD) is available in the UCI Repository of Machine Learning Databases (https://archive.ics.uci.edu/ml/datasets /Pima+Indians+Diabetes).Some of the stated works in the same dataset or related to diabetes are briefly described.

(Dogantekin et al., 2010) used Linear Discriminant Analysis (LDA) and Adaptive Neuro–Fuzzy Inference System (ANFIS) for diagnosis of diabetes. LDA is used to separate feature variables between healthy and patient (diabetes) data, and ANFIS is used for classification.

(Polat and Gunes, 2007) used Principal Component Analysis (PCA) and ANFIS in which PCA is used to reduce the dimensions of diabetes and ANFIS apply classification on that to reduce features of diabetes datasets.

(Seera and Lim, 2014) introduced Fuzzy Min-Max neural network, Classification and Regression Tree (CART), Random Forest (RF) for the classification of medical data. These combined methodologies were implemented on various datasets i.e., Breast Cancer Wisconsin, Pima Indian Diabetes Dataset (PIDD), and Liver Disorders and performed better as compared to other existing methods.

(Orkcu and Bal, 2011) used Back propogation neural network, binary-coded genetic algorithms, real coded genetic algorithm for the classifications of medical datasets.

(Barakat et al., 2010) worked on SVM method as the classification of diabetes. The authors stated SQRex-SVMand Electic method for rule extraction to enable SVMs to be more intelligible. The experimental results are performed on the real life datasets that shows the performance of the methodology.

(Aslam et al., 2013) generates a number of features using genetic based rules extraction and then compares the results for the diabetes classification. The rules generation based technique realized generates a new set of rules without any knowledge of diabetes. The methodology applied works in stages consisting of various tests including t-test and then selection of F-score on the basis of which accuracy can be predicted and finally applying Genetic programming.

(Polat et al., 2008) proposed and executed an efficient technique of diabetes classification using the cascaded learning approach based on Discriminate Analysis and Least square based support vector machine. The preprocessing is done on the real dataset for the discrimination of the features variable so that the patients belonging to healthy category and diabetes patients and finally LS-SVM (Least Square-Support Vector Machine) is applied for the classification of the diabetes patients. It provides accuracy of 82.05% on applied on 10-folds cross validations.

(Luukka,2011) used Fuzzy entropy measure, similarity classifier for the classification of diabetic disease. Fuzzy entropy was used as a feature selection and similarity classifier was used for the classification on those selected features.

In order to improve the performance of classification techniques, feature selection has proved to be one of the suitable methods by which good classification accuracy can be achieved. Feature selection is an important part of a pattern recognition system. It is important to note that all the features may not always be beneficial for classification and some of the features may not contribute meaningful information in any pattern recognition problem. Actually, these features are irrelevant or redundant. It affects the classification accuracy as well as adds noise to the dataset distribution. A high dimension dataset has high computational cost which results in many processing challenges. Some form of dimension reduction is necessary to minimize these effects as a preprocessing step.

(Dash and Liu, 1997) presented a survey on different feature selection methods. Effectiveness of the features can be evaluated by using one of the following feature selection criteria: distance, information, dependence, consistency and classifier error rate. Some of the feature selection methods employing these criteria are discussed in (Nandi et al., 2006).

Wrapper type and filter type are two main types of feature selection methods as discussed by (Muni et al., 2006). Wrapper method is computationally expensive and it can result in over-fitting the model because it is biased to its underlying classification engine.

Feature selection is performed in the first stage in filter type methods, irrespective of the classifier used for classification in the second stage. This method minimizes the computational complexity at the cost of reduced classification accuracy. Machine learning algorithms including Neural Network (NN), Support Vector Machine (SVM), and Genetic Algorithms (GA) have also been used in the past for feature selection (Siedlecki&Sklansky, 1989; Setiono& Liu, 1997).

(Temurtas et al., 2009) presented Levenberg-Marquardt (LM) algorithm and Probabilistic neural network (PNN) to train a multilayer neural network and Ten fold cross validation technique for estimation of result. LM, PNN, 10-Fold cross validation provided better correct training pattern than conventional validation method.

(Aslam and Nandi, 2010) have a proposed a method uses Genetic Programming (GP) and a modified version of GP with Comparative Partner Selection (CPS) for the classification of diabetes.

(Aslam et al., 2013) implemented an expert system for the classification of diabetes data using Genetic Programming (GP). The methods implemented here consists of three stages: the first stage includes feature selection using t-test, kolmogorov-smirnov test and kulback-Leibler divergence test whereas the next stage uses GP for non-linear combination of selected attributes from the first stage. At the final stage the generated features using GP is compared with K-Nearest Neighbor (KNN) and SVM. The classification is done on Pima Indian Diabetes Dataset (PIDD) consists of 768 instance values in the dataset and 8 attributes and one output variable (class variable) which have either a value '1' or '0' available in the dataset. The selected features are then used for the classification of diabetes patients with high classification accuracy.

(Karegowda et al., 2011) used a hybrid method i.e. GA with BPN where GA is used to initialize and optimize connection weights of BPN. The hybrid method shows the substantial improvement.

(Ramesh andPadmini,2017) have used several classification algorithms (MLP NN, Random Forest, Bayers Net, Decision Stump, Naive Bayes) for determining the correlation among the various risk factors and design a model to predict the risk level of diabetic retinopathy. They have compared the risk factors with & without diabetic retinopathy patients. Among all the classification algorithms, MLP algorithm found is more suitable to predict the risk factor.

(Goncalves et al., 2006) also implemented a new neuro-fuzzy model for the classification of diabetes patients. Here, inverted hierarchical neuro-fuzzy based system is implemented which is based on binary space partitioning model and it provided embodies for the continue recursive of the input space and automatically generates own structure for the classification of inputs. This method finally generates a series of rules extraction on the basis of which classification can be done.

(Selvakuberan et al.,2011)used Ranker search method, K star, REP tree, Naive bayes, Logisitic, Dagging, Multiclass model in which Ranker search approach is used for attribute selection and K star, REP tree, Naive bayes, Logisitic, Dagging, Multiclass are used for classification. The methods provide a reduced feature set with higher classification accuracy.

(Kayaer and Yildirim, 2003) used General Regression Neural Network (GRNN) to classify a medical data in which the optimum spread values were found by trial and error and used for training and classification of test data.

(Kahramanli and Allahverdi, 2008) used Artificial Neural Network (ANN) and Fuzzy Neural Network (FNN) for the classification of heart and diabetes disease. This method when applied on PIDD and Cleveland heart disease dataset, achieved 84.24% classification accuracy for diabetes and 86.8% for heart disease respectively.

(Naser and Ola, 2008) proposed an expert system for diagnosing eye disease using CLIPS (C Language Integrated Production System). CLIPS language was used as a tool for implementing this expert system.

(Lee and Wang, 2011) used Fuzzy Ontology (FO), Fuzzy Diabetes Ontology (FDO), Semantic Decision Support Agent (SDSA) for the diagnosis of diabetes disease.

(Ephzibah, 2011) used GA and Fuzzy Logic (FL) for diagnosis of diabetes in which GA has been used as an attribute selection tool and FL is used for classification.

(Qasem and Shamsuddin,2011) introduced a Time Variant Multi–Objective Particle Swarm Optimization (TVMOPSO) of Radial basis function (RBF) network for diagnosing the medical disease. RBF networks training to determine whether RBF networks can be developed using TVMOPSO, and the performance is validated based on accuracy and complexity.

(Jayalakshmi and Santhakumaran,2010) introduced an Artificial Neural Network (ANN) method for the classification of diabetes.

(Li,2006) used GA and NN for the classification of medical data and Glass identification which is obtained from the UCI repository of machine learning databases in which GA was used as a feature selection and NN for classification.

(Bala et al.2017, 2018) have summarized different soft computing and data mining techniques for prediction of thunderstorm.

(Jia et al., 2014) described RBF, GA-RBF, GA-RBF-L for the classification on waveform database, wine data set where RBF was used as a classification technique and GA was used for optimizing the neural network structure and weights of RBF algorithm.

(Tukur andShamsuddin, 2014) used RBFN and Modified Backpropagation algorithm on continuous and discretized dataset i.e., XOR, Ballon, Iris, Cancer, Ionosphere where RBFN was used for the classification on the mentioned dataset and Modified Backpropagation was used to improve the learning speed of RBF. This work was implemented on C programming and performs T-test statistical analysis for experimental studies to check the significance and satisfactory significance was found.

(Borgohain and Sanyal, 2012) proposed a questionnaire rule based expert system for the diagnosis of neuromuscular disorders i.e. cerebral palsy, parkinson's disease, muscular dystrophy, multiple sclerosis which was implemented by using Java Expert System Shell (JESS). This rule based expert system uses backward chaining and RETE algorithm. Backward chaining is used for inference engine and RETE algorithm is used for searching the knowledge base.

(Patil et al., 2010) implemented an association rule based method for the classification of type -2 diabetic patients. The classification is implemented for PIDD containing eight attributes and one class. This methodology generated rules using Apriori algorithm on the basis of some support and confidence. In the first stage the numeric attributes were converted into categorical form which is based on the input parameters. Lastly generated rules was used to identify the associations in between the data to understand the relationship between the measured fields whether the patient goes on to develop diabetes or not. The authors presented step-by-step approach to help the physicians to explore their data and to understand the discovered rules better way.

(Kala et al.,2010) used RBFN for classification of Pima Indian Diabetes Dataset and achieved the accuracy 82.37% which is greater than several other existed techniques.

(Comak et al.,2007) stated fuzzy weighting preprocessing and LSSVM in which fuzzy weighting preprocessing is used for pre-processed liver disorder dataset and then LS–SVM is used for classification on that and obtained 94.29% classification accuracy which is the highest classification rate in literature. Without preprocessed 60.0% classification accuracy has been achieved with LSSVM.

(Palivela and Thotadara, 2012) used K-means clustering, SMO, Fuzzy "C" mean, Random Forest, Rotation Forest, Bagging, AdaBoost M1, Naive Bayes, J48 algorithm, Cross–validation methods for the prediction of diabetes by clustering and classification approach.

(Sathasivam et al., 2011) used Hopfield networks and Radial Basis Function networks for the comparison in several different aspects.

(Wang et al., 2007) implemented an ontology based fuzzy interface for the classification of diabetes dataset. The ontology contains all the required knowledge of personal diabetes ontology repository from an expert system for classification of diabetes disease.

(Ganji et al., 2010) was used Ant Colony Optimization (ACO) and Fuzzy Logic for diagnosis of diabetes disease. ACO has been used for feature extraction and Fuzzy If Then rules for classification.

(Revett et al., 2005) used a hybrid decision support system, combining the reductionist approach of rough sets in combination with a probabilistic neural network (PNN). Rough sets have been used in various medical diagnostic systems with a large degree of success. One of the hallmark features of rough sets is the ability to remove redundant attributes. After removing redundant attributes, PNN has been applied for the final classification task.

(Zhi-Xing et al., 1997) designed Fuzzy Neural Network (FNN) to translate directly the expert knowledge into neural network structure by using a fuzzy model.

(Choubey, 2017) have used weighted fuzzy rule based system for the diagnosis of diabetes. In this research paper, an expert system have been presented which is finding the type of diabetes (Type 1, Type 2, Pre diabetes, Gestational) with probability of occurrences.

(Senol andyildirim,2009) stated a new hybrid structure in which NN and Fuzzy Logic are combined worked as a classification technique for diabetes.

(Margret et al., 2013) stated Rough set technique for developing of a diabetic diagnosis system in which firstly approximation sets are generated and the diagnosis is done by taking only those objects into account.

(Acording toKarahoca et al., 2009) used ANFIS, and Multinomial Logistic Regression (MLR). ANFIS is used as an estimation method which has fuzzy input and output parameters, whereas MLR is used as a non–linear regression method and has fuzzy input and output parameters.

(Ein Oh et al., 2013) stated the learning models including ridge, elastic net, and Least Absolute Shrinkage and Selection Operator (LASSO) for diabetic retinopathy risk prediction.

(Dhanushkodi et al., 2013) described NN to detect and diagnose lesions or abnormalities associated with diabetic retinopathy which facilitate the Ophthalmologists in accurate diagnosis and early treatment to prevent vision loss in diabetic patients.

(Priya and Aruna,2013)described a diagnosis system for diabetic retinopathy where three models like PNN, Bayesian Classification and SVM are introduced and their results are compared.

(Soundararajan et al., 2012) used fuzzy logic for the decision support system in tuberculosis medicine. This method is well suitable for developing knowledge-based systems in tuberculosis. It will be helpful for physicians to detect class of tuberculosis and to reduce the time for diagnostic process.

(Saloni et al., 2015) used various classifiers i.e ANN, linear, quadratic and SVM for the classification of Parikson disease in which SVM provides the best accuracy of 96%.

(Marisol et al., 2006) proposed a supervised learning approach for the prediction and classification of type 2 diabetes mellitus patients. The methodology implemented here is a combinatorial method of applying GA and KNN for the classification of type 2 diabetes mellitus patients. A GA is used as an initialization technique that integrates medical expert knowledge with traditional data-driven GA initialization techniques. The GA is also used as the learning of attribute input with an optimized fitness function and KNN is used for the classification of diabetes disease patients.

(Balakrishnan et al., 2008) implemented an SVM ranking based algorithm for the classification of diabetes disease.

(Revett, and Salem, 2010) proposed a new and efficient framework for the classification of type-2 diabetes disease patients using rough set of glycosylated Hemoglobin. The dataset is collected for 403 patients and it contains a range of physiological features particularly diagnosing diabetes including glycosylated hemoglobin. A number of rules are extracted from the dataset which can be used for the classification of diabetes patients.

The author (Yu et al., 2010) described SVM based approach to predict common disease for the case of diabetes or pre-diabetes patient. A final goal was to demonstrate the applicability of the SVM approach by using web-based classification tool.

The combination of some stochastic nature based optimization methods (Singh and Jain, 2016, 2018) and neural network is developed with the scope of creating an improved balance between premature convergence and stagnation.

(Aibinu et al., 2010) implemented a new and efficient technique for the classification of diabetes diagnosis. New expert systems have been suggested for the automatic diagnosis and classification of diabetes by using the Complex–Valued Neural Networks (CVNN) and Real–Valued Neural Network (RVNN) based parametric modeling approaches. Application of complex data normalization technique uses the process of phase encoding over unity magnitude to convert the real valued input data to complex valued data (CVD). CVNN described the relationship between the input and output phase encoded data which is extracted from the complex-valued weights and coefficients of the trained network during training and the coefficients of Complex-valued autoregressive (CAR) model. Similarly operations can be performed for real-valued autoregressive technique except for CVD normalization. In this paper, the effect of data normalization techniques, activation functions, learning rate, number of neurons in the hidden layer and the number of epoch using the suggested techniques on Pima Indian Diabetes Dataset have been evaluated.

Fuzzy counter propagation network (FCPN) model (Sakhre et al. 2017) is used to control different nonlinear, uncertain systems with unknown disturbances. Fuzzy competitive learning (FCL) is used to process the weight connection and make adjustments between the instar and the outstar of the network.

(Kala et al., 2011) proposed a new methodology for the diagnosis of Breast Cancer using the concept of NN. In the paper, a mixture of various expert models is grouped to solve various problems. The decision from each of the individual expert system is mixed to give a final output. The proposed architecture implemented here is used for the solving of Breast Cancer Diagnosis by individually evolving neural network into GA. The experimental results performed on the methodology are highly scalable and provides efficient results on attributes and data items.

(Ahmad et al., 2014) analyzed and generate reports for the evaluation of the bio-artificial liver reactor. Here Fuzzy Analytic Hierarchy Process (FAHP) is implemented for the uncertainty of detecting bio-artificial liver (BAL). The methodology implemented here is more scalable as compared to other existing techniques. The method also provides an efficient final score of detecting bio - artificial liver.

(Miller and Leroy, 2008) also proposed a new and efficient technique for the dynamic generation of Health Topics. The paper implemented a dynamic health topics based web pages that maintains information of four consumer-preferred categories. The methodology implemented here provides efficient precision of 82%, recall of 75% and f-score of 78%.

(Choubey et al., 2012) proposed a method of integrating network security with criterion based access control to handle network and fine grained web database access control simultaneously.

(Choubey et al., 2013) have stated the same above work and implemented in college databases and then evaluated the performance. Whenever any unauthorized user altered our data a system called web-secure report to the authorized user via E-mail or Short Message Service (SMS). Basically, they are protecting the databases in the web server through cells which we call the fine grains. Here, the implemented results show that how this model is suitable for web database security.

(Tomar andSaxena,2011) presented a rule base diagnostic decision support system for medical disease diagnosis. The rule-based expert system will assist to the physician for determining the best course of treatment.

(Zeki et al., 2012) designed a rule based expert system for diagnosis of all kinds of diabetes. This rule based expert system has been also tested and validated.

(Choubey and Paul, 2015) used GA_J48graft DT for the classification of Pima Indian Diabetes Dataset. The method J48graft Decision Tree (J48graft DT) for the classification of data, and GA used as a feature selection and then have performed once again classification on the selected feature.

(Choubey and Paul, 2016) introduced GA_MLP NN for the classification of Pima Indian Diabetes Dataset. This work consists in two stages firstly GA has been used as a feature selection then MLP NN has been used for classification on the selected features by GA and on all the features. The authors have compared the result with MLP NN and GA_MLP NN to assure that the benefit of feature selection.

They have analyzed and compared the several existed work on diabetes with their advantages, issues, technique, tool used, existed work, future work. The used technique, tool has also been discussed on the basis of following parameter i.e., advantages, issues, application.

(Choubey and Paul, 2017) used GA as an attribute selection and RBF NN for the classification on Pima Indian Diabetes Dataset. GA is filtering the significant features, reducing the computation cost and time, improving the accuracy, ROC of the classification.

(Mishra et al., 2014) have used fuzzy logic for designing rule based to determine the type of diabetes occur in patients such as Type 1, Type 2, Pre diabetes, Gestational. The rule based system will help to the physicians in determining the best course of treatment and reduce time consumptions.

The summary of various existing classification algorithms on diabetes are given in Table 3.

PROPOSED METHODOLOGY

The Proposed approach consists of the following phases:

1. The Pima Indian Diabetes Dataset obtained from the UCI repository of machine learning databases.
2. Perform the classification technique by using Fuzzy Decision Tree on Pima Indian Diabetes Dataset. Apply PSO_SVM as a Feature Selection Technique followed by the classification technique by using Fuzzy Decision Tree on Pima Indian Diabetes Dataset.

The proposed system of block diagram is shown below. In the proposed approach, PSO_SVM is implemented as a Feature selection technique and Fuzzy Decision Tree is used as the Classification technique on Pima Indian Diabetes Dataset.

Table 3. Summary of Existing Classification Algorithms on Diabetes

S. No.	Paper	Dataset Used	Tool Used	Technique Used	Advantages	Issues	Accuracy
1.	An Intelligent Diagnosis System For Diabetes on Linear Discriminant Analysis and Adaptive Network Based Fuzzy Inference System: LDA–ANFIS.	Pima Indian Diabetes Dataset.	MATLAB.	LDA–ANFIS is used for diagnosis of diabetes. LDA is used to separate feature variables between healthy and patient (diabetes) data, ANFIS is used forclassification on the result produced by LDA.	The techniques used provide good accuracy then the previous existing results. So, the physicians can perform very accurate decisions by using such an efficient tool.	May be achieved more accuracy then existing by using different technique, may be this technique also not as suitable as in Pima Indian Diabetes Dataset.	84.61%.
2.	A hybrid intelligent system for medical data classification.	Breast Cancer Wisconsin, Pima Indian Diabetes, and Liver Disorders.	WEKA.	Fuzzy Min-Max neural network, Classification and Regression Tree (CART), Random Forest (RF) for the classification of medical data using hybrid intelligence system.	The techniques provide an accurate prediction with explanatory rules in the form of a decision tree as well as it provide an online learning of expert system.	The techniques implemented may require robustness of FMM-CART-RF for the classification of real world implementations.	78.39% (Pima Indian Diabetes).
3.	Comparing performances of backpropagati on and genetic algorithmsin the data classification.	Breast Cancer, Bupa liver, Boston housing, Pima diabetes, Iris, Vehicle, Dermatology, Glass, E,coli, Yeast.	....	Backpropogation neural network, binary-coded genetic algorithms, real-coded genetic algorithm for theclassifications of medical datasets.	The comparison between these techniques involves classification of several dataset to prove that these used techniques may provide better accuracy.	BP algorithm has negative features such as being captured in the local solutions and having low classification performance in some cases.	Variable for several datasets.
4.	Feature selection using fuzzy entropy measures with similarity classifier.	Dermatology, Pima-Indian diabetes, Breast cancer and Parkinsons dataset.	MATLAB.	Fuzzy entropy measure, similarity classifier for the better classification of diabetic disease.	The techniques used provide computation time much lower, enhance classification accuracy by the process to reduce noise, reduced computational cost, more transparent and comprehensible by removing insignificant features from the dataset.	The same techniques used provide less accuracy with breast cancer dataset while increases in remaining all datasets.	75.97% (Pim-Indian diabetes data set).
5.	A comparative study on diabetes disease diagnosis using neuralnetworks.	Pima Indian Diabetes Dataset.	MATLAB.	Levenberg-Marquardt (LM) algorithm and Probabilistic neural network (PNN) were used to train a multilayer neural network, Ten fold cross validation technique were used for estimation of result.	Author found that LM, PNN, 10-Fold cross validation provide better correct training pattern than conventional validation method.	For 10-Fold Cross validation method, the classification accuracies was good but not better than the classification accuracy by Polat and Gunes (2007).	79.62%.
6.	Feature generation using genetic programming with comparative partner selection for diabetes Classification.	Pima Indian Diabetes Dataset	....	Genetic Programming-K-Nearest Neighbor (GPKNN), Genetic Programming-Support Vector Machines (GPSVM) have been used, inwhich KNN andSVM tested thenew features generated by GP for performance evaluation.	GP improves the performance and it also reduces the eight input dimensions to a singledimension.	Ignoring the missing values without giving anydetails which Values were ignored.	80.5% (GPKNN). 87.0% (GPSVM).
7.	An efficient feature selection method for classification in Health care Systems using Machine Learning Techniques.	Pima Indian Diabetes Dataset.	WEKA.	Ranker search method, K star, REP tree, Naive bayes,Logisitic, Dagging, Multiclass in which Ranker search approach is used for feature selection and K star, REP tree, Naive bayes, Logisitic, Dagging, Multiclass are used for classification.	The techniques implemented here provide a reduced feature set with higher classification accuracy.	The technique implemented provides classification accuracy of 81% only which needs to be improved further and also the technique is not suitable for missing attributes.	81%.

continued on following page

Table 3. Continued

S. No.	Paper	Dataset Used	Tool Used	Technique Used	Advantages	Issues	Accuracy
8.	Medical Diagnosis on Pima Indian Diabetes Using General Regression Neural Networks.	Pima Indian Diabetes Dataset.	MATLAB 5.3.	General Regrssion Neural Network (GRNN) has been used to classify a medical data in which the optimum spread values were found by trial anderror and used for training and the classification of test data.	GRNN is a simple and practical method to classify Medical data.	GRNN require more memory space to store the model.	80.21%, 82.29% (Mean total prediction).
9.	A Fuzzy Expert System for Diabetes Decision Support Application.	Pima Indian Diabetes Dataset.	C++ Builder 2007.	Fuzzy Ontology (FO), Fuzzy Diabetes Ontology (FDO), Semantic Decision Support Agent (SDSA) for the diabetes disease using fuzzy expert based system.	The maximum number of rules are generated hence provides bestclassification accuracy.	In FO technique may do further improvement for the Pima Indian Diabetes Dataset to make the prediction much mature.	Variable for several parameters.
10.	Comparison of Clinical and Textural Approach for Diabetic Retinopathy Grading.	Messidor benchmarked database.	MATLAB 2009b.	SVM used for the comparison with both the clinical a textual approach for performance analysis of diabetic retinopathy.	The technique used to compare both approach for performance analysis to a standard dataset with 82.74% and 83.87% for clinical and textural approach respectively.	Through this technique, may investigate combination both approaches using assemble based classifier to be used to increase the accuracy of classification of DR (Diabetic Retinopathy) grading.	82.74% and 83.87% for clinical and textural approach respectively.
11.	Cost Effective Approach on Feature Selection using Genetic Algorithms and Fuzzy Logic for Diabetes Diagnosis.	Pima Indian Diabetes Dataset.	MATLAB.	GA and Fuzzy Logic (FL) are are used for diabetes diagnosis in which GA has been used as a feature selection and FL is used for classification.	The techniques used improve the accuracy and reduced the cost.	May be this technique also not as suitable as in Pima Indian Diabetes Dataset.	87%.
12.	Recognition of Diabetes Disease Using a New Hybrid Learning Algorithm for Nefclass.	Pima Indian Diabetes Dataset.	....	PSO-NEFCLASS which is used for the recognition of diabetes disease using hybrid learning approach.	The techniques provides a substantial improvement in the recognition rate of diabetics and non-diabetics cases, specifically in the recognition of true positives, i.e, a lower number of false negatives.	The classification accuracy depends on the input parameters of the Neuro-fuzzy classifier.	82.32%.
13.	DREAM: Diabetic Retinopathy Analysis Using Machine Learning.	Messidor dataset.	....	Gaussian Mixture Model (GMM) and K-Nearest Neighbor (KNN) and Support vector machine (SVM), AdaBoost for the prediction of diabetic disease using machine learning approach.	The techniques providereduction in the number of features used for lesion classification by feature ranking using Adaboost where 30 top features are selected out of 78.	Analyzing the impact of cost sensitive SVM and AdaBoost for lesion classification.	100% (sensitivity, 53.16% (specificity), 0.904 (AUC).
14.	An Integrated Approach towards the prediction of Likelihood of Diabetes.	Diabetes Dataset taken from SGPGI, Lucknow (A super specialty hospital in Lucknow, Uttar Pradesh, India).	WEKA.	Newly clustering algorithm, Likelihood for the prediction of diabetic's dataset using an integrated approach.	The techniques used to predicts an unknown class label for the dataset under consideration would be of low risk, medium risk or high risk with efficient accuracy, sensitivity, specificity, kappa value for classification	Not implemented for the real application framework.	83.2%.
15.	Region based Support Vector Machine Algorithm for MedicalDiagnosis on PIMA Indian Diabetes Dataset.	Pima Indian Diabetes Dataset.	MATLAB.	Modified support vector machine for the diagnosis of Pima Indian Diabetic Dataset.	Achieves satisfactory performance while avoiding excess tuning, can be applied without further consideration or modifications to any "hard" classification problem that seems difficult to solve with high successful classification rates.	The algorithm doesn't work with the dataset of small size, another issue that region based SVM must deal with is the execution time of the GA when the dataset is large, finally algorithm's performance was not tested on multiclass problems.	82.2%.

continued on following page

Table 3. Continued

S. No.	Paper	Dataset Used	Tool Used	Technique Used	Advantages	Issues	Accuracy
16.	Bijectives Soft set based Classification of Medical Data .	Breast Cancer, Pima Indians Diabetes, Liver Disorder Datasets.	MATLAB.	Bijective soft set for the classification of Medical Data.	Provides high precision, recall, f – measure, for the Breast Cancer, Pima Indians Diabetes datasets, and, recall, f – measure, for liver disorder datasets.	The technique used does not provide high precision for liver disorder datasets.	Variable for several datasets.
17.	Efficient Chronic Disease Prediction and Recommendation System.	Diabetes dataset collected from hospitals in oman.	....	Decision tree algorithms, unified Collaborative Filtering (CF) for the Prediction of chronic disease and expert system.	Provides more efficient correctly classified instances.	As per the author other technique may be used to improve the accuracy for the Chronic Disease Diagnosis (CDD) of prediction and recommendation.	90%.
18.	A novel approach to predict diabetes by Cascading Clustering and Classification.	Pima Indian Diabetes Dataset.	WEKA.	K-means clustering, SMO, Fuzzy "C" mean, Random Forest, Rotation Forest, Bagging, AdaBoost M1, Naive Bayes, J48 algorithm, Cross–validation used for the prediction of diabetes by clustering and classification.	The techniques used provide to improve the accuracy in the prediction of positive & negative test, also achieved the maximum cost/benefit of 34.895% and minimum cost/benefit of 73.82%.	The processing time is more since it combined i.e. k means clustering with several differentclassifiers for the classification and also applied on a particular Pima Indian Diabetes Dataset only.	76.54%.
19.	Using fuzzy Ant Colony Optimization forDiagnosis of Diabetes Disease.	Pima Indian Diabetes Dataset.	WEKA.	Ant Colony Optimization (ACO) has been used to feature extraction and Fuzzy If Then rules for Classification.	Good Comprehensibility and quality of each rule improve with every iteration.	Very strong rules of ACO have been diluted to improve the cooperation between rules.	79.48 (Mean classificationrate).

Figure 4. Block Diagram of Proposed System

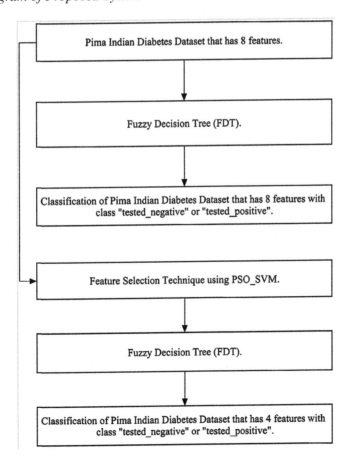

217

Used Diabetes Disease Dataset

The Pima Indian Diabetes Database (PIDD) was obtained from the UCI Repository of Machine Learning Databases (https://archive.ics.uci.edu/ml/datasets/Pima+Indians+Diabetes). The same data dataset has been used in the references(Temurtas et al., 2009; Barakat et al., 2010; Aslam et al., 2013; Polat et al., 2008; Polat and Gunes, 2007; Goncalves, 2006; Choubey and Paul, 2015, 2016, 2017; Seera and Lim, 2014; Orkcu and Bal, 2011; Selvakuberan et al., 2011; Kahramanli and Allahverdi, 2008; Luukka, 2011; Choubey et al., 2014, 2017;Kalaiselvi and Nasira, 2014;Barakat and Bradley, 2007;Aslam and Nandi, 2010; Ganji and Abadeh, 2010, 2011;Patil et al., 2010;Palivela, and Thotadara, 2012;Karegowda et al., 2011; Lee and Wang, 2011;Ephzibah, 2011;Qasem and Shamsuddin, 2011;Jayalakshmi and Santhakumaran, 2010;Kala et al., 2010; Wang et al., 2007; Kumar et al., 2013;Karatsiolis and Schizas, 2012;Daho et al., 2013;Kayaer and Yildirim, 2003;Dogantekin et al., 2010; Choubey et al., 2017).The National Institute of Diabetes, Digestive, and Kidney Diseases originally owned this data and received it on 9 May 1990. All Patients in this database are Pima Indian Women at least 21 years old and living near Phoenix, Arizona, USA. The features of this database are given in below:

- Number of instances: 768
- Number of attributes: 8
- Attributes:
  - Number of times pregnant
  - Plasma glucose concentration a 2 hours in an oral glucose tolerance test
  - Diastolic blood pressure (mm Hg)
  - Triceps skin fold thickness (mm)
  - 2 – hour serum insulin (mu U/ml)
  - Body mass index (weight in kg/ (height in m)2)
  - Diabetes pedigree function
  - Age (years)
  - Class or Output (tested_negative or tested_positive)

There are eight all numeric-valued attributes and last one is class. There are no missing values of any attribute.

Here class distribution is tested_negative and tested_positive:

```
Class Distribution      Number of Instances
tested_negative         500 (65.1%)
tested_positive         268 (34.9%)
```

Use Classification Technique

A Decision Tree consists of root nodes and leaves which shows the dataset dependent attributes and their respective values. It is constructed on the basis of attributes dependency value in which the root node is the most dependent attribute of the dataset. Here Fuzzy Logic is used as the superset of Boolean logic that is used for the identification and classification of classes from the dataset. Here the computation of Total Gain can be done on the basis of objective function.

The fuzzy optimization constraints can be given by:

Fuzzy maximize $[f_1(x), f_2(x)...............f_n(x)]$

Subject to $g_i(x) <= 0; i = 1, 2, 3, ...m$

FDT (T, F, O)

T - Training Dataset Attributes

F - Pima Indian Input Dataset attributes selected from PSO_SVM

O - Output classified attributes

1. Initially an empty tree $'t't \to \varphi$
2. For each of the training attributes present in the dataset
3. Calculate the probability of weighted factor of a particular attribute in the data and is given by:

$$I(A_1 A_2) = -\frac{A_1}{(A_1 + A_2)} \log\left(\frac{A_1}{(A_1 + A_2)}\right) - \frac{A_2}{(A_1 + A_2)} \log\left(\frac{A_2}{(A_1 + A_2)}\right) \qquad (9)$$

where I denote Information of the dataset based on classes A_1 & A_2.

4. Calculate Information Gain based on which the most dependent featuree is chosen is given by:

$$Information\,Gain(feature) = I(feature) - E(feature) \qquad (10)$$

where, I is information & E is the entropy of the feature

5. Select the feature with the highest information gain
6. Update the tree $'t'$ the feature as the root node to $'t'$.
7. Remove the feature from the relation set
8. End

USE OF SVM FOR FEATURES SELECTION OPTIMIZED BY PSO FOLLOWED BY CLASSIFICATION TECHNIQUES IN PIMA INDIAN DIABETES DATASET (PIDD)

Feature Selection Using SVM Optimized by PSO

The methodology applied here using the concept of feature selection from the PIDD so that the selection of features is done more accurately using the concept SVM which is a supervised machine learning approach and is based on the statistical learning theory optimized by PSO. The feature selection using SVM provides a decision surface that efficiently separates the two classes in the PIDD. The input training dataset consist of tuples $\{x_i, y_i\}$, where $i = 1 \rightarrow n$ and $'x'$ denotes the input vector (attributes of the training dataset) and $'y'$ contains the class labels $\{+1, -1\}$. SVM contains a hyper plane of the form $wo.p + bs = 0$ where $'p'$ is the dynamic point lying on the considered hyper plane and $'bs'$ denotes the bias value of the distance of hyper plane from origin and $'wo'$ denotes orientation of hyper plane. The feature selection process repeats till the optimum hyper plane is detected.

PSO is stochastic population based optimization technique which is based on the simulation behavior of birds within a group of flocks. PSO contains a number of particles from which the problem can be solved. It contains personal best solution denotes as $'Pbest'$ which provides position of particle so that the maximum value used by the attributes can be predicted used for classification of attributes. It also contains local best particle denoted as $'Lbest'$ indicating position of entire swarm best position. The leader particle is used for the best search space from the set of attributes. The Vector velocity contains the direction of the particle it needs to move to another position from the current position. The weighted factor $'W'$ is the inertia is used to control the particle movement position depending on the previous particle position. PSO contains two learning constant factors C_1 & C_2 which denotes the cognitive learning factor and social learning factor.

Pseudo Code for Feature Selection Process Using PSO Based SVM

```
Start with the Initialization of Population
While! (Ngen || Sc)
For  p = 1 : Np
If fitness  Xp > fitness pbestp
Update  pbestp = Xp
For  K ∈ NX_p
If fitness X_k > gbest
Update  gbest = X_k
Next  K
For each dimension d
```

$$v_{pd}^{new} = w * v_{pd}^{old} + c_1 * rand_1 * (pbest_{pd} - x_{pd}^{old}) + c_2 * rand_2 * (gbest_d - x_{pd}^{old}) \qquad (11)$$

$$v_{pd} \notin (V_{\min}, V_{\max}) \tag{12}$$

$$v_{pd} = \max(\min(V_{\max}, v_{pd}), V_{\min}) \tag{13}$$

$$x_{pd} = x_{pd} + v_{pd} \tag{14}$$

```
Next d
Next  p
Next generation till stop
```

The particles are first encoding into a bit string $S = F1F2....Fn, n = 1,2...m$ and the bit {1} represents for the selected feature from the dataset and the bit string {0} is the non-selected feature from the dataset. The evaluation parameters can be computed using SVM. Let us suppose in the dataset the available feature set is 10 then set {F1F2F3…..F10} is then analyzed using PSO and selection of any number of features say 5 a dimensional evaluation of these 5 features is computed using SVM. Each particle in PSO is renewed using adaptive computation of SVM, hence on the basis of which $pbest$ is chosen. Now for the final feature selection each of the particles is then updated according to operation.

$$v_{pd}^{new} = w * v_{pd}^{old} + c_1 * rand_1 * (pbest_{pd} - x_{pd}^{old}) + c_2 * rand_2 * (gbest_d - x_{pd}^{old}) \tag{15}$$

$$S(v_{pd}^{new}) = \frac{1}{1 + e^{-v_{pd}^{new}}} \tag{16}$$

$$(rand < S(v_{pd}^{new})) \tag{17}$$

$$x_{pd}^{new} = 1 \, elsex_{pd}^{old} = 0 \tag{18}$$

The Table 4 describes the used notations in pseudo code.

The renewed features are then calculated using Eq. (7) and hence on the basis of renewal calculation of 'S' and depending on the previous value of 'S' the features are selected as {1} otherwise {0} means the feature is not selected.

1. Initialization of parameters such as number of particles, their velocity and the cross folds used by SVM.

Table 4. Various Notations used in Pseudo Code

Parameter	Summary
$Ngen$	Number of generations or iterations
S_c	Stopping Criteria
N_p	Number of particles
X_p	Current position of pheromone
P_{bestp}	Pheromone with best fitness
x_{pd}^{old}	Previous fitness value
X_k	Current particle position
G_{best}	Best fitness value
K	Current particle number
v_{pd}^{new}	Updated particle velocity
v_{pd}^{old}	Current particle velocity
$rand1$	Random number 1
$rand2$	Random number 2
a_1	Acceleration factor 1
a_2	Acceleration factor 2
V_{max}	Maximum Velocity

2. From the dataset, choose a random sample values for each of the particle, objects and their respective moving position. After initialization step the particles or attributes of the PIDD is chosen so that the better or dependent features are selected.

3. Best position can be the considered as the particle current position means as the best sample value.

The random attribute selected supposed to be the better attribute of the dataset and so its fitness value as best.

4. For each of the particle for max_iterations.

   Now calculate for all the attributes of the PIDD.

5. Selection of the position of particle in the PIDD as asample values as (r, s).

   The attribute to be selected (Particle) moves along $'X'$ and $'Y'$ axis for the next better attribute from the PIDD depending upon the fitness value.

6. Now Initialize the Input Parameters of SVM such as kinds of kernel used, margin width of SVM and number of iterations have to be done.
7. ker = '@linear Kernel' OR 'Gaussian Kernel'

   Selection of kernel as linear or Gaussian (RBF) on the basis of which SVM iterates and select attributes.

8. $I_1 = r$;

   Here $'r'$ is selected as the particle or attribute of the dataset.

9. $P = s$;

   $'s'$ is assumed to be the class index of SVM.

10. $trnX = X$;

    Select the $'X'$ as the training value of the SVM.

11. $trnY = Y$;

    Select $'Y'$ as the training classes of SVM.

12. $tstX = X'$;
13. $tstY = Y'$;
14. Training is performed on the basis of $(trnX, trnY, P)$

    The selection of features starts with the basic input to SVM as the training values and class index.

15. On the basis of training parameters as $(trnX, trnY, tstX, \text{ker}, alpha, bias, actfunc)$;

    A predefined function is defined which calculates the attributes on the basis of above parameters.

16. Selection of 'Y' as the values of attributes values can be predicted.

The Figure 5 is the proposed approach applied here for the classification of Pima Indian Diabetes Dataset.

Since the proposed methodology includes optimization algorithm such as PSO hence various parameters needs to be initialized such as number of particles and particle velocity and number of iterations. The input training dataset is passed to the supervised learning approach with a number of cross fold validations. The generated or selected features from SVM are then optimized using PSO. Finally a decision tree based classification approach is applied on the selected features using Fuzzy so that the classification of testing dataset is done.

RESULTS AND DISCUSSION OF PROPOSED METHODOLOGY

In experimental studies, the dataset has been partitioned 60-40% (461-307) for training & test for diagnosis of diabetes. As per the Table 4, GA technique provides four features among eight features. It means

Figure 5. Flow of the Overview of PSO_SVM-FDT

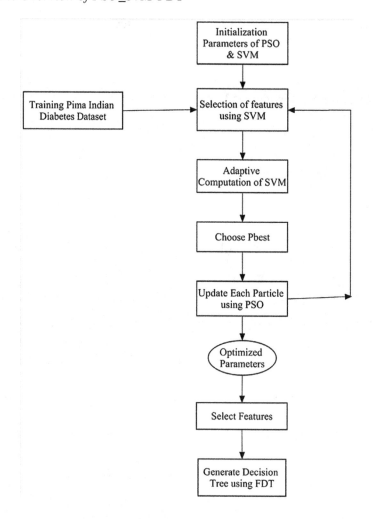

that it reduced the cost to s(x) = 4/8 = 0.5 from 1 and have obtained an improvement on the training and classification by a factor of 2.

It is well known that the diagnostic performance is usually evaluated in terms of Classification Accuracy, Precision, Recall, Fallout and F–Measure, Receiver Operating Curve graph (ROC), kappa statistics, Mean Absolute Error (MAE), Root Mean Square Error (RMSE), Relative Absolute Error (RAE), Root Relative Squared Error (RRSE). These terms are briefly explained below:

- **Classification Accuracy (Acc):** Classification accuracy is the ratio of total number of correctly diagnosed cases to the total number of cases.

$$Classification\ accuracy\left(\%\right) = \left(TP + TN\right) / \left(TP + FP + TN + FN\right) \tag{19}$$

TP (True Positive): Diabetic people correctly detected as diabetic people.
FP (False Positive): Healthy people incorrectly detected as diabetic people.
TN (True Negative): Healthy people correctly detected as healthy people.
FN (False Negative): Diabetic people incorrectly detected as healthy people.

- **Precision:** Precision is also called Positive Predictive Value (PPV). It may be defined as the measures of the rate of correctly classified samples that are predicted as diabetic samples or precision is the ratio of true positive to the sum of true positive and false positive.

$$or\ Precision = TP\ /\ TP + FP \tag{20}$$

- **Recall:** Recall is also called Sensitivity or True Positive Rate or Hit Rate. It may be defined as the total number of positive cases correctly diagnosed to the total of positive cases or recall is the ratio of true positive to the sum of true positive and false negative.

$$or\ Recall = TP\ /\ TP + FN \tag{21}$$

- **Fallout:** Fallout is also known as False Positive Rate (FPR). The term fallout is used to check true negative of the dataset during classification.

$$Fallout = \frac{FP}{FP + TN} = 1 - TNR(Specificity) \tag{22}$$

- **Specificity:** Specificity is also known as True Negative Rate (TNR). Specificity may be defined as the total number of negative cases correctly diagnosed to the total number of negative cases.

$$Specificity = \frac{TN}{(FP + TN)} \tag{23}$$

- **F-Measure:** F-Measure is also called F1 score or F score. The F–Measure computes some average of the information retrieval precision and recall metrics. The F–Measure (F–Score) is calculated based on the precision and recall. It is a trade-off between precision and recall. It is the harmonic–mean of precision and recall. The calculation is as follow:

$$F - Measure = \frac{2 * Precision * Recall}{Precision + Recall} \tag{24}$$

- **Area Under Curve (AUC):** It is defined as the metric used to measure the performance of classifier with relevant acceptance. It is calculated from area under curve based on true positives and false positives.

$$AUC = \frac{1}{2}\left(\frac{TP}{TP + FN} + \frac{TN}{TN + FP}\right) \tag{25}$$

An example of its application is ROC (Receiver operating curve graph) curves. ROC is an effective method of evaluating the performance of diagnostic tests. ROC is defined as a plot of test or relationship between Sensitivity or True Positive Rate (TPR) as the Y coordinate and 1-Specificity or False Positive Rate (FPR) as the X coordinate.

- **Confusion Matrix:** Confusion Matrix is also known as an Error Matrix. A confusion matrix [12] [2] contains information regarding actual and predicted classifications done by a classification system. It is a table that is often used to describe visualization of the performance of an algorithm or model. Each column of the matrix represents the instance in a predicted class while each row represents instance an actual class or vice versa. It provides summary or performance of prediction results on a classification problem.
- **Kappa Statistics (KS):** It is defined as performance to measure the true classification or accuracy of the algorithm.

$$K = \frac{T_O - T_C}{1 - T_C} \tag{26}$$

where, T_O is the total agreement probability and T_C is the agreement probability due to change.

- **Mean Absolute Error (MAE):** MAE means the average of the absolute errors. MAE is a quantity used to measure how close forecasts or predictions are to the eventual outcomes. MAE is a common measure of forecasts errors. MAE can be compared between models whose errors are measured in the same units. It is usually similar in magnitude to RMSE, but slightly smaller.

It is defined as:

$$\text{MAE} = \frac{\left|t_1 - q_1\right| + \ldots + \left|t_n - q_n\right|}{n} \tag{27}$$

- **Root Mean-Squared Error (RMSE):** The square root of the mean /average of the square of all of the error. RMSE is used to assess how well a system learns a given model. RMSE can be compared between models whose errors are measured in same units.

It is defined as:

$$\text{RMSE} = \sqrt{\frac{\left(t_1 - q_1\right)^2 + \ldots + \left(t_n - q_n\right)^2}{n}} \tag{28}$$

- **Relative Absolute Error (RAE):** Like RSE, RAE can be compared between models whose errors are measured in the different units.

It is defined as:

$$\text{RAE} = \frac{\left|t_1 - q_1\right| + \ldots + \left|t_n - q_n\right|}{\left|\bar{q} - q_1\right| + \ldots + \left|\bar{q} - q_n\right|} \tag{29}$$

- **Relative Squared Error (RSE):** Unlike RMSE, RSE can be compared between models whose errors are measured in different units.

It is defined as:

$$\text{RSE} = \frac{\left(t_1 - q_1\right)^2 + \ldots + \left(t_n - q_n\right)^2}{\left(\bar{q} - q_1\right)^2 + \ldots + \left(\bar{q} - q_n\right)^2} \tag{30}$$

where, $q_1, q_2, \ldots q_n$, are the actual target values and $t_1, t_2, \ldots t_n$, are the predicted target values. These terms are briefly explained in (Choubey and Paul, 2015, 2016, 2017).

The result evaluations of training and testing dataset are mentioned below:

The Table 5 shows the results of the training and testing set evaluation by using FDT technique for Pima Indian Diabetes Dataset based on some parameters.

The Table 6 shows the number of features reduced after applying PSO with SVM and without applying PSO with SVM. The methodology implemented here provides efficient selection of features from Pima Indian Diabetes dataset. The dataset contains 8 attributes one output variable (Class variable) which

Table 5. Training and Testing set evaluations of FDT classifier techniques Performance for Pima Indian Diabetes Dataset

Measure	Training Set Evaluations	Testing Set Evaluations
Time Taken to Build Model (In Sec.)	0.31	0.28
Precision	0.91	0.81
Recall	0.91	0.81
F–Measure	0.91	0.80
Accuracy	91.17%	80.85%
ROC	0.90	0.87
Kappa statistics	0.78	0.54
MAE	0.08	0.25
RMSE	0.29	0.37
RAE	21.60%	55.44%
RRSE	66.12%	76.64%

Table 6. PSO_SVM Feature Reduction

Data Set	Number of Attributes	Feature Set (Name of Attributes)
Without PSO_SVM	8	1. Number of times pregnant 2. Plasma glucose concentration a 2 hours in an oral glucose tolerance test 3. Diastolic blood pressure 4. Triceps skin fold thickness 5. 2 – hour serum insulin 6. Body mass index 7. Diabetes pedigree function 8. Age (years)
With PSO_SVM	4	1. Diastolic blood pressure. 2. Triceps skin fold thickness. 3. 2-Hour serum insulin. 4. Diabetes pedigree function.

has either a value '1' or '0' which defines the patient's to be tested positive or negtaive depending on 8 attributes, but most of the attributes in the dataset are independent to take decision hence reduction of the features is done using PSO-SVM.

The Table 7 shows the results of the training and testing set evaluation by using FDT technique for Pima Indian Diabetes Dataset based on the selected features by using PSO_SVM of some parameters.

Figure 6 is the ROC Curve with PSO_SVM in Pima Indian Diabetes Dataset. The analysis is done on Pima Indian dataset, with the increase of False Positive Rate the True Positive Rate also increases up to 1 and gets constant at certain interval when false positive rate becomes 1. The figures are implemented using Weka library. The Pima Indian Diabetes Dataset when classified using Fuzzy Decision tree provides high rate of classification and takes less error rate as shown in Figure 6.

Table 7. Training and Testing set evaluations of FDT classifier techniques Performance for Pima Indian Diabetes Dataset

Measure	Training Set Evaluations	Testing Set Evaluations
Time Taken to Build Model (In Sec.)	0.27	0.21
Precision	0.97	0.93
Recall	0.97	0.92
F–Measure	0.97	0.92
Accuracy	96.76%	92.43%
ROC	0.96	0.9112
Kappa statistics	0.92	0.81
MAE	0.03	0.07
RMSE	0.18	0.27
RAE	7.84%	18.52%
RRSE	39.60%	61.22%

Figure 6. ROC Curve with PSO_SVM

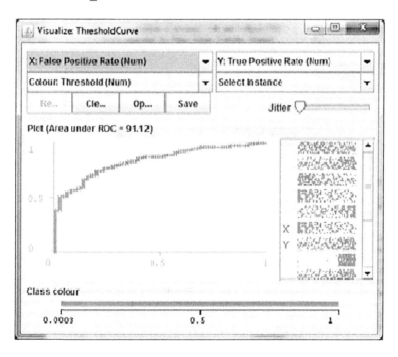

The Figure 7 is the decision tree generated when classification is done using fuzzy decision tree in the selected features produced by PSO_SVM on Pima Indian diabetes dataset. The figure shows the dependent attributes of the dataset so that the classification is done easily and quickly.

The rules generated using FDT on the selected features by PSO_SVM technique of Pima Indian Diabetes Dataset for Figure 7 are as shown in Table 8.

Figure 7. Generation of decision tree using FDT

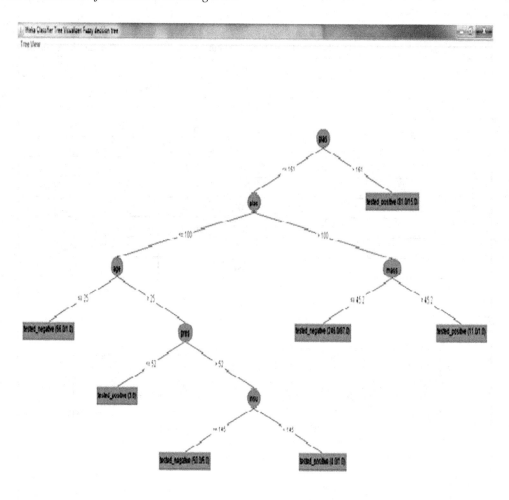

Table 8.

Rule 1:
If (plas<=151)
If (plas<=100)
If (age <=25)
"tested_negative"
	Rule 2:
	If (plas>151)
	"tested_positive"
		Rule 3:
		If (plas<=151)
		If (plas>100)
		If (mass >45.2)
		"tested_positiive"
			Rule 4:
			If (plas<=151)
			If(plas>100)
			If (mass <=45.2)
			"tested_negative"

Rule 5:
If (plas<=151)
If (plas<=100)
If (age >25)
If (pres<=52)
"tested_positive"
	Rule 6:
	If (plas<=151)
	If (plas<=100)
	If (age >25)
	If (pres>52)
	If (insu<=145)
	"tested_negative"
		Rule 7:
		If (plas<=151)
		If (plas<=100)
		If (age >25)
		If (pres>52)
		If (insu>145)
		"tested_positive"	

The Table 7 shows the result analysis and comparison of various techniques implemented on PIDD. The proposed approach outperforms better accuracy to existing techniques as it may be observed in Table 9.

The Table 10 shows analysis of ROC for the Pima Indian dataset including proposed methodology and existing methodologies implemented. The proposed methodology outperforms better accuracy to other techniques implemented as it may be observed in below table.

Table 9. Results and Comparison with other methods for the Pima Indians Diabetes Data set

Source	Method	Accuracy
PasiLuukka (2011)	Sim	75.29%
	Sim + F1	75.84%
	Sim + F2	75.97%
H. HasanOrkcu et al. (2011)	Binary–coded GA	74.80%
	BP	73.80%
	Real–coded GA	77.60%
ManjeevanSeera et al. (2014)	FMM	69.28%
	FMM–CART	71.35%
	FMM-CART–RF	78.39%
Dilip Kumar Choubey and Sanchita Paul (2015)	J48graft DT	76.5217%
	GA_J48grft DT	74.7826%
Dilip Kumar Choubey and Sanchita Paul (2016)	MLP NN	78.2609%
	GA_MLP NN	79.1304%
Dilip Kumar Choubey and Sanchita Paul (2017)	RBF NN	76.087%
	GA_RBF NN	77.3913%
	Polynomial Kernel SVM	64.7826%
	GA _Polynomial Kernel SVM	74.3478%
	RBF Kernel SVM	65.6522%
	GA_RBF Kernel SVM	63.913%
	Sigmoid Function Kernel SVM	65.6522%
	GA_ Sigmoid Function Kernel SVM	65.6522%
	Liner Kernel SVM	77.3913%
	GA_Linear Kernel SVM	79.5652%
	NBs	76.9565%
	GA_NBs	78.6957%
Dilip Kumar Choubey et al. (2017)	NBs	76.9565%
	GA_NBs	78.6957%
Our Study	FDT	80.85%
	PSO_SVM-FDT	92.43%

Table 10. Comparison of ROC with other Existing Techniques for the PIDD

Source	Method	ROC
PasiLuukka (2011)	Sim	0.762
	Sim + F1	0.703
	Sim + F2	0.667
ManjeevanSeera et al. (2014)	FMM	0.661
	FMM – CART	0.683
	FMM-CART – RF	0.732
Dilip Kumar Choubey and Sanchita Paul (2015)	J48graft DT	0.765
	GA_J48grft DT	0.786
Dilip Kumar Choubey and Sanchita Paul (2016)	MLP NN	0.853
	GA_MLP NN	0.842
Dilip Kumar Choubey and Sanchita Paul (2017)	RBF NN	0.813
	GA_RBF NN	0.848
	Polynomial Kernel SVM	0.554
	GA _Polynomial Kernel SVM	0.672
	RBF Kernel SVM	0.5
	GA_RBF Kernel SVM	0.487
	Sigmoid Function Kernel SVM	0.5
	GA_ Sigmoid Function Kernel SVM	0.5
	Liner Kernel SVM	0.716
	GA_Linear Kernel SVM	0.748
Dilip Kumar Choubey et al. (2017)	NBs	0.846
	GA_NBs	0.844
Our Study	FDT	0.87
	PSO _SVM -FDT	0.912

CONCLUSION AND FUTURE WORK

Diabetes means blood sugar is above the desired level on a sustained basis. This is one of the most world's widespread diseases, now a day's very common. According to "Diabetes Atlas 2013" released by the International Diabetes Federation, there are 382 million people in the world with diabetes and this is projected to increase to 592 million by the year 2035. After China (98.4 million), India has the largest numbers of individuals with diabetes in the world (65.1 million). Diabetes means blood sugar is above the desired level on a sustained basis. Diabetes occurs when insulin is not being properly produced or responded by the body, which is indispensable to maintain the prescribed level of sugar. Diabetes can be moderated with the help of insulin injections, taking oral medications (pills), controlled diet (changing eating habits), and doing regular physical exercise but no complete cure is yet available.

Diabetes can cause serious health complications such as blindness, blood pressure, heart disease, kidney disease and nerve damage, etc. which is hazardous to health. The proposed approach implemented here for the classification on Pima Indian Diabetes Dataset provides efficient results. The approach implemented here for the optimization of SVM using PSO improves the classification ratio of SVM and then rules are generated using Fuzzy based decision tree so that quick and accurate prediction is done. The proposed methodology improves the accuracy and ROC of classification diabetes as compared to other existing methodologies. In this work with the feature selection technique the improvement has been observed in every parameter.

PSO_SVM is not only reducing the cost and computation time, but the proposed approach also improved the accuracy and ROC of classification. Feature selection technique once again facilitates to preserve the storage capacity or memory, reduce computation time (shorter training time and test time), decrease computation cost, lesser processor requirements meanwhile sustain accuracy and ROC.

The experimental results obtained classification accuracy and ROC show that Feature selection and classification can be successfully used for the classification of diabetes.

Although the proposed methodology implemented here for the classification of Diabetes Patient's using Fuzzy Decision Tree is efficient but there are certain future direction for the betterment of the methodology such as accuracy and ROC may be increased further and can be applied for any dataset.

The limitations of this work may be that there is no guarantee that the classification techniques which is providing good accuracy as presented here for Pima Indian Diabetes Dataset or Localized Diabetes Dataset will also provide the same coherency for any other such dataset. The same thing is also applicable with feature selection techniques, which may be suitable for Pima Indian Diabetes Dataset or Localized Diabetes Dataset but not be that beneficial in case of any other dataset.

For the future research work, it is proposed to develop such a classification technique, which provides the same result or even better as the result received in the manuscript, which could significantly decrease healthcare costs via early prediction and diagnosis of diabetes disease. The proposed technique can be used for other kinds of medical diseases but not sure that in all the medical diseases either same or greater than the existing results can be achieved. Results that are more interesting may also happen from the exploration of the datasets also.

REFERENCES

Abraham, R., Simha, J. B., & Iyengar, S. (2007). Medical data mining with a new algorithm for feature selection and Naive Bayesian classifier. *10th International Conference on Information Technology.*

Ahmad, S. (2014). A bio-artificial liver reactor evaluation method. *International Journal of Biomedical Engineering and Technology, 14*(1), 1–12. doi:10.1504/IJBET.2014.059055

Aibinu, A. M., Salami, M. J. E., & Shafie, A. A. (2010). Application of Modeling Techniques to Diabetes Diagnosis. *IEEE EMBS Conference on Biomedical Engineering & Sciences (IECBES 2010)*, 194-198. 10.1109/IECBES.2010.5742227

American Diabetes Association. (2009). Available: https://archive.ics.uci.edu/ml/datasets/Pima+Indians+Diabetes

Aslam, A. W., Zhu, Z., & Nandi, A. K. (2013). Feature generation using genetic programming with comparative partner selection for diabetes classification. *Expert Systems With Applications, Elsevier, 40*(13), 5402–5412. doi:10.1016/j.eswa.2013.04.003

Aslam, M. W., & Nandi, A. K. (2010). Detection of diabetes using genetic programming. *18th European Signal Processing Conference (EUSIPCO-2010)*, 1184-1188.

Bala, K., Choubey, D. K., & Paul, S. (2017). Soft computing and data mining techniques for thunderstorms and lightning prediction: A survey. *International Conference of Electronics, Communication and Aerospace Technology (ICECA 2017)*, *1*, 42-46.

Bala, K., Choubey, D. K., Paul, S., & Ghosh Nee Lala, M. (2018). Classification techniques for thunderstorms and lightning prediction-A survey. In Soft Computing-Based Nonlinear Control Systems Design. IGI Global.

Balakrishnan, S., Narayanaswamy, R., Savarimuthu, N., & Samikannu, R. (2008). SVM Ranking with Backward Search for Feature Selection in Type II Diabetes Databases. *International Conference on Systems, Man and Cybernetics*, 2628-2633. 10.1109/ICSMC.2008.4811692

Barakat, N. (2007). *Rule extraction from support vector machines: Medical diagnosis prediction and explanation* (Ph.D. thesis). School Inf. Technol. Electr. Eng. (ITEE), Univ. Queensland, Brisbane, Australia.

Barakat, N. H., & Bradley, A. P. (2007). Rule extraction from support vector machines: A sequential covering approach. *IEEE Transactions on Knowledge and Data Engineering*, *19*(6), 729–741. doi:10.1109/TKDE.2007.190610

Barakat, N. H., Bradley, A. P., & Barakat, M. N. H. (2010). Intelligible support vector machines for diagnosis of diabetes mellitus. *IEEE Transactions on Information Technology in Biomedicine*, *14*(4), 1114–1120. doi:10.1109/TITB.2009.2039485 PMID:20071261

Borgohain, R., & Sanyal, S. (2012). Rule Based Expert System for Diagnosis of Neuromuscular Disorders. *International Journal Advanced Networking and Applications*, *4*(1), 1509–1513.

Brank, J., Grobelnik, M., & Mladenic, D. (2002). *Feature selection using linear support vector Machin*. Technical Report Microsoft Research Corporation.

Chen, Z., Li, J., & Wei, L. (2007). A multiple kernel support vector machine scheme for feature selection and rule extraction from gene expression data of cancer tissue. *Artificial Intelligence in Medicine*, *41*(2), 161–175. doi:10.1016/j.artmed.2007.07.008 PMID:17851055

Choubey, D. K., Bhattacharjee, J., & Soni, R. (2013). Loss Minimization of Web Databases by Fine Grain Approach. *International Journal of Engineering Research and Applications*, *3*(1), 1437–1444.

Choubey, D.K., & Paul, S. (2015). GA_J48graft DT: A hybrid intelligent system for diabetes disease diagnosis. *International Journal of Bio-Science and Bio-Technology (IJBSBT)*, *7*(5), 135–150.

Choubey, D. K., & Paul, S. (2016). GA_MLP NN: A hybrid intelligent system for diabetes disease diagnosis. *International Journal of Intelligent Systems and Applications (IJISA)*, *8*(1), 49–59.

Choubey, D. K., & Paul, S. (2016). Classification techniques for diagnosis of diabetes disease: A Review. *International Journal of Biomedical Engineering and Technology (IJBET)*, *21*(1), 15–39.

Choubey, D. K., & Paul, S. (2017). GA_SVM-A classification system for diagnosis of diabetes. In Handbook of Research on Nature Inspired Soft Computing and Algorithms. IGI Global.

Choubey, D. K., & Paul, S. (2017). GA_RBF NN: A classification system for diabetes. *International Journal of Biomedical Engineering and Technology (IJBET), 23*(1), 71–93.

Choubey, D. K., Paul, S., & Bhattacharjee, J. (2014). Soft computing approaches for diabetes disease diagnosis: A Survey. *International Journal of Applied Engineering Research, RIP, 9*, 11715–11726.

Choubey, D. K., Paul, S., & Dhandhania, V. K. (2017). GA_NN: An intelligent classification system for diabetes. *Proceedings AISC Series, 7th International Conference on Soft Computing for Problem Solving-SocProS 2017.*

Choubey, D. K., Paul, S., & Dhandhenia, V. K. (2017). Rule based diagnosis system for diabetes, Biomedical Research. *Allied Academies, 28*(12), 5196–5209.

Choubey, D. K., Paul, S., Kumar, S., & Kumar, S. (2017). *Classification of Pima Indian Diabetes Dataset using Naive Bayes with Genetic Algorithm as an Attribute Selection*. CRC Press.

Choubey, D. K., Soni, R., & Bhattacharjee, J. (2012). A Novel approach for Security of Web Databases. *International Journal of Computer Science and Technology, 3*(4), 110–113.

Comak, E., Polat, K., Gunes, S., & Arslan, A. (2007). A new medical decision making system: Least square support vector machine (LSSVM) with fuzzy weighting pre-processing. *Expert Systems with Applications, Elsevier, 32*(2), 409–414. doi:10.1016/j.eswa.2005.12.001

Daho, M. E. H., Settouti, N., Lazouni, M. E. A., & Chikh, M. A. (2013). Recognition of diabetes disease using a New hybrid learning algorithm for nefclass. *8th International Workshop on Systems, Signal Processing and their Applications (WoSSPA)*, 239-243.

Dash, M., & Liu, H. (1997). Feature selection for classification. *Intelligent Data Analysis Elsevier, 1*(1-4), 131–156. doi:10.1016/S1088-467X(97)00008-5

Anouncia, Madonna, Clara, Jeevitha, & Nandhini. (2013). Design of a Diabetic Diagnosis System Using Rough Sets. *Cybernetics and Information Technologies, 13*(3), 124–139.

Dhanushkodi, S. S. R., & Manivannan, V. (2013). Diagnosis System for Diabetic Retinopathy to Prevent Vision Loss. *Applied Medical Informatics Original Research, 33*(3), 1–11.

Dogantekin, E., Dogantekin, A., Avci, D., & Avci, L. (2010). An intelligent diagnosis system for diabetes on linear discriminant analysis and adaptive network based fuzzy inference system. *LDA–ANFIS, Digital Signal Processing, Elsevier, 20*(4), 1248–1255. doi:10.1016/j.dsp.2009.10.021

Eberhart, R., & Kennedy, J. (1995). A new optimizer using particle swarm theory. *Proc. 6th Int. Symp. Micro Machine and Human Science (MHS)*, 39–43. 10.1109/MHS.1995.494215

Engelbrecht, A. P. (2006). Particle swarm optimization: Where does it belong? *Proc. IEEE Swarm Intell. Symp*, 48–54.

Ephzibah, E. P. (2011). Cost effective approach on feature selection using genetic algorithms and fuzzy logic for diabetes diagnosis. *International Journal on Soft Computing, 2*(1), 1–10. doi:10.5121/ijsc.2011.2101

Ganji, M. F., & Abadeh, M. S. (2010). Using fuzzy ant colony optimization for diagnosis of diabetes disease. *Proceedings of ICEE 2010*, 501-505.

Ganji, M. F., & Abadeh, M. S. (2011). A fuzzy classification system based on ant colony optimization for diabetes disease diagnosis. *Expert Systems with Applications, Elsevier, 38*(12), 14650–14659. doi:10.1016/j.eswa.2011.05.018

Goncalves, L. B., Vellasco, M. M. B. R., & Pacheco, M. A. C. (2006). Inverted hierarchical neuro-fuzzy BSP System: A novel neuro-fuzzy model for pattern classification and rule extraction in databases. *IEEE Transactions on Systems, Man and Cybernetics. Part C, Applications and Reviews, 36*(2), 236–248. doi:10.1109/TSMCC.2004.843220

Goncalves, L., Bernardes, M. M., & Vellasco, R. (2006). Inverted Hierarchical Neuro-Fuzzy BSP System: A Novel Neuro-Fuzzy Model for Pattern Classification and Rule Extraction in Databases. *IEEE Transactions on Systems, Man, and Cybernetics—Part C: Applications and Reviews, 36*(2), 236-248.

Imran, M., Hashim, R., & Khalid, R. N. E. A. (2012). An overview of particle swarm optimization variants. In *Malaysian Technical Universities Conference on Engineering & Technology*. Elsevier.

International Diabetes Federation. (2007). *Diabetes Atlas* (3rd ed.). Brussels, Belgium: International Diabetes Federation.

Jayalakshmi, T., & Santhakumaran, A. (2010). A novel classification method for diagnosis of diabetes mellitus using artificial neural networks. *International Conference on Data Storage and Data Engineering*, 159-163. 10.1109/DSDE.2010.58

Jia, W., Zhao, D., Shen, T., Su, C., Hu, C., & Zhao, Y. (2014). A new optimized GA-RBF neural network algorithm, Computational Intelligence and Neuroscience. *Hindawi Publishing Corporation, 2014*, 1–6.

Kahramanli, H., & Allahverdi, N. (2008). Design of a hybrid system for the diabetes and heart diseases. *Expert Systems with Applications, Elsevier, 35*(1-2), 82–89. doi:10.1016/j.eswa.2007.06.004

Kala, R., Janghel, R. R., Tiwari, R., & Shukla, A. (2011). A. Diagnosis of Breast Cancer by Modular Evolutionary Neural Networks. *International Journal of Biomedical Engineering and Technology, 7*(2), 194–211. doi:10.1504/IJBET.2011.043179

Kala, R., Vazirani, H., Khanwalkar, N., & Bhattacharya, M. (2010). Evolutionary radial basis function network for classificatory problems. *International Journal of Computer Science and Applications, 7*(4), 34-49.

Kalaiselvi, C., & Nasira, G. M. (2014). A new aproach for diagnosis of diabetes and prediction of cancer using ANFIS. *IEEE: World Congress on Computing and Communication Technologies*, 188-190.

Karahoca, A., Karahoca, D., & Kara, A. (2009). Diagnosis of Diabetes by using Adaptive Neuro Fuzzy Inference Systems. *Fifth International Conference on Soft Computing, Computing with Words and Perceptions in System Analysis, Decision and Control*, 1-4. 10.1109/ICSCCW.2009.5379497

Karatsiolis, S., & Schizas, C. N. (2012). Region based support vector machine algorithm for medical diagnosis on pima Indian diabetes dataset. *Proceedings of the 2012 IEEE 12th International Conference on Bioinformatics & Bioengineering (BIBE)*, 139-144. 10.1109/BIBE.2012.6399663

Karegowda, A. G., Manjunath, A. S., & Jayaram, M. A. (2011). Application of genetic algorithm optimized neural network connection weights for medical diagnosis of pima Indians diabetes. *International Journal on Soft Computing, 2*(2), 15–23. doi:10.5121/ijsc.2011.2202

Kayaer, K., & Yildirim, T. (2003). Medical diagnosis on pima indian diabetes using general regression neural networks. *Proceedings of the International Conference on Artificial Neural Networks and Neural Information Processing*, 181-184.

Kennedy, J., & Eberhart, R. (1995). Particle swarm optimization. *Proc. IEEE Int. Conf. Neural Netw. (ICNN), 4*, 1942–1948.

Kumar, S. U., Inbarani, H. H., & Kumar, S. S. (2013). Bijectives soft based classification of medical data. *Proceedings of the 2013 International Conference on Pattern Recognition, Informatics and Mobile Engineering*, 517-521. 10.1109/ICPRIME.2013.6496725

Lee, C. S., & Wang, M. H. (2011). A fuzzy expert system for diabetes decision support application. *IEEE Transactions on Systems, Man, and Cybernetics. Part B, Cybernetics, 41*(1), 139–153. doi:10.1109/TSMCB.2010.2048899 PMID:20501347

Li, T. S. (2006). Feature selection for classification by using a GA-based neural network approach. *Journal of the Chinese Institute of Industrial Engineers, 23*(1), 55–64. doi:10.1080/10170660609508996

Liu, H., & Sentino, R. (1998). Some issues on scalable feature selection. *Expert Systems with Applications, 15*(3-4), 333–339. doi:10.1016/S0957-4174(98)90049-5

Luukka, P. (2011). Feature Selection using fuzzy entropy measures with similarity classifier. *Expert Systems with Applications, Elsevier, 38*(4), 4600–4607. doi:10.1016/j.eswa.2010.09.133

Mandal, I., & Sairam, N. (2012). SVM-PSO based feature selection for improving medical diagnosis reliability using machine learning ensembles. School of Computing, 267-276.

Marisol, Azuaje, McCullagh, & Harper. (2006). A Supervised Learning Approach to Predicting Coronary Heart Disease Complications in Type 2 Diabetes Mellitus Patients. *Sixth IEEE Symposium on BionInformatics and BioEngineering (BIBE'06)*, 325-331.

Miller, T., & Leroy, G. (2008). Dynamic generation of a Health Topics Overview from consumer health information documents. *International Journal of Biomedical Engineering and Technology, 1*(4), 395–414. doi:10.1504/IJBET.2008.020069

Mishra, P., Singh, D.B.V., Rana, N.S., & Sengar, S. (2014). Clinical decision support system for diabetes disease diagnosis. *International Journal of Engineering Research and Applications (IJERA)*, 105-110.

Morik, K., Brockhausen, P., & Joachims, T. (1998). Combining statistical learning with knowledge-based approach-A case study in intensive care monitoring. *Proc. Eur. Conf. Mach. Learn*, 268–277.

Muni, D. P., Pal, N. R., & Das, J. (2006). Genetic Programming for Simultaneous Feature Selection and Classifier Design. *IEEE Transactions on Systems, Man, and Cybernetics. Part B, Cybernetics, 36*(1), 106–117. doi:10.1109/TSMCB.2005.854499 PMID:16468570

Nandi, D., Tahiliani, P., Kumar, A., & Chandu, D. (2006). The Ubiquitin-Proteasome System. *Journal of Biosciences*, *31*(1), 137–155. doi:10.1007/BF02705243 PMID:16595883

Oh, E., Tae KeunYoo, T.K., & Park, E.C. (2013). Diabetic retinopathy risk prediction for fundus examination using sparse learning: A cross-sectional study. *BMC Medical Informatics and Decision Making*, 1–14. PMID:24033926

Orkcu, H. H., & Bal, H. (2011). Comparing performances of backpropagation and genetic algorithms in the data classification. *Expert Systems with Applications, Elsevier*, *38*(4), 3703–3709. doi:10.1016/j.eswa.2010.09.028

Palivela, H., & Thotadara, P. (2012). A novel approach to predict diabetes by cascading clustering and classification. *Computing Communication & Networking Technologies (ICCCNT)*, 1-7.

Patil, B. M., Joshi, R. C., & Toshniwal, D. (2010). Association rule for classification of type-2 diabetic patients. *Second International Conference on Machine Learning and Computing*, 330-334. 10.1109/ICMLC.2010.67

Polat, K., Guneh, S., & Arslan, A. (2008). A cascade learning system for classification of diabetes disease: Generalized discriminant analysis and least square support vector machine. *Expert Systems with Applications, Elsevier*, *34*(1), 482–487. doi:10.1016/j.eswa.2006.09.012

Polat, K., & Gunes, S. (2007). An expert system approach based on principal component analysis and adaptive neuro–fuzzy inference system to diagnosis of diabetes disease. *Digital Signal Processing, Elsevier*, *17*(4), 702–710. doi:10.1016/j.dsp.2006.09.005

Priya, R., & Aruna, P. (2013). Diagnosis of diabetic retinopathy using machine learning techniques. *Ictact Journal on Soft Computing*, *3*(4), 563–575. doi:10.21917/ijsc.2013.0083

Qasem, S. N., & Shamsuddin, S. M. (2011). Radial basis function network based on time variant multi-objective particle swarm optimization for medical diseases diagnosis. *Applied Soft Computing, Elsevier*, *11*(1), 1427–1438. doi:10.1016/j.asoc.2010.04.014

Ramesh, V., & Padmini, R. (2017). Risk level prediction system of diabetic retinopathy using classification algorithms. *International Journal of Scientific Development and Research*, *2*(6).

Revett, K., Gorunescu, F., Gorunescu, M., El-Darzi, E., & Ene, M. (2005). A Breast Cancer Diagnosis System: A Combined Approach Using Rough Sets and Probabilistic Neural Networks. *The International Conference on Computer as a Tool*, 1124-1127. 10.1109/EURCON.2005.1630149

Revett, K., & Salem, A-B. (2010). Exploring the Role of Glycosylated Hemoglobin as a marker for Type-2 Diabetes Mellitus using Rough Sets. *7th International Conference on Informatics and Systems (INFOS)*, 1-7.

Sakhre, V., Singh, U. P., & Jain, S. (2017). FCPN Approach for Uncertain Nonlinear Dynamical System with Unknown Disturbance. *International Journal of Fuzzy Systems (Springer)*, *19*(2), 452–469. doi:10.100740815-016-0145-5

Saloni, Sharma, R. K., & Gupta, A. K. (2015). Voice Analysis for Telediagnosis of Parkinson Disease Using Artificial Neural Networks and Support Vector Machines. *MECS: International Journal of Intelligent Systems and Applications (IJISA)*, 41-47.

Samy, S., Naser, A., & Ola, A. Z. A. (2008). An expert system for diagnosing eye diseases using clips. *Journal of Theoretical and Applied Information Technology (JATIT)*, 923-930.

Sathasivam, S., Hamadneh, N., & Choon, O. H. (2011). Comparing neural networks: Hopfield network and RBF network. *Applied Mathematical Sciences*, *5*(69), 3439–3452.

Seera, M., & Lim, C. P. (2014). A hybrid intelligent system for medical data classification. *Expert Systems with Applications, Elsevier*, *41*(5), 2239–2249. doi:10.1016/j.eswa.2013.09.022

Selvakuberan, K., Kayathiri, D., Harini, B., & Devi, M. I. (2011). An efficient feature selection method for classification in health care systems using machine learning techniques. IEEE.

Senol, C., & Yildirim, T. (2009). Thyroid and breast cancer disease diagnosis using fuzzy-neural networks. *International Conference on Electrical and Electronics Engineering*, 390-393.

Setino, R. (1997). Neural-Network Feature Selector. *IEEE Transactions on Neural Networks*, *8*(3).

Siedlecki, W., & Skylansky, J. (1989). A Note on Genetic Algorithms for Large Scale Feature Selection, Elsevier. *Pattern Recognition Letters*, *10*(5), 335–347. doi:10.1016/0167-8655(89)90037-8

Singh, U. P., & Jain, S. (2016). Modified Chaotic Bat Algorithm-Based Counter Propagation Neural Network for Uncertain Nonlinear Discrete Time System. *International Journal of Computational Intelligence and Applications*, *15*(3), 1–15.

Singh, U. P., & Jain, S. (2018). Optimization of Neural Network for Nonlinear Discrete Time System Using Modified Quaternion Firefly Algorithm: Case Study of Indian Currency Exchange Rate Prediction. *Soft Computing*, *22*(8), 2667–2681.

Soundararajan, K., Kumar, S., & Anusuya, C. (2012). Diagnostics Decision Support System for Tuberculosis using Fuzzy Logic. *International Journal of Computer Science and Information Technology & Security*, *2*(3), 684–689.

Temurtas, H., Yumusak, N., & Temurtas, F. (2009). A Comparative study on diabetes disease diagnosis using neural networks. Expert Systems With Applications, 36, 8610–8615.

Tomar, P. P. S., & Saxena, P. K. (2011). Architecture for medical diagnosis using rule-based technique. *The First International Conference on Interdisciplinary Research and Development*, 25.1-25.5.

Tukur, U. M., & Shamsuddin, S. M. (2014). Radial basis function network learning with modified backpropagation algorithm. *Telkomnika Indonesian Journal of Electrical Engineering*, *13*(2), 369–378.

Vapnik, V. N. (1995). *The nature of statistical learning theory*. New York, NY: Springer-Verlag New York, Inc. doi:10.1007/978-1-4757-2440-0

Wang, Lee, Li, & Ko. (2007). Ontology-based Fuzzy Inference Agent for Diabetes Classification. *Annual Meetings of the North American Fuzzy Information Processing Society*, 79-83.

Wang, M. H., Lee, C. S., Huan–Chung Li, H. C., & Ko, W. M. (2007). Ontology-based fuzzy inference agent for diabetes classification. *Annual Meetings of the North American Fuzzy Information Processing Society*, 79-83.

WHO/IDF. (2006). *Definition and diagnosis of diabetes mellitus and intermediate hyperglycemia*. World Health Organization. Available: http://www.who.int/diabetes /publications/Definition%20and%20diagnosis%20of%20diabetes_new.pdf

Wyatt, C. J., & Altman, D. G. (1995). Prognostic models: Clinically useful or quickly forgotten? *BMJ (Clinical Research Ed.)*, *311*(7019), 1539–1541. doi:10.1136/bmj.311.7019.1539

Xie, Xie, & Ning. (1997). Application of Fuzzy Neural Network to ECG Diagnosis. *International Conference on Neural Networks*, 62-66.

Ye, R. L., & Johnson, P. E. (1997). The impact of explanation facilities on user acceptance of expert systems advise. *IS Q.*, *19*, 157–172.

Yu, W., Liu, T., Valdez, R., Gwinn, M., & Khoury, M. J. (2010). Application of support vector machine modeling for prediction of common diseases: The case of diabetes and pre-diabetes. *BMC Medical Informatics and Decision Making*, 1–7. PMID:20307319

Zeki, T.S., MalaKooti, M.V., Ataeipoor, Y., & Tabibi, S.T. (2012). An expert system for diabetes diagnosis. *American Academic & Scholarly Research Journal*, *4*(5), 1–13.

Chapter 10
Melanoma Identification Using MLP With Parameter Selected by Metaheuristic Algorithms

Soumen Mukherjee
RCC Institute of Information Technology, India

Arunabha Adhikari
West Bengal State University, India

Madhusudan Roy
Saha Institute of Nuclear Physics, India

ABSTRACT

Nature-inspired metaheuristic algorithms find near optimum solutions in a fast and efficient manner when used in a complex problem like finding optimum number of neurons in hidden layers of a multi-layer perceptron (MLP). In this chapter, a classification work is discussed of malignant melanoma, which is a type of lethal skin cancer. The classification accuracy is more than 91% with visually imperceptible features using MLP. The results found are comparably better than the related work found in the literature. Finally, the performance of two metaheuristic algorithms (i.e., particle swarm optimization [PSO] and simulated annealing [SA]) are compared and analyzed with different parameters to show their searching nature in the two-dimensional search space of hidden layer neurons.

INTRODUCTION

Melanoma, a small subset of skin cancer is very deadly, and can be a cause of death if not detected in early stages (Marks, 2000). For diagnosis of Melanoma disease dermatologists need to relate many of their visual observations such as color, size, border and shape of the lesion. Image processing and computer vision can be used for enhanced visualization of skin surface and subsurface area for clinical analysis of dermatological problems. Using image processing tools some features of the morphology of the skin become detectable which are not visible otherwise by naked eyes. Machine learning methods

DOI: 10.4018/978-1-5225-7107-0.ch010

can be used to analyze the data extracted from these image processing techniques. In the proposed work, Melanoma and nevus or benign images of standard dataset is taken from different sources and considerable number of attributes including visually imperceptible features are extracted from each class of images which is used further for classification using machine learning based methods with optimized parameter generated by nature inspired metaheuristic approaches. In this work ordinary images are used for the work though dermoscopy image can also be used for better visualization of the lesion area. In recent time Deep learning plays a major role for achieving good result for large dataset of skin cancer but requires huge training time.

This chapter is organized in the following manner. In the second section different related research in this field are discussed. In the third section detailed discussion from medical perspective on malignant Melanoma is done. In fourth section different sources of dataset in this field of research are discussed. In the fifth section discussion are done on image preprocessing and different image features used in this work in detail. Sixth section deals with the metaheuristic algorithm including Particle Swarm Optimization (PSO) and Simulated Annealing (SA) which are used in this work. In seventh section, discussion on multi layer perceptron (MLP) is done with the use of hidden layer and neuron size. Eighth and ninth section has discussion on proposed methodology and result and analysis respectively of the present work. In the tenth section future research directions are given. In conclusion part the importance of the present work and some light on the future direction is given.

BACKGROUND

Automatic detection of malignant Melanoma is carried out by several researchers starting from the last decade. In 2015 Giotis (Giotis et al. 2015) used only 675 features to attain 81% of accuracy with MED-NODE dataset of 170 images. After pre-processing all the images are converted to 50 square patches of 15 X 15 pixels size which finally classified by CLAM classifier. In the year 2016 Tan (Tan et al. 2016) reached to 88% accuracy rate using Dermofit image library of 1300 images using SVM classifier. Preprocessing steps like removal of hair, enhancement of contrast are done in each image. Genetic Algorithm used as feature selector to select 1472 features out of 3914 features extracted. Laskaris (Laskaris et al., 2010) and McDonagh (McDonagh et al., 2008) worked on Dermofit dataset and achieved accuracy of 80.64% with only 31 images and accuracy of 83.7% with 234 images respectively. An online Melanoma detection system is developed by Iyatomi (Iyatomi et al., 2005, 2006) using neural network with a classification accuracy of 97.3% with dermoscopy image unlike the present work. Esteva et al. (Esteva et al., 2017) recently used Deep Convolutional Neural Networks (CNN) for skin cancer classification. They have used 129450 number of image dataset in their work. Codella et al. (Codella et al., 2017) achieved 76% accuracy using deep learning with standard dataset.

Nature inspired metaheuristic algorithms are used by numerous researchers for the optimization of parameters of different classifiers. Blondin and Saad (Blondin & Saad, 2010) have used *PSO and Ant Colony Optimization (ACO)* for optimal parameter selection of Support Vector Machine (SVM). In their work they show that classification accuracy increased to 96% from 55% by optimized SVM parameter selection. Pericles (Pericles et al., 2014) has used the *I/F-Race* algorithm for selection of γ parameter of RBF kernel. Hassanat (Hassanat et al., 2014) has used *Ensemble Learning Algorithm* for the selection of k Parameter for kNN Classifier. Lamba (Lamba & Kumar, 2016) modified the kNN algorithm using *firefly algorithm* to select representatives of different classes. In case of Multi Layer Perceptron the most important parameter is the hidden layer neuron. Nature inspired metaheuristic algorithms like *PSO, SA, ACO, Tabu Search (TS), Bee Colony Optimization (BCO)* are used in some research works for optimization of MLP parameters. Rere et al. (Rere et al., 2016) in their work have used *Differential Evolution (DE), Simulated Annealing (SA), and Harmony Search (HS)* for bias and weight optimization of hidden layers in Convolution Neural Network (CNN) and found DE gives best result than *SA and HS*. Name of all metaheuristic algorithms is given in italic in this section.

As the complexity of the problem grows sufficient number of hidden layers required and number of neuron required in each layer of neural network architecture becomes a very frequently asked question by the research fraternity (Stathakis, 2009) of machine learning domain. The neuron number and hidden layer size of neural network depends on the concept of Kolmogorov's (Kolmogorov, 1957) theorem which states that any n dimensional continuous function easily be represented using superposition and sum of one variable continuous function. Hecht-Nielsen (Hecht-Nielsen, 1987) stated that this function can be implemented by one hidden layer of 2i+1 hidden node, when i is taken as number of input node, when a complex activation function is taken instead of usual sigmoidal function. Kurkova (Kurkova, 1992) suggested that if regular sigmoidal activation function is taken then two layer neural network gives better accuracy. Jinchuan and Xinzhe (Jinchuan & Xinzhe, 2008) has given a function $N_{hi}=(N_i+\sqrt{N_s})/L_a$ where N_{hi} is the hidden layer neuron N_i is the input neuron number, N_s is the number of sample and L_a is the hidden layer number. One of the popular but primitive methods of choosing hidden layer number and size is by trial and error, where a small portion of the search space is being utilized by naive users (Sheela & Deepa, 2013). Another method is called heuristic search, where close optimal solution is being searched by some formula considering number of samples, number of input, number of output class to find the node of the hidden layer. The most time consuming method is the exhaustive search of the solution space, which is not feasible to implement in complex problems. Pruning method creates an efficient network topology by changing the weights of a network by decreasing the training error. Stathakis (Stathakis, 2009) searched the two dimensional solution space of hidden layer 1 and 2 neuron using Genetic Algorithm (GA). The detailed research in this field for last 20 years is reviewed by Gnana Sheela (Sheela & Deepa, 2013). A comprehensive survey paper is published by Ojha (Ojha et al., 2017) for the research work on nature inspired algorithm in neural networks parameter design in last two decade.

MALIGNANT MELANOMA

Malignant Melanoma primarily a type of skin cancer causes due to excessive UV ray exposure in skin melanocytes cell (McCourt et al., 2014) It is also found in the eyes, ears and oral part (McCourt et al., 2014). Though Melanoma is least common skin cancer but has highest mortality rate mainly in the Europe, US and Australia (McCourt et al., 2014). The increase in cases of occurrence of malignant Melanoma is due to depletion in ozone layer due to pollution and change in life style. There are mainly four subtypes of Melanoma, superficial spreading Melanoma, nodular Melanoma, lentigo maligna Melanoma (sun tanned body parts) and acral lentiginous Melanoma (Garbe et al, 2016). Melanoma is a curable disease if detected in early stages, but may become deadly later. There is only 5 year survival rate in United States if it is detected in later stages. The most important risk factors of malignant Melanoma is changing mole color, shape and size, sun sensitivity etc (Beth et al., 2001)(U.S. Department of Health and Human Services). In general one can calculate different dermatology score used for different skin diseases to identify the disease and severity. Dermatologists use Menzies method, ABCD rule (Maglogiannis et al., 2005), 7-point checklist (Zanotto, 2010) and C.A.S.H. rule (Bhor & Pande, 2006) frequently for the determination of malignant Melanoma. The details of different dermatological scoring system are given in the Table 1.

ABCD rule is among the most frequently used scoring methods for identification of melanocytic lesions. In ABCD, A means asymmetry, B means border, C means color, D means differential structural components. In this rule, each criterion (i.e. A, B, C and D) has a corresponding score which is given by the dermatologist depending upon investigation of the lesion and they are multiplied by some weight factors and summed over to generate a total dermatoscopy score (TDS). The details of ABCD rule are given in the Table 2.

If the TDS mentioned above is less than 4.76, the lesion is benign. If it is in between 4.76 to 5.45 the lesion is suspicious. The lesion is malignant if the TDS is greater than 5.45.

MALIGNANT MELANOMA IMAGE DATASET

This present system deals with processing of melanocyitc images and automated identification of the image using machine learning tools. So standard image data sources are very important is this work. There are two types of image data sources primary and secondary. Primary data sources are hospitals and clinics. They provide better control over the settings and quality of images, but it is very time consuming to build the data base. The collection of primary data has to be done in a standardized way to make all collected data in the same format. On the other hand, available secondary data banks have standardization. There are different sources of secondary data present in the internet. These dataset can be used in education and research with proper acknowledgement and permission from the concerned authority.

Table 1. Melanoma scoring system depending on skin features.

Scoring System	Skin Features to Be Scored
ABCD Rule (Maglogiannis et al., 2005)	Asymmetry, Borders, Colors and Differential structural.
7-point checklist (Zanotto, 2010)	Atypical pigment network, Atypical vascular pattern, Blue-whitish veil, Irregular streaks, Irregular dots, Irregular blotches and Regression structures.
Menzies method (Bhor & Pande, 2006)	Melanoma negative features like: Symmetrical pattern, Single color Melanoma positive features like: Blue-white veil, Multiple brown dots, Scar-like depigmentation, Multiple colors, Multiple blue or grey dots and Broadened network.
C.A.S.H. (Bhor & Pande, 2006)	Colors, Architecture, Symmetry, Homogeneity.

Table 2. The ABCD rule score, weight factor for the detection of malignant Melanoma.

ABCD Criteria	Choice of Score	Weight Value
Asymmetry	0 to 2	1.3
Borders	0 to 8	0.1
Colors	1 to 6	0.5
Differential structural components	1 to 5	0.5

There are lots of secondary data sources from where images of melanocytic lesion can be found. There are quite a few general skin image dataset from where Melanoma image can be collected. DermQuest has around 22500 secondary clinical images. Dermatology image atlas has over 9000 secondary skin disease images. DermNet case photo library has more than 7500 images with live interaction with the users. Pediatric dermatology online image atlas has a repository of over 7000 images in alphabetical order. There are some image libraries specifically meant for malignant Melanoma. In this section the details about some of the Melanoma image library are given. In this proposed work image data of two of them are (MED-NODE and Dermofit) taken for the work.

MED-NODE Dataset

MED-NODE dataset of melanoma has 170 good quality, high resolution color macroscopic images, which includes 70 images of malignant melanoma, and 100 images of benign lesion type. MED-NODE is an image dataset for skin cancer identification, taken from a large collection of around 50 thousand images prepared by University Medical Center Groningen. All the images are collected by either Nikon D1x or Nikon D3 camera with a distance of $2^1/_2$ feet from the lesion. All the images are in .JPG format with different pixel size. This MED-NODE library images are verified by the pathologist and dermatologist and identified as gold standard.

Dermofit Dataset

Dermofit image library (Ballerini et al., 2013) has 1300 melanocytic lesion images copyrighted by University of Edinburgh. Edinburgh innovations center which is a part of University of Edinburgh has collected and prepared the image library for use in research and non-commercial educational purpose. Dermofit image dataset are marked as gold standard data by dermatologists and derma-pathologists. Total 10 types of melanocytic lesion images are stored in the Dermofit image library, which can be further categorized into 2 groups, malignant melanoma and nevus type. A total 526 images of malignant melanoma and 774 images of benign type are present in the dataset. NHS national ethics permission is taken for carrying out the Dermofit research project.

ISIC Dataset

ISIC is a project of International Society for Digital Imaging of the Skin (ISDIS) which was founded by some U.S. dermatologists in the year 1992. In this ISIC archive easy downloadable total 13791 numbers of dermatoscopic images are stored. Each image has its metadata like diagnostic attributes (benign, intermediate or malignant and type of lesion), clinical attributes (age, size, medical diagnosis and family history) and technological attributes attached with it. The images can be used for teaching and for development of non-commercial melanoma diagnostic system. This archive maintains quality, interoperability and privacy. Appropriate patient consent is taken before including each image in the dataset. Each image collected in similar environment like lighting arrangement and magnification.

PH² Dataset

The PH² is a project (Mendonça et al., 2013) where dermatologist from Pedro Hispano hospital and researchers from Computer Science Engineering of different Universities are involved. The database has a total 200 images of melanocytic lesions. Each lesion is assessed by an expert dermatologist.

Skin Cancer Dataset of University of Waterloo

This dataset is created by University of Waterloo (Amelard et al., 2015) by taking melonocytic lesion images either from DermIS website or DermQuest website. There are total 119 Melanoma images and 87 benign images in the dataset.

In this present work 170 images of MEDNODE dataset and 1300 images of Dermofit dataset are used. Sample images used in the work are shown in the Figure 1.

IMAGE PREPROCESSING AND FEATURE EXTRACTION

Image preprocessing is the initial but costly step in any image processing work. Type of image preprocessing depends upon the image to deal with. Skin image require preprocessing steps like hair removal (Tan et al. 2016), skin color normalization, noise reduction, contrast enhancement etc. To find the lesion

Figure 1. a), b), c), d) Sample images used in the present work.

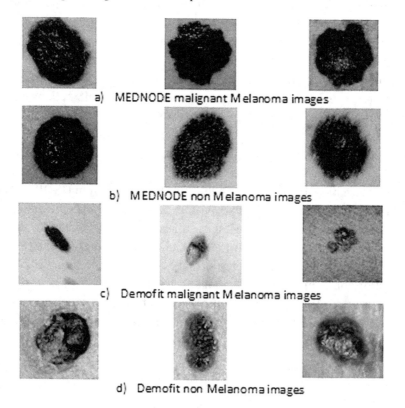

a) MEDNODE malignant Melanoma images

b) MEDNODE non Melanoma images

c) Demofit malignant Melanoma images

d) Demofit non Melanoma images

area different image segmentation algorithms (De et al., 2016) can be used like k-means and Otsu's which follows thresholding method. Some edge detection based segmentation techniques like Sobel and Canny methods are also used. There are some popular region-based method like split and merge available for image segmentation. Certain soft computing based new methods i.e. neural network based, fuzzy logic based and genetic algorithm based methods are available in the literature. In this work MATLAB version R2016b is used for writing scripts for image segmentation, all feature extraction, metaheuristic algorithm like SA and PSO and multilayer perceptron classifier. The work is done in Windows 10 OS of 64 bit and Core i5 processor with 8 GB primary memory. In this work Otsu's algorithm (Otsu, 1979) is used for image segmentation as it performs better in bimodal images used in this problem. Otsu's algorithm is used for the segmentation of lesion area from its boundary. Otsu algorithm is very fast as it acts on 8 bit gray level image bimodal histogram. Otsu algorithm finds the threshold intensity value which maximize inter class variance and minimize the intra class variance. In this work total 1898 numbers of lesion shape, color and texture features are extracted after segmentation. In these total 1898 features, 10 lesion shape features (Tan et al. 2016), 36 color features (Pereira et al., 2013) and 88 Gray Level Run Length Matrix (GLRLM) texture (Tang, 1998) feature and 1764 Gray Level Co-occurrence Matrix (GLCM) texture (Haralick et al. 1973),(Soh, & Tsatsoulis, 1999), (Clausi, 2002) feature are present. The details about the 10 shape features are given in Table 3.

In the group of color feature, standard deviation and mean features of 3 different color channels for each six color model namely RGB, XYZ, HSV, Lab, YIQ and YCbCr are used. This makes another 36 color feature (2X6X3) in total.

The largest group of features used in the work is the human imperceptible second order statistical feature which could not be seen by human eye. In this group 1764 GLCM texture feature are present. GLCM stands for Gray Level Co-occurrence Matrix. It is proposed by Haralick (Haralick et al. 1973) in 1973 and further new features are proposed by Soh (Soh, & Tsatsoulis, 1999) and Clausi (Clausi, 2002) in the year 1999 and 2002 respectively. Using GLCM one can find the number of "i" gray level pixel occurrence in a distance d with an angle Θ with respect to "j" gray level in the image texture for

Table 3. Details of shape features

Shape Feature	Description
Lesion Area	Number of pixel in ROI (lesion)
Major axis	Number of pixel in a line in major axis of ROI (lesion) when approximated as an ellipse
Minor axis	Number of pixel in a line in minor axis of ROI (lesion) when approximated as an ellipse
Irregularity metric I	Perimeter of ROI (lesion) /Area of ROI (lesion)
Irregularity metric II	Perimeter of ROI (lesion) /Major axis length of ROI (lesion);
Irregularity metric III	Perimeter of ROI (lesion) *((1/ Minor axis length of ROI (lesion))-(1/ Major axis length of ROI (lesion)));
Irregularity metric IV	Major axis length of ROI (lesion) - Minor axis length of ROI (lesion);
Perimeter	Number of pixel in the boundary of the ROI (lesion)
Solidity	Calculated as the ratio of Area and convex Area of the ROI (lesion)
Circularity metric	((4*Area of ROI (lesion) *$\prod$)/(Perimeter of ROI (lesion))2)

quantization level L. Before extracting features of GLCM the matrix is to be normalized i.e.
$\sum_{j=1}^{L}\sum_{i=1}^{L}G(i,j)=1$.

Thus GLCM creates a co-occurrence matrix G (i,j|d,Θ|L) for the whole image, where L is the image quantization level. In the Figure 2(a) an image with 5 gray levels is shown. The corresponding GLCM matrix is shown in the Figure 2(b) with a distance 1 and angle 0°. In Figure 2(c) the pixel of interest is represented by P and the pixel with distance 1 and angle 0°, 45°, 90° and 135° are represented by the corresponding values. In this work 21 GLCM features are calculated with 6 pixel pair distance d (1, 2, 3, 4, 5, 6) and 1 angle Θ (0°) with 2 quantization level 64 and 128 for gray level and six color channels (3 channels of HSV and 3 channels of RGB). In this respect total 1764 (21X6X1X2X7) features are calculated altogether.

The details about the 21 GLCM features are given in the Table 4 where G(i, j) represents the (i, j)th entry in GLCM matrix, where i and j are the intensity level in row and column in the GLCM matrix. N_{gr} is the number of grey level in quantization level. σ_x, σ_y, are the standard deviation and μ_x, μ_y are means of G_x and G_y.

$$\mu_x=\sum_{j=1}^{N_{gr}}G(i,j) \text{ and } \mu_y=\sum_{i=1}^{N_{gr}}G(i,j)$$

$$G_{x+y}(k)=\sum_{\substack{i=1 \\ i+j=k}}^{N_{gr}}\sum_{j=1}^{N_{gr}}G(i,j) \quad \text{and} \quad G_{x-y}(k)=\sum_{\substack{i=1 \\ |i-j|=k}}^{N_{gr}}\sum_{j=1}^{N_{gr}}G(i,j)$$

The details about the 11 GLRLM features are given in the Table 5 where Gr (i, j) represents the (i, j)th entry in GLRLM matrix, where i is the intensity level and j is the length of run. n_{rg} is the number of gray level in quantization level.

There are 88 GLRLM features (Tang, 1998) present in the work. GLRLM stands for Gray Level Run Length Matrix. GLRLM is very similar like GLCM used to extract second order run length statistical

Figure 2. a) Image with 5 gray levels, b) Corresponding GLCM matrix, c) Pixel of interest and pixel with angle 0°, 45°, 90° and 135°

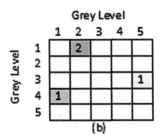

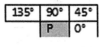

Table 4. Formulae for calculating 21 GLCM features

Feature	Description
Auto-correlation	$\sum_i \sum_j (ij)G(i,j)$
Contrast	$\sum_{n=0}^{N_{gr}-1} n^2 \left(\sum_{i=1}^{N_{gr}} \sum_{j=1}^{N_{gr}} G(i,j) \right)$ $\lvert i-j \rvert = n$
Correlation	$\dfrac{\sum_i \sum_j (ij)G(i,j) - \mu_x \mu_y}{\sigma_x \sigma_y}$
Homogeneity	$\sum_i \sum_j \dfrac{1}{(i-j)^2 + 1} G(i,j)$
Max probability	$\underset{i,j}{MAX}\, G(i,j)$
Sum of squares (variance)	$\sum_i \sum_j (i-\mu)^2 G(i,j)$
Sum average	$\sum_{i=2}^{2N_{gr}} i G_{x+y}(i)$
Sum variance	$\sum_{i=2}^{2N_{gr}} (i - SumEntropy)^2 G_{x+y}(i)$
Sum entropy	$-\sum_{i=2}^{2N_{gr}} G_{x+y}(i) \log\left\{ G_{x+y}(i) \right\}$
Difference variance	Variance of G_{x-y}
Difference entropy	$-\sum_{i=0}^{N_{gr}-1} G_{x-y}(i) \log\left\{ G_{x-y}(i) \right\}$

continued on following page

Table 4. Continued

Feature	Description
Information measure correlation A	$\dfrac{IXY - IXY1}{\max imum\{IY, IX\}}$ when IXY$= -\sum_i \sum_j G(i,j)\log(G(i,j))$ and IX and IY are the entropies of G_x and G_y, and IXY1 is $-\sum_i \sum_j G(i,j)\log\{G_x(i)G_y(j)\}$ IXY2 is $-\sum_i \sum_j G_x(i)G_y(j)\log\{G_x(i)G_y(j)\}$
Information measure correlation B	$(1 - \exp[-2.0(IXY2 - IXY)])^{1/2}$ 5.
Clustering prominence	$\sum_i \sum_j ((i+j) - \mu_x - \mu_y)^4 G(i,j)$
Clustering shade	$\sum_i \sum_j ((i+j) - \mu_x - \mu_y)^3 G(i,j)$
Dissimilarity	$\sum_i \sum_j |i - j| * G(i,j)$
Energy	$\sum_i \sum_j G(i,j)^2$
Entropy	$-\sum_i \sum_j G(i,j)\log(G(i,j))$
Inverse difference	$\sum \dfrac{T_{ij}}{1 + |i - j|}$ where $T_{ij} = \dfrac{G(i,j)}{\sum\limits_{i,j=1}^{N_{gr}} G(i,j)}$
Inverse difference normalize	$\sum\limits_{i,j=1}^{N_{gr}} \dfrac{T_{ij}}{|i - j|^2 + 1 / N_{gr}^2}$
Inverse difference normalize of moment	$\sum\limits_{i,j=1}^{N_{gr}} \dfrac{T_{ij}}{(i - j)^2 + 1 / N_{gr}^2}$

features from 2D image texture. It is proposed by Tang in 1998. With GLRLM one can find the number of runs (same gray level value) "j" of "i" gray level pixel in an angle Θ within the image texture for quantization level L. Before extracting features of GLRLM the matrix is to be normalized i.e.

$$\sum_{j=1}^{L} \sum_{i=1}^{L} Gr(i,j) = 1$$

Thus GLRLM creates a run length matrix Gr (i,j|ϴ|L) for the whole image, where L is the image quantization level. In the Figure 3(a) an image with 5 gray levels is shown. The corresponding GLRLM matrix is shown in the Figure 3(b) with an angle 0°. In Figure 3(c) the pixel of interest is represented by P and the pixel with angle 0°, 45°, 90° and 135° are represented by the corresponding values. In this work 11 GLRLM features are calculated with 4 angle ϴ (0°, 45°, 90°, 135°) with 2 quantization level 64 and 128 for gray level. In this respect total 88 (11X4X2) features are calculated altogether.

METAHEURISTIC ALGORITHM

Finding the optimal solution of the NP-hard problem is computationally infeasible in nature. The time taken by the problem is non-deterministic. These problems can categorize as single objective or multi objective optimization problem. One of the popularly used methods to solve this type of problem is to use metaheuristic algorithm. Advantage of metaheuristic algorithm is it doesn't depend on problem unlike heuristic algorithms which are problem specific. Metaheuristic is used in those type of problem where there is no specific single solution exists. Metaheuristic algorithms have two common characteristic, presence of random variable and inspiration from nature. Metaheuristic algorithms are very popular for solving optimization problem as they efficiently searches the solution space in a non-deterministic way to find near–optimal solutions. This Metaheuristic term first coined by Glover (Glover, 1986) in the year 1986. There are various well known metaheuristic algorithms found in the literature like Simulated Annealing (SA), Genetic Algorithm (GA), Particle Swarm Optimization (PSO), Ant Colony Optimization (ACO), Taboo Search (TS), Teaching-Learning-Based Optimization (TLBO), Firefly Algorithm (FA), Shuffled Frog Leaping (SFL), Scatter Search (SS), Artificial Immune System (AIS), Gravitational Search Algorithm (GSA), Harmony Search Algorithm (HSA), Cuckoo Search Algorithm (CSA) etc. (Silberholz & Golden). Metaheuristic algorithms can be classified in different ways. Metaheuristic algorithms can be of single solution based like simulated annealing, variable neighborhood search etc. where improvement is done on a single candidate solution in each iteration. In single solution based

Figure 3. a) Image with 5 gray levels, b) Corresponding GLRLM matrix, c) Pixel of interest and pixel with angle 0°, 45°, 90° and 135°

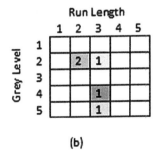

Table 5. Formulae for calculating 11 GLRLM features

Feature	Description
Short run emphasis	$\frac{1}{n_{rg}}\sum_{i=1}^{P}\sum_{j=1}^{Q}\frac{Gr(i,j)}{j^2}$
Long run emphasis	$\frac{1}{n_{rg}}\sum_{i=1}^{P}\sum_{j=1}^{Q}Gr(i,j)*j^2$
High gray level run emphasis	$\frac{1}{n_{rg}}\sum_{i=1}^{P}\sum_{j=1}^{Q}Gr(i,j)*i^2$
Low gray level short run emphasis	$\frac{1}{n_{rg}}\sum_{i=1}^{P}\sum_{j=1}^{Q}\frac{Gr(i,j)}{i^2*j^2}$
High gray level short run emphasis	$\frac{1}{n_{rg}}\sum_{i=1}^{P}\sum_{j=1}^{Q}\frac{Gr(i,j)*i^2}{j^2}$
Gray-level non uniformity	$\frac{1}{n_{rg}}\sum_{i=1}^{P}(\sum_{j=1}^{Q}Gr(i,j))^2$
Run length non uniformity	$\frac{1}{n_{rg}}\sum_{j=1}^{Q}\left(\sum_{i=1}^{P}Gr(i,j)\right)^2$
Run %	$\frac{n_{rg}}{Gr(i,j)*j}$
Low gray-level run emphasis	$\frac{1}{n_{rg}}\sum_{i=1}^{P}\sum_{j=1}^{Q}\frac{Gr(i,j)}{i^2}$
Low gray level long run emphasis	$\frac{1}{n_{rg}}\sum_{i=1}^{P}\sum_{j=1}^{Q}\frac{Gr(i,j)*j^2}{i^2}$
High gray level long run emphasis	$\frac{1}{n_{rg}}\sum_{i=1}^{P}\sum_{j=1}^{Q}Gr(i,j)*i^2*j^2$

strategy, a solution trajectory is created starting from a single solution to a better solution in the search space. There can be population based search like particle swarm optimization or ant colony optimization where in each iteration multiple candidate solution is evaluated. Unlike single solution strategies in population based strategies initially a population of solution is considered. Then these solutions are modified to a better solution by crossover and mutation. Metaheuristic algorithm can also be categories as local search based like hill climbing which find local optimum solutions or global search based like tabu search or simulated annealing. Recently research community gives more focus is on nature inspired metaheuristic algorithms like ant colony optimization, simulated annealing, particle swarm optimization and evolutionary algorithms. Recently a new domain of research trends deals with hybrid metaheuristic algorithms which combines the advantages of two or more metaheuristic algorithm and try to curtail the disadvantage of the same. The main aim of hybridization is fast convergence and better accuracy percentage. Silberholz and Golden (Silberholz & Golden) has done an elaborated comparison of the metaheuristic algorithms with their standard parameters, solution quality and run-time environments. They found that large parameter of metaheuristic algorithm degrades the performance of the algorithm. Madić (Madić et al., 2013) compared the performance of four metaheuristic algorithm namely SA, GA, CSA and Improved HSA for five machine optimization problems. In our work we have used two popular metaheuristic algorithms PSO and SA. The basics of those algorithms are discussed in the next section.

Particle Swarm Optimization (PSO)

The concept of Particle Swarm Optimization (PSO) which is proposed by Kennedy and Eberhart (Kennedy & Eberhart, 1995) is a very popular natured inspired metaheuristic technique modeled upon the actions of animals. It is a simple but powerful optimization technique which uses two techniques for optimization namely communication and learning. To understand the PSO let X is a vector of n dimension, which is the solution of the function $f\left(x_1, x_2, \ldots x_n\right)$. So we can write $X = \left(x_1, x_2, \ldots x_n\right)$ now a function $f\left(x_1, x_2, \ldots x_n\right)$ can be considered as a cost function. The aim is to minimize the cost of the function $f\left(x_1, x_2, \ldots x_n\right)$ in the n dimensional solution search space. This above problem can be considered as an optimization problem. In this search space of solution (SP) of the optimization problem, every solution is known as a particle (PAR), which is a vector X of n dimension, has a position PS_{PAR}, shown as $PS_{PAR} \in SP$. In time t the position of the particle can be written as $PS_{PAR}(t)$. Each particle has a velocity $V_{PAR}(t)$, personal best position, $PB_{PAR}(t)$ (best solution of that particle up to time t) and a global best position, $GB(t)$(best solution of any particle in the search space up to time t). The particle $PS_{PAR}(t)$ with velocity $V_{PAR}(t)$ may traverse from location A to C due to its inertia as per the Figure 4.

Figure 4. Schematic diagram of the particle swarm optimization

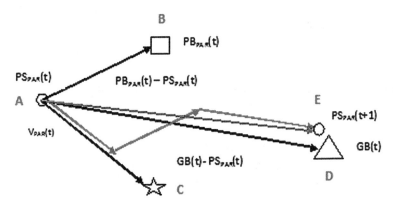

The personal best and the global best positions of the particles are located in B and D respectively. For the presence of three vectors $V_{PAR}(t)$, $(PB_{PAR}(t) - PS_{PAR}(t))$ and $(GB(t) - PS_{PAR}(t))$ the particle changes its position from the position A to position E instead of A to C.

Position of the particle is updated by the equations 1 and 2:

$$PS_{PAR}(t+1) = PS_{PAR}(t) + V_{PAR}(t+1) \tag{1}$$

when

$$V_{PAR}(t+1) = ir.V_{PAR}(t) + a1.ran1.\left(PB_{PAR}(t) - PS_{PAR}(t)\right) + a2.ran2.\left(GB(t) - PS_{PAR}(t)\right) \tag{2}$$

In equation (2) ir is known as inertia co-efficient and a1 (individual particle learning rate), a2 (social learning rate) are called acceleration co-efficient and ran1 and ran2 are random number within 1 to 0.

PSO algorithm steps are:

Step 1: Take n number of particles in the search space.
Step 2: Start with the position $PS_{PAR}(t)$ and velocity $V_{PAR}(t)$ for every particle PAR in time t.
Step 3: Find the personal best position, $PB_{PAR}(t)$ of each particle and the global best GB(t) at time t.
Step 4: Improve each particle's position $PS_{PAR}(t)$ and the velocity vector $V_{PAR}(t)$ by equation 1 and 2 in t+1 time.
Step 5: Repeat step 3 and step 4 until the target threshold of the cost function is achieved or maximum iteration is fulfilled.
Step 6: Display the final value of the solution.

Simulated Annealing (SA)

Simulated Annealing (SA) (Kirkpatrick et al., 1983) is another method to optimize a function $f(x_1, x_2, ...x_n)$. A point $X = (x_1, x_2, ...x_n)$ in the n dimensional search space is called a solution. SA is a popular single solution metaheuristic algorithm which has a background of Statistical Mechanics. A physical system equilibrates at its minimum energy at absolute zero temperature but has a probability to climb up to higher energy state increases with temperature. At a sufficiently high temperature the system is free to explore the entire phase space but as the temperature is reduced it settles down to a deep valley in the energy surface. Optimization by SA makes use of this concept. The function $f(x_1, x_2, ...x_n)$ is taken as the energy analog and temperature is a parameter that determines the probability to go to a worse solution. As the system at high temperature roams around throughout the search space it does not get trapped into shallow local minima and more likely to go to global minima. The algorithm of Simulated Annealing is as follows:

Step 1: Select a random starting solution X_i and temperature TEMP (>0).
Step 2: Until temperature is zero executes the following steps Step 3.A and Step 3.B.
    Step 3.A: Iterate the following statement n times.

Step 3.A.i: Select another random solution X_i+1 from the search space.

Step 3.A.ii: Find out the error value ε which is equal to $f(X_{i+1}) - f(X_i)$

Step 3.A.iii: if ε <= 0 then $X_i = X_i$+1

Step 3.A.iV: if ε > 0 then $X_i = X_i$+1 with a probability function $e^{-ε/TEMP}$

Step 3.B: Decrease the temperature TEMP in a small step

Step 4: Terminate the algorithm with returning the solution X_i

MULTI LAYER PERCEPTRON

This present work deals with multi layer perceptron (MLP) (Rosenblatt, 1961) as a classifer. The schematic diagram of multi layer perceptron is shown in Figure 5. The multi layer perceptron has one input layer where features of the dataset are being feed. The input layer size is same with feature dimension of the problem. The input layer is connected with the hidden layer with each input value is multiplied with a weight and summed over and finally a bias value is added with the sum. Each and every node in the MLP except the input node is primarily called a neuron which uses a nonlinear activation function. The multilayer perceptron can have one or more hidden layers. In this work the system has two hidden layers. The hidden layer size depends on the neuron size. All the hidden layer node is fully connected with the next hidden layer node, finally the last hidden layer is connected with the output layer. The output layer size is same with the number of class in which the classification is done. Searching the optimal number of hidden layer neuron or node in MLP is an extremely difficult and time consuming task in any problem where the number of input and output is large. In the present work Metaheuristic algorithm like SA and PSO are used the find the optimal number of neuron in each layer as it is an optimization problem. As suggested by Kurkova (Kurkova, 1992) two hidden layers in MLP are taken in this problem with at least 1 neuron and at most 500 neurons present in each hidden layer. This maximum amount of 500

Figure 5. Schematic diagram of multi layer Perceptron

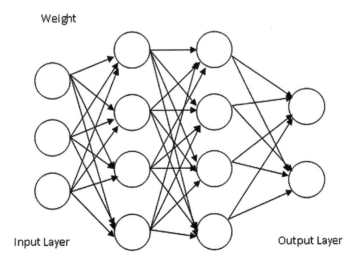

neurons in each layer is taken as per the formulae suggested by Jinchuan & Xinzhe (Jinchuan & Xinzhe, 2008). In this work when Dermofit and MED-NODE dataset is used total neuron size is 960 and 950 respectively as per the formulae. As the neuron is divided in two layers, around half of the neuron is taken in each layer. To run the whole experiment with all combination of neuron in two hidden layer an exhaustive search of 250000 solution are to be tested. In the present work only 500 solutions are tested (5 population and 100 iteration), which is only 1/500th combination of the exhaustive search, which saves considerable amount of time.

PROPOSED METHODOLOGY

The present work is done separately on two popular standard image data sets namely Dermofit and MEDNODE. The Dermofit image library has 1300 melanocytic lesion images with 526 images of malignant Melanoma and 774 images of benign type. The MEDNODE has 170 melanocytic images with 70 images of malignant Melanoma and 100 images of benign type. The Melanoma (or, malignant Melanoma) images are skin cancer image, whereas benign or nevus are non-cancerous type. In this work the aim is to classify between cancerous and non-cancerous lesion image. Out of the total 1898 features, 12 features are not taken in the final experiment as they are giving constant value in the dataset. With total 1886 number of features extracted from each melanocytic lesion image the classification work has been done. The classification work is done for two classes i.e. Malignant or benign melanocytic lesion image identification. For this classification work feed-forward Multi Layer Perceptron is used with one-step secant network training function and cross entropy neural network performance function. The classification work is done with 3 fold cross validation. For both the dataset 70% of the images are used for testing, 15% for validation and 15% for testing. Table 6 shows all the details of the training and testing image count for the present work.

There are total 4 layers in the MLP architecture used in this present work. This neural network has one input layer fixed with 1886 neuron and 2 neurons in the output layer. Due to large number of features and samples present in this classification work, two hidden layers are used in the topology of the neural network architecture. The topology of the MLP is designed in such a way that in each hidden layer of MLP the neuron can be varied between minimum 1 to maximum 500. Finding the exact number of neuron in the hidden layer suitable for classifications are done in different ways as found in the literature. Different approaches are like trial and error, exhaustive search, heuristic search and pruning algorithms by the researchers. In this present work two popular nature inspired metaheuristic algorithms i.e. Simulated Annealing (SA) and Particle Swarm Optimization (PSO) are used for the heuristic search. The algorithms are used to optimize the neuron number in the two hidden layers.

Table 6. Images used for training and testing for both dataset

Image Dataset	Total Image in the Dataset	Image Used in Training (70%)	Image Used in Validation (15%)	Image Used in Testing (15%)
MED-NODE	170	119	26	25
Dermofit	1300	910	195	195

RESULT AND DISCUSSION

When the neuron size of the hidden layer is chosen randomly by trial and error the classification accuracy is not satisfactory, but use of metaheuristic algorithm in choosing hidden layer neuron gives better result. In the case of Dermofit dataset the classification accuracy reaches to 88% with 5 particle search in 100 iterations using PSO. The Iteration versus accuracy curve is shown in the Figure 6. The optimal neuron number found in hidden layer 1 and hidden layer 2 are 437 and 429 respectively.

When the same work is repeated with SA the accuracy reaches to 88.5%. The Iteration versus accuracy curve is shown in the Figure 7. The optimal neuron number found in hidden layer 1 and hidden layer 2 are 481 and 351 respectively by SA.

When MEDNODE image dataset is used for the same work similar good accuracy is found. Highest accuracy of 88.46% is reached with MEDNODE dataset of 170 images and 1886 features with optimal neuron number in hidden layer 1 and hidden layer 2 are 276 and 143 respectively using PSO algorithm for neuron number optimization in two hidden layers. In this case the PSO personal learning coefficient and social learning coefficient is fixed at 1.5 and 2.0 respectively which is a standard value. The iteration versus accuracy curve is shown in Figure 8.

Figure 6. The iteration versus accuracy curve for Dermofit dataset with 1300 image samples and 1886 features and optimization of hidden layer neuron using PSO (5 particle search in 100 iterations), accuracy reaches to 88%.

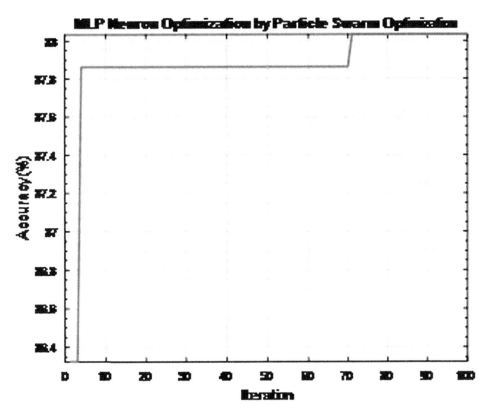

Figure 7. The iteration versus accuracy curve for Dermofit dataset with 1300 image samples and 1886 features and optimization of hidden layer neuron using SA (5 particle search in 100 iterations), accuracy reaches to 88.5%.

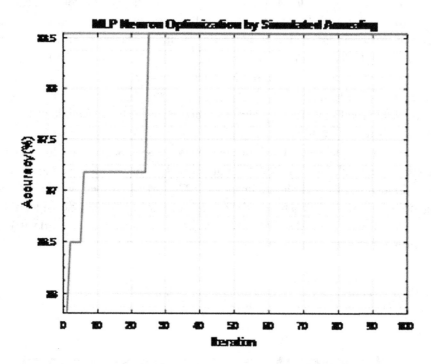

Figure 8. The iteration versus accuracy curve for MEDNODE dataset with 170 image samples and 1886 features and optimization of hidden layer neuron using PSO (5 particle search in 100 iterations), accuracy reaches to 88.46%.

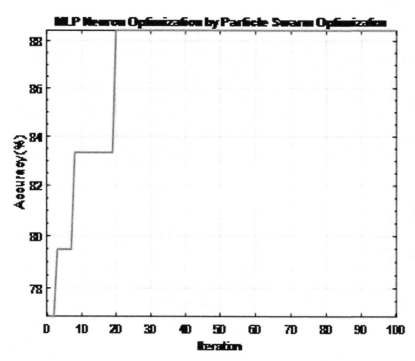

With the use of SA algorithm for neuron number optimization in NN hidden layer the present system achieves accuracy of 89.74% with optimal neuron number in hidden layer 1 and hidden layer 2 are 400 and 343 respectively. The iteration versus accuracy curve is shown in Figure 9.

The search space of the two hidden layer neuron can be represented as a two dimensional space. The X axis and Y axis can be taken as the search dimension of hidden layer 1 neuron and hidden layer 2 neuron respectively. In this work the search space have 250000 (500 X 500) points. In each point of the search space an accuracy value is present. The PSO and SA algorithm searches only 500 points within these 250000 points. In the present work, only 1/500th of the exhaustive search is being done, which makes the system very fast but efficient. The 2D search space of each 5 particles in 100 iterations of PSO algorithm with personal learning coefficient 1.5 and social learning coefficient 2.0 for MEDNODE dataset is shown in Figure 10 (Yarpiz Project). The starting position of each 5 particle is in different location. Four of them have started from four corner of the search space and one have stated from the middle. The details of the metaheuristic algorithm parameters used initially in the present work are given in Table 7.

It can be seen from the graph in Figure 10 that all particles have merged to a single location after 100 iterations. In Figure 11 the plot of 5 particles in 100 iterations of SA algorithm is shown. It can be seen from Figure 10 and Figure 11 that the search path of PSO and SA is totally different. In SA the searching is done apparently throughout the whole search space, whereas in PSO searching is confined

Figure 9. The iteration versus accuracy curve for MEDNODE dataset with 170 image samples and 1886 features and optimization of hidden layer neuron using SA (5 particle search in 100 iterations), accuracy reaches to 89.74%.

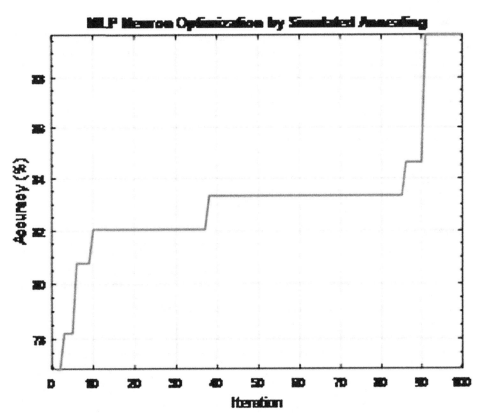

Table 7. Metaheuristic algorithm parameter used in the present work

Metaheuristic	Parameter Value
SA	Initial temperature: 0.1 Temperature reduction rate: 0.99 Maximum iteration: 100 Population size: 5 Starting position of 5 particles in 2D space: (1, 500), (500, 1), (250, 250), (1, 1) (500, 500)
PSO	Initial inertia: 1 Inertia damping: 0.99 Individual particle learning rate: 1.5 Social learning rate: 2.5 Maximum iteration: 100 Population Size: 5 Starting position of 5 particles in 2D space: (1, 500), (500, 1), (250, 250), (1, 1) (500, 500)

Figure 10. The run of 5 particles in the 2D search space with 100 iterations using PSO with personal learning coefficient 1.5 and social learning coefficient 2.0 for MEDNODE dataset having 170 image samples and 1886 features achieving an accuracy of 88.46% with optimal neuron number in hidden layer 1 and hidden layer 2 are 276 and 143 respectively.

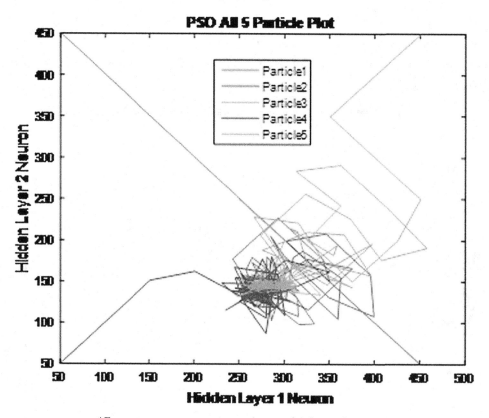

For a more accurate representation see the electronic version.

to local optima. So in SA better possibility of finding global optima is present in the scenario of the present work. This is quite observable from the result found. In SA the classification accuracy is 89.74%, which is greater than PSO (88.46%).

The local or global optima search of PSO heavily depends on the ratio of personal learning coefficient and social learning coefficient used in PSO. In the present experiment when the personal learning coefficient (20) is taken as 2000 times of social learning coefficient (0.01) then the accuracy reaches to 91.02% (Figure 12). The Figure 13 shows the plot of 5 particles in 100 iterations of PSO algorithm with personal learning to social learning ratio to 2000. It is observable that the 5 particles in this case give more weight on local optima search and doesn't merge to a particular location. It can be also observed that the points of the search space are very similar to each other.

When the same experiment is done with PSO with 10 times social learning coefficient (15) than personal learning coefficient (1.5) then the 5 particle merges to the middle of the search space very fast after a few iteration. Figure 14 shows the run of 5 particles in the 2D space using PSO with 10 times of social learning coefficient than personal learning coefficient.

Figure 11. The run of 5 particles in the 2D search space with 100 iterations using SA for MEDNODE dataset having 170 image samples and 1886 features achieving an accuracy of 89.74% with optimal neuron number in hidden layer 1 and hidden layer 2 are 400 and 343 respectively.

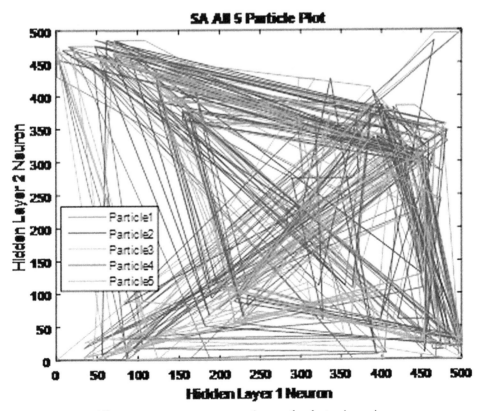

For a more accurate representation see the electronic version.

Figure 12. The Iteration versus accuracy curve for MEDNODE dataset with 170 image samples and 1886 features and optimization of hidden layer neuron using PSO (5 particle search in 100 iterations), Accuracy reaches to 91.02%.

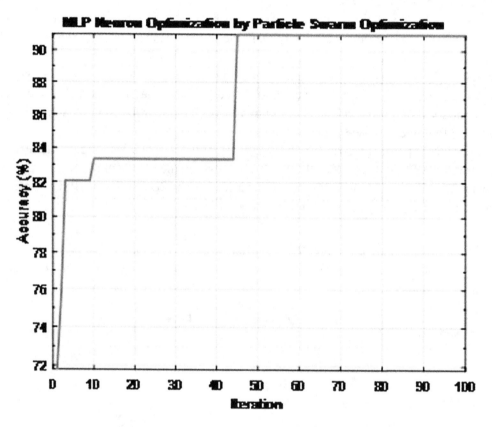

RESULT COMPARISON WITH RELATED WORK

The Table 8 and Table 9 give the comparisons of different classification result of Dermofit and MED-NODE dataset. It can be found that the present works achieves better classification than other related work using both the dataset. In the previous work with MEDNODE dataset the authors have taken the quantization level of GLCM and GLRLM texture features as 4 and 8 (Mukherjee et al., 2018). In the present work the quantization level of GLCM and GLRLM are taken as 64 and 128, which is yields better classification accuracy.

Iyatomi (Iyatomi et al., 2005, 2006) using neural network achieved a classification accuracy of 97.3% but they have used different dataset other than the dataset used in this work. Iyatomi have used dermoscopy images but in this work simple image collected by camera is used.

Figure 13. The run of 5 particles in the 2D search space with 100 iterations using PSO with personal learning coefficient (20) 2000 times of social learning coefficient (0.01) for MEDNODE dataset having 170 image samples and 1886 features achieving an accuracy of 91.02% with optimal neuron number in hidden layer 1 and hidden layer 2 are 442 and 500 respectively.

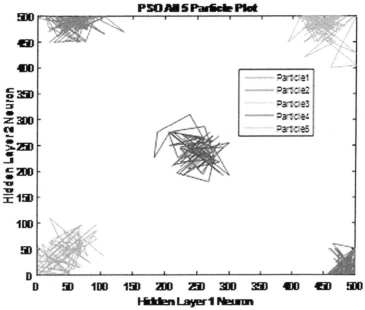

For a more accurate representation see the electronic version.

Figure 14. The run of 5 particles in the 2D search space with 100 iterations using PSO with social learning coefficient (15) 10 times of personal learning coefficient (1.5) for MEDNODE dataset having 170 image samples and 1886 features achieving an accuracy of 87.18% with optimal neuron number in hidden layer 1 and hidden layer 2 are 274 and 265 respectively

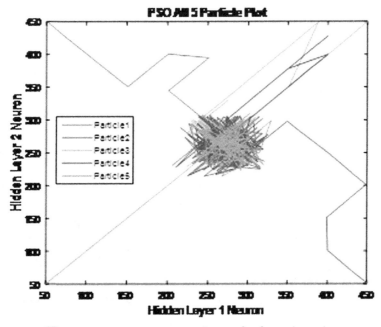

For a more accurate representation see the electronic version.

Table 8. Result comparison of related work for Dermofit Dataset

Related Work	Number of Sample	Feature Dimension	Accuracy (%)
Tan et al., 2016	1300	1472	88
Mukherjee et al., 2018	1300	163	86.2
Present work with NN parameter optimization by SA	1300	1886	88.5
Present work with NN parameter optimization by PSO	1300	1886	88

Table 9. Result comparison of related work for MEDNODE Dataset

Related Work	Number of Sample	Feature Dimension	Accuracy (%)
Giotis et al., 2015	170	675	81
Mukherjee et al., 2016	170	1875	85.9
Present work with NN parameter optimization by SA	170	1886	89.74
Present work with NN parameter optimization by PSO	170	1886	91.02

FUTURE RESEARCH DIRECTIONS

This work can be extended by applying Deep Neural Network, although there are some disadvantages of Deep learning. There are some challenges of Deep learning. Bengio et al. (Bengio et al., 2009) discussed some of them e.g. Deep learning training is more difficult than its shallow counterpart. The Deep learning requires a large number of images in the dataset to give satisfying result.

CONCLUSION

This present chapter shows how nature inspired metaheuristic algorithms can be used in optimized parameter tuning of neural network topology. In this work, two popular metaheuristic algorithms show different results due to their fundamental difference in searching the solution space. Rising the temperature in SA can bring it out of the influence of the local minima and therefore it is closer to uniform exhaustive search. While if the communication dominates the personal learning in PSO an entrapment in the local minima inevitable (refer Figure 10 and 14). The hidden layer size of two-layer MLP is optimized with PSO and SA. The two dimensional solution space have multiple optima which are very near to each other in respect to classification accuracy level, which is taken as solution in this optimization problem. When the local learning rate parameter and social learning rate parameter of PSO is taken close to each other all the particles of PSO search and meet in a single location. As there are multiple very near solutions exist, the PSO particles are unable to search the entire local optimal which may have good solution (classification accuracy level). In case of SA which searches the whole solution space is able to find better solution (classification accuracy level). When the local learning rate of PSO is fixed at a very higher value (2000 times of social learning rate) then the PSO is able to find better solution as all the particle search its local area thoroughly rather than going for global optima. From the point of classification accuracy it can be seen that the higher the quantization level of GLCM and GLRLM texture feature taken better the accuracy level found. This work is done with only two metaheuristic algorithms PSO and SA. The work can be extended to other algorithms and hybrid metaheuristic algorithm can also be used for parameter optimization.

REFERENCES

Amelard, R., Glaister, J., Wong, A., & Clausi, D. A. (2015, October). High-level intuitive features (HLIFs) for intuitive skin lesion description. *IEEE Transactions on Biomedical Engineering*, 62(3), 820–831. doi:10.1109/TBME.2014.2365518 PMID:25361498

Ballerini, L., Fisher, R. B., Aldridge, R. B., & Rees, J. (2013). A Color and Texture Based Hierarchical K-NN Approach to the Classification of Non-melanoma Skin Lesions. In M. E. Celebi & G. Schaefer (Eds.), *Color Medical Image Analysis, Lecture Notes in Computational Vision and Biomechanics 6*. Springer. doi:10.1007/978-94-007-5389-1_4

Bengio, Y. (2009). Learning Deep Architectures for AI. *Foundations and Trends in Machine Learning*, 2(1), 1–127. doi:10.1561/2200000006

Beth, G., Goldstein, M. D., & Goldstein, M. D. (2001). Diagnosis and Management of Malignant Melanoma. *American Family Physician*, 63, 1359–1368, 1374. PMID:11310650

Bhor, U., & Pande, S. (2006). Scoring systems in dermatology. *IJDVL*, 72, 315–321. PMID:16880586

Blondin, J., & Saad, A. (2010). Metaheuristic Techniques for Support Vector Machine Model Selection. *10th International Conference on Hybrid Intelligent Systems*, 197-200. 10.1109/HIS.2010.5600086

Clausi, D. A. (2002). An analysis of co-occurrence texture statistics as a function of grey level quantization. *Canadian Journal of Remote Sensing*, 28(1), 45–62. doi:10.5589/m02-004

Codella, N. C. F., Nguyen, Q. B., Pankanti, S., Gutman, D. A., Helba, B., Halpern, A. C., & Smith, J. R. (2017). Deep learning ensembles for melanoma recognition in dermoscopy images. *IBM Journal of Research and Development, Volume*, 61(4). doi:10.1147/JRD.2017.2708299

De, S., Bhattacharyya, S., Chakraborty, S., & Dutta, P. (2016). *Image Segmentation: A Review*. Hybrid Soft Computing for Multilevel Image and Data Segmentation, Computational Intelligence Methods and Applications. doi:10.1007/978-3-319-47524-0_2

Esteva, A., Kuprel, B., Novoa, R. A., Ko, J., Swetter, S. M., Blau, H. M., & Thrun, S. (2017). *Dermatologist-level classification of skin cancer with deep neural networks, Springer Nature. Macmillan Publishers Limited*. doi:10.1038/nature21056

Garbe, C., Peris, K., Hauschild, A., Saiag, P., Middleton, M., Bastholt, L., ... Pehamberger, H. (2016). Diagnosis and treatment of melanoma. European consensus-based interdisciplinary guideline. *European Journal of Cancer*, 63, 201–217. doi:10.1016/j.ejca.2016.05.005 PMID:27367293

Giotis, I., Molders, N., Land, S., Biehl, M., Jonkman, M. F., & Petkov, N. (2015). MED-NODE: A computer-assisted melanoma diagnosis system using non-dermoscopic images. Expert Systems with Applications, 42, 6578–6585.

Glover, F. (1986). Future paths for integer programming and links to artificial intelligence. *Computers & Operations Research, 13*(5), 533–549. doi:10.1016/0305-0548(86)90048-1

Haralick, R. M., Shanmugam, K., & Dinstein, I. (1973, November). Textural Features of Image Classification. *IEEE Transactions on Systems, Man, and Cybernetics, SMC-3*(6), 610–621. doi:10.1109/TSMC.1973.4309314

Hassanat, A. B., Abbadi, M. A., & Altarawneh, G. A. (2014). Solving the Problem of the K Parameter in the KNN Classifier Using an Ensemble Learning Approach. *International Journal of Computer Science and Information Security, 12*(8), 2014.

Hecht-Nielsen, R. (1987). Kolmogorov's mapping neural network existence theorem. *IEEE First Annual International Conference on Neural Networks*, 11-13.

Iyatomi, H., Oka, H., Hashimoto, M., Tanaka, M., & Ogawa, K. (2005). *An Internet-based Melanoma Diagnostic System toward the Practical Application.* IEEE. doi:10.1109/CIBCB.2005.1594952

Iyatomi, H., Tanahashi, Y., Oka, H., Tanaka, M., & Ogawa, K. (2006). Classification of blue nevus from other lesions for Internet-based melanoma diagnostic system. *SCIS & ISIS2006*, 1995-2000.

Jinchuan, K., & Xinzhe, L. (2008). Empirical analysis of optimal hidden neurons in neural network modeling for stock prediction. *Proceedings of the Pacific-Asia Workshop on Computational Intelligence and Industrial Application, 2*, 828–832.

Kennedy, J., & Eberhart, R. C. (1995). Particle Swarm Optimization. *Proceedings of the IEEE international conference on neural networks IV*, 1942–1948. 10.1109/ICNN.1995.488968

Kirkpatrick, S., Gelatt, C. D., & Vecchi, M. P. (1983, May 13). Optimization by Simulated Annealing, Science. *New Series, 220*(4598), 671–680. PMID:17813860

Kolmogorov, A. N. (1957). *On the representational of continuous functions of many variables by superpositions of continuous functional of one variable and addition.* Doklady Akademii Nauk, USSR.

Kurkova, V. (1992). Kolmogorov's theorem and multilayer neural networks. *Neural Networks, 5*(3), 501–506. doi:10.1016/0893-6080(92)90012-8

Lamba, A., & Kumar, D. (2016). Optimization of KNN with Firefly Algorithm. *BIJIT - BVICAM's International Journal of Information Technology*, 997–1003.

Laskaris, N., Ballerini, L., Fisher, R. B., Aldridge, B., & Rees, J. (2010). Fuzzy Description of Skin Lesions. *SPIE Proceedings, 7627.*

Madić, M., Marković, D., & Radovanović, M. (2013). Comparison of Meta-Heuristic Algorithms for Solving Machining Optimization Problems. *Facta Universitatis Series. Mechanical Engineering (New York, N.Y.), 11*(1), 29–44.

Maglogiannis, I., Pavlopoulos, S., & Koutsouris, D. (2005, March). An Integrated Computer Supported Acquisition, Handling, and Characterization System for Pigmented Skin Lesions in Dermatological Images. *IEEE Transactions on Information Technology in Biomedicine*, *9*(1), 86–98. doi:10.1109/TITB.2004.837859 PMID:15787011

Marks, R. (2000). Epidemiology of melanoma. *Clinical and Experimental Dermatology*, 459–463. 10.1046/j.1365-2230.2000.00693.x

McCourt, C., Dolan, O., & Gormley, G. (2014). Malignant Melanoma: *A Pictorial Review*. *The Ulster Medical Journal*, *83*(2), 103–110. PMID:25075139

McDonagh, S., Fisher, R. B., & Rees, J. (2008). *Using 3D information for classification of non-melanoma skin lesions. In Proc. Medical Image Understanding and Analysis* (pp. 164–168). BMVA Press.

Mendonça, T., Ferreira, P. M., Marques, J., Marcal, A. R. S., & Rozeira, J. (2013). PH2 - A dermoscopic image database for research and benchmarking. *35th International Conference of the IEEE Engineering in Medicine and Biology Society*.

Mukherjee, S., Adhikari, A., & Roy, M. (2018). Malignant Melanoma Identification using Best Visually Imperceptible Features from Dermofit Dataset. *1st International Conference on Emerging Trends in Engineering and Science*.

Mukherjee, S., Adhikari, A., & Roy, M. (2018). Malignant Melanoma Detection using Multi Layer Perceptron with Optimized Network Parameter Selection by PSO. *1st International Conference on Contemporary Advances in Innovative & Applicable Information Technology*.

Ojha, V. K., Abraham, A., & Snasel, V. (2017). Metaheuristic Design of Feedforward Neural Networks: A Review of Two Decades of Research. *Engineering Applications of Artificial Intelligence*, *60*, 97–116. doi:10.1016/j.engappai.2017.01.013

Otsu, N. (1979). A threshold selection method from gray-level histograms. *IEEE Transactions on Systems, Man, and Cybernetics*, *9*(1), 62–66. doi:10.1109/TSMC.1979.4310076

Pereira, S. M., Frade, M. A. C., Rangayyan, R. M., & Marques, P. M. A. (2013, January). Classification of Color Images of Dermatological Ulcers. *IEEE Journal of Biomedical and Health Informatics*, *17*(1), 136–142. doi:10.1109/TITB.2012.2227493 PMID:23193315

Pericles, B. C., Silva, R. C., & Prudencio, R. C. (2014). Fine-Tuning of Support Vector Machine Parameters using Racing Algorithms. *European Symposium on Artificial Neural Networks 2014, Computational Intelligence and Machine Learning*.

Rere, L. M. R., Fanany, M. I., & Arymurthy, A. M. (2016). Metaheuristic Algorithms for Convolution Neural Network. *Computational Intelligence and Neuroscience*, *2016*, 1537325. doi:10.1155/2016/1537325 PMID:27375738

Rosenblatt, F. (1961). *Principles of Neurodynamics: Perceptrons and the Theory of Brain Mechanisms*. Washington, DC: Spartan Books. doi:10.21236/AD0256582

Sheela, K.G., & Deepa, S. N. (2013). Review on Methods to Fix Number of Hidden Neurons in Neural Networks. *Mathematical Problems in Engineering*. .10.1155/2013/425740

Soh, L., & Tsatsoulis, C. (1999, March). Texture Analysis of SAR Sea Ice Imagery Using Gray Level Co-Occurrence Matrices. *IEEE Transactions on Geoscience and Remote Sensing, 37*(2), 780–795. doi:10.1109/36.752194

Stathakis, D. (2009, April 20). How many hidden layers and nodes? *International Journal of Remote Sensing, 30*(8), 2133–2147. doi:10.1080/01431160802549278

Tan, T. Y., Zhang, L., & Jiang, M. (2016). An Intelligent Decision Support System for Skin Cancer Detection from Dermoscopic Images. *Proceedings of the 12th International Conference on Natural Computation, Fuzzy Systems and Knowledge Discovery (ICNC-FSKD)*, 2194-2199. 10.1109/FSKD.2016.7603521

Tang, X. (1998, November). Texture Information in Run-Length Matrices. *IEEE Transactions on Image Processing, 7*(11), 1602–1609. doi:10.1109/83.725367 PMID:18276225

U.S. Department of Health and Human Services. (n.d.). *What You Need To Know About Melanoma and Other Skin Cancers.* National Institutes of Health.

Yarpiz Project. (2018). Retrieved February 01, 2018, from http://www.yarpiz.com

Zanotto, M. (2010). *Visual Description of Skin Lesions* (Master's dissertation). University of Edinburgh.

KEY TERMS AND DEFINITIONS

GLCM: Gray level co-occurrence matrix is used to find pixel intensity co-occurrence texture feature in an image.

GLRLM: Gray level run length matrix is used to find pixel intensity run length texture feature in an image.

Hidden Layer Neuron: Number of neuron in the hidden layer of the multi-layer perceptron.

Malignant Melanoma: A type of skin cancer causes due to excessive UV ray exposure in skin melanocytes cell.

Otsu Algorithm: An algorithm to finds the threshold intensity value which maximize inter class variance and minimize the intra class variance.

Particle Swarm Optimization: A popular natured inspired metaheuristic technique modeled upon the actions of animals.

Simulated Annealing: A popular single solution metaheuristic algorithm which has a background of statistical mechanics.

Compilation of References

Aamodt, A., & Plaza, E. (1994). Case-based reasoning: Foundational issues, methodological variations, and system approaches. *AI Communications*, *7*(1), 39–59.

Abbas, S. A., El Arif, T. I. B., Ghaleb, F. F. M., & Khamis, S. M. (2015). *Optimized video steganography using Cuckoo Search algorithm*. IEEE. doi:10.1109/IntelCIS.2015.7397279

Abdallah, M. A., Samu, T. I., & Grisson, W. A. (1995). Automatic target identification using neural networks. *SPIE Proceedings Intelligent Robots and Computer Vision XIV*, *2588*, 556–565.

Abraham, R., Simha, J. B., & Iyengar, S. (2007). Medical data mining with a new algorithm for feature selection and Naive Bayesian classifier. *10th International Conference on Information Technology*.

Achanta, R., Hemami, S., Estrada, F., & Susstrunk, S. (2009). Frequency-tuned salient region detection. *IEEE CVPR*.

Acharya, A. K., Paul, R., Batham, S., & Yadav, V. K. (2013). *Hiding large amount of data using a new approach of video steganography*. Institution of Engineering and Technology. 10.1049/cp.2013.2338

Acharya, R., Bhat, P. S., Kumar, S., & Min, L. C. (2003). Transmission and storage of medical images with patient information. *Computers in Biology and Medicine*, *33*(4), 303–310. doi:10.1016/S0010-4825(02)00083-5 PMID:12791403

Acharya, R., Niranjan, U. C., Iyengar, S. S., Kannathal, N., & Min, L. C. (2004). Simultaneous storage of patient information with medical images in the frequency domain. *Computer Methods and Programs in Biomedicine*, *76*(1), 13–19. doi:10.1016/j.cmpb.2004.02.009 PMID:15313538

Acharya, U. R., Acharya, D., Bhat, P. S., & Niranjan, U. C. (2001). Compact storage of medical images with patient information. *IEEE Transactions on Information Technology in Biomedicine*, *5*(4), 320–323. doi:10.1109/4233.966107 PMID:11759838

Agatonovic-Kustrin, S., & Beresford, R. (2000). Basic concepts of artificial neural network (ANN) modeling and its application in pharmaceutical research. *Journal of Pharmaceutical and Biomedical Analysis*, *22*(5), 717–727. doi:10.1016/S0731-7085(99)00272-1 PMID:10815714

Ahmad, M., Shahid, A., Qadri, M. Y., Hussain, K., & Qadri, N. N. (2017). Fingerprinting non-numeric datasets using row association and pattern generation. *2017 International Conference on Communication Technologies (ComTech)*, 149-155. 10.1109/COMTECH.2017.8065765

Ahmad, S. (2014). A bio-artificial liver reactor evaluation method. *International Journal of Biomedical Engineering and Technology*, *14*(1), 1–12. doi:10.1504/IJBET.2014.059055

Aibinu, A. M., Salami, M. J. E., & Shafie, A. A. (2010). Application of Modeling Techniques to Diabetes Diagnosis. *IEEE EMBS Conference on Biomedical Engineering & Sciences (IECBES 2010)*, 194-198. 10.1109/IECBES.2010.5742227

Ajili, S., Hajjaji, M. A., & Mtibaa, A. (2015). Hybrid SVD-DWT watermarking technique using AES algorithm for medical image safe transfer. *2015 16th International Conference on Sciences and Techniques of Automatic Control and Computer Engineering (STA)*, 69-74. 10.1109/STA.2015.7505164

Alattar, A. M. (2004). Reversible watermark using the difference expansion of a generalized integer transform. *IEEE Transactions on Image Processing*, 13(8), 1147–1156. doi:10.1109/TIP.2004.828418 PMID:15326856

Al-Qershi, O. M., & Khoo, B. E. (2011). Authentication and data hiding using a hybrid ROI-based watermarking scheme for DICOM images. *Journal of Digital Imaging*, 24(1), 114–125. doi:10.100710278-009-9253-1 PMID:19937363

Amelard, R., Glaister, J., Wong, A., & Clausi, D. A. (2015, October). High-level intuitive features (HLIFs) for intuitive skin lesion description. *IEEE Transactions on Biomedical Engineering*, 62(3), 820–831. doi:10.1109/TBME.2014.2365518 PMID:25361498

American Diabetes Association. (2009). Available: https://archive.ics.uci.edu/ml/datasets/Pima+Indians+Diabetes

Amin, M. M., Salleh, M., Ibrahim, S., Katmin, M. R., & Shamsuddin, M. Z. I. (2003). Information hiding using steganography. *4th National Conference of Telecommunication Technology, 2003. NCTT 2003 Proceedings*, 21-25. 10.1109/NCTT.2003.1188294

Anand, D., & Niranjan, U. C. (1998, October). Watermarking medical images with patient information. In *Engineering in Medicine and Biology Society, 1998. Proceedings of the 20th Annual International Conference of the IEEE* (Vol. 2, pp. 703-706). IEEE.

Anand, D., & Niranjan, U. C. (1998). Watermarking medical images with patient information. *Proceedings of the 20th Annual International Conference of the IEEE Engineering in Medicine and Biology Society*, 20, 703-706. doi: 10.1109/IEMBS.1998.745518

Annadurai, S. (2007). *Fundamentals of digital image processing*. Pearson Education India.

Anouncia, Madonna, Clara, Jeevitha, & Nandhini. (2013). Design of a Diabetic Diagnosis System Using Rough Sets. *Cybernetics and Information Technologies*, 13(3), 124–139.

Antani, S., Kasturi, R., & Jain, R. (2002). A survey on the use of pattern recognition methods for abstraction, indexing and retrieval of images and video. *Pattern Recognition*, 35(4), 945–965. doi:10.1016/S0031-3203(01)00086-3

Antonucci, M., Tirozzi, B., Yarunin, N. D., & Dotsenko, V. S. (1994). Numerical simulation of neural networks with translation and rotation invariant pattern recognition. *International Journal of Modern Physics B*, 8(11–12), 1529–1541. doi:10.1142/S0217979294000658

Arora, P., Srivastava, S., Arora, K., & Bareja, S. (2015). Improved Gait Recognition using Gradient Histogram Gaussian Image. *Procedia Computer Science*, 58, 408–413. doi:10.1016/j.procs.2015.08.049

Arsalan, M., Malik, S. A., & Khan, A. (2012). Intelligent reversible watermarking in integer wavelet domain for medical images. *Journal of Systems and Software*, 85(4), 883–894. doi:10.1016/j.jss.2011.11.005

Artz, D. (2001). Digital steganography: Hiding data within data. *IEEE Internet Computing*, 5(3), 75–80. doi:10.1109/4236.935180

Aslam, A. W., Zhu, Z., & Nandi, A. K. (2013). Feature generation using genetic programming with comparative partner selection for diabetes classification. *Expert Systems With Applications, Elsevier*, 40(13), 5402–5412. doi:10.1016/j.eswa.2013.04.003

Aslam, M. W., & Nandi, A. K. (2010). Detection of diabetes using genetic programming. *18th European Signal Processing Conference (EUSIPCO-2010)*, 1184-1188.

Assini, I., Badri, A., Safi, K., Sahel, A., & Baghdad, A. (2017). Hybrid multiple watermarking technique for securing medical image using DWT-FWHT-SVD. *2017 International Conference on Advanced Technologies for Signal and Image Processing (ATSIP)*, 1-6. 10.1109/ATSIP.2017.8075569

Atkinson, L., Kamalabadi, F., & Jones, D. (2003). Wavelet-based hyperspectral image estimation. *Proc. IGARSS, 2,* 743–745.

Aurenhammer, F., & Klein, R. (2000). Voronoi Diagrams. In J.-R. Sack & J. Urrutia (Eds.), *Handbook of Computational Geometry* (pp. 201–290). Amsterdam: North-Holland. doi:10.1016/B978-044482537-7/50006-1

Avcibas, I., Bayram, S., Memon, N., Ramkumar, M., & Sankur, B. (2004, October). A classifier design for detecting image manipulations. In *Image Processing, 2004. ICIP'04. 2004 International Conference on* (Vol. 4, pp. 2645-2648). IEEE.

Badran, E. F., Sharkas, M. A., & Attallah, O. A. (2009, March). Multiple watermark embedding scheme in wavelet-spatial domains based on ROI of medical images. In *Radio Science Conference, 2009. NRSC 2009. National* (pp. 1-8). IEEE.

Baeth, M. J., & Aktas, M. (2015). On the Detection of Information Pollution and Violation of Copyrights in the Social Web. *2015 IEEE 8th International Conference on Service-Oriented Computing and Applications (SOCA)*, 252-254. 10.1109/SOCA.2015.27

Bala, K., Choubey, D. K., & Paul, S. (2017). Soft computing and data mining techniques for thunderstorms and lightning prediction: A survey. *International Conference of Electronics, Communication and Aerospace Technology (ICECA 2017), 1,* 42-46.

Bala, K., Choubey, D. K., Paul, S., & Ghosh Nee Lala, M. (2018). Classification techniques for thunderstorms and lightning prediction-A survey. In Soft Computing-Based Nonlinear Control Systems Design. IGI Global.

Balakrishnan, S., Narayanaswamy, R., Savarimuthu, N., & Samikannu, R. (2008). SVM Ranking with Backward Search for Feature Selection in Type II Diabetes Databases. *International Conference on Systems, Man and Cybernetics*, 2628-2633. 10.1109/ICSMC.2008.4811692

Ballerini, L., Fisher, R. B., Aldridge, R. B., & Rees, J. (2013). A Color and Texture Based Hierarchical K-NN Approach to the Classification of Non-melanoma Skin Lesions. In M. E. Celebi & G. Schaefer (Eds.), *Color Medical Image Analysis, Lecture Notes in Computational Vision and Biomechanics 6.* Springer. doi:10.1007/978-94-007-5389-1_4

Bamgbade, B. J., Akintola, B. A., Agbenu, D. O., Ayeni, C. O., Fagbami, O. O., Abubakar, H. O., ... Škaron, K. (2013). Cyber crime and violation of copyright. *36th International Convention on Information and Communication Technology, Electronics and Microelectronics (MIPRO)*, 1127-1130.

Bao, F., Deng, R. H., Ooi, B. C., & Yang, Y. (2005). Tailored reversible watermarking schemes for authentication of electronic clinical atlas. *IEEE Transactions on Information Technology in Biomedicine, 9*(4), 554–563. doi:10.1109/TITB.2005.855556 PMID:16379372

Barakat, N. (2007). *Rule extraction from support vector machines: Medical diagnosis prediction and explanation* (Ph.D. thesis). School Inf. Technol. Electr. Eng. (ITEE), Univ. Queensland, Brisbane, Australia.

Barakat, N. H., & Bradley, A. P. (2007). Rule extraction from support vector machines: A sequential covering approach. *IEEE Transactions on Knowledge and Data Engineering, 19*(6), 729–741. doi:10.1109/TKDE.2007.190610

Barakat, N. H., Bradley, A. P., & Barakat, M. N. H. (2010). Intelligible support vector machines for diagnosis of diabetes mellitus. *IEEE Transactions on Information Technology in Biomedicine, 14*(4), 1114–1120. doi:10.1109/TITB.2009.2039485 PMID:20071261

Barni, M., & Bartolini, F. (2004). Data hiding for fighting piracy. *IEEE Signal Processing Magazine, 21*(2), 28–39. doi:10.1109/MSP.2004.1276109

Barni, M., Bartolini, F., & Piva, A. (2002). Multichannel watermarking of color images. *IEEE Transactions on Circuits and Systems for Video Technology, 12*(3), 142–156. doi:10.1109/76.993436

Barre, S. (n.d.). *DICOM Medical image samples*. Retrieved from http://barre.nom.fr/medical/samples/

Barreto, P. S., Kim, H. Y., & Rijmen, V. (2002). Toward secure public-key blockwise fragile authentication watermarking. *IEE Proceedings. Vision Image and Signal Processing, 149*(2), 57–62. doi:10.1049/ip-vis:20020168

Basalla, G. (1988). *The evolution of technology*. Cambridge University Press.

Basu, A., Chatterjee, A., Datta, S., Sarkar, S., & Karmakar, R. (2016, October). FPGA implementation of Saliency based secured watermarking framework. In *Intelligent Control Power and Instrumentation (ICICPI), International Conference on* (pp. 273-277). IEEE. 10.1109/ICICPI.2016.7859716

Basu, A., Karmakar, R., Chatterjee, A., Datta, S., Sarkar, S., & Mondal, A. (2017, March). Implementation of salient region based secured digital image watermarking. In *Computer, Communication and Electrical Technology: Proceedings of the International Conference on Advancement of Computer Communication and Electrical Technology (ACCET 2016)* (p. 9). CRC Press. 10.1201/9781315400624-4

Basu, A. (2015). On the implementation of a secure medical image watermarking. *National Conference on Frontline Research in Computer, Communication and Device (FRCCD)*.

Basu, A. (2016). Some Studies on Quality Metrics for Information Hiding. *National Conference on Recent Innovations in Computer Science & Communication Engineering*.

Bayram, S., Avcibas, I., Sankur, B., & Memon, N. (2005, September). Image manipulation detection with binary similarity measures. In *Signal Processing Conference, 2005 13th European* (pp. 1-4). IEEE.

Beer, G. (1992). Topological completeness of function spaces arising in the Hausdorff approximation of functions. *Canadian Mathematical Bulletin, 35*(4), 439–448. doi:10.4153/CMB-1992-058-1

Ben Hamza, A., Luque, P., Martinez, J., & Roman, R. (1999, October). Removing noise and preserving details with relaxed median filters. *Journal of Mathematical Imaging and Vision, 11*(2), 161–177. doi:10.1023/A:1008395514426

Benbakreti, S., & Benyettou, M. (2012). Gait Recognition Based on Leg motion and Contour Of Silhouette. *International Conference on Information Technology and e-Services*. 10.1109/ICITeS.2012.6216626

Bender, Gruhl, Morimoto, & Lu. (1996). Techniques for data hiding. *IBM Systems Journal, 35*(3-4), 313-336. doi:10.1147j.353.0313

Bengio, Y. (2009). Learning Deep Architectures for AI. *Foundations and Trends in Machine Learning, 2*(1), 1–127. doi:10.1561/2200000006

Berbecel, G., Cooklev, T., & Venetsanopoulos, A. N. (1997). A Multiresolution Technique For Watermarking Digital Images. *1997 International Conference on Consumer Electronics*, 354-355. 10.1109/ICCE.1997.625997

Beth, G., Goldstein, M. D., & Goldstein, M. D. (2001). Diagnosis and Management of Malignant Melanoma. *American Family Physician, 63*, 1359–1368, 1374. PMID:11310650

Bhattacharyya, S., Maulik, U., & Dutta, P. (2011). Multilevel image segmentation with adaptive image context based thresholding. *Applied Soft Computing, 11*(1), 946–962. doi:10.1016/j.asoc.2010.01.015

Bhattacharyya, S., Pal, P., & Bhowmick, S. (2014). Binary image denoising using a quantum multilayer self-organizing neural network. *Applied Soft Computing, 24*, 717–729. doi:10.1016/j.asoc.2014.08.027

Bhole, A. T., & Patel, R. (2012). *Steganography over video file using Random Byte Hiding and LSB technique.* IEEE. doi:10.1109/ICCIC.2012.6510230

Bhor, U., & Pande, S. (2006). Scoring systems in dermatology. *IJDVL, 72*, 315–321. PMID:16880586

Biermann, C. J. (1996). *7. In Handbook of Pulping and Papermaking* (2nd ed.; p. 171). San Diego, CA: Academic Press.

Bing, B. (2015). *Video Coding Fundamentals, Next-Generation Video Coding and Streaming.* Hoboken, NJ: John Wiley & Sons, Inc.; doi:10.1002/9781119133346.ch2

Blondin, J., & Saad, A. (2010). Metaheuristic Techniques for Support Vector Machine Model Selection. *10th International Conference on Hybrid Intelligent Systems*, 197-200. 10.1109/HIS.2010.5600086

Boho, A., van Wallendael, G., Dooms, A., de Cock, J., Braeckman, G., Schelkens, P., ... Van de Walle, R. (2013). End-to-end security for video distribution. *IEEE Signal Processing Magazine, 30*(2), 97–107. doi:10.1109/MSP.2012.2230220

Boncelet, C. G. (2006). The NTMAC for authentication of noisy messages. *IEEE Transactions on Information Forensics and Security, 1*(1), 35–42. doi:10.1109/TIFS.2005.863506

Boney, L., Tewfik, A. H., & Hamdy, K. N. (1996). Digital watermarks for audio signals. *Proceedings of the Third IEEE International Conference on Multimedia Computing and Systems*, 473-480. 10.1109/MMCS.1996.535015

Bora, D. J., & Gupta, A. K. (2014). Effect of Different Distance Measures on the Performance of K-Means Algorithm: An Experimental Study in Matlab. *International Journal of Computer Science and Information Technologies, 5*(2), 2501–2506.

Borgohain, R., & Sanyal, S. (2012). Rule Based Expert System for Diagnosis of Neuromuscular Disorders. *International Journal Advanced Networking and Applications, 4*(1), 1509–1513.

Borji, A., & Itti, L. (2012). Exploiting local and global patch rarities for saliency detection. *2012 IEEE Conference on Computer Vision and Pattern Recognition*, 478-485. 10.1109/CVPR.2012.6247711

Boucherkha, S., & Benmohamed, M. (2004). A Lossless Watermarking Based Authentication System For Medical Images. In *International Conference on Computational Intelligence* (pp. 240-243). Academic Press.

Bounkong, S., Toch, B., Saad, D., & Lowe, D. (2003). ICA for watermarking digital images. *Journal of Machine Learning Research, 4*(Dec), 1471–1498.

Bradley, P. S., & Mangasarian, O. L. (1998). Feature Selection via Concave Minimization and Support Vector Machines. *ICML - Proceedings of the Fifteenth International Conference on Machine Learning*, 82-90.

Brank, J., Grobelnik, M., & Mladenic, D. (2002). *Feature selection using linear support vector Machin.* Technical Report Microsoft Research Corporation.

Brummer, M. E., Mersereau, R. M., Eisner, R. L., & Lewine, R. R. J. (1993, June). Automatic detection of brain contours in MRI data sets. *IEEE Transactions on Medical Imaging, 12*(2), 153–166. doi:10.1109/42.232244 PMID:18218403

Burlacu, A & Lazar, C. (2008). *Image Features Detection using Phase Congruency and Its Application in Visual Servoing.* Academic Press. .10.1109/ICCP.2008.4648353

BW, T.A., & Permana, F.P. (2012, July). Medical image watermarking with tamper detection and recovery using reversible watermarking with LSB modification and run length encoding (RLE) compression. In *Communication, Networks and Satellite (ComNetSat), 2012 IEEE International Conference on* (pp. 167-171). IEEE.

Canagarajah, C. N., Faernando, W. A. C., & Bull, D. R. (2001). Scene change detection algorithms for content-based video indexing and retrieval. *Electronics & Communication Engineering Journal, 13*(3), 117–126. doi:10.1049/ecej:20010302

Candes & Wakin. (2007). An Introduction To Compressive Sampling. *IEEE Signal Processing Magazine, 25*(2), 21-30. doi: 10.1109/MSP.2007.914731

Cao, F., Huang, H. K., & Zhou, X. Q. (2003). Medical image security in a HIPAA mandated PACS environment. *Computerized Medical Imaging and Graphics, 27*(2-3), 185–196. doi:10.1016/S0895-6111(02)00073-3 PMID:12620309

Cao, P., Hashiba, M., Akazawa, K., Yamakawa, T., & Matsuto, T. (2003). An integrated medical image database and retrieval system using a web application server. *International Journal of Medical Informatics, 71*(1), 51–55. doi:10.1016/S1386-5056(03)00088-1 PMID:12909158

Cao, Y., Zhang, H., Zhao, X., & Yu, H. (2015a). Covert Communication by Compressed Videos Exploiting the Uncertainty of Motion Estimation. *IEEE Communications Letters, 19*(2), 203–206. doi:10.1109/LCOMM.2014.2387160

Cao, Y., Zhang, H., Zhao, X., & Yu, H. (2015b). *Video Steganography Based on Optimized Motion Estimation Perturbation.* ACM Press. doi:10.1145/2756601.2756609

Cauvin, J. M., Le Guillou, C., Solaiman, B., Robaszkiewicz, M., Le Beux, P., & Roux, C. (2003). Computer-assisted diagnosis system in digestive endoscopy. *IEEE Transactions on Information Technology in Biomedicine, 7*(4), 256–262. doi:10.1109/TITB.2003.823293 PMID:15000352

Celik, M. U., Sharma, G., Tekalp, A. M., & Saber, E. (2002). Reversible data hiding. In *Image Processing. 2002. Proceedings. 2002 International Conference on* (Vol. 2, pp. II-II). IEEE. 10.1109/ICIP.2002.1039911

Celik, M., Sharma, G., Tekalp, A., & Saber, E. (2005). Lossless generalized-LSB data embedding. *IEEE Transactions on Image Processing, 14*(2), 253–266. doi:10.1109/TIP.2004.840686 PMID:15700530

Chae, J. J., Mukherjee, D., & Manjunath, B. S. (1998). A robust data hiding technique using multidimensional lattices. *Research and Technology Advances in Digital Libraries, 1998. ADL 98. Proceedings. IEEE International Forum on,* 319-326. 10.1109/ADL.1998.670432

Chamlawi, R., Usman, I., & Khan, A. (2009, December). Dual watermarking method for secure image authentication and recovery. In *Multitopic Conference, 2009. INMIC 2009. IEEE 13th International* (pp. 1-4). IEEE. 10.1109/INMIC.2009.5383118

Chang, G., Yu, B., & Vetterli, M. (2000). Adaptive wavelet thresholding for image denoising and compression. *IEEE Transactions on Image Processing, 9,* 1532–1546. doi:10.1109/83.862633 PMID:18262991

Chang, S., & Vetterli, M. (1997). Spatial adaptive wavelet thresholding for image denoising. *Proc. of the IEEE-ICIP,* 374–377. 10.1109/ICIP.1997.638782

Channalli & Jadhav. (2009). Steganography An Art of Hiding Data. *International Journal on Computer Science and Engineering, 1*(3), 137-141.

Chao, H. M., Hsu, C. M., & Miaou, S. G. (2002). A data-hiding technique with authentication, integration, and confidentiality for electronic patient records. *IEEE Transactions on Information Technology in Biomedicine, 6*(1), 46–53. doi:10.1109/4233.992161 PMID:11936596

Charalambous, C. P. (2014). Walking Patterns of Normal Men. In P. Banaszkiewicz & D. Kader (Eds.), *Classic Papers in Orthopaedics* (pp. 393–395). Springer. doi:10.1007/978-1-4471-5451-8_99

Chaudhary, A., & Vasavada, J. (2012). *A hash based approach for secure keyless image steganography in lossless RGB images*. IEEE. doi:10.1109/ICUMT.2012.6459795

Chawla, Saini, & Kamaldeep. (2012). Classification of Watermarking Based upon Various Parameters. *International Journal of Computer Applications & Information Technology, 1*(2).

Chen, C., Ni, J., & Huang, J. (2009). Temporal statistic based video watermarking scheme robust against geometric attacks and frame dropping. *Digital Watermarking: 8th. International Workshop IWDW 2009, Guildford, UK, August 24-16, 2009, Proceedings*, 81-95.

Chen, B., & Wornell, G. W. (2001). Quantization Index Modulation: A class of provably good methods for digital watermarking and information embedding. *IEEE Transactions on Information Theory, 47*(4), 1423–1443. doi:10.1109/18.923725

Cheng, S., Wu, Q., & Castleman, K. R. (2005, September). Non-ubiquitous digital watermarking for record indexing and integrity protection of medical images. In *Image Processing, 2005. ICIP 2005. IEEE International Conference on* (Vol. 2). IEEE. 10.1109/ICIP.2005.1530242

Chen, G., Mao, Y., & Chui, C. K. (2004). A symmetric image encryption scheme based on 3D chaotic cat maps. *Chaos, Solitons, and Fractals, 21*(3), 749–761. doi:10.1016/j.chaos.2003.12.022

Chen, J., Shan, S., He, C., Zhao, G., Pietikainen, M., Chen, X., & Gao, W. (2010). WLD: A robust local image descriptor. *IEEE Transactions on Pattern Analysis and Machine Intelligence, 32*(9), 1705–1720. doi:10.1109/TPAMI.2009.155 PMID:20634562

Chen, K., & Ramabadran, T. V. (1994). Near-lossless compression of medical images through entropy-coded DPCM. *IEEE Transactions on Medical Imaging, 13*(3), 538–548. doi:10.1109/42.310885 PMID:18218529

Chen, Z., Li, J., & Wei, L. (2007). A multiple kernel support vector machine scheme for feature selection and rule extraction from gene expression data of cancer tissue. *Artificial Intelligence in Medicine, 41*(2), 161–175. doi:10.1016/j.artmed.2007.07.008 PMID:17851055

Chiang, K. H., Chang-Chien, K. C., Chang, R. F., & Yen, H. Y. (2008). Tamper detection and restoring system for medical images using wavelet-based reversible data embedding. *Journal of Digital Imaging, 21*(1), 77–90. doi:10.100710278-007-9012-0 PMID:17333416

Chikkerur, S., Sundaram, V., Reisslein, M., & Karam, L. J. (2011). Objective Video Quality Assessment Methods: A Classification, Review, and Performance Comparison. *IEEE Transactions on Broadcasting, 57*(2), 165–182. doi:10.1109/TBC.2011.2104671

Choubey, D. K., & Paul, S. (2017). GA_SVM-A classification system for diagnosis of diabetes. In Handbook of Research on Nature Inspired Soft Computing and Algorithms. IGI Global.

Choubey, D. K., Paul, S., & Dhandhania, V. K. (2017). GA_NN: An intelligent classification system for diabetes. *Proceedings AISC Series, 7th International Conference on Soft Computing for Problem Solving-SocProS 2017.*

Choubey, D. K., Paul, S., Kumar, S., & Kumar, S. (2017). *Classification of Pima Indian Diabetes Dataset using Naive Bayes with Genetic Algorithm as an Attribute Selection*. CRC Press.

Choubey, D.K., & Paul, S. (2015). GA_J48graft DT: A hybrid intelligent system for diabetes disease diagnosis. *International Journal of Bio-Science and Bio-Technology (IJBSBT), 7*(5), 135–150.

Choubey, D. K., Bhattacharjee, J., & Soni, R. (2013). Loss Minimization of Web Databases by Fine Grain Approach. *International Journal of Engineering Research and Applications, 3*(1), 1437–1444.

Choubey, D. K., & Paul, S. (2016). Classification techniques for diagnosis of diabetes disease: A Review. *International Journal of Biomedical Engineering and Technology (IJBET), 21*(1), 15–39.

Choubey, D. K., & Paul, S. (2016). GA_MLP NN: A hybrid intelligent system for diabetes disease diagnosis. *International Journal of Intelligent Systems and Applications (IJISA), 8*(1), 49–59.

Choubey, D. K., & Paul, S. (2017). GA_RBF NN: A classification system for diabetes. *International Journal of Biomedical Engineering and Technology (IJBET), 23*(1), 71–93.

Choubey, D. K., Paul, S., & Bhattacharjee, J. (2014). Soft computing approaches for diabetes disease diagnosis: A Survey. *International Journal of Applied Engineering Research, RIP, 9*, 11715–11726.

Choubey, D. K., Paul, S., & Dhandhenia, V. K. (2017). Rule based diagnosis system for diabetes, Biomedical Research. *Allied Academies, 28*(12), 5196–5209.

Choubey, D. K., Soni, R., & Bhattacharjee, J. (2012). A Novel approach for Security of Web Databases. *International Journal of Computer Science and Technology, 3*(4), 110–113.

Chrysochos, E., Fotopoulos, V., Skodras, A. N., & Xenos, M. (2007). Reversible image watermarking based on histogram modification. *Proc. 11th Panhellenic Conf. Informatics*, 93-104.

Chung, T.-Y., Hong, M.-S., Oh, Y.-N., Shin, D.-H., & Park, S.-H. (1998, August). Digital watermarking for copyright protection of MPEG2 compressed video. *IEEE Transactions on Consumer Electronics, 44*(3), 895–901. doi:10.1109/30.713211

Clausi, D. A. (2002). An analysis of co-occurrence texture statistics as a function of grey level quantization. *Canadian Journal of Remote Sensing, 28*(1), 45–62. doi:10.5589/m02-004

Coatrieux, G., Lecornu, L., Sankur, B., & Roux, C. (2006, August). A review of image watermarking applications in healthcare. In *Engineering in Medicine and Biology Society, 2006. EMBS'06. 28th Annual International Conference of the IEEE* (pp. 4691-4694). IEEE. 10.1109/IEMBS.2006.259305

Coatrieux, G., Maitre, H., Sankur, B., Rolland, Y., & Collorec, R. (2000). Relevance of watermarking in medical imaging. In *Information Technology Applications in Biomedicine, 2000. Proceedings. 2000 IEEE EMBS International Conference on* (pp. 250-255). IEEE. 10.1109/ITAB.2000.892396

Coatrieux, G., Montagner, J., Huang, H., & Roux, C. (2007, August). Mixed reversible and RONI watermarking for medical image reliability protection. In *Engineering in Medicine and Biology Society, 2007. EMBS 2007. 29th Annual International Conference of the IEEE* (pp. 5653-5656). IEEE. 10.1109/IEMBS.2007.4353629

Coatrieux, G., Puentes, J., Lecornu, L., Le Rest, C. C., & Roux, C. (2006, April). Compliant secured specialized electronic patient record platform. In *Distributed Diagnosis and Home Healthcare, 2006. D2H2. 1st Transdisciplinary Conference on* (pp. 156-159). IEEE. 10.1109/DDHH.2006.1624820

Coatrieux, G., Puentes, J., Roux, C., Lamard, M., & Daccache, W. (2006, January). A low distorsion and reversible watermark: application to angiographic images of the retina. In *Engineering in Medicine and Biology Society, 2005. IEEE-EMBS 2005. 27th Annual International Conference of the* (pp. 2224-2227). IEEE.

Coatrieux, G., Huang, H., Shu, H., Luo, L., & Roux, C. (2013). A watermarking-based medical image integrity control system and an image moment signature for tampering characterization. *IEEE Journal of Biomedical and Health Informatics, 17*(6), 1057–1067. doi:10.1109/JBHI.2013.2263533 PMID:24240724

Coatrieux, G., Le Guillou, C., Cauvin, J. M., & Roux, C. (2009). Reversible watermarking for knowledge digest embedding and reliability control in medical images. *IEEE Transactions on Information Technology in Biomedicine, 13*(2), 158–165. doi:10.1109/TITB.2008.2007199 PMID:19272858

Coatrieux, G., Maitre, H., & Sankur, B. (2001, August). Strict integrity control of biomedical images. In *Security and watermarking of multimedia contents III* (Vol. 4314, pp. 229–241). International Society for Optics and Photonics. doi:10.1117/12.435403

Codella, N. C. F., Nguyen, Q. B., Pankanti, S., Gutman, D. A., Helba, B., Halpern, A. C., & Smith, J. R. (2017). Deep learning ensembles for melanoma recognition in dermoscopy images. *IBM Journal of Research and Development, Volume, 61*(4). doi:10.1147/JRD.2017.2708299

Cole. (2003). *Hiding in plain sight: Steganography and the Art of covert communication.* Academic Press.

Coltuc, D. (2011). Improved Embedding for Prediction-Based Reversible Watermarking. *IEEE Transactions on Information Forensics and Security, 6*(3), 873–882. doi:10.1109/TIFS.2011.2145372

Coltuc, D., & Bolon, P. (1999). Robust watermarking by histogram specification. *Proc. Int. Conf. Image Processing, 2*, 236-239.

Coltuc, D., & Chassery, J. M. (2007). Very fast watermarking by reversible contrast mapping. *IEEE Signal Processing Letters, 14*(4), 255–258. doi:10.1109/LSP.2006.884895

Comak, E., Polat, K., Gunes, S., & Arslan, A. (2007). A new medical decision making system: Least square support vector machine (LSSVM) with fuzzy weighting pre-processing. *Expert Systems with Applications, Elsevier, 32*(2), 409–414. doi:10.1016/j.eswa.2005.12.001

Conti, M., Dehghantanha, A., Franke, K., & Watson, S. (2018). *Internet of Things security and forensics: Challenges and opportunities.* Academic Press.

Cox, I. J., Kilian, J., Leighton, F. T., & Shamoon, T. (1997). Secure spread spectrum watermarking for multimedia. *IEEE Transactions on Image Processing, 6*(12), 1673–1687. doi:10.1109/83.650120 PMID:18285237

Cox, I. J., Kilian, J., Leighton, T., & Shamoon, T. (1996). Secure spread spectrum watermarking for images, audio and video. *Proceedings of 3rd IEEE International Conference on Image Processing*, 243-246. 10.1109/ICIP.1996.560429

Cox, I. J., Miller, M., Bloom, J., Fridrich, J., & Kalker, T. (2007). *Digital Watermarking and Steganography.* Morgan Kaufman.

Crespi, M., Delvaux, M., Schaprio, M., Venables, C., & Zwiebel, F. (1996). Working Party Report by the Committee for Minimal Standards of Terminology and Documentation in Digestive Endoscopy of the European Society of Gastrointestinal Endoscopy. Minimal standard terminology for a computerized endoscopic database. Ad hoc Task Force of the Committee. *The American Journal of Gastroenterology, 91*(2), 191. PMID:8607482

Criminisi, A., Pérez, P., & Toyama, K. (2004). Region filling and object removal by exemplar-based image inpainting. *IEEE Transactions on Image Processing, 13*(9), 1200–1212. doi:10.1109/TIP.2004.833105 PMID:15449582

Dagadu, J. C., & Li, J. (2018). (2018). Context-based watermarking cum chaotic encryption for medical images in telemedicine applications. *Multimedia Tools and Applications.* doi:10.100711042-018-5725-y

Daho, M. E. H., Settouti, N., Lazouni, M. E. A., & Chikh, M. A. (2013). Recognition of diabetes disease using a New hybrid learning algorithm for nefclass. *8th International Workshop on Systems, Signal Processing and their Applications (WoSSPA)*, 239-243.

Dandapat, S., Chutatape, O., & Krishnan, S. M. (2004, October). Perceptual model based data embedding in medical images. In *Image Processing, 2004. ICIP'04. 2004 International Conference on* (Vol. 4, pp. 2315-2318). IEEE. 10.1109/ICIP.2004.1421563

Das, D., & Saharia, S. (2014). Human Gait Analysis and Recognition using Support Vector Machines. *ICCSEA, SPPR, VLSI, WiMoA, SCAI, CNSA, WeST, 2014*, 187–195.

Dash, M., & Liu, H. (1997). Feature selection for classification. *Intelligent Data Analysis Elsevier*, *1*(1-4), 131–156. doi:10.1016/S1088-467X(97)00008-5

de Carvalho, D. F., Chies, R., Freire, A. P., Martimiano, L. A. F., & Goularte, R. (2008). *Video steganography for confidential documents: integrity, privacy and version control*. ACM Press. doi:10.1145/1456536.1456578

De Vleeschouwer, C., Delaigle, J. F., & Macq, B. (2003). Circular interpretation of bijective transformations in lossless watermarking for media asset management. *IEEE Transactions on Multimedia*, *5*(1), 97–105. doi:10.1109/TMM.2003.809729

Delp, E. J. (2005). Multimedia security: The 22nd century approach. *Multimedia Systems*, *11*(2), 95–97. doi:10.100700530-005-0193-4

Deng, L., & Poole, M. S. (2003, January). Learning through telemedicine networks. In *System Sciences, 2003. Proceedings of the 36th Annual Hawaii International Conference on* (pp. 8-pp). IEEE.

De, S., Bhattacharyya, S., Chakraborty, S., & Dutta, P. (2016). *Image Segmentation: A Review*. Hybrid Soft Computing for Multilevel Image and Data Segmentation, Computational Intelligence Methods and Applications. doi:10.1007/978-3-319-47524-0_2

Desai, H. V. (2012, December). Steganography, Cryptography, Watermarking: A Comparative Study. *Journal of Global Research in Computer Science*, *3*(12). doi:10.1109/ICAETR.2014.7012790

Deshmukh, P. R., & Rahangdale, B. (2014). Hash Based Least Significant Bit Technique For Video Steganography. *Int. Journal of Engineering Research and Applications*, *4*(1), 44-49.

Dhanushkodi, S. S. R., & Manivannan, V. (2013). Diagnosis System for Diabetic Retinopathy to Prevent Vision Loss. *Applied Medical Informatics Original Research*, *33*(3), 1–11.

Dhengre, N., Upla, K. P., Patel, H., & Chudasama, V. M. (2017). Bio-medical image fusion based on phase-congruency and guided filter. *2017 Fourth International Conference on Image Information Processing (ICIIP)*, 1-5.10.1109/ICIIP.2017.8313792

Diffie, W., & Hellman, M. (1976, November). New directions in cryptography. *IEEE Transactions on Information Theory*, *22*(6), 644–654. doi:10.1109/TIT.1976.1055638

Dilijonaite, A., Flaglien, A., Sunde, I. M., Hamm, J., Sandvik, J. P., Bjelland, P., & Axelsson, S. (2017). Digital Forensic Readiness. *Digital Forensics*, 117-145.

Dillon, T., Wu, C., & Chang, E. (2010). Cloud Computing: Issues and Challenges. *2010 24th IEEE International Conference on Advanced Information Networking and Applications*, 27-33. 10.1109/AINA.2010.187

Divecha, N. H., & Jani, N. N. (2015). Reversible Watermarking Technique for Medical Images Using Fixed Point Pixel. *2015 Fifth International Conference on Communication Systems and Network Technologies*, 725-730. 10.1109/CSNT.2015.287

Dogantekin, E., Dogantekin, A., Avci, D., & Avci, L. (2010). An intelligent diagnosis system for diabetes on linear discriminant analysis and adaptive network based fuzzy inference system. *LDA–ANFIS, Digital Signal Processing, Elsevier*, *20*(4), 1248–1255. doi:10.1016/j.dsp.2009.10.021

Dong, C., Chen, Y. W., Li, J., & Bai, Y. (2012, May). Zero watermarking for medical images based on DFT and LFSR. In *Computer Science and Automation Engineering (CSAE), 2012 IEEE International Conference on* (Vol. 1, pp. 22-26). IEEE. 10.1109/CSAE.2012.6272540

Dragoi, I., & Coltuc, D. (2014). Local-Prediction-Based Difference Expansion Reversible Watermarking. *IEEE Transactions on Image Processing*, *23*(4), 1779–1790. doi:10.1109/TIP.2014.2307482 PMID:24808346

Durward, B. R., Baer, G. D., & Rowe, P. J. (1999). *Functional Human Movement* (3rd ed.). Edinburgh, UK: Elsevier Science Ltd.

Eberhart, R., & Kennedy, J. (1995). A new optimizer using particle swarm theory. *Proc. 6th Int. Symp. Micro Machine and Human Science (MHS)*, 39–43. 10.1109/MHS.1995.494215

Egmont-Petersen, M., de Ridder, D., & Handels, H. (2002). Image processing using neural networks – a review. *Pattern Recognition*, *35*(10), 2279–2301. doi:10.1016/S0031-3203(01)00178-9

Ekici, O., Coskun, B., Naci, U., & Sankur, B. (2001, November). Comparative assessment of semifragile watermarking techniques. In *Multimedia Systems and Applications IV* (Vol. 4518, pp. 177–189). International Society for Optics and Photonics. doi:10.1117/12.448202

Engelbrecht, A. P. (2006). Particle swarm optimization: Where does it belong? *Proc. IEEE Swarm Intell. Symp*, 48–54.

Ephzibah, E. P. (2011). Cost effective approach on feature selection using genetic algorithms and fuzzy logic for diabetes diagnosis. *International Journal on Soft Computing*, *2*(1), 1–10. doi:10.5121/ijsc.2011.2101

Esteva, A., Kuprel, B., Novoa, R. A., Ko, J., Swetter, S. M., Blau, H. M., & Thrun, S. (2017). *Dermatologist-level classification of skin cancer with deep neural networks, Springer Nature. Macmillan Publishers Limited*. doi:10.1038/nature21056

Eswaraiah, R., & Reddy, E. S. (2014). A Fragile ROI-Based Medical Image Watermarking Technique with Tamper Detection and Recovery. *2014 Fourth International Conference on Communication Systems and Network Technologies*, 896-899. 10.1109/CSNT.2014.184

Farias, Q. M. C. (2010). Video Quality Metrics. In F. De (Ed.), Digital Video. InTech. doi:10.5772/8038

Farid, H., & Lyu, S. (2003, June). Higher-order wavelet statistics and their application to digital forensics. In *Computer Vision and Pattern Recognition Workshop, 2003. CVPRW'03. Conference on* (Vol. 8, pp. 94-94). IEEE. 10.1109/CVPRW.2003.10093

Farid, H. (2009). Image forgery detection. *IEEE Signal Processing Magazine*, *26*(2), 16–25. doi:10.1109/MSP.2008.931079

Filler, T., Judas, J., & Fridrich, J. (2011). Minimizing Additive Distortion in Steganography Using Syndrome-Trellis Codes. *IEEE Transactions on Information Forensics and Security*, *6*(3), 920–935. doi:10.1109/TIFS.2011.2134094

Firmansyah, D. M., & Ahmad, T. (2016). *An improved neighbouring similarity method for video steganography*. IEEE. doi:10.1109/CITSM.2016.7577528

Fontaine, C., & Galand, F. (2007). A survey of homomorphic encryption for nonspecialists. EURASIP Journal on Information Security.

Franke, K., Årnes, A., Flaglien, A., Sunde, I. M., Dilijonaite, A., Hamm, J., & Axelsson, S. (2018). Challenges in Digital Forensics. *Digital Forensics*, 313-317.

Fridrich, J., Goljan, M., & Du, R. (2001, April). Invertible authentication watermark for JPEG images. In *Information Technology: Coding and Computing, 2001. Proceedings. International Conference on* (pp. 223-227). IEEE. 10.1109/ITCC.2001.918795

Fridrich, J., Goljan, M., & Du, R. (2001, August). Invertible authentication. In *Security and Watermarking of Multimedia contents III* (Vol. 4314, pp. 197–209). International Society for Optics and Photonics. doi:10.1117/12.435400

Fu, D., Shi, Y. Q., & Su, W. (2006, November). Detection of image splicing based on hilbert-huang transform and moments of characteristic functions with wavelet decomposition. In *International workshop on digital watermarking* (pp. 177-187). Springer. 10.1007/11922841_15

Furht, B., Smoliar, S. W., & Zhang, H. (1995). *Video and Image Processing in Multimedia Systems*. Boston, MA: Springer US. doi:10.1007/978-1-4615-2277-5

Gaba, J., & Kumar, M. (2013). Implementation of steganography using CES technique. *2013 IEEE Second International Conference on Image Information Processing (ICIIP-2013)*, 395-399. 10.1109/ICIIP.2013.6707622

Ganji, M. F., & Abadeh, M. S. (2010). Using fuzzy ant colony optimization for diagnosis of diabetes disease. *Proceedings of ICEE 2010*, 501-505.

Ganji, M. F., & Abadeh, M. S. (2011). A fuzzy classification system based on ant colony optimization for diabetes disease diagnosis. *Expert Systems with Applications, Elsevier*, *38*(12), 14650–14659. doi:10.1016/j.eswa.2011.05.018

Garbe, C., Peris, K., Hauschild, A., Saiag, P., Middleton, M., Bastholt, L., ... Pehamberger, H. (2016). Diagnosis and treatment of melanoma. European consensus-based interdisciplinary guideline. *European Journal of Cancer*, *63*, 201–217. doi:10.1016/j.ejca.2016.05.005 PMID:27367293

Garimella, A., Satyanarayana, M. V. V., Kumar, R. S., Murugesh, P. S., & Niranjan, U. C. (2003, January). VLSI implementation of online digital watermarking technique with difference encoding for 8-bit gray scale images. In *VLSI Design, 2003. Proceedings. 16th International Conference on* (pp. 283-288). IEEE.

Ghosh Dastidar, J., & Biswas, R. (2015). Tracking human intrusion through a CCTV. In IEEE conference CICN. IEEE. doi:10.1109/CICN.2015.95

Ghosh, S., Kundu, B., Datta, D., Maity, S. P., & Rahaman, H. (2014, February). Design and implementation of fast FPGA based architecture for reversible watermarking. In *Electrical Information and Communication Technology (EICT), 2013 International Conference on* (pp. 1-6). IEEE. 10.1109/EICT.2014.6777819

Ghosh, A., Pal, N. R., & Pal, S. K. (1993). Self organization for object extraction using a multilayer neural network and fuzziness measures. *IEEE Transactions on Fuzzy Systems*, *1*(1), 54–68. doi:10.1109/TFUZZ.1993.390285

Giakoumaki, A., Pavlopoulos, S., & Koutouris, D. (2003, September). A medical image watermarking scheme based on wavelet transform. In *Engineering in medicine and biology society, 2003. Proceedings of the 25th annual international conference of the IEEE* (Vol. 1, pp. 856-859). IEEE. 10.1109/IEMBS.2003.1279900

Giakoumaki, A., Pavlopoulos, S., & Koutsouris, D. (2006). Multiple image watermarking applied to health information management. *IEEE Transactions on Information Technology in Biomedicine*, *10*(4), 722–732. doi:10.1109/TITB.2006.875655 PMID:17044406

Giotis, I., Molders, N., Land, S., Biehl, M., Jonkman, M. F., & Petkov, N. (2015). MED-NODE: A computer-assisted melanoma diagnosis system using non-dermoscopic images. Expert Systems with Applications, 42, 6578–6585.

Girdhar, A., & Kumar, V. (2018). Comprehensive survey of 3D image steganography techniques. IET Image Processing, 12(1), 1-10. doi:10.1049/iet-ipr.2017.0162

Glover, F. (1986). Future paths for integer programming and links to artificial intelligence. *Computers & Operations Research, 13*(5), 533–549. doi:10.1016/0305-0548(86)90048-1

Goljan, M., Fridrich, J., & Du, R. (2001). Distortion-free data embedding for images. *Information Hiding, 2137*, 27–41. doi:10.1007/3-540-45496-9_3

Goncalves, L., Bernardes, M. M., & Vellasco, R. (2006). Inverted Hierarchical Neuro-Fuzzy BSP System: A Novel Neuro-Fuzzy Model for Pattern Classification and Rule Extraction in Databases. *IEEE Transactions on Systems, Man, and Cybernetics—Part C: Applications and Reviews, 36*(2), 236-248.

Goncalves, L. B., Vellasco, M. M. B. R., & Pacheco, M. A. C. (2006). Inverted hierarchical neuro-fuzzy BSP System: A novel neuro-fuzzy model for pattern classification and rule extraction in databases. *IEEE Transactions on Systems, Man and Cybernetics. Part C, Applications and Reviews, 36*(2), 236–248. doi:10.1109/TSMCC.2004.843220

Gonzalez, R. C., & Woods, R. E. (2009). Digital Image Processing (3rd ed.). Pearson Education.

Gosalia, S., Shetty, S. A., & Revathi, S. (2016). Embedding Audio inside a Digital Video Using LSB Steganography. *3rd IEEE International Conference on Computing for Sustainable Global Development (INDIACom)*, 2650 – 2653.

Guo, X., & Zhuang, T. G. (2009). Lossless watermarking for verifying the integrity of medical images with tamper localization. *Journal of Digital Imaging, 22*(6), 620–628. doi:10.100710278-008-9120-5 PMID:18473141

Gupta & Brar. (2013). An Enhanced Security Technique for Storage of Multimedia Content over Cloud Server. *International Journal of Engineering Research and Applications, 3*(4), 2273-2277.

Gupta Banik, B., & Bandyopadhyay, S. K. (2015). Review on Steganography in Digital Media. *International Journal of Science and Research, 4*(2), 265–274. doi:10.21275/SUB151127

Gupta, B. B. (2017). *Advances in Security and Privacy of Multimedia Big Data in Mobile and Cloud Computing*. Springer.

Hamed, G., Marey, M., El-Sayed, S. A., & Tolba, M. F. (2016). Comparative study for various DNA based steganography techniques with the essential conclusions about the future research. *2016 11th International Conference on Computer Engineering & Systems (ICCES)*, 220-225. 10.1109/ICCES.2016.7822003

Hamid, N., Yahya, A., Ahmad, R. B., & Al-Qershi, O. (2012). Characteristic region based image steganography using Speeded-Up Robust Features technique. *2012 International Conference on Future Communication Networks*, 141-146. 10.1109/ICFCN.2012.6206858

Hamm, J., Flaglien, A., Sunde, I. M., Dilijonaite, A., Sandvik, J. P., Bjelland, P., & Axelsson, S. (2018). Computer Forensics. *Digital Forensics*, 147-190.

Hanafy, A. A., Salama, G. I., & Mohasseb, Y. Z. (2008). *A secure covert communication model based on video steganography*. IEEE. doi:10.1109/MILCOM.2008.4753107

Han, G., & Jiao, Y. (2016). Feature selection and regional labeling of significant detection for pulmonary nodules in CT images. *2016 IEEE International Conference on Signal and Image Processing (ICSIP)*, 60-63. 10.1109/SIPROCESS.2016.7888224

Hao-Bin, Li-Yi, & Wei-Dong. (2011). *A novel steganography algorithm based on motion vector and matrix encoding*. IEEE. 10.1109/ICCSN.2011.6013622

Haralick, R. M., Shanmugam, K., & Dinstein, I. (1973, November). Textural Features of Image Classification. *IEEE Transactions on Systems, Man, and Cybernetics*, *SMC-3*(6), 610–621. doi:10.1109/TSMC.1973.4309314

Hardie, R. C., & Barner, K. E. (1994, March). Rank conditioned rank selection filters for signal restoration. *IEEE Transactions on Image Processing*, *3*(2), 192–206. doi:10.1109/83.277900 PMID:18291919

Hartley, R. V. L. (1942). A More Symmetrical Fourier Analysis Applied to Transmission Problems. *Proceedings of the IRE.*, *30*(3), 144–150. doi:10.1109/JRPROC.1942.234333

Hartung, F., & Kutter, M. (1999, July). Multimedia watermarking techniques. *Proceedings of the IEEE*, *87*(7), 1079–1107. doi:10.1109/5.771066

Haskell, B. G., & Puri, A. (2012). MPEG Video Compression Basics. In L. Chiariglione (Ed.), *The MPEG Representation of Digital Media* (pp. 7–38). New York, NY: Springer New York. doi:10.1007/978-1-4419-6184-6_2

Hassanat, A. B., Abbadi, M. A., & Altarawneh, G. A. (2014). Solving the Problem of the K Parameter in the KNN Classifier Using an Ensemble Learning Approach. *International Journal of Computer Science and Information Security*, *12*(8), 2014.

Haykin, S. (1999). *Neural Networks: A Comprehensive Foundation* (2nd ed.). Upper Saddle River, NJ: Prentice Hall.

Hecht-Nielsen, R. (1987). Kolmogorov's mapping neural network existence theorem. *IEEE First Annual International Conference on Neural Networks*, 11-13.

He, D., Zhang, Y., & Song, H. (2010). A novel saliency map extraction method based on improved Itti's model. *2010 International Conference on Computer and Communication Technologies in Agriculture Engineering*, 323-327. doi: 10.1109/CCTAE.2010.5544608

He, H. J., Zhang, J. S., & Tai, H. M. (2009, June). Self-recovery fragile watermarking using block-neighborhood tampering characterization. In *International Workshop on Information Hiding* (pp. 132-145). Springer. 10.1007/978-3-642-04431-1_10

Hernandez, J. R., Amado, M., & Perez-Gonzalez, F. (2000, January). DCT-domain watermarking techniques for still images: Detector performance analysis and a new structure. *IEEE Transactions on Image Processing*, *9*(1), 55–68. doi:10.1109/83.817598 PMID:18255372

Herrera-Joancomarti, J., Katzenbeisser, S., Megias, D., Minguillon, J., Pommer, A., Steinebach, M., & Uhl, A. (2005). *First summary report on hybrid systems*. EU project ECRYPT (European Network of Excellence in Cryptology), Deliverable D.WVL.5.

Hilbert, M., & López, P. (2011). The world's technological capacity to store, communicate, and compute information. *Science, 332*(6025), 60-65.

Hong, I., & Potkonjak, M. (1998). Techniques for intellectual property protection of DSP designs. *Acoustics, Speech and Signal Processing, 1998. Proceedings of the 1998 IEEE International Conference on*, 3133-3136. 10.1109/ICASSP.1998.678190

Hong, W., Chen, T., & Shiu, C. (2009). Reversible data hiding for high quality images using modification of prediction errors. *Journal of Systems and Software*, *82*(11), 1833–1842. doi:10.1016/j.jss.2009.05.051

Honsinger, C. (2002). Digital watermarking. *Journal of Electronic Imaging*, *11*(3), 414. doi:10.1117/1.1494075

Hopfield, J. J. (1984). Neurons with graded response have collective computational properties like those of two state neurons. *Proceedings of the National Academy of Sciences of the United States of America*, *1984*(10), 3088–3092. doi:10.1073/pnas.81.10.3088 PMID:6587342

Hou, X., & Zhang, L. (2007). Saliency detection: a spectral residual approach. *IEEE Conference on Computer Vision and Pattern.*

Hrsa.gov. (2014). *HHS Budget Makes Smart Investments, Protects the Health and Safety America's Families.* Available at: http://www.hrsa.gov/about/news/pressreleases/2010/100201a.html http://www.internetlivestats.com/internet-users/ https://pulse.embs.org/january-2017/electronic-health-records-data-delivers-better-patient-outcomes/

Hsu, C.-T., & Wu, J.-L. (1999, January). Hidden digital watermarks in images. *IEEE Transactions on Image Processing,* 8(1), 58–68. doi:10.1109/83.736686 PMID:18262865

Hu, S. D., & U, K. T. (2011). *A Novel Video Steganography Based on Non-Uniform Rectangular Partition.* IEEE. 10.1109/CSE.2011.24

Huang, H., Coatrieux, G., Shu, H. Z., Luo, L. M., & Roux, C. (2010, July). Medical image tamper approximation based on an image moment signature. In *e-Health Networking Applications and Services (Healthcom), 2010 12th IEEE International Conference on* (pp. 254-259). IEEE. 10.1109/HEALTH.2010.5556561

Huang, H., Coatrieux, G., Shu, H., Luo, L., & Roux, C. (2012). Blind integrity verification of medical images. *IEEE Transactions on Information Technology in Biomedicine,* 16(6), 1122–1126. doi:10.1109/TITB.2012.2207435 PMID:22801523

Huang, J., & Shi, Y. Q. (1998). Adaptive Image Watermarking Scheme Based on Visual masking. *Electronics Letters,* 34(8), 748–750. doi:10.1049/el:19980545

Huang, Y., Lin, S., Stan, Z., Lu, H., & Shum, V. (2004). Face Alignment under Variable Illumination. *IEEE International Conference on Automatic Face and Gesture Recognition.*

Huang, Y., Lin, S., Stan, Z., Lu, H., & Shum, V. (2004). Noise removal and impainting model for iris image. *International Conference on Image Processing.*

Hu, M. K. (1962). Visual pattern recognition by moment invariants. *I.R.E. Transactions on Information Theory,* 8(2), 179–187. doi:10.1109/TIT.1962.1057692

Hussain, N., Wageeh, B., & Colin, B. (2013). A Review of Medical Image Watermarking Requirements for Teleradiology. *Journal of Digital Imaging,* 26(2), 326–343. doi:10.100710278-012-9527-x PMID:22975883

Hu, Y., Lee, H., & Li, J. (2009). DE-Based Reversible Data Hiding with Improved Overflow Location Map. *IEEE Transactions on Circuits and Systems for Video Technology,* 19(2), 250–260. doi:10.1109/TCSVT.2008.2009252

Hwai-Tsu, H., & Ling-Yuan, H. (2016). A mixed modulation scheme for blind image watermarking. *International Journal of Electronics and Communications,* 70(2), 172–178. doi:10.1016/j.aeue.2015.11.003

Idbeaa, T. F., Samad, S. A., & Husain, H. (2015). *An adaptive compressed video steganography based on pixel-value differencing schemes.* IEEE. doi:10.1109/ATC.2015.7388379

Imran, M., Hashim, R., & Khalid, R. N. E. A. (2012). An overview of particle swarm optimization variants. In *Malaysian Technical Universities Conference on Engineering & Technology.* Elsevier.

Imran, U., Asifullah, K., Rafiullah, C., & Abdul, M. (2008). *Towards a Better Robustness-Imperceptibility Tradeoff in Digital Watermarking.* Innovations and Advanced Techniques in Systems, Computing Sciences and Software Engineering.

International Diabetes Federation. (2007). *Diabetes Atlas* (3rd ed.). Brussels, Belgium: International Diabetes Federation.

İsmail, A. (2001). *Image Quality Statistics And Their Use In Steganalysis and Compression* (PhD Thesis). Institute for Graduate Studies in Science and Engineering, Uludağ University.

Ismail, A., Bulent, S., & Khalid, S. (2002). Statistical Evaluation of Image Quality Measures. *Journal of Electronic Imaging*, *11*(2), 206–223. doi:10.1117/1.1455011

Itti, L., & Koch, C. (2000). A saliency-based search mechanism for overt and covert shifts of visual attention. *Vision Research*, *40*(10-12), 1489–1506. doi:10.1016/S0042-6989(99)00163-7 PMID:10788654

Itti, L., & Koch, C. (2001). Computational Modeling of Visual Attention. Nature Reviews. *Neuroscience*, *2*(3), 194–203. doi:10.1038/35058500 PMID:11256080

Itti, L., Koch, C., & Niebur, E. (1998, November). A model of saliency-based visual attention for rapid scene analysis. *IEEE Transactions on Pattern Analysis and Machine Intelligence*, *20*(11), 1254–1259. doi:10.1109/34.730558

Iyatomi, H., Tanahashi, Y., Oka, H., Tanaka, M., & Ogawa, K. (2006). Classification of blue nevus from other lesions for Internet-based melanoma diagnostic system. *SCIS & ISIS2006*, 1995-2000.

Iyatomi, H., Oka, H., Hashimoto, M., Tanaka, M., & Ogawa, K. (2005). *An Internet-based Melanoma Diagnostic System toward the Practical Application*. IEEE. doi:10.1109/CIBCB.2005.1594952

Izquierdo, E., & Macq, B. (2003, August). Introduction to the special issue on authentication, copyright protection, and information hiding. *IEEE Transactions on Circuits and Systems for Video Technology*, *13*(8), 729–731. doi:10.1109/TCSVT.2003.817838

Jaiswal, S. P., Au, O. C., Jakhetiya, V., Guo, Y., Tiwari, A. K., & Yue, K. (2013). Efficient adaptive prediction based reversible image watermarking. *IEEE International Conference on Image Processing*, 4540-4544. 10.1109/ICIP.2013.6738935

Jalal, F., Jalil, F., & Peter, W. (1999). *Digital Certificates: Applied Internet Security* (Vol. 1). Addison- Wesley.

James, B. D. (2008). *A Multimedia – Based Threat Management and Information Security Framework*. IGI Global.

James, B. D., & Joshi, A. (2006). *Multimedia – Based Threat Management and Information Security Framework*. IGI Global.

Janeczko Paul, B. (2006). *Top Secret: A Handbook of Codes, Ciphers and Secret Writing*. Candlewick Press.

Jaseena & John. (2011). Text Watermarking using Combined Image and Text for Authentication and Protection. *International Journal of Computer Applications, 20*(4).

Jasim Mohammed, S. (2013). Implementation of Encoder for (31, k) Binary BCH Code based on FPGA for Multiple Error Correction Control. *International Journal of Computers and Applications*, *76*(11), 23–28. doi:10.5120/13291-0815

Jayalakshmi, T., & Santhakumaran, A. (2010). A novel classification method for diagnosis of diabetes mellitus using artificial neural networks. *International Conference on Data Storage and Data Engineering*, 159-163. 10.1109/DSDE.2010.58

Jianquan, X., Qing, X., Dazu, H., & Duosi, X. (2010). Research on imperceptibility index of image Information Hiding. *Second International Conference on Networks Security Wireless Communications and Trusted Computing (NSWCTC)*. 10.1109/NSWCTC.2010.148

Jiansheng, Q., Dong, W., Li, L. C. D., & Xuesong, W. (2014). Image quality assessment based on multiscale representation of structure. *Digital Signal Processing*, *33*, 125–133. doi:10.1016/j.dsp.2014.06.009

Jianzhong, L., & Xiaojing, C. (2009). An adaptive secure watermarking scheme using double randomphase encoding technique. *2nd International Congress on Image and Signal Processing, CISP '09*.

Jia, W., Zhao, D., Shen, T., Su, C., Hu, C., & Zhao, Y. (2014). A new optimized GA-RBF neural network algorithm, Computational Intelligence and Neuroscience. *Hindawi Publishing Corporation*, *2014*, 1–6.

Jinchuan, K., & Xinzhe, L. (2008). Empirical analysis of optimal hidden neurons in neural network modeling for stock prediction. *Proceedings of the Pacific-Asia Workshop on Computational Intelligence and Industrial Application, 2*, 828–832.

Job, D., & Paul, V. (2016). *An efficient video Steganography technique for secured data transmission.* IEEE. doi:10.1109/SAPIENCE.2016.7684125

Johnson, N. F., Duric, Z., & Jajodia, S. (2001). *Information Hiding: Steganography and Watermarking-Attacks and Countermeasures: Steganography and Watermarking: Attacks and Countermeasures* (Vol. 1). Springer Science & Business Media. doi:10.1007/978-1-4615-4375-6

Jose, J. A., & Titus, G. (2013). *Data hiding using motion histogram.* IEEE. doi:10.1109/ICCCI.2013.6466269

Joshi, M., Raval, M. S., Dandawate, Y., Joshi, K., & Metkar, S. (2014). *Image and video compression* (1st ed.). Boca Raton, FL: CRC Press, Taylor and Francis. doi:10.1201/b17738

Joshi, V., Raval, M. S., Gupta, D., Rege, P., & Parulkar, S. (2015). A multiple reversible watermarking technique for fingerprint authentication. *Multimedia Systems, 22*(3), 367–378. doi:10.100700530-015-0465-6

Jouini, Rabai, & Aissa. (2014). Classification of security threats in information systems. *ScienceDirect 5th International Conference on Ambient Systems, Networks and Technologies (ANT-2014).* doi: 10.1016/j.procs.2014.05.452

Jouini, M., & Latifa, B. A. R. (2016). Comparative Study of Information Security Risk Assessment Models for Cloud Computing systems. *Procedia Computer Science, 83*, 1084–1089. doi:10.1016/j.procs.2016.04.227

Jue, W., Min-qing, Z., & Juan-li, S. (2011). *Video steganography using motion vector components.* IEEE. doi:10.1109/ICCSN.2011.6013642

Kahn, D. (1996). The history of steganography. In R. Anderson (Ed.), Lecture Notes in Computer Science: Vol. 1174. *Information Hiding. IH 1996.* Berlin: Springer.

Kahramanli, H., & Allahverdi, N. (2008). Design of a hybrid system for the diabetes and heart diseases. *Expert Systems with Applications, Elsevier, 35*(1-2), 82–89. doi:10.1016/j.eswa.2007.06.004

Kala, R., Vazirani, H., Khanwalkar, N., & Bhattacharya, M. (2010). Evolutionary radial basis function network for classificatory problems. *International Journal of Computer Science and Applications, 7*(4), 34-49.

Kalaiselvi, C., & Nasira, G. M. (2014). A new aproach for diagnosis of diabetes and prediction of cancer using ANFIS. *IEEE: World Congress on Computing and Communication Technologies*, 188-190.

Kalaivani, K., & Sivakumar, B. R. (2012). Survey on Multimedia Data Security. *International Journal of Modeling and Optimization, 2*(1).

Kalaivani, K., & Sivakumar, R. (2011). Survey on Multimedia Data Security. *International Conference on Signal, Image Processing and Applications With workshop of ICEEA 2011.*

Kala, R., Janghel, R. R., Tiwari, R., & Shukla, A. (2011). A. Diagnosis of Breast Cancer by Modular Evolutionary Neural Networks. *International Journal of Biomedical Engineering and Technology, 7*(2), 194–211. doi:10.1504/IJBET.2011.043179

Kamgar-Parsi, B. (1995). Automatic target extraction in infrared images. *NRL Review*, 143–146.

Kamp, S., Heyden, D., & Ohm, J.-R. (2007). *Inter-temporal vector prediction for motion estimation in scalable video coding.* IEEE. doi:10.1109/ISPACS.2007.4445955

Kamstra, L., & Heijmans, H. J. A. M. (2005, December). Reversible data embedding into images using wavelet techniques and sorting. *IEEE Transactions on Image Processing*, *14*(12), 2082–2090. doi:10.1109/TIP.2005.859373 PMID:16370461

Kanithi, A. K. (2011). *Study of Spatial and Transform Domain Filters for Efficient Noise Reduction* (Master's thesis). NIT Rourkela, India.

Karahoca, A., Karahoca, D., & Kara, A. (2009). Diagnosis of Diabetes by using Adaptive Neuro Fuzzy Inference Systems. *Fifth International Conference on Soft Computing, Computing with Words and Perceptions in System Analysis, Decision and Control*, 1-4. 10.1109/ICSCCW.2009.5379497

Karatsiolis, S., & Schizas, C. N. (2012). Region based support vector machine algorithm for medical diagnosis on pima Indian diabetes dataset. *Proceedings of the 2012 IEEE 12th International Conference on Bioinformatics & Bioengineering (BIBE)*, 139-144. 10.1109/BIBE.2012.6399663

Karegowda, A. G., Manjunath, A. S., & Jayaram, M. A. (2011). Application of genetic algorithm optimized neural network connection weights for medical diagnosis of pima Indians diabetes. *International Journal on Soft Computing*, *2*(2), 15–23. doi:10.5121/ijsc.2011.2202

Karthigaikumar, P., & Baskaranc Anumol, K. (2011). FPGA Implementation of High Speed Low Area DWT Based Invisible Image Watermarking Algorithm. *International Conference on Communication Technology and System Design*.

Katariya. (2012). Digital Watermarking: Review. *International Journal of Engineering and Innovative Technology*, *1* (2).

Kaur, Pooja, & Varsha. (2016). *A hybrid approach for video steganography using edge detection and identical match techniques*. IEEE. 10.1109/WiSPNET.2016.7566255

Kaur, H., & Kaur, V. (2016). *Invisible video multiple watermarking using optimized techniques*. IEEE. doi:10.1109/GET.2016.7916675

Kaur, N., & Behal, S. (2014). A Survey on various types of Steganography and Analysis of Hiding Techniques. *International Journal of Engineering Trends and Technology*, *11*(8), 388–392. doi:10.14445/22315381/IJETT-V11P276

Kaushal, S., Upamanyu, M., Manjunath, B. S., & Shiv, C. (2005). Modeling the Print-Scan Process for Resilient Data Hiding, Security, Steganography, and Watermarking of Multimedia Contents. *SPIE*, *5681*, 418–429.

Kautilya. (1992). *The Arthashastra* (L. N. Rangarajan, Trans.). Penguin Books India.

Kayaer, K., & Yildirim, T. (2003). Medical diagnosis on pima indian diabetes using general regression neural networks. *Proceedings of the International Conference on Artificial Neural Networks and Neural Information Processing*, 181-184.

Ke, N., & Zhong, W. (2013). *A video steganography scheme based on H.264 bitstreams replaced*. IEEE. doi:10.1109/ICSESS.2013.6615345

Kennedy, J., & Eberhart, R. (1995). Particle swarm optimization. *Proc. IEEE Int. Conf. Neural Netw. (ICNN)*, *4*, 1942–1948.

Kennedy, J., & Eberhart, R. C. (1995). Particle Swarm Optimization. *Proceedings of the IEEE international conference on neural networks IV*, 1942–1948. 10.1109/ICNN.1995.488968

Keskinarkaus, A., Pramila, A., & Seppänen, T. (2012). Image watermarking with feature point based synchronization robust to print–scan attack. *Journal of Visual Communication and Image Representation*, *23*(3), 507–515. doi:10.1016/j.jvcir.2012.01.010

Kester, Q. A., Nana, L., Pascu, A. C., Gire, S., Eghan, J. M., & Quaynor, N. N. (2015, June). A Security Technique for Authentication and Security of Medical Images in Health Information Systems. In *Computational Science and Its Applications (ICCSA), 2015 15th International Conference on* (pp. 8-13). IEEE. 10.1109/ICCSA.2015.8

Khan, A., & Malik, S. A. (2014). A high capacity reversible watermarking approach for authenticating images: Exploiting down-sampling, histogram processing, and block selection. *Information Sciences, 256,* 162–183. doi:10.1016/j.ins.2013.07.035

Khare, R., Mishra, R., & Arya, I. (2014). *Video Steganography Using LSB Technique by Neural Network.* IEEE. doi:10.1109/CICN.2014.189

Kharittha, T., Pipat, S., & Thumrongrat, A. (2015). Digital Image Watermarking based on Regularized Filter. *14th IAPR International Conference on Machine Vision Applications.*

Ki-Hyeok, B., & Sung-Hwan, J. (2001). A study on the robustness of watermark according to frequency band. *IEEE International Symposium on Industrial Electronics.* 10.1109/ISIE.2001.932024

Kim, B. S., Kwon, K. K., Kwon, S. G., Park, K. N., Song, K. I., & Lee, K. I. (2002, July). A robust wavelet-based digital watermarking using statistical characteristic of image and human visual system. In *Proc. of ITC-CSCC* (Vol. 2, pp. 1019-1022). Academic Press.

Kim, C. Y. (1998). Compression of color medical images in gastrointestinal endoscopy: A review. *Studies in Health Technology and Informatics, 52,* 1046–1050. PMID:10384620

Kirkpatrick, S., Gelatt, C. D., & Vecchi, M. P. (1983, May 13). Optimization by Simulated Annealing, Science. *New Series, 220*(4598), 671–680. PMID:17813860

Kobayashi, L. O., & Furuie, S. S. (2009). Proposal for DICOM multiframe medical image integrity and authenticity. *Journal of Digital Imaging, 22*(1), 71–83. doi:10.100710278-008-9103-6 PMID:18266035

Kohonen, T. (1984). *Self-organization and Associative Memory.* London: Springer-Verlag.

Kolmogorov, A. N. (1957). *On the representational of continuous functions of many variables by superpositions of continuous functional of one variable and addition.* Doklady Akademii Nauk, USSR.

Kong, X., & Feng, R. (2001). Watermarking medical signals for telemedicine. *IEEE Transactions on Information Technology in Biomedicine, 5*(3), 195–201. doi:10.1109/4233.945290 PMID:11550841

Kononenko, I. (1997). Overcoming the myopia of inductive learning algorithms with RELIEFF. *Applied Intelligence, 7*(1), 39–55.

Kothari, L., Thakkar, R., & Khara, S. (2017). Data hiding on web using combination of Steganography and Cryptography. *2017 International Conference on Computer, Communications and Electronics (Comptelix),* 448-452. 10.1109/COMPTELIX.2017.8004011

Kother Mohideen, S., Arumuga Perumal, S., & Mohamed Sathik, M. (2008). Image De-noising using Discrete Wavelet transform. *International Journal of Computer Science and Network Security, 8*(1).

Kovesi, P. (1996). *Invariant Measures of Image Features From Phase Information* (PhD Thesis). The University of Western Australia.

Kovesi, P. (1997). Symmetry and Asymmetry From Local Phase. *AI'97, Tenth Australian Joint Conference on Artificial Intelligence. 2 - 4 December 1997. Proceedings - Poster Papers,* 185-190.

Kovesi. (1999). Image Features From Phase Congruency. *Videre: A Journal of Computer Vision Research, 1*(3).

Kovesi, P. (2002). Edges Are Not Just Steps. *Proceedings of ACCV2002 The Fifth Asian Conference on Computer Vision,* 822-827.

Kovesi, P. (2003). Phase Congruency Detects Corners and Edges. *The Australian Pattern Recognition Society Conference: Digital Image Computing: Techniques and Applications DICTA 2003*, 309-318.

Kumar, S. U., Inbarani, H. H., & Kumar, S. S. (2013). Bijectives soft based classification of medical data. *Proceedings of the 2013 International Conference on Pattern Recognition, Informatics and Mobile Engineering*, 517-521. 10.1109/ICPRIME.2013.6496725

Kumar, S., & Dutta, A. (2016). A study on robustness of block entropy based digital image watermarking techniques with respect to various attacks. *2016 IEEE International Conference on Recent Trends in Electronics, Information & Communication Technology (RTEICT)*, 1802-1806. 10.1109/RTEICT.2016.7808145

Kundu, M., Sengupta D., & Ghosh Dastidar, J. (2014). Tracking direction of human movement – an efficient implementation using skeleton. *International Journal of Computer Applications*, *96*(13), 27-33.

Kundur & Okorafor. (2008). Security and Privacy for Distributed Multimedia Sensor Networks. *Proceedings of the IEEE*, *96*(1).

Kundur, D., & Hatzinakos, D. (1998, May). Digital watermarking using multiresolution wavelet decomposition. In *Acoustics, Speech and Signal Processing, 1998. Proceedings of the 1998 IEEE International Conference on* (Vol. 5, pp. 2969-2972). IEEE.

Kundur, D., & Hatzinakos, D. (1997). A robust digital image watermarking method using wavelet-based fusion. *Proceedings of International Conference on Image Processing*, 544-547. 10.1109/ICIP.1997.647970

Kundur, D., & Hatzinakos, D. (1998). Improved robust watermarking through attack characterization. *Optics Express*, *3*(12), 485–490. doi:10.1364/OE.3.000485 PMID:19384399

Kundur, D., & Hatzinakos, D. (1999). Digital watermarking for telltale tamper proofing and authentication. *Proceedings of the IEEE*, *87*(7), 1167–1180. doi:10.1109/5.771070

Kurkova, V. (1992). Kolmogorov's theorem and multilayer neural networks. *Neural Networks*, *5*(3), 501–506. doi:10.1016/0893-6080(92)90012-8

Kutter, M., & Petitcolas, F. A. (1999, April). Fair benchmark for image watermarking systems. In *Security and Watermarking of Multimedia Contents* (Vol. 3657, pp. 226–240). International Society for Optics and Photonics. doi:10.1117/12.344672

Lach, J., Mangione-Smith, W. H., & Potkonjak, M. (1998). Signature hiding techniques for FPGA intellectual property protection. *1998 IEEE/ACM International Conference on Computer-Aided Design. Digest of Technical Papers*, 186-189. 10.1145/288548.288606

Lagendijk, R.-L., Erkin, Z., & Barni, M. (2013). Encrypted signal processing for privacy protection. *IEEE Signal Processing Magazine*, *30*(1), 82–105. doi:10.1109/MSP.2012.2219653

Lai, D., Xiong, B., & Kuang, G. (2017). Weak target detection in SAR images via improved itti visual saliency model. *2017 2nd International Conference on Frontiers of Sensors Technologies (ICFST)*, 260-264. 10.1109/ICFST.2017.8210515

Lai, C. C., & Tsai, C. C. (2010, November). Digital Image Watermarking Using Discrete Wavelet Transform and Singular Value Decomposition. *IEEE Transactions on Instrumentation and Measurement*, *59*(11), 3060–3063. doi:10.1109/TIM.2010.2066770

Lakshmi, K., & Hemalatha, J., & Basha, F. (2017). K-Anonymous Privacy Preserving Technique for Participatory Sensing With Multimedia Data Over Cloud Computing. *International Journal of Computer Engineering In Research Trends*, *4*(2), 48-52.

Lamba, A., & Kumar, D. (2016). Optimization of KNN with Firefly Algorithm. *BIJIT - BVICAM's International Journal of Information Technology*, 997–1003.

Laskaris, N., Ballerini, L., Fisher, R. B., Aldridge, B., & Rees, J. (2010). Fuzzy Description of Skin Lesions. *SPIE Proceedings, 7627*.

Latham, A. (1999). *Steganography*. Retrieved from http://linux01.gwdg.de/ alatham/stego.html

Le Guillou, C., Cauvin, J. M., Solaiman, B., Robaszkiewicz, M., & Roux, C. (2000, November). Information processing in upper digestive endoscopy. In *Information Technology Applications in Biomedicine, 2000. Proceedings. 2000 IEEE EMBS International Conference on* (pp. 183-188). IEEE. 10.1109/ITAB.2000.892383

Lee, H. K., Kim, H. J., Kwon, K. R., & Lee, J. K. (2005, June). Digital watermarking of medical image using ROI information. In *Enterprise networking and Computing in Healthcare Industry, 2005. HEALTHCOM 2005. Proceedings of 7th International Workshop on* (pp. 404-407). IEEE.

Lee, C. S., & Wang, M. H. (2011). A fuzzy expert system for diabetes decision support application. *IEEE Transactions on Systems, Man, and Cybernetics. Part B, Cybernetics, 41*(1), 139–153. doi:10.1109/TSMCB.2010.2048899 PMID:20501347

Lehmann, T. M., Güld, M. O., Thies, C., Fischer, B., Spitzer, K., Keysers, D., ... Wein, B. B. (2004). Content-based image retrieval in medical applications. *Methods of Information in Medicine, 43*(4), 354–361. doi:10.1055-0038-1633877 PMID:15472746

Leon-Garcia, A. (1994). *Probability and random processes for electrical engineering*. Addison-Wesley.

Letaba, P., Pretorius, M. W., & Pretorius, L. (2015). Analysis of the intellectual structure and evolution of technology roadmapping literature. *2015 Portland International Conference on Management of Engineering and Technology (PIC-MET)*, 2248-2254. 10.1109/PICMET.2015.7273147

Li, C., & Liu, L. (2008, May). An image authentication scheme with localization and recovery. In Image and Signal Processing, 2008. CISP'08. Congress on (Vol. 5, pp. 669-673). IEEE. doi:10.1109/CISP.2008.374

Li, D., Yang, C., Li, C., Jiang, Q., Chen, X., Ma, J., & Ren, J. (2017). A Client – based Secure Deduplication of Multimedia Data. *IEEE ICC 2017 Communication and Information Systems Security Symposium.*

Lian, Kanellopoulos, & Ruffo. (2009). Recent Advances in Multimedia Information System Security. *Informatica, 33*, 3-24.

Lian, S. (2008). *Multimedia Content Encryption: Techniques and Applications*. CRC Press, Auerbach Publications.

Lian, S. (2009). Quasi-commutative watermarking and encryption for secure media content distribution. *Multimedia Tools and Applications, 43*(1), 91–107. doi:10.100711042-008-0258-4

Lian, S., Liu, Z., Zhen, R., & Wang, H. (2006). Commutative watermarking and encryption for media data. *Optical Engineering (Redondo Beach, Calif.), 45*(8), 080510. doi:10.1117/1.2333510

Li, C. T., & Yang, F. M. (2003). One-dimensional neighborhood forming strategy for fragile watermarking. *Journal of Electronic Imaging, 12*(2), 284–292. doi:10.1117/1.1557156

Li, E., Xu, C., Gui, C., & Fox, M. D. (2005). *Level set evolution without re-initialization: a new variational formulation.* IEEE CVPR.

Liew, S. C., & Zain, J. M. (2010, July). Reversible medical image watermarking for tamper detection and recovery. In *Computer Science and Information Technology (ICCSIT), 2010 3rd IEEE International Conference on* (Vol. 5, pp. 417-420). IEEE.

Li, M., Poovendran, R., & Narayanan, S. (2005). Protecting patient privacy against unauthorized release of medical images in a group communication environment. *Computerized Medical Imaging and Graphics*, *29*(5), 367–383. doi:10.1016/j.compmedimag.2005.02.003 PMID:15893452

Lim, Y., Xu, C., & Feng, D. D. (2001, May). Web based image authentication using invisible fragile watermark. In *Proceedings of the Pan-Sydney area workshop on Visual information processing-Volume 11* (pp. 31-34). Australian Computer Society, Inc.

Lin, C. H., Chan, D. Y., Su, H., & Hsieh, W. S. (2006). Histogram-oriented watermarking algorithm: Colour image watermarking scheme robust against geometric attacks and signal processing. *IEE Proceedings. Vision Image and Signal Processing*, *153*(4), 483–492. doi:10.1049/ip-vis:20050107

Lin, C. Y., & Chang, S. F. (2000, May). Semifragile watermarking for authenticating JPEG visual content. In *Security and Watermarking of Multimedia Contents II* (Vol. 3971, pp. 140–152). International Society for Optics and Photonics. doi:10.1117/12.384968

Lin, C., Tai, W., & Chang, C. (2008). Multilevel reversible data hiding based on histogram modification of difference images. *Pattern Recognition*, *41*(12), 3582–3591. doi:10.1016/j.patcog.2008.05.015

Lin, C.-Y., & Chang, S.-F. (2001, February). A robust image authentication method distinguishing JPEG compression from malicious manipulation. *IEEE Transactions on Circuits and Systems for Video Technology*, *11*(2), 153–168. doi:10.1109/76.905982

Lin, E. T., Podilchuk, C. I., & Delp, E. J. (2000, May). Detection of image alterations using semifragile watermarks. In *Security and Watermarking of Multimedia Contents II* (Vol. 3971, pp. 152–164). International Society for Optics and Photonics. doi:10.1117/12.384969

Lippmann, R. P. (1987). An introduction to computing with neural nets. *IEEE ASSP Magazine*, 3–22.

Li, T. S. (2006). Feature selection for classification by using a GA-based neural network approach. *Journal of the Chinese Institute of Industrial Engineers*, *23*(1), 55–64. doi:10.1080/10170660609508996

Liu, B., Liu, F., Yang, C., & Sun, Y. (2008). *Secure Steganography in Compressed Video Bitstreams*. IEEE. doi:10.1109/ARES.2008.140

Liu, H., & Sentino, R. (1998). Some issues on scalable feature selection. *Expert Systems with Applications*, *15*(3-4), 333–339. doi:10.1016/S0957-4174(98)90049-5

Li, Y. (2017). *Crowdsensing Multimedia Data: Security and Privacy Issues*. IEEE.

Loudon, J., Swift, M., & Bell, S. (2008). *The clinical orthopedic assessment guide* (2nd ed.). Human Kinetics.

Lu, C. S., & Liao, H. Y. (2001). Multipurpose watermarking for image authentication and protection. *IEEE Transactions on Image Processing*, *10*(10), 1579–1592. doi:10.1109/83.951542 PMID:18255500

Luo, X., & Cheng, Q. (2003, October). Health information integrating and size reducing. 2003 IEEE nuclear science symposium,'medical imaging conference, and workshop of room-temperature semiconductor detectors'. In *Nuclear Science Symposium Conference Record, 2003 IEEE* (Vol. *4*, pp. 3014-3018). IEEE.

Luo, X., Cheng, Q., & Tan, J. (2003, September). A lossless data embedding scheme for medical images in application of e-diagnosis. In *Engineering in Medicine and Biology Society, 2003. Proceedings of the 25th Annual International Conference of the IEEE* (Vol. *1*, pp. 852-855). IEEE.

Luo, L., Chen, Z., Chen, M., Zeng, X., & Xiong, Z. (2010, March). Reversible Image Watermarking Using Interpolation Technique. *IEEE Transactions on Information Forensics and Security*, 5(1), 187–193. doi:10.1109/TIFS.2009.2035975

Luukka, P. (2011). Feature Selection using fuzzy entropy measures with similarity classifier. *Expert Systems with Applications, Elsevier*, 38(4), 4600–4607. doi:10.1016/j.eswa.2010.09.133

Ma, Y., & Zhang, H. (2003). Contrast-based image attention analysis by using fuzzy growing. *ACM Trans. Multimedia*.

Mabuza-Hocquet, G., & Nelwamondo, F. (2015). Fusion of Phase Congruency and Harris Algorithm for Extraction of Iris Corner Points. *2015 3rd International Conference on Artificial Intelligence, Modelling and Simulation (AIMS)*, 315-320. 10.1109/AIMS.2015.57

Macq, B., & Dewey, F. (1999, October). Trusted headers for medical images. In DFG VIII-D II Watermarking Workshop (Vol. 10). Erlangen.

Madić, M., Marković, D., & Radovanović, M. (2013). Comparison of Meta-Heuristic Algorithms for Solving Machining Optimization Problems. *Facta Universitatis Series. Mechanical Engineering (New York, N.Y.)*, 11(1), 29–44.

Madsen, M. T., Berbaum, K. S., Ellingson, A. N., Thompson, B. H., Mullan, B. F., & Caldwell, R. T. (2006). A new software tool for removing, storing, and adding abnormalities to medical images for perception research studies. *Academic Radiology*, 13(3), 305–312. doi:10.1016/j.acra.2005.11.041 PMID:16488842

Maeder, A. J., & Eckert, M. P. (1999, July). Medical image compression: Quality and performance issues. In *New Approaches in Medical Image Analysis* (Vol. 3747, pp. 93–102). International Society for Optics and Photonics. doi:10.1117/12.351629

Maes, M. J. J. J. B., & van Overveld, C. W. A. M. (1998). Digital watermarking by geometric warping. *Proceedings 1998 International Conference on Image Processing. ICIP98*, 424-426. 10.1109/ICIP.1998.723408

Maglogiannis, I., Pavlopoulos, S., & Koutsouris, D. (2005, March). An Integrated Computer Supported Acquisition, Handling, and Characterization System for Pigmented Skin Lesions in Dermatological Images. *IEEE Transactions on Information Technology in Biomedicine*, 9(1), 86–98. doi:10.1109/TITB.2004.837859 PMID:15787011

Maitya, H. K., & Maity, S. P. (2012). Joint Robust and Reversible Watermarking for Medical Images. *2nd International Conference on Communication, Computing & Security*. 10.1016/j.protcy.2012.10.033

Mandal, I., & Sairam, N. (2012). SVM-PSO based feature selection for improving medical diagnosis reliability using machine learning ensembles. School of Computing, 267-276.

Marisol, Azuaje, McCullagh, & Harper. (2006). A Supervised Learning Approach to Predicting Coronary Heart Disease Complications in Type 2 Diabetes Mellitus Patients. *Sixth IEEE Symposium on BionInformatics and BioEngineering (BIBE'06)*, 325-331.

Marks, R. (2000). Epidemiology of melanoma. *Clinical and Experimental Dermatology*, 459–463. 10.1046/j.1365-2230.2000.00693.x

Marvel, L. M., Boncelet, C. G., & Retter, C. T. (1999, August). Spread spectrum image steganography. *IEEE Transactions on Image Processing*, 8(8), 1075–1083. doi:10.1109/83.777088 PMID:18267522

Mashalkar, A. M. S. D., & Shirgan, S. S. (2017). Design of watermarking scheme in medical image authentication using DWT and SVD technique. *2017 International Conference on Computing Methodologies and Communication (ICCMC)*, 955-960. 10.1109/ICCMC.2017.8282609

Mason, E. J., Traore, I., & Woungang, I. (2016). Gait Biometric Recognition. In *Machine Learning Techniques for Gait Biometric Recognition*. Springer.

Mathur, A., Modh, D., Kulkarni, P., & Roy, S. (2016). Multimedia Big Data Security. *Survey (London, England)*.

Mathur, E., & Mathuria, M. (2017). Unbreakable digital watermarking using combination of LSB and DCT. *2017 International conference of Electronics, Communication and Aerospace Technology (ICECA)*, 351-354. 10.1109/ICECA.2017.8212832

McCay-Peet, Toms, & Marchionini. (2017). Researching Serendipity in Digital Information Environments. *Researching Serendipity in Digital Information Environments, 1*, 91. doi: 10.2200/S00790ED1V01Y201707ICR059

McCourt, C., Dolan, O., & Gormley, G. (2014). Malignant Melanoma: *A Pictorial Review*. *The Ulster Medical Journal, 83*(2), 103–110. PMID:25075139

McDonagh, S., Fisher, R. B., & Rees, J. (2008). *Using 3D information for classification of non-melanoma skin lesions. In Proc. Medical Image Understanding and Analysis* (pp. 164–168). BMVA Press.

Medical Identity Theft in Healthcare. (2010). Retrieved 09, July, 2013. https://www.securetechalliance.org/publications-medical-identity-theft-in-healthcare/

Medical Image Database. https://medpix.nlm.nih.gov/home

Meerwald, P., & Uhl, A. (2001, August). Survey of wavelet-domain watermarking algorithms. In *Security and Watermarking of Multimedia Contents III* (Vol. 4314, pp. 505–517). International Society for Optics and Photonics. doi:10.1117/12.435434

Me, L., & Arce, G. R. (2001). A class of authentication digital watermarks for secure multimedia communication. *IEEE Transactions on Image Processing, 10*(11), 1754–1764. doi:10.1109/83.967402 PMID:18255516

Mendonça, T., Ferreira, P. M., Marques, J., Marcal, A. R. S., & Rozeira, J. (2013). PH2 - A dermoscopic image database for research and benchmarking. *35th International Conference of the IEEE Engineering in Medicine and Biology Society*.

Mestiri, A., Kricha, A., Sakly, A., & Mtibaa, A. (2017). *Watermarking for integrity, authentication and security of Medical Imaging. 2017 14th International Multi-Conference on Systems, Signals & Devices*.

Miaou, S. G., Hsu, C. M., Tsai, Y. S., & Chao, H. M. (2000). A secure data hiding technique with heterogeneous data-combining capability for electronic patient records. In *Engineering in Medicine and Biology Society, 2000. Proceedings of the 22nd Annual International Conference of the IEEE* (Vol. 1, pp. 280-283). IEEE.

Miller, T., & Leroy, G. (2008). Dynamic generation of a Health Topics Overview from consumer health information documents. *International Journal of Biomedical Engineering and Technology, 1*(4), 395–414. doi:10.1504/IJBET.2008.020069

Mintzer, F., Braudaway, G. W., & Yeung, M. M. (1997). Effective and ineffective digital watermarks. *Proceedings of International Conference on Image Processing*, 9-12. 10.1109/ICIP.1997.631957

Mishra, P., Singh, D.B.V., Rana, N.S., & Sengar, S. (2014). Clinical decision support system for diabetes disease diagnosis. *International Journal of Engineering Research and Applications (IJERA)*, 105-110.

Mohanty, S. P., Ranganathan, N., & Namballa, R. K. (2003, August). VLSI implementation of invisible digital watermarking algorithms towards the development of a secure JPEG encoder. In *Signal Processing Systems, 2003. SIPS 2003. IEEE Workshop on* (pp. 183-188). IEEE. 10.1109/SIPS.2003.1235666

Mohanty, S. P. (1999). *Digital watermarking: a tutorial review. Report*. Bangalore, India: Department of Electrical Engineering, Indian Institute of Science.

Mohanty, S. P., Ranganathan, N., & Namballa, R. K. (2005). A VLSI architecture for visible watermarking in a secure still digital camera (S/sup 2/DC) design (Corrected). *IEEE Transactions on Very Large Scale Integration (VLSI) Systems, 13*(8), 1002–1012.

Moon, S. K., & Raut, R. D. (2013). *Analysis of secured video steganography using computer forensics technique for enhance data security*. IEEE. doi:10.1109/ICIIP.2013.6707677

Morik, K., Brockhausen, P., & Joachims, T. (1998). Combining statistical learning with knowledge-based approach-A case study in intensive care monitoring. *Proc. Eur. Conf. Mach. Learn*, 268–277.

Morrone, M. C., & Burr, D. C. (1988). Feature detection in human vision: A phase-dependent energy model. *Proceedings of the Royal Society of London. Series B, Biological Sciences*, 235(1280), 221–245. doi:10.1098/rspb.1988.0073 PMID:2907382

Morrone, M. C., & Owens, R. A. (1987). Feature detection from local energy. *Pattern Recognition Letters*, 6(5), 303–313. doi:10.1016/0167-8655(87)90013-4

Mostafa, S. A., El-Sheimy, N., Tolba, A. S., Abdelkader, F. M., & Elhindy, H. M. (2010). Wavelet packets-based blind watermarking for medical image management. *The Open Biomedical Engineering Journal*, 4(1), 93–98. doi:10.2174/1874120701004010093 PMID:20700520

Motwani, M. C., Gadiya, M. C., & Motwani, R. C. (2010). *Survey of Image Denoising Techniques*. Retrieved from https://www.cse.unr.edu/~fredh/papers/conf/034-asoidt/paper.pdf

Moulin, P., & Ivanovic, A. (2003). The zero-rate spread-spectrum watermarking game. *IEEE Transactions on Signal Processing*, 51(4), 1098–1117. doi:10.1109/TSP.2003.809370

Msolli, A., Helali, A., Ameur, H., & Maaref, H. (2017). Secure Encryption for Wireless Multimedia Sensors Network. *International Journal of Advanced Computer Science and Applications*, 8(6). doi:10.14569/IJACSA.2017.080643

Mstafa, R. J., & Elleithy, K. M. (2015). *A high payload video steganography algorithm in DWT domain based on BCH codes (15, 11)*. IEEE. doi:10.1109/WTS.2015.7117257

Mstafa, R. J., & Elleithy, K. M. (2015). *A novel video steganography algorithm in the wavelet domain based on the KLT tracking algorithm and BCH codes*. IEEE. doi:10.1109/LISAT.2015.7160192

Mstafa, R. J., & Elleithy, K. M. (2015c). *A New Video Steganography Algorithm Based on the Multiple Object Tracking and Hamming Codes*. IEEE. doi:10.1109/ICMLA.2015.117

Mstafa, R. J., & Elleithy, K. M. (2016a). *A DCT-based robust video steganographic method using BCH error correcting code*. IEEE. doi:10.1109/LISAT.2016.7494111

Mstafa, R. J., & Elleithy, K. M. (2016b). *A novel video steganography algorithm in DCT domain based on hamming and BCH codes*. IEEE. doi:10.1109/SARNOF.2016.7846757

Mukherjee, S., Adhikari, A., & Roy, M. (2018). Malignant Melanoma Detection using Multi Layer Perceptron with Optimized Network Parameter Selection by PSO. *1st International Conference on Contemporary Advances in Innovative & Applicable Information Technology*.

Mukherjee, S., Adhikari, A., & Roy, M. (2018). Malignant Melanoma Identification using Best Visually Imperceptible Features from Dermofit Dataset. *1st International Conference on Emerging Trends in Engineering and Science*.

Mukundan, R., & Ramakrishnan, K. R. (1998). *Moment functions in image analysis-theory and applications*. World Scientific. doi:10.1142/3838

Munasinghe, A., Dharmaratne, A., & De Zoysa, K. (2013). *Video steganography*. IEEE. doi:10.1109/ICTer.2013.6761155

Muni, D. P., Pal, N. R., & Das, J. (2006). Genetic Programming for Simultaneous Feature Selection and Classifier Design. *IEEE Transactions on Systems, Man, and Cybernetics. Part B, Cybernetics*, *36*(1), 106–117. doi:10.1109/TSMCB.2005.854499 PMID:16468570

Murat, E. I. (2006). *Human Identification using Gait* (Vol. 14). Turkey Journal of Elec. Engg.

Muro-de-la-Herran, A., Garcia-Zapirain, B., & Mendez-Zorrilla, A. (2014). Gait Analysis Methods: An Overview of Wearable and Non-Wearable Systems, Highlighting Clinical Applications. *Sensors (Basel)*, *14*(2), 3362–3394. doi:10.3390140203362 PMID:24556672

Mustafa, A.E., ElGamal, A.M.F., ElAlmi, M.E., & Ahmed, B.D. (2011). A Proposed Algorithm For Steganography In Digital Image Based on Least Significant Bit. *Research Journal Specific Education*, (21).

Mwangi, E. (2007, December). A geometric attack resistant image watermarking scheme based on invariant centroids. In *Signal Processing and Information Technology, 2007 IEEE International Symposium on* (pp. 190-193). IEEE. 10.1109/ISSPIT.2007.4458073

Nair, U. R., & Birajdar, G. K. (2016). Audio watermarking in wavelet domain using Fibonacci numbers. *2016 International Conference on Signal and Information Processing (IConSIP)*, 1-5. 10.1109/ICONSIP.2016.7857479

Nambakhsh, M. S., Ahmadian, A., Ghavami, M., Dilmaghani, R. S., & Karimi-Fard, S. (2006, August). A novel blind watermarking of ECG signals on medical images using EZW algorithm. In *Engineering in Medicine and Biology Society, 2006. EMBS'06. 28th Annual International Conference of the IEEE* (pp. 3274-3277). IEEE. 10.1109/IEMBS.2006.259603

Namdev, D., & Bansal, A. (2015). Frequency Domain Analysis for Audio Data Forgery Detection. *2015 Fifth International Conference on Communication Systems and Network Technologies*, 702-705. 10.1109/CSNT.2015.168

Nandi, D., Tahiliani, P., Kumar, A., & Chandu, D. (2006). The Ubiquitin-Proteasome System. *Journal of Biosciences*, *31*(1), 137–155. doi:10.1007/BF02705243 PMID:16595883

Narendra, K. C., & Satyanarayana, S. (2016). Hartley transform based correlation filters for face recognition. *Proc of the International Conference on Signal Processing and Communications (SPCOM)*. 10.1109/SPCOM.2016.7746699

Navas, K. A., & Sasikumar, M. (2007, March). Survey of medical image watermarking algorithms. In *Proc. International Conf. Sciences of Electronics, Technologies of Information and Telecommunications* (pp. 25-29). Academic Press.

Navas, K. A., Sasikumar, M., & Sreevidya, S. (2007, June). A benchmark for medical image watermarking. In *Systems, Signals and Image Processing, 2007 and 6th EURASIP Conference focused on Speech and Image Processing, Multimedia Communications and Services. 14th International Workshop on* (pp. 237-240). IEEE. 10.1109/IWSSIP.2007.4381197

Nayak, J., Bhat, P. S., Kumar, M. S., & Acharya, U. R. (2004, December). Reliable and robust transmission and storage of medical images with patient information. In *Signal Processing and Communications, 2004. SPCOM'04. 2004 International Conference on* (pp. 91-95). IEEE. 10.1109/SPCOM.2004.1458363

Nayak, J., Bhat, P. S., Kumar, M. S., & Acharya, U. R. (2004, December). Reliable transmission and storage of medical images with patient information using error control codes. In *India Annual Conference, 2004. Proceedings of the IEEE INDICON 2004. First* (pp. 147-150). IEEE. 10.1109/INDICO.2004.1497726

Nayak, J., Bhat, P. S., Acharya, R., & Niranjan, U. C. (2004). Simultaneous storage of medical images in the spatial and frequency domain: A comparative study. *Biomedical Engineering Online*, *3*(1), 17. doi:10.1186/1475-925X-3-17 PMID:15180899

Neelima, M., & Mahaboob Pasha, M. (2014). Wavelet Transform Based On Image Denoising Using Thresholding Techniques. *International Journal of Advanced Research in Computer and Communication Engineering*, *3*(9).

Negroponte, N. (1995). The digital revolution: Reasons for optimism. *The Futurist, 29*(6), 68.

Nguyen, T. H., & Duong, D. M. (2015). Reversible Medical Image Watermarking Technique Based on Choosing Threshold Values in Histogram Shifting. *2015 Seventh International Conference on Knowledge and Systems Engineering (KSE)*, 204-209. 10.1109/KSE.2015.75

Nikolaidis, A., Tsekeridou, S., Tefas, A., & Solachidis, V. (2001). A survey on watermarking application scenarios and related attacks. In *Image Processing, 2001. Proceedings. 2001 International Conference on* (Vol. 3, pp. 991-994). IEEE. 10.1109/ICIP.2001.958292

Ni, Z., Shi, Y. Q., Ansari, N., & Su, W. (2006). Reversible data hiding. *IEEE Transactions on Circuits and Systems for Video Technology, 16*(3), 354–362. doi:10.1109/TCSVT.2006.869964

Oh, E., Tae KeunYoo, T.K., & Park, E.C. (2013). Diabetic retinopathy risk prediction for fundus examination using sparse learning: A cross-sectional study. *BMC Medical Informatics and Decision Making*, 1–14. PMID:24033926

Oh, G. T., Lee, Y. B., & Yeom, S. J. (2004, June). Security mechanism for medical image information on PACS using invisible watermark. In *International Conference on High Performance Computing for Computational Science* (pp. 315-324). Springer.

Ojha, V. K., Abraham, A., & Snasel, V. (2017). Metaheuristic Design of Feedforward Neural Networks: A Review of Two Decades of Research. *Engineering Applications of Artificial Intelligence, 60*, 97–116. doi:10.1016/j.engappai.2017.01.013

Olivares, J., Hormigo, J., Villalba, J., & Benavides, I. (2004). Minimum Sum of Absolute Differences Implementation in a Single FPGA Device. In J. Becker, M. Platzner, & S. Vernalde (Eds.), *Field Programmable Logic and Application* (Vol. 3203, pp. 986–990). Berlin: Springer Berlin Heidelberg. doi:10.1007/978-3-540-30117-2_112

Oosterkamp, W. J., & Ardran, G. M. (1955, November). Discussion on image intensification in radiology. *Proceedings of the IEE - Part B: Radio and Electronic Engineering, 102*(6), 845–849. doi:10.1049/pi-b-1.1955.0169

Oppenheim, A. V., & Lim, J. S. (1981). The importance of phase in signals. *Proceedings of the IEEE, 69*(5), 529–541. doi:10.1109/PROC.1981.12022

Orkcu, H. H., & Bal, H. (2011). Comparing performances of backpropagation and genetic algorithms in the data classification. *Expert Systems with Applications, Elsevier, 38*(4), 3703–3709. doi:10.1016/j.eswa.2010.09.028

Osada, M., & Tsukui, H. (2002, August). Development of ultrasound/endoscopy pacs (picture archiving and communication system) and investigation of compression method for cine images. In *Electronic Imaging and Multimedia Technology III* (Vol. 4925, pp. 99–103). International Society for Optics and Photonics. doi:10.1117/12.481574

Otsu, N. (1979). A threshold selection method from gray-level histograms. *IEEE Transactions on Systems, Man, and Cybernetics, 9*(1), 62–66. doi:10.1109/TSMC.1979.4310076

Ou, B., Li, X., Zhao, Y., Ni, R., & Shi, Y. (2013). Pairwise Prediction-Error Expansion for Efficient Reversible Data Hiding. *IEEE Transactions on Image Processing, 22*(12), 5010–5021. doi:10.1109/TIP.2013.2281422 PMID:24043388

Ouelati, S., & Solaiman, B. (2018). Watermarking medical images with patient identificationto verify authenticity. *International Journal of Medical Engineering and Informatics, 10*(1).

Palivela, H., & Thotadara, P. (2012). A novel approach to predict diabetes by cascading clustering and classification. *Computing Communication & Networking Technologies (ICCCNT)*, 1-7.

Pan, F., Xiang, L., Yang, X.-Y., & Guo, Y. (2010). *Video steganography using motion vector and linear block codes.* IEEE. doi:10.1109/ICSESS.2010.5552283

Pappa, C. K., Vijayaraj, M., & Subbulakshmi, M. (2017). (2017), An optimal approach for watermarking using MRC4 encryption scheme. *Cluster Computing*. doi:10.100710586-017-1349-7

Parah, S. A., Ahad, F., Sheikh, J. A., Loan, N. A., & Bhat, G. M. (2017). A New Reversible and high capacity data hiding technique for E-healthcare applications. *Multimedia Tools and Applications*, 76(3), 3943–3975. doi:10.100711042-016-4196-2

Parameswaran, L., & Anbumani, K. (2008). Content-based watermarking for image authentication using independent component analysis. *Informatica, 32*(3).

Pardalos, P. M., & Schnitger, G. (1988). Checking local optimality in constrained quadratic programming is NP-hard. *Operations Research Letters*, 7(1), 33–35. doi:10.1016/0167-6377(88)90049-1

Patel, R., & Patel, M. (2014). Steganography over video file by hiding video in another video file, random byte hiding and LSB technique. *2014 IEEE International Conference on Computational Intelligence and Computing Research*, 1-5. 10.1109/ICCIC.2014.7238343

Patil, B. M., Joshi, R. C., & Toshniwal, D. (2010). Association rule for classification of type-2 diabetic patients. *Second International Conference on Machine Learning and Computing*, 330-334. 10.1109/ICMLC.2010.67

Peerzada & Chawla. (2014). An Analytical Review of the Multimedia Data and Encryption Mechanism at Cloud Server. *International Journal of Innovative Research in Computer and Communication Engineering*, 2(2).

Pereira, S. M., Frade, M. A. C., Rangayyan, R. M., & Marques, P. M. A. (2013, January). Classification of Color Images of Dermatological Ulcers. *IEEE Journal of Biomedical and Health Informatics*, 17(1), 136–142. doi:10.1109/TITB.2012.2227493 PMID:23193315

Pereira, S., Voloshynovskiy, S., Madueno, M., Marchand-Maillet, S., & Pun, T. (2001, April). Second generation benchmarking and application oriented evaluation. In *International Workshop on Information Hiding* (pp. 340-353). Springer. 10.1007/3-540-45496-9_25

Pericles, B. C., Silva, R. C., & Prudencio, R. C. (2014). Fine-Tuning of Support Vector Machine Parameters using Racing Algorithms. *European Symposium on Artificial Neural Networks 2014, Computational Intelligence and Machine Learning*.

Perlovsky, L. I., Schoendor, W. H., & Burdick, B. J. (1997). Model-based neural network for target detection in SAR images. *IEEE Transactions on Image Processing*, 6(1), 203–216. doi:10.1109/83.552107 PMID:18282889

Petitcolas, F. A. P., Anderson, R. J., & Kuhn, M. G. (1999, July). Information hiding-a survey. *Proceedings of the IEEE*, 87(7), 1062–1078. doi:10.1109/5.771065

Pham, D. T., & Bayro-Corrochano, E. J. (1998). Neural computing for noise filtering, edge detection and signature extraction. *J. Syst. Eng.*, 2(2), 666–670.

Pinson, M. H., & Wolf, S. (2004). A New Standardized Method for Objectively Measuring Video Quality. *IEEE Transactions on Broadcasting*, 50(3), 312–322. doi:10.1109/TBC.2004.834028

Piva, A., Barni, M., Bartolini, F., & Cappellini, V. (1997). DCT-based watermark recovering without resorting to the uncorrupted original image. *Proceedings of International Conference on Image Processing*, 520-523. 10.1109/ICIP.1997.647964

Piva, A., Barni, M., Bartolini, F., & De Rosa, A. (2005). Data hiding technologies for digital radiography. *IEE Proceedings. Vision Image and Signal Processing*, 152(5), 604–610. doi:10.1049/ip-vis:20041240

Planitz, B., & Maeder, A. (2005, February). Medical image watermarking: a study on image degradation. In *Proc. Australian Pattern Recognition Society Workshop on Digital Image Computing*. WDIC.

Podilchuk, C. I., & Delp, E. J. (2001). Digital watermarking: Algorithms and applications. *IEEE Signal Processing Magazine, 18*(4), 33–46. doi:10.1109/79.939835

Podilchuk, C. I., & Zeng, W. (1998, May). Image-adaptive watermarking using visual models. *IEEE Journal on Selected Areas in Communications, 16*(4), 525–539. doi:10.1109/49.668975

Polat, K., Guneh, S., & Arslan, A. (2008). A cascade learning system for classification of diabetes disease: Generalized discriminant analysis and least square support vector machine. *Expert Systems with Applications, Elsevier, 34*(1), 482–487. doi:10.1016/j.eswa.2006.09.012

Polat, K., & Gunes, S. (2007). An expert system approach based on principal component analysis and adaptive neuro–fuzzy inference system to diagnosis of diabetes disease. *Digital Signal Processing, Elsevier, 17*(4), 702–710. doi:10.1016/j.dsp.2006.09.005

Pomponiu, V., Cavagnino, D., & Botta, M. (2018). Data Hiding in the Wild: Where Computational Intelligence Meets Digital Forensics. In *Surveillance in Action* (pp. 301–331). Cham: Springer. doi:10.1007/978-3-319-68533-5_15

Poobathy, D., & Chezian, R. M. (2014). Edge Detection Operators: Peak Signal to Noise Ratio Based Comparison. International Journal of Image. *Graphics and Signal Processing, 6*(10), 55–61. doi:10.5815/ijigsp.2014.10.07

Poornima, R., & Ishwarya, R.J. (2013). An Overview of Digital Image Steganography. *International Journal of Computer Science & Engineering Survey, 4*(1).

Popescu, A. C., & Farid, H. (2004, May). Statistical tools for digital forensics. In *International Workshop on Information Hiding* (pp. 128-147). Springer. 10.1007/978-3-540-30114-1_10

Porwik, P., & Lisowska, A. (2004). The Haar-wavelet transform in digital image processing: Its status and achievements. *Machine Graphics and Vision, 13*(1-2).

Potdar, V. M., Han, S., & Chang, E. (2005). A survey of digital image watermarking techniques. *INDIN '05. 2005 3rd IEEE International Conference on Industrial Informatics*, 709-716. 10.1109/INDIN.2005.1560462

Prashanti, G., Jyothirmai, B. V., & Chandana, K. S. (2017). Data confidentiality using steganography and cryptographic techniques. *2017 International Conference on Circuit, Power and Computing Technologies (ICCPCT)*, 1-4. 10.1109/ICCPCT.2017.8074276

Priya, R., & Aruna, P. (2013). Diagnosis of diabetic retinopathy using machine learning techniques. *Ictact Journal on Soft Computing, 3*(4), 563–575. doi:10.21917/ijsc.2013.0083

Prokop, R. J., & Reeves, A. P. (1992). A survey of moment-based techniques for unoccluded object representation and recognition. *CVGIP. Graphical Models and Image Processing, 54*(5), 438–460. doi:10.1016/1049-9652(92)90027-U

Provos, N., & Honeyman, P. (2003, May-June). Hide and seek: An introduction to steganography. *IEEE Security and Privacy, 1*(3), 32–44. doi:10.1109/MSECP.2003.1203220

Puech, W., & Rodrigues, J. M. (2004, September). A new crypto-watermarking method for medical images safe transfer. In *Signal Processing Conference, 2004 12th European* (pp. 1481-1484). IEEE.

Qasem, S. N., & Shamsuddin, S. M. (2011). Radial basis function network based on time variant multi-objective particle swarm optimization for medical diseases diagnosis. *Applied Soft Computing, Elsevier, 11*(1), 1427–1438. doi:10.1016/j.asoc.2010.04.014

Qi, X., & Qi, J. (2007). A robust content-based digital image watermarking scheme. *Signal Processing, 87*(6), 1264-1280.

Qian, L., Li, Z., Zhou, P., & Chen, J. (2016). *An Improved Matrix Encoding Steganography Algorithm Based on H.264 Video*. IEEE. doi:10.1109/CSCloud.2016.8

Qiao, L., & Nahrstedt, K. (1998). Watermarking methods for MPEG encoded video: towards resolving rightful ownership. *Proceedings. IEEE International Conference on Multimedia Computing and Systems*, 276-285. 10.1109/MMCS.1998.693656

Qu, G., & Potkonjak, K. (1998). Analysis of watermarking techniques for graph coloring problem. *1998 IEEE/ACM International Conference on Computer-Aided Design. Digest of Technical Papers*, 190-193. 10.1145/288548.288607

Quellec, G., Russell, S. R., & Abramoff, M. D. (2011). Optimal filter framework for automated, instantaneous detection of lesions in retinal images. *IEEE Transactions on Medical Imaging*, *30*(2), 523–533. doi:10.1109/TMI.2010.2089383 PMID:21292586

Queluz, M. P. (2001). Authentication of digital images and video: Generic models and a new contribution. *Signal Processing Image Communication*, *16*(5), 461–475. doi:10.1016/S0923-5965(00)00010-2

Radharani, S., & Valarmathi, M. L. (2010). A study on watermarking schemes for image authentication. *International Journal of Computers and Applications*, *2*(4), 24–32. doi:10.5120/658-925

Radwan, N. I., Salem, N. M., & El Adawy, M. I. (2012). Histogram Correlation for Video Scene Change Detection. In D. C. Wyld, J. Zizka, & D. Nagamalai (Eds.), *Advances in Computer Science, Engineering & Applications* (Vol. 166, pp. 765–773). Berlin: Springer Berlin Heidelberg; doi:10.1007/978-3-642-30157-5_76

Rahimi, F., & Rabbani, H. (2011). A dual adaptive watermarking scheme in contourlet domain for DICOM images. *Biomedical Engineering Online*, *10*(1), 53. doi:10.1186/1475-925X-10-53 PMID:21682862

Ramesh, V., & Padmini, R. (2017). Risk level prediction system of diabetic retinopathy using classification algorithms. *International Journal of Scientific Development and Research*, *2*(6).

Rao & Hasan. (2017). Secure Multimedia Data Storage in Cloud Computing. *International Journal of Engineering Sciences & Research Technology*, *6*(5).

Raval, M. S. (2009). A Secure Steganographic Technique for Blind Steganalysis Resistance. In *Seventh International Conference on Advances in Pattern Recognition* (pp. 25-28). Kolkata: Academic Press.

Raval, M. S., Joshi, M., Rege, P. P., & Parulkar, S. (2011). Image tampering detection using compressive sensing based watermarking scheme. In *National Conference on Machine Vision and Image Processing* (pp. 5-9). Pune: IET.

Raval, M. S., & Rege, P. P. (2005). Scalar Quantization Based Multiple Patterns Data Hiding Technique for Gray Scale Images. *ICGST Journal of Graphics, Vision and Image Processing*, *5*(9), 55–61.

Rayachoti, E., & Edara, S. R. (2014). A novel medical image watermarking technique for detecting tampers inside ROI and recovering original ROI. *2014 IEEE International Symposium on Signal Processing and Information Technology (ISSPIT)*, 321-326. 10.1109/ISSPIT.2014.7300608

Read, P., & Meyer, M.-P. (2000). *Restoration of Motion Picture Film*. Burlington: Elsevier. Retrieved from http://www.123library.org/book_details/?id=36001

Reena, Shah, & Bhavna. (2014). Multimedia Security Techniques. International Journal of Innovative Research In Electrical, Electronics, Instrumentation And *Control Engineering*, *2*(5).

Rere, L. M. R., Fanany, M. I., & Arymurthy, A. M. (2016). Metaheuristic Algorithms for Convolution Neural Network. *Computational Intelligence and Neuroscience*, *2016*, 1537325. doi:10.1155/2016/1537325 PMID:27375738

Revett, K., & Salem, A-B. (2010). Exploring the Role of Glycosylated Hemoglobin as a marker for Type-2 Diabetes Mellitus using Rough Sets. *7th International Conference on Informatics and Systems (INFOS)*, 1-7.

Revett, K., Gorunescu, F., Gorunescu, M., El-Darzi, E., & Ene, M. (2005). A Breast Cancer Diagnosis System: A Combined Approach Using Rough Sets and Probabilistic Neural Networks. *The International Conference on Computer as a Tool*, 1124-1127. 10.1109/EURCON.2005.1630149

Rey, C., & Dugelay, J. L. (2002). A survey of watermarking algorithms for image authentication. *EURASIP Journal on Applied Signal Processing*, (1): 613–621.

Rezagholipour, K., & Eshghi, M. (2016). *Video steganography algorithm based on motion vector of moving object.* IEEE. doi:10.1109/IKT.2016.7777764

Riasat, R., Bajwa, I. S., & Ali, M. Z. (2011). *A hash-based approach for colour image steganography.* IEEE. doi:10.1109/ICCNIT.2011.6020886

Ritenour, E. R., & Maidment, A. D. (1999). Lossy compression should not be used in certain imaging applications such as chest radiography. *Medical Physics*, *26*(9), 1773–1775. doi:10.1118/1.598783 PMID:10505862

Rodriguez-Colin, R., Claudia, F. U., & Trinidad-Blas, G. D. J. (2007, February). Data hiding scheme for medical images. In *Electronics, Communications and Computers, 2007. CONIELECOMP'07. 17th International Conference on* (pp. 32-32). IEEE. 10.1109/CONIELECOMP.2007.14

Rosenblatt, F. (1961). *Principles of Neurodynamics: Perceptrons and the Theory of Brain Mechanisms*. Washington, DC: Spartan Books. doi:10.21236/AD0256582

Roy, S., & Chang, E. C. (2004). Watermarking color histograms. *Proc. 2004 Int. Conf. Image Processing*, 2191-2194.

Ruanaidh, J. J. K. O., Dowling, W. J., & Boland, F. M. (1996). Phase watermarking of digital images. *Proceedings of 3rd IEEE International Conference on Image Processing*, 239-242. 10.1109/ICIP.1996.560428

Sachnev, V., Kim, H. J., Nam, J., Suresh, S., & Shi, Y. Q. (2009). Reversible Watermarking Algorithm Using Sorting and Prediction. *IEEE Transactions on Circuits and Systems for Video Technology*, *19*(7), 989–999. doi:10.1109/tcsvt.2009.2020257

Sakhre, V., Singh, U. P., & Jain, S. (2017). FCPN Approach for Uncertain Nonlinear Dynamical System with Unknown Disturbance. *International Journal of Fuzzy Systems (Springer)*, *19*(2), 452–469. doi:10.100740815-016-0145-5

Saloni, Sharma, R. K., & Gupta, A. K. (2015). Voice Analysis for Telediagnosis of Parkinson Disease Using Artificial Neural Networks and Support Vector Machines. *MECS: International Journal of Intelligent Systems and Applications (IJISA)*, 41-47.

Samy, S., Naser, A., & Ola, A. Z. A. (2008). An expert system for diagnosing eye diseases using clips. *Journal of Theoretical and Applied Information Technology (JATIT)*, 923-930.

Sandaruwan, G. W. R., & Ranathunga, L. (2017). Robust and adaptive watermarking technique for digital images. *2017 IEEE International Conference on Industrial and Information Systems (ICIIS)*, 1-6. 10.1109/ICIINFS.2017.8300387

Sarani, N., & Amudha, K. (2015). A security technique based on watermarking and encryption for medical image. *2015 International Conference on Innovations in Information, Embedded and Communication Systems (ICIIECS)*, 1-4. 10.1109/ICIIECS.2015.7192934

Sarkar, A., Sullivan, K., & Manjunath, B. S. (2008). Steganographic capacity estimation for the statistical restoration framework. Academic Press. doi:10.1117/12.767841

Sathasivam, S., Hamadneh, N., & Choon, O. H. (2011). Comparing neural networks: Hopfield network and RBF network. *Applied Mathematical Sciences, 5*(69), 3439–3452.

Saturwar, J. H., & Chaudhari, D. N. (2017). Review of models, issues and applications of digital watermarking based on visual cryptography. *2017 International Conference on Inventive Systems and Control (ICISC)*, 1-4. 10.1109/ICISC.2017.8068588

Schmidhuber, J. (2015). Deep learning in neural networks: An overview. *Neural Networks, 61*, 85–117. doi:10.1016/j.neunet.2014.09.003 PMID:25462637

Schmitz, R., Li, S., Grecos, C., & Zhang, X. (2012). A new approach to commutative watermarking-encryption. *Communications and Multimedia Security: 13th IFIP TC 6/TC 11 International Conf., CMS 2012, Canterbury, UK, September 3-5, 2012. Proceedings*, 117-130.

Schmitz, R., & Gruber, J. (2017). Commutative Watermarking Encryption of Audio Data with Minimum Knowledge Verification. *Advances in Multimedia, 2017*, 5879257. doi:10.1155/2017/5879257

Schmitz, R., Li, S., Grecos, C., & Zhang, X. (2013). Towards more robust commutative watermarking-encryption. *Proceedings of 2013 IEEE International Symposium on Multimedia*, 283-286. 10.1109/ISM.2013.54

Schmitz, R., Li, S., Grecos, C., & Zhang, X. (2014). Towards Robust Invariant Commutative Watermarking-Encryption based on Image Histograms. *International Journal of Multimedia Data Engineering and Management, 5*(4), 36–52. doi:10.4018/ijmdem.2014100103

Schmitz, R., Li, S., Grecos, C., & Zhang, X. (2015). Content-Fragile Commutative Watermarking-Encryption Based on Pixel Entropy. *Lecture Notes in Computer Science, 9386*, 474–485. doi:10.1007/978-3-319-25903-1_41

Schneider, M., & Chang, S. F. (1996): A robust content based digital signature for image authentication, *Proc. International Conference on Image Processing*, 3, 227–230. 10.1109/ICIP.1996.560425

Schneier, B. (1996). *Applied cryptography: protocols, algorithms, and source code in C*. Wiley.

Schneier, B. (1997). *Applied Cryptography* (2nd ed.). Paris: International Thomson Publishing.

Schou, C. D., Frost, J., & Maconachy, W. V. (2004). Information assurance in biomedical informatics systems. *IEEE Engineering in Medicine and Biology Magazine, 23*(1), 110–118. doi:10.1109/MEMB.2004.1297181 PMID:15154266

Scott, P. D., Young, S. S., & Nasrabadi, N. M. (1997). Object recognition using multilayer hop-field neural network. *IEEE Transactions on Image Processing, 6*(3), 357–372. doi:10.1109/83.557336 PMID:18282932

Sebald, D. J., & Bucklew, J. A. (2000). Support vector machine techniques for nonlinear equalization. *IEEE Transactions on Signal Processing, 48*(11), 3217–3226. doi:10.1109/78.875477

Seema, & Chaudhary, J. (2014). *A Multi Phase Model to Improve Video Steganography*. IEEE. 10.1109/CICN.2014.158

Seera, M., & Lim, C. P. (2014). A hybrid intelligent system for medical data classification. *Expert Systems with Applications, Elsevier, 41*(5), 2239–2249. doi:10.1016/j.eswa.2013.09.022

Seitz, J. (2005). *Digital watermarking for digital media*. IGI Global. doi:10.4018/978-1-59140-518-4

Selvakuberan, K., Kayathiri, D., Harini, B., & Devi, M. I. (2011). An efficient feature selection method for classification in health care systems using machine learning techniques. IEEE.

Selvigrija, P., & Ramya, E. (2015). *Dual steganography for hiding text in video by linked list method*. IEEE. doi:10.1109/ICETECH.2015.7275018

Senol, C., & Yildirim, T. (2009). Thyroid and breast cancer disease diagnosis using fuzzy-neural networks. *International Conference on Electrical and Electronics Engineering*, 390-393.

Setino, R. (1997). Neural-Network Feature Selector. *IEEE Transactions on Neural Networks, 8*(3).

Sharifzadeh, M., & Schonfeld, D. (2015). *Statistical and information-theoretic optimization and performance bounds of video steganography.* IEEE. doi:10.1109/ALLERTON.2015.7447179

Sharma, S., Gupta, A., Trivedi, M. C., & Yadav, V. K. (2016). Analysis of Different Text Steganography Techniques: A Survey. *2016 Second International Conference on Computational Intelligence & Communication Technology (CICT)*, 130-133. 10.1109/CICT.2016.34

Sheela, K.G., & Deepa, S. N. (2013). Review on Methods to Fix Number of Hidden Neurons in Neural Networks. *Mathematical Problems in Engineering.* .10.1155/2013/425740

Shih, F. Y., & Wu, Y. T. (2005). Robust watermarking and compression for medical images based on genetic algorithms. *Information Sciences, 175*(3), 200–216. doi:10.1016/j.ins.2005.01.013

Shiozaki, A. (1986, October). Edge extraction using entropy operator. *Elsevier Journal of Computer Vision, Graphics, and Image Processing, 36*(1), 1–9. doi:10.1016/S0734-189X(86)80025-1

Siedlecki, W., & Skylansky, J. (1989). A Note on Genetic Algorithms for Large Scale Feature Selection, Elsevier. *Pattern Recognition Letters, 10*(5), 335–347. doi:10.1016/0167-8655(89)90037-8

Silvestre, G. C. M., & Dowling, W. J. (1997). Image watermarking using digital communication techniques. *1997 Sixth International Conference on Image Processing and Its Applications*, 443-447. 10.1049/cp:19970933

Singh, A., & Dutta, M. K. (2014, November). A blind & fragile watermarking scheme for tamper detection of medical images preserving ROI. In *Medical Imaging, m-Health and Emerging Communication Systems (MedCom), 2014 International Conference on* (pp. 230-234). IEEE. 10.1109/MedCom.2014.7006009

Singh, A., Nigam, J., Thakur, R., Gupta, R., & Kumar, A. (2016). Wavelet Based Robust Watermarking Technique for Integrity Control in Medical Images. *2016 International Conference on Micro-Electronics and Telecommunication Engineering (ICMETE)*, 222-227. 10.1109/ICMETE.2016.103

Singh, D., & Kanwal, N. (2016) Dynamic video steganography using LBP on CIELAB based K-means clustering. *International Conference on Computing for Sustainable Global Development (INDIACom)*, 2684 – 2689.

Singh, U. P., & Jain, S. (2016). Modified Chaotic Bat Algorithm-Based Counter Propagation Neural Network for Uncertain Nonlinear Discrete Time System. *International Journal of Computational Intelligence and Applications, 15*(3), 1–15.

Singh, U. P., & Jain, S. (2018). Optimization of Neural Network for Nonlinear Discrete Time System Using Modified Quaternion Firefly Algorithm: Case Study of Indian Currency Exchange Rate Prediction. *Soft Computing, 22*(8), 2667–2681.

Singla, D., & Juneja, M. (2014). *An analysis of edge based image steganography techniques in spatial domain. In 2014 Recent Advances in Engineering and Computational Sciences* (pp. 1–5). Chandigarh: RAECS; doi:10.1109/RAECS.2014.6799604

Smith, S. W. (1997). *The scientist and engineer's guide to digital signal processing* (1st ed.). San Diego, CA: California Technical Pub.

Smolka, B., Malik, K., & Malik, D. (2012). Adaptive rank weighted switching filter for impulsive noise removal in color images. *Journal of Real-Time Image Processing*, 1–23.

Sobti, R., & Geetha, G. (2012). Cryptographic Hash Functions: A Review. *International Journal of Computer Science Issues, 9*(2).

Soh, L., & Tsatsoulis, C. (1999, March). Texture Analysis of SAR Sea Ice Imagery Using Gray Level Co-Occurrence Matrices. *IEEE Transactions on Geoscience and Remote Sensing, 37*(2), 780–795. doi:10.1109/36.752194

Solachidis, V., Tefas, A., Nikolaidis, N., Tsekeridou, S., Nikolaidis, A., & Pitas, I. (2001). A benchmarking protocol for watermarking methods. In *Image Processing, 2001. Proceedings. 2001 International Conference on* (Vol. 3, pp. 1023-1026). IEEE. 10.1109/ICIP.2001.958300

Sommer, P. (2018). *Accrediting digital forensics: What are the choices?* Academic Press.

Song, G., Li, Z., Zhao, J., Tu, H., & Cheng, J. (2014). *A video steganography algorithm for MVC without distortion drift.* IEEE. doi:10.1109/ICALIP.2014.7009893

Soni, K., & Singh, A. (2016). A Survey Paper on Human Gait Recognition Techniques. *International Journal of Science Technology & Engineering, 2*(10).

Soundararajan, K., Kumar, S., & Anusuya, C. (2012). Diagnostics Decision Support System for Tuberculosis using Fuzzy Logic. *International Journal of Computer Science and Information Technology & Security, 2*(3), 684–689.

Srinivasan, Y., Nutter, B., Mitra, S., Phillips, B., & Ferris, D. (2004, June). Secure transmission of medical records using high capacity steganography. In *Computer-Based Medical Systems, 2004. CBMS 2004. Proceedings. 17th IEEE Symposium on* (pp. 122-127). IEEE. 10.1109/CBMS.2004.1311702

Stathakis, D. (2009, April 20). How many hidden layers and nodes? *International Journal of Remote Sensing, 30*(8), 2133–2147. doi:10.1080/01431160802549278

Su, Zhang, Yue, Chang, Jiang, & Yao. (2018). SNR-Constrained Heuristics for Optimizing the Scaling Parameter of Robust Audio Watermarking. *IEEE Transactions on Multimedia.* doi: 10.1109/TMM.2018.2812599

Subramanyam, A. V., Emmanuel, S., & Kankanhalli, M. S. (2012). Robust watermarking of compressed and encrypted JPEG2000 images. *IEEE Transactions on Multimedia, 14*(3), 703–716. doi:10.1109/TMM.2011.2181342

Suganya, G., & Amudha, K. (2014). Medical image integrity control using joint encryption and watermarking techniques. *2014 International Conference on Green Computing Communication and Electrical Engineering (ICGCCEE),* 1-5. 10.1109/ICGCCEE.2014.6922265

Sujatha, C. N., & Satyanarayana, P. (2016). Analysis of robust watermarking techniques: A retrospective. *International Conference on Communication and Signal Processing (ICCSP),* 336-341. 10.1109/ICCSP.2016.7754151

Sumathi, C. P., Santanam, T., & Umamaheswari, G. (2013, December). A Study of Various Steganographic Techniques Used for Information Hiding. *International Journal of Computer Science & Engineering Survey, 4*(6). doi:10.5121/ijcses.2013.4602

Supriya & Shetty. (2017). A Survey on Multimedia Content Protection. International Research *Journal of Engineering Technology, 4*(5).

Surse, N. M., & Vinayakray-Jani, P. (2017). A comparative study on recent image steganography techniques based on DWT. *2017 International Conference on Wireless Communications, Signal Processing and Networking (WiSPNET),* 1308-1314. 10.1109/WiSPNET.2017.8299975

Susanto & Muhaya. (2010). Multimedia Information Security Architecture Framework. In *5th International Conference on Future Information Technology.* IEEE.

Swanson, M., Kobayashi, M., & Tewfik, A. (1998). Multimedia data-embedding and watermarking technologies. *Proceedings of the IEEE, 86*(6), 1064–1087. doi:10.1109/5.687830

Tagliasacchi, M., Valenzise, G., & Tubaro, S. (2009). Hash-based identification of sparse image tampering. *IEEE Transactions on Image Processing, 18*(11), 2491–2504. doi:10.1109/TIP.2009.2028251 PMID:19635704

Tanaka, K. (2011). Embedding of computer-generated hologram in a dithered image. *Applied Optics, 50*(34), H315. doi:10.1364/AO.50.00H315 PMID:22193023

Tang, W., & Aoki, Y. (1997). A DCT-based coding of images in watermarking. *Proceedings of ICICS, 1997 International Conference on Information, Communications and Signal Processing. Theme: Trends in Information Systems Engineering and Wireless Multimedia Communications*, 510-512. doi: 10.1109/ICICS.1997.647150

Tang, X. (1998, November). Texture Information in Run-Length Matrices. *IEEE Transactions on Image Processing, 7*(11), 1602–1609. doi:10.1109/83.725367 PMID:18276225

Tan, T. Y., Zhang, L., & Jiang, M. (2016). An Intelligent Decision Support System for Skin Cancer Detection from Dermoscopic Images. *Proceedings of the 12th International Conference on Natural Computation, Fuzzy Systems and Knowledge Discovery (ICNC-FSKD)*, 2194-2199. 10.1109/FSKD.2016.7603521

Tao, W., Liu, T., Zheng, R., & Feng, H. (2012). Gait Analysis Using Wearable Sensors. *Sensors (Basel), 12*(2), 2255–2283. doi:10.3390120202255 PMID:22438763

Temurtas, H., Yumusak, N., & Temurtas, F. (2009). A Comparative study on diabetes disease diagnosis using neural networks. Expert Systems With Applications, 36, 8610–8615.

Terry, M. (2009). Medical identity theft and telemedicine security. *Telemedicine Journal and e-Health, 15*(10), 928–933. doi:10.1089/tmj.2009.9932 PMID:19908998

Thakur, V., & Saikia, M. (2013). *Hiding secret image in video*. IEEE. doi:10.1109/ISSP.2013.6526892

Thiemert, S., Sahbi, H., & Steinebach, M. (2006). Using entropy for image and video authentication watermarks. *Proceedings of the Society for Photo-Instrumentation Engineers, 6072*, 607218–1, 607218–10. doi:10.1117/12.643053

Thodi, D., & Rodriguez, J. (2004). Prediction-error based reversible watermarking. In *International Conference on Image Processing* (pp. 1549-1552). IEEE.

Thodi, D., & Rodriguez, J. (2007). Expansion Embedding Techniques for Reversible Watermarking. *IEEE Transactions on Image Processing, 16*(3), 721–730. doi:10.1109/TIP.2006.891046 PMID:17357732

Thuraisingham. (2007). Security and Privacy for multimedia database management systems. *Springer Science, 33*, 13-29.

Tian, J. (2002, April). Wavelet-based reversible watermarking for authentication. In *Security and Watermarking of Multimedia Contents IV* (Vol. 4675, pp. 679–691). International Society for Optics and Photonics. doi:10.1117/12.465329

Tian, J. (2003). Reversible data embedding using a difference expansion. *IEEE Transactions on Circuits and Systems for Video Technology, 13*(8), 890–896. doi:10.1109/TCSVT.2003.815962

Tirkel, A. Z., Rankin, G. A., Van Schyndel, R. M., Ho, W. J., Mee, N. R. A., & Osborne, C. F. (1993). Electronic Water Mark. In *DICTA 93* (pp. 666–673). Macquarie University.

Tomar, P. P. S., & Saxena, P. K. (2011). Architecture for medical diagnosis using rule-based technique. *The First International Conference on Interdisciplinary Research and Development*, 25.1-25.5.

Trithemius, J. (1499). *Steganographia, a treatise on cryptography and steganography.* Retrieved from Jonathan Harel, A Saliency Implementation in MATLAB: http://www.klab.caltech.edu/~harel/share/gbvs.php and http://www.klab.caltech.edu/harel/share/simpsal.zip

Tsai, P., Hu, Y., & Yeh, H. (2009). Reversible image hiding scheme using predictive coding and histogram shifting. *Signal Processing, 89*(6), 1129–1143. doi:10.1016/j.sigpro.2008.12.017

Tukur, U. M., & Shamsuddin, S. M. (2014). Radial basis function network learning with modified backpropagation algorithm. *Telkomnika Indonesian Journal of Electrical Engineering, 13*(2), 369–378.

Tyagi, S., Singh, H. V., Agarwal, R., & Gangwar, S. K. (2016). Digital watermarking techniques for security applications. *2016 International Conference on Emerging Trends in Electrical Electronics & Sustainable Energy Systems (ICETEESES),* 379-382. 10.1109/ICETEESES.2016.7581413

U.S. Department of Health and Human Services. (n.d.). *What You Need To Know About Melanoma and Other Skin Cancers.* National Institutes of Health.

Uhrina, M., Hlubik, J., & Vaculik, M. (2013). Correlation between Objective and Subjective Methods Used for Video Quality Evaluation. *Advances in Electrical and Electronic Engineering, 11*(2). doi:10.15598/aeee.v11i2.775

Umadevi, R. (2016). Joint Approach For Secure Communication Using Video Steganography. *3rd International Conference on Computing for Sustainable Global Development (INDIACom),* 3104 – 3106.

Umamaheswari, M., Sivasubramanian, S., & Pandiarajan, S. (2010). Analysis of Different Steganographic Algorithms for Secured Data Hiding. *International Journal of Computer Science and Network Security, 10*(8).

Unser, M., & Aldroubi, A. (1996). A review of wavelets in biomedical applications. *Proceedings of the IEEE, 84*(4), 626–638. doi:10.1109/5.488704

Van Leest, A. R. N. O., van der Veen, M., & Bruekers, F. (2003, September). Reversible image watermarking. In *Image Processing, 2003. ICIP 2003. Proceedings. 2003 International Conference on* (Vol. 2, pp. II-731). IEEE. 10.1109/ICIP.2003.1246784

van Schyndel, R. G., Tirkel, A. Z., & Osborne, C. F. (1994). A digital watermark. *Proceedings of 1st International Conference on Image Processing,* 86-90. doi: 10.1109/ICIP.1994.413536

Vapnik, V. N. (1995). *The nature of statistical learning theory.* New York, NY: Springer-Verlag New York, Inc. doi:10.1007/978-1-4757-2440-0

Vasudev. (2016). A Review on Digital Image Watermarking and its Technique. *India Journal of Image and Graphics, 4*(2).

Venkateswarlu, L., Reddy, B. E., & Rao, N. V. (2016). Arnold - wavelet based robust watermarking technique for medical images. *2016 International Conference on ICT in Business Industry & Government (ICTBIG),* 1-5. 10.1109/ICTBIG.2016.7892689

Venkateswarlu, L., Rao, N. V., & Reddy, B. E. (2017). A Robust Double Watermarking Technique for Medical Images with Semi-fragility. *2017 International Conference on Recent Advances in Electronics and Communication Technology (ICRAECT),* 126-131. 10.1109/ICRAECT.2017.40

Verhelst, M., & Bahai, A. (2015, Summer). Where Analog Meets Digital: Analog?to?Information Conversion and Beyond. *IEEE Solid-State Circuits Magazine, 7*(3), 67–80. doi:10.1109/MSSC.2015.2442394

Vidal, J., & Sayrol, E. (1998). Optimum watermark detection and embedding in digital images. *1998 IEEE Second Workshop on Multimedia Signal Processing,* 285-290. 10.1109/MMSP.1998.738948

Voloshynovskiy, S., Pereira, S., Iquise, V., & Pun, T. (2001). Attack modelling: Towards a second generation watermarking benchmark. *Signal Processing, 81*(6), 1177–1214. doi:10.1016/S0165-1684(01)00039-1

Wakatani, A. (2002, January). Digital watermarking for ROI medical images by using compressed signature image. In *System Sciences, 2002. HICSS. Proceedings of the 35th Annual Hawaii International Conference on* (pp. 2043-2048). IEEE. 10.1109/HICSS.2002.994129

Walia, E., & Suneja, A. (2013). Fragile and blind watermarking technique based on Weber's law for medical image authentication. *IET Computer Vision, 7*(1), 9–19. doi:10.1049/iet-cvi.2012.0109

Walia, E., & Suneja, A. (2014). A robust watermark authentication technique based on Weber's descriptor. *Signal, Image and Video Processing, 8*(5), 859–872. doi:10.100711760-012-0312-6

Walters, W., & Betz, A. (2012). Medical identity theft. *Journal of Consumer Education*, 75.

Wang, C., Li, X., & Yang, B. (2010). Efficient reversible image watermarking by using dynamical prediction-error expansion. In *International conference on Image processing* (pp. 3673– 3676). Academic Press. 10.1109/ICIP.2010.5652508

Wang, Lee, Li, & Ko. (2007). Ontology-based Fuzzy Inference Agent for Diabetes Classification. *Annual Meetings of the North American Fuzzy Information Processing Society*, 79-83.

Wang, M. H., Lee, C. S., Huan–Chung Li, H. C., & Ko, W. M. (2007). Ontology-based fuzzy inference agent for diabetes classification. *Annual Meetings of the North American Fuzzy Information Processing Society*, 79-83.

Wang, S., Kubota, T., Siskind, J.M., & Wang, J. (2005). Salient closed boundary extraction with ratio contour. *IEEE Pattern Anal. Mach. Intell., 27*, 546–561.

Wang, J., Li, T., Shi, Y. Q., Lian, S., & Ye, J. (2017). Forensics feature analysis in quaternion wavelet domain for distinguishing photographic images and computer graphics. *Multimedia Tools and Applications, 76*(22), 23721–23737. doi:10.100711042-016-4153-0

Wang, P., Zhang, H., Cao, Y., & Zhao, X. (2016). *A Novel Embedding Distortion for Motion Vector-Based Steganography Considering Motion Characteristic, Local Optimality and Statistical Distribution*. ACM Press. doi:10.1145/2909827.2930801

Wang, Z., Bovik, A. C., Sheikh, H. R., & Simoncelli, E. P. (2004). Image quality assessment: From error visibility to structural similarity. *IEEE Transactions on Image Processing, 13*(4), 600–612. doi:10.1109/TIP.2003.819861 PMID:15376593

Wang, Z., Lu, L., & Bovik, A. C. (2004). Video quality assessment based on structural distortion measurement. *Signal Processing Image Communication, 19*(2), 121–132. doi:10.1016/S0923-5965(03)00076-6

Watson, A. B. (1993, September). DCT quantization matrices visually optimized for individual images. In *Human vision, visual processing, and digital display IV* (Vol. 1913, pp. 202–217). International Society for Optics and Photonics. doi:10.1117/12.152694

Watson, S., & Dehghantanha, A. (2016). Digital forensics: The missing piece of the Internet of Things promise. *Computer Fraud & Security, 2016*(6), 5–8. doi:10.1016/S1361-3723(15)30045-2

Weinberger, M., Seroussi, G., & Sapiro, G. (2000). The LOCO-I lossless image compression algorithm: Principles and standardization into JPEG-LS. *IEEE Transactions on Image Processing, 9*(8), 1309–1324. doi:10.1109/83.855427 PMID:18262969

White, L. A. E., Krousel-Wood, M. A., & Mather, F. (2001). Technology meets healthcare: Distance learning and telehealth. *The Ochsner Journal, 3*(1), 22–29. PMID:21765713

Whittle, M. W. (2013). *Gait analysis. In The Soft Tissues* (pp. 187–199). Elsevier. doi:10.1016/B978-0-7506-0170-2.50017-0

WHO/IDF. (2006). *Definition and diagnosis of diabetes mellitus and intermediate hyperglycemia*. World Health Organization. Available: http://www.who.int/diabetes /publications/Definition%20and%20diagnosis%20of%20diabetes_new.pdf

Wong, K. K., Tse, C. H., Ng, K. S., Lee, T. H., & Cheng, L. M. (1997, November). Adaptive water marking. *IEEE Transactions on Consumer Electronics, 43*(4), 1003–1009. doi:10.1109/30.642365

Woo, C.S., Du, J., & Pham, B.L. (2005). *Multiple watermark method for privacy control and tamper detection in medical images*. Academic Press.

Wu, M., & Liu, B. (1998, October). Watermarking for image authentication. In *Image Processing, 1998. ICIP 98. Proceedings. 1998 International Conference on* (Vol. 2, pp. 437-441). IEEE.

Wu, H., Dugelay, J., & Shi, Y. (2015). Reversible Image Data Hiding with Contrast Enhancement. *IEEE Signal Processing Letters, 22*(1), 81–85. doi:10.1109/LSP.2014.2346989

Wu, J. H., Chang, R. F., Chen, C. J., Wang, C. L., Kuo, T. H., Moon, W. K., & Chen, D. R. (2008). Tamper detection and recovery for medical images using near-lossless information hiding technique. *Journal of Digital Imaging, 21*(1), 59–76. doi:10.100710278-007-9011-1 PMID:17393256

Wu, X., Liang, X., Liu, H., Huang, J., & Qiu, G. (2006). Reversible semi-fragile image authentication using zernike moments and integer wavelet transform. In *Digital Rights Management. Technologies, Issues, Challenges and Systems* (pp. 135–145). Berlin: Springer. doi:10.1007/11787952_11

Wu, X., Memon, N., & Sayood, K. (1995). *A context- based, adaptive, lossless/nearly-lossless coding scheme for continuous-tone images*. ISO.

Wyatt, C. J., & Altman, D. G. (1995). Prognostic models: Clinically useful or quickly forgotten? *BMJ (Clinical Research Ed.), 311*(7019), 1539–1541. doi:10.1136/bmj.311.7019.1539

Xiang, S., Kim, H. J., & Huang, J. (2008). Invariant image watermarking based on statistical features in the low-frequency domain. *IEEE Transactions on Circuits and Systems for Video Technology, 18*(6), 777–790. doi:10.1109/TCSVT.2008.918843

Xie, Xie, & Ning. (1997). Application of Fuzzy Neural Network to ECG Diagnosis. *International Conference on Neural Networks*, 62-66.

Xin, Y., Liao, S., & Pawlak, M. (2007). Circularly orthogonal moments for geometrically robust image watermarking. *Pattern Recognition, 40*(12), 3740–3752. doi:10.1016/j.patcog.2007.05.004

Xu, B., Wang, J., Liu, X., & Zhang, Z. (2007, August). Passive steganalysis using image quality metrics and multi-class support vector machine. In *Natural Computation, 2007. ICNC 2007. Third International Conference on* (Vol. 3, pp. 215-220). IEEE. 10.1109/ICNC.2007.544

Xu, N., Bansal, R., & Ahuja, N. (2003). Object segmentation using graph cuts based active contours. *IEEE CVPR*.

Xu, Q., Wang, L., & Wang, Z. (2016). Ultrasound Image Features Detection Using Phase Congruency Based Dimensionality Reduction. *2016 6th International Conference on Digital Home (ICDH)*, 68-73. 10.1109/ICDH.2016.024

Xuan, G., Yang, C., Zhen, Y., Shi, Y. Q., & Ni, Z. (2005). Reversible data hiding using integer wavelet transform and companding technique. In Lecture Notes in Computer Science: Vol. 3304. *Digital Watermarking* (pp. 115–124). Berlin: Springer. doi:10.1007/978-3-540-31805-7_10

Xu, Y. (2013). *An improved mean-shift moving object detection and tracking algorithm based on segmentation and fusion mechanism*. IEEE. doi:10.1109/SPC.2013.6735136

Xu, Z., Xiong, L., & Xu, Y. (2014). On the provably secure CEW based on orthogonal decomposition. *Signal Processing Image Communication, 29*(5), 607–617. doi:10.1016/j.image.2013.10.007

Yadav, N., Pahal, N., Kalra, P., Lall, B., & Chaudhury, S. (2011, February). A Novel Approach for Securing Forensic Documents Using Rectangular Region-of-Interest (RROI). In *Emerging Applications of Information Technology (EAIT), 2011 Second International Conference on* (pp. 198-201). IEEE.

Yadav, P., Mishra, N., & Sharma, S. (2013). *A secure video steganography with encryption based on LSB technique.* IEEE. doi:10.1109/ICCIC.2013.6724212

Yang, H., & Kot, A. C. (2006). Binary image authentication with tampering localization by embedding cryptographic signature and block identifier. *IEEE Signal Processing Letters, 13*(12), 741–744. doi:10.1109/LSP.2006.879829

Yang, M., Trifas, M., Chen, L., Song, L., Aires, D. B., & Elston, J. (2010). Secure patient information and privacy in medical imaging. *Journal of Systemics, Cybernetics and Informatics, 8*(3), 63–66.

Yang, R., Yin, L., Gabbouj, M., Astola, J., & Neuvo, Y. (1995, March). Optimal weighted median filters under structural constraints. *IEEE Transactions on Signal Processing, 43*(3), 591–604. doi:10.1109/78.370615

Yarpiz Project. (2018). Retrieved February 01, 2018, from http://www.yarpiz.com

Yeh, C. H., & Kuo, C. J. (1999). Digital watermarking through quasi m-arrays. *1999 IEEE Workshop on Signal Processing Systems. SiPS 99. Design and Implementation*, 456-461. doi: 10.1109/SIPS.1999.822351

Ye, R. L., & Johnson, P. E. (1997). The impact of explanation facilities on user acceptance of expert systems advise. *IS Q., 19*, 157–172.

Yeung, M. M., & Mintzer, F. (1997, October). An invisible watermarking technique for image verification. In *Image Processing, 1997. Proceedings., International Conference on* (Vol. 2, pp. 680-683). IEEE. 10.1109/ICIP.1997.638587

Yeung, M. M., Mintzer, F. C., Braudaway, G. W., & Rao, A. R. (1997). Digital watermarking for high-quality imaging. *Proceedings of First Signal Processing Society Workshop on Multimedia Signal Processing*, 357-362. 10.1109/MMSP.1997.602661

Yi, H., Rajan, D., & Chia, L.-T. (2005). A new motion histogram to index motion content in video segments. *Pattern Recognition Letters, 26*(9), 1221–1231. doi:10.1016/j.patrec.2004.11.011

Yi, X., & Ling, N. (2005). *Fast Pixel-Based Video Scene Change Detection.* IEEE. doi:10.1109/ISCAS.2005.1465369

Yu, H., Li, J., Tian, Y., & Huang, T. (2010). Automatic interesting object extraction from images using complementary saliency maps. *Proc. of the MM'10.* doi:10.1145/1873951.1874105

Yu, W., Liu, T., Valdez, R., Gwinn, M., & Khoury, M. J. (2010). Application of support vector machine modeling for prediction of common diseases: The case of diabetes and pre-diabetes. *BMC Medical Informatics and Decision Making*, 1–7. PMID:20307319

Zabih, R., Miller, J., & Mai, K. (1995). *A feature-based algorithm for detecting and classifying scene breaks.* ACM Press. doi:10.1145/217279.215266

Zain, J. M., & Fauzi, A. R. (2006, August). Medical image watermarking with tamper detection and recovery. In *Engineering in Medicine and Biology Society, 2006. EMBS'06. 28th Annual International Conference of the IEEE* (pp. 3270-3273). IEEE. 10.1109/IEMBS.2006.260767

Zain, J., & Clarke, M. (2005). Security in telemedicine: issues in watermarking medical images. Sciences of Electronic, Technologies of Information and Telecommunications, Tunisia.

Zanotto, M. (2010). *Visual Description of Skin Lesions* (Master's dissertation). University of Edinburgh.

Zeki, T.S., MalaKooti, M.V., Ataeipoor, Y., & Tabibi, S.T. (2012). An expert system for diabetes diagnosis. *American Academic & Scholarly Research Journal, 4*(5), 1–13.

Zhang, F., & Zhang, X. (2014). EBR Analysis of Digital Image Watermarking. In S. Patnaik & X. Li (Eds.), *Proceedings of International Conference on Computer Science and Information Technology* (Vol. 255, pp. 11–18). New Delhi: Springer India. 10.1007/978-81-322-1759-6_2

Zhang, H., Cao, Y., & Zhao, X. (2016). Motion vector-based video steganography with preserved local optimality. *Multimedia Tools and Applications, 75*(21), 13503–13519. doi:10.100711042-015-2743-x

Zhang, H., Cao, Y., Zhao, X., Zhang, W., & Yu, N. (2014). *Video steganography with perturbed macroblock partition.* ACM Press. doi:10.1145/2600918.2600936

Zhang, M., & Guo, Y. (2014). *Video steganography algorithm with motion search cost minimized.* IEEE. doi:10.1109/ICIEA.2014.6931298

Zhang, W., Hu, X., Li, X., & Yu, N. (2013). Recursive Histogram Modification: Establishing Equivalency Between Reversible Data Hiding and Lossless Data Compression. *IEEE Transactions on Image Processing, 22*(7), 2775–2785. doi:10.1109/TIP.2013.2257814 PMID:23591495

Zhang, Y., Zhang, M., Niu, K., & Liu, J. (2015). *Video Steganography Algorithm Based on Trailing Coefficients.* IEEE. doi:10.1109/INCoS.2015.47

Zhang, Z., Ma, S., Liu, H., & Gong, Y. (2009, April). An edge detection approach based on directional wavelet transform. *Elsevier Journal of Computers and Mathematics with Applications, 57*(8), 1265–1271. doi:10.1016/j.camwa.2008.11.013

Zhao, X., Ho, A. T., Treharne, H., Pankajakshan, V., Culnane, C., & Jiang, W. (2007, November). A novel semi-fragile image watermarking, authentication and self-restoration technique using the slant transform. In *Intelligent Information Hiding and Multimedia Signal Processing, 2007. IIHMSP 2007. Third International Conference on* (Vol. 1, pp. 283-286). IEEE. 10.1109/IIH-MSP.2007.50

Zhou, X. Q., Huang, H. K., & Lou, S. L. (2001). Authenticity and integrity of digital mammography images. *IEEE Transactions on Medical Imaging, 20*(8), 784–791. doi:10.1109/42.938246 PMID:11513029

About the Contributors

Arunabha Adhikari is an M.Sc. in Physics. He worked on the computational models of Biological Neuron and its network for his Ph.D. He then joined Neuroscience laboratories in Indian Institute of Science, Bangalore and in University of Saarland, Germany. He taught Physics in Gobardanga Collge, West Bengal University of Technology before joining West Bengal State University where he serves as an Associate Professor in Physics. His interests include Non-linear Dynamics, Biological Neuron Network, Computational Physics, Pattern Recognition.

Kanchan Bala did her Bachelors in Engineering in Computer Science and Engineering from Rajasthan University, followed by Master of Technology in Computer science and pursuing Ph.D from Birla Institute of Technology, Mesra in 2005, 2009 and 2015 respectively . She is currently the Research Scholar in Department of Computer Science and Engineering, Birla Institute of Technology, Mesra, Jharkhand, India. She has 4 research publications in international journals, book and conference proceedings to her credit. She has been the member of CSI. Her research interests include soft computing, data mining, Big Data.

Abhishek Basu received his B. Tech. in Electronics and Telecommunication Engineering from West Bengal University of Technology in year 2005, M. Tech. in VLSI Design from Institute of Radio Physics, Calcutta University, India in 2008 and Ph. D (Engg) from Jadavpur University in 2015. At present he is an Assistant Professor in the department of Electronics and Communication Engineering at RCC Institute of Information Technology, Kolkata, India. His field of interest spans visual information hiding, IP protection technique, FPGA based system design and low power VLSI Design.

Arup Kumar Bhattacharjee did his MCA from Kalyani University and MTech from West Bengal University of Technology. He is currently working as an Assistant Professor in RCC Institute of Information Technology, Kolkata, India. He has more than 14 years teaching experience. He has over 10 research publication in different National and International journals and conference proceedings. He has contributed in over 20 internationally acclaimed books. He has edited 2 books. His research areas are data mining and machine learning.

Debangshu Chakraborty is a student of the Post Graduate Department of Computer Science in St. Xavier's College, Kolkata. He completed his graduation in Computer Science from Ananda Chandra College, Jalpaiguri. He has been awarded the University Gold Medal for securing first position in first class in Computer Science in the Bachelor of science with Honours examination, 2016 by University of North Bengal. His research area of interest is Digital Image Processing.

Dilip Kumar Choubey submitted his Ph.D in Engineering from Birla Institue of Technology (B.I.T), Mesra, Ranchi, India. He received his M.Tech degree in Computer Science and Engineering from Oriental College of Technology (O.C.T), Bhopal, India in 2012 and has B.E. degree in Information Technology from Bansal Institute of Science and Technology (B.I.S.T), Bhopal, India in 2010. Currently, He is working as an Assistant Professor (On Contract) in NIT Patna, India. He worked as an Asst. Prof. in Lakshmi Narain College of Technology (L.N.C.T), Bhopal, India and Oriental College of Technology (O.C.T), Bhopal, India. He has more than 6 years of teaching and research experience. He is a author of 1 book and has more than 14 research publications in international journals, book chapters and conference proceedings to his credit. He has been the member of the organizing and technical program committees of some conferences and Workshop. He has reviewed several research papers in reputed journal. He has been attended so many workshop's/Seminar's/Conference's. He is the lifetime members of several professional bodies such as The International Association of Engineers (IAENG), The Internet Society Switzerland (ISOC), The Society of Digital Information and Wireless Communications (SDIWC), Universal Association of Computers and Electronics Engineers (UACEE), Associate Member (till 4 May, 2019), Computer Science Teachers Association (CSTA), Member (Individual III, till 11/08/2016), etc. His research interests include Machine Learning, Soft Computing, Bioinformatics, Data Mining, Pattern Recognition, and Database Management System, etc. Ph. No. 7033789676.

Soumadeb Dutta is pursuing B.Tech in the department of Electronics and Communication Engineering at RCC Institute of Information Technology, Kolkata, India. His field of interest spans Medical image Watermarking and Copyright Protection.

Jayati Ghosh Dastidar has been working in the education sector for over 15 years. She is currently serving as an Assistant Professor in the Department of Computer Science, St. Xavier's College, Kolkata. Her teaching experience includes both theoretical as well as practical Computer Science topics both at the UG as well as the PG level. She specializes in the teaching of courses such as Object Oriented Technology, Compiler Design, Automata Theory, Digital Image Processing, Digital Electronics, Computer Organisation, Data Structure, Mobile Communication, Parallel Architecture, etc. Her research interests are in the area of Digital Image Processing and Pattern Recognition. She has several publications in reputed International Journals and Conference proceedings. She has also contributed several chapters in edited books of publishers like Springer, CRC Press (Taylor and Francis), etc.

Christos Grecos is currently a tenured full time Professor and Chair of the Computer Science Department of Central Washington University (CWU) in US. Previously, he was the Dean of the Faculty of Computing and Information Technology and Full Professor of Visual Communication Standards at Sohar University, Oman. Prior to that he was employed in the United Kingdom as a Full Professor of Visual Communications Standards and Head of School of Computing in the University of the West of Scotland, Dr Grecos holds a Bachelor's degree in Computer Science (Systems Software Option) from Concordia University in Montreal, Canada, a Master's of Science degree in Human Computer Interaction from Heriot Watt University in Edinburgh, Scotland (UK). His PhD degree in Image and Video Coding algorithms for standards is from Glamorgan University (later renamed University of South Wales in Wales, UK). For his contributions in his research field, Dr Grecos was elevated to a Senior Member of the Institute of Electronic and Electrical Engineers (IEEE) in 2006.Dr Grecos was also elevated to a Senior Member of the International Society of Optics and Photonics (SPIE) in 2008 for specific achievements in digital image processing. Dr Grecos has received the best poster award in the 2012 IEEE Conference in Consumer Electronics and the First Place Student paper award in the 2014 IEEE Conference in Consumer Electronics. He has also received the best student paper award in the 2014 International Conference on Signal Processing and Multimedia Applications (SIGMAP and the best student paper prize in the 2014 Irish Machine Vision and Image Processing Conference. Dr Grecos has been a reviewer of research proposals for the UK Engineering and Physical Sciences Research Councils (UK EPSRC) since 2003. He is a member of the EPSRC College of Peers and on September 22nd 2016, he was invited to continue his tenure. Dr Grecos is an associate editor of the Journal of Real Time Image Processing (Springer publishing) and of many other international journals. Dr Grecos was a member of the International Program Committee of the Real Time Image and Video Processing (RTIVP) conferences in 2009 – 18 under the umbrellas of IS&T and SPIE and of many other international conferences. Dr Grecos's research interests include image/video compression standards, image/video processing and analysis, image/video networking and computer vision. He has published widely in top-tier international outlets.

Barnali Gupta Banik, B.Tech (Computer Science & Engineering), M.Tech (Software Engineering), Ph.D. (pursuing in Computer Science and Engineering from University of Calcutta, Kolkata, India), currently Assistant Professor of Computer Science & Engineering department at St. Thomas' College of Engineering & Technology, Kolkata. She has over 9 years of teaching experience and over 2 years of industrial experience working for MNCs in India & UK. She has authored several research papers in Network Security domain, including 7 Scopus indexed and 2 SCIE indexed articles as of date.

Ranit Karmakar received his B. Tech. in ECE from West Bengal University of Technology in year 2016. At present he is working as Assistant System Engineer with TATA Consultancy Services, Kolkata, India. His field of interest spans from image processing to computer vision and machine learning.

Amit Khan has obtained his B.Tech (IT) from HIT, Haldia, in the year 2004 and his M.E. from WBUT, Kolkata in the year 2006 and currently working as Assistant Professor in the Department of Information Technology at RCC Institute of Information Technology, Kolkata.

Manish Kumar received the B.Tech. Degree in Applied Electronics and Instrumentation Engineering from Biju Patnaik University, Rourkela, India, in 2010 and the M.Tech. Degree in Biomedical Engineering from the Manipal University, Udupi, India, in 2013. He is currently pursuing Ph.D. degree in Electrical and Electronics engineering. His area of interests are image & signal processing and computational intelligence.

Shujun Li is Professor of Cyber Security and Director of Kent Interdisciplinary Research Centre in Cyber Security (KirCCS), University of Kent, UK. Before joining the University of Kent, he was a Deputy Director of the Surrey Centre for Cyber Security (SCCS) at the University of Surrey, a UK government recognised Academic Centres of Excellence in Cyber Security Research (ACE-CSR), from 2014 to 2017. His research interests are mostly around interdisciplinary topics covering cyber security, digital forensics and cybercrime, human factors and human-centric computing, multimedia computing and information visualization, and applications of artificial intelligence and discrete optimization. Due to the interdisciplinary nature of his research, he is actively working with researchers from other disciplines such as Electronic Engineering, Psychology, Law, Business and Sociology. He is also working very closely with industry and public bodies such as police forces. More about his research can be found at http://www.hooklee.com/.

Dipankar Majumdar has obtained his B.E (Electrical Engg) from REC, Silchar, in the year 1999 and his M.Tech. from JU, Kolkata in the year 2006 followed by PhD(Engg) in the year 2011 and currently working as Associate Professor in the Department of Information Technology at RCC Institute of Information Technology, Kolkata.

Soumen Mukherjee did his B.Sc (Physics Honours) from Calcutta University, M.C.A. from Kalyani University and ME in Information Technology from West Bengal University of Technology. He is the silver medalist for ME examination in the university. He has done his Post-Graduate Diploma in Business Management from Institute of Management Technology, Center of Distance Learning, Ghaziabad. He is now working as an Assistant Professor in RCC Institute of Information Technology, Kolkata. He has 14 years teaching experience in the field of Computer Science and Application. He has over 30 research paper published in different National and International Journal and Conferences. He has contributed in over 20 internationally acclaimed books in the field of Computer Science and Engineering. He has edited 2 books. His research fields are Image Processing and Machine Learning. He is a life member of several institutions like IETE, CSI, ISTE, FOSET, etc.

Sanchita Paul did her Bachelors in Engineering in Computer Science and Engineering from Burdwan University, followed by Master of Engineering in Software Engineering and Ph.D from Birla Institute of Technology, Mesra in 2004, 2006 and 2012 respectively . She is currently the Assistant Professor in Department of Computer Science and Engineering, Birla Institute of Technology, Mesra, Jharkhand, India. She is a co-author of 1 book and has 50 research publications in international journals, book chapters and conference proceedings to her credit. She has been the member of the organizing and technical program committees of several International conferences and Workshop. She has also acted as Principal Investigator in an AICTE funded project. Her research interests include soft computing, cloud computing, Big Data, IoT and NLP and Bioinformatics.

Mehul Raval joined Ahmedabad University in 2013. During 2008-2013, he served at DA-IICT, Gandhinagar and from 1997 - 2008 he was associated with Sarvajanik College of Engineering and Technology (SCET), Surat, India. He was visiting faculty to Sardar Vallabhbhai National Institute of Technology Surat (2005 - 2007) and Veer Narmad South Gujarat University (2004 - 2008), Surat, India. Dr. Raval visited Graduate School of Natural Science and Technology, Okayama University, Japan during July- August 2016 under Sakura science exchange program sponsored by Japan Science and Technology (JST), Govt. of Japan. He was an Argosy visiting Associate Professor at Olin College of Engineering, MA, US during Fall 2016. He is an alumnus of Electronics & Telecommunication Engineering Department, College of Engineering Pune (COEP), one of the oldest engineering institute in Asia (established in 1854) and University of Pune. He obtained Bachelor of Engineering (B.E) - Electronics and Telecommunication (E&TC) in 1996 and Master of Engineering (M.E.) - Digital Systems in 2002. Dr. Raval co-authored a book on Image and Video Compression: Fundamentals, Techniques and Applications for CRC press and he has published extensively in journals, magazines, conferences, workshops at national and international stage. Dr. Raval is an associate editor for IEEE Access: a leading open access publication by IEEE. He serve as member of technical program committees for leading national and international conferences, workshops and symposium and reviews journals articles of IEEE, ACM, Springer, Elsevier, IET. He has received research funds from Board of Research in Nuclear Science (BRNS), Department of Atomic Energy, Government of India and IEEE. He is supervising three doctoral students and many completed M. Tech theses and B. Tech projects under his supervision. He also served on Board of Studies(BoS) for various universities. He is a senior member of IEEE and a Fellow of IETE. Dr. Raval served IEEE Gujarat section during 2008 - 2015 and also served IEEE signal processing society (SPS) chapter as vice chair and exe-com member in 2014.

Roland Schmitz holds a diploma degree and a Ph.D. in mathematics, both from the Technical University of Braunschweig, Germany. From 1995 to 2001 he worked as a senior researcher at the research center of Deutsche Telekom in Darmstadt, Germany, where he was mainly concerned with mobile communications security and digital signature standardization. Since 2001, Roland Schmitz is a professor of Internet Security at Stuttgart Media University. He has authored and co-authored more than 60 peer-reviewed journal and conference publications. Currently, his main research interests are multimedia security and usable security.

Uday Pratap Singh was born on February 6, 1979 in Sultanpur, U.P., India. Dr. Singh graduated in Mathematics from Dr. Ram Manohar Lohiya (Awadh) University, Faizabad, U.P. in 1998. He obtained his first M.Sc. degree in Mathematics & Statistics (Gold Medalist) in 2000, from Dr. Ram Manohar Lohiya (Awadh) University, Faizabad, U.P. and Second M.Sc. degree in Mathematics & Computing from Indian Institute of Technology, Guwahati. He later received his Doctorate Degree in Computer Science from Barkatullah University, Bhopal, in 2013. He is currently working as an Assistant Professor in the Department of Applied Mathematics, Madhav Institute of Technology & Science, Gwalior, India. Dr. Singh has published/presented about 83 research papers (including 16 SCI and SCOPUS indexed) in International/National Journals and Conferences, 02 Books and 11 Book Chapters in the area of Evolutionary Computation, Soft Computing and Image Processing etc. His area of research includes Nature and Bio Inspired Metaheuristic Algorithm, Soft Computing, and Image Processing etc. He has also qualified CSIR (NET). He is managing editor, associate editor and reviewer in various reputed journals and conferences. He is a life member of the Computer Society of India (CSI) and IAENG.

Kanimozhi Suguna S. has completed her M.C.A., from College of Engineering Guindy, Anna University, Chennai by 2008. She has started her research experience with M.Phil degree from Vinayaka Missions Deemed University, Salem and continued with Ph.D from Anna University, Chennai. She completed the research degrees by 2009 and 2015 respectively. She has 8 years of teaching experience from Anna University, Regional Campus Coimbatore and currently working as Assistant Professor in SASTRA Deemed University. She has a good number of journal publications to her credit.

Dhanya V. S. is a student of II year, Department of Computer Science and Engineering, School of Computing, SASTRA University.

Xinpeng Zhang received the B.S. degree in computational mathematics from Jilin University, China, in 1995, and the M.E. and Ph.D. degrees in communication and information system from Shanghai University, China, in 2001 and 2004, respectively. Since 2004, he has been with the faculty of the School of Communication and Information Engineering, Shanghai University, where he is currently a Professor. He was with the State University of New York at Binghamton as a visiting scholar from January 2010 to January 2011, and Konstanz University as an experienced researcher sponsored by the Alexander von Humboldt Foundation from March 2011 to May 2012. He is an Associate Editor for IEEE Transactions on Information Forensics and Security. His research interests include multimedia security, image processing, and digital forensics. He has published more than 200 papers in these areas.

Index

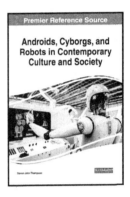

Ensure Quality Research is Introduced to the Academic Community

Become an IGI Global Reviewer for Authored Book Projects

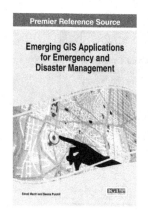

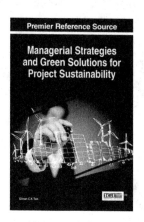

The overall success of an authored book project is dependent on quality and timely reviews.

In this competitive age of scholarly publishing, constructive and timely feedback significantly expedites the turnaround time of manuscripts from submission to acceptance, allowing the publication and discovery of forward-thinking research at a much more expeditious rate. Several IGI Global authored book projects are currently seeking highly qualified experts in the field to fill vacancies on their respective editorial review boards:

Applications may be sent to:
development@igi-global.com

Applicants must have a doctorate (or an equivalent degree) as well as publishing and reviewing experience. Reviewers are asked to write reviews in a timely, collegial, and constructive manner. All reviewers will begin their role on an ad-hoc basis for a period of one year, and upon successful completion of this term can be considered for full editorial review board status, with the potential for a subsequent promotion to Associate Editor.

If you have a colleague that may be interested in this opportunity, we encourage you to share this information with them.

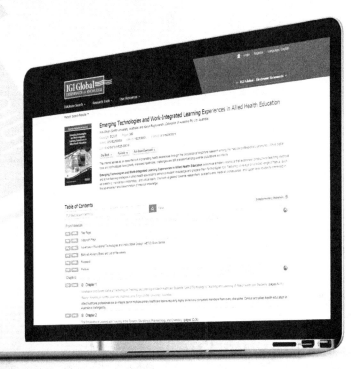

Printed in the United States
By Bookmasters